CASS LIBRARY OF AFRICAN STUDIES

GENERAL STUDIES

No. 75

LAND LAW AND CUSTOM IN THE COLONIES

BY

C. K. MEEK

With an Introduction by

LORD HAILEY

SECOND EDITION

FRANK CASS & CO. LTD.

1968

Published by
FRANK CASS AND COMPANY LIMITED
67 Great Russell Street, London WC1
by arrangement with Oxford University Press

First edition	1946
Second edition	1949
New impression	1968

SBN 7146 1698 2

Printed in Great Britain by
Thomas Nelson (Printers) Ltd., London and Edinburgh

Author's Preface

THIS book deals only with the tenure of agricultural lands in the Colonies. No attempt has been made to describe the conditions of urban tenure. Moreover, the study is confined to certain selected Colonies, since any attempt to cover all the Colonies would require many books.

It would be impossible to exaggerate the importance of the subject of land tenure in the Colonies. In the industrialized civilizations of the West the people have many sources of income, but in the British Colonies land is, for the most part, the only form of capital and its exploitation the only means of livelihood. Such manufacturing industries as exist are almost solely concerned with the products of agriculture. Land therefore has something of a sacred character and rights over land are more jealously treasured than any other form of rights.

Until recently the vast majority of the Colonial peoples have practised a subsistence system of agriculture. They have grown all that they required. And so they have remained owners of the land and kept themselves free from the booms and depressions of world trade. But their standards of living have remained correspondingly low. If these are to be raised, as raised they must be, then commercial crops must be grown for export, and self-subsistence economies replaced by those of a wider kind. This has already happened in many territories, and the rate of progress has been enormously increased by the requirements of the war. New types of crops and new methods of agriculture are transforming the systems of tenure; land is being commercialized; the basis of holding land is changing from one of community and custom to one of individualism and contract; wealthy native capitalists are appearing; agricultural debt is already in full swing, and many peasants are becoming labourers on lands which were once their own.

In some territories the legal status of the Colonial governments regarding land has enabled them to assume the rôle of landlord and engage in extensive schemes of long-range planning, but in others their powers of control have been strictly limited by the vested interests of the local political authorities or the heads of kinship groups. In others again the situation may be complicated by the demands of different racial groups, as for example in East Africa where there are the competing claims of Europeans, Negroes, Arabs and Indians, or in Malaya those of Europeans, Malays and Chinese.

It is clear then that the problems of land in the Colonies are many and that they are complex and pressing. The local or Native Authorities who are faced with the difficulties of adjusting their land systems to the new conditions have a right to look for guidance and assistance from the British Administrations. There is a need in many territories for much more knowledge of the indigenous systems of tenure and of the changes they are undergoing; for more positive policies in the planning of land use; for the preservation and if possible the extension of community rights; for greater control over sale and mortgage; for the establishment of suitable systems of agricultural credit; for greater protection of tenants and the extension of the principle of compensation for unexhausted improvements; and for the general building-up of a tradition of good husbandry which will prevent the present occupiers from attempting to exploit their trust.

In its original form this book consisted of a series of memoranda written between 1941 and 1943 for the information of a Colonial Office committee on post-war problems of which Lord Hailey was the chairman. Lord Hailey suggested that if these memoranda were recast and enlarged they might prove of use to Colonial governments, since they had brought together a great deal of widely scattered information. Colonial governments have no readily accessible means of ascertaining each others' problems regarding land and in the Colonial Office itself there is no machinery for the pooling of information. Steps are now being taken to remedy this defect and if this book should contribute towards this end and lead eventually to other more comprehensive and authoritative works it will have served a useful purpose. At the same time it is hoped that the book may be of use outside official circles; to students of agriculture, law, economics, and sociology, as well as to others who are interested in the general welfare of the peoples of the Colonial Empire. It should be clearly understood, however, that the views expressed in this study are not those of the Colonial Office, unless the contrary has been made clear by the context.

30 November 1945 C. K. MEEK

PREFACE TO SECOND EDITION

Since this book was written, in 1945, there have been many changes. Ceylon is no longer a 'colony'; in Africa many new developments, such as the ground-nut scheme of Tanganyika, have introduced new conceptions of land tenure; in Cyprus the Ottoman system described in the first edition has been abolished; and so on.

I should have liked in this new edition to have revised many of the previous chapters. But this must await some future occasion, and, apart from the chapter on Cyprus, which has been completely rewritten, this second edition is an exact reproduction of the first.

23 August, 1948. C. K. MEEK

CONTENTS

Introduction by Lord Hailey

I WELCOME the publication of Dr. Meek's work, for it has long been apparent that we need a comprehensive study of the systems of land tenure in the Colonies and the rights associated with them. I am indebted to him for giving me the opportunity of making, in this Introduction, some observations both on the general significance of the subject, and on the problems of policy to which it gives rise. Such views as are expressed here are of course my own; but they occupy, I fear, an undue space, and I apologize for this abuse of the hospitality Dr. Meek has extended to me.

The extensive programme of development which has now become the outstanding feature of our Colonial policy has given prominence to many aspects of administration which, though by no means neglected in the past, nevertheless did not seem to make the same claim on our attention as they demand to-day. The expansion of labour inspectorates, the foundation of Universities and technical institutions, improvements in urban housing and sanitation, the organization of marketing, the stimulation of secondary industries—all these are now in progress or in active contemplation. It is natural that the public of a highly industrialized country such as ours should view these matters with special interest, and it is all to the good that they should do so. But the increase of primary production still remains the basic problem in any endeavour to improve the general standards of life in the Colonies.

The issues which this problem involves are many-sided, and I am concerned here mainly with only one of the factors which have to be taken into account, namely, the general bearing which different systems of land tenure and the rights associated with them may have on the utilization of the land and the development of production. But this matter has wide implications affecting the social no less than the material life of the community, and its study demands a broader and in some sense a more fundamental approach than that adopted by the Colonial Administrations in dealing with some of the problems with which they have been faced. If I may take an illustration from a different but not dissimilar field of administrative policy, the type of approach which I have in mind would have insured a more careful study of the social factors underlying indigenous institutions before they were modified or replaced . It would have estimated the value of the alienation of land for European farming by its effect on the life of native societies, rather than by the extent to which it might increase the resources of the territory. Or to take another example, such an approach would have assessed the value of new systems of justice, not so much by their similarity to the methods followed in

Europe, as by the promise they held out of a capacity to win the confidence of native communities and thus to assist in moulding their conceptions of social conduct.

These reflections do not necessarily imply a criticism of either the goodwill or the competence of the earlier administrations. It is, indeed, only of recent years that we have seen in Europe itself an appreciation of the value of a systematic study of social factors as a basis for legislative and administrative action. One of the most characteristic developments of modern political philosophy is seen in the widening of the range assigned to governmental activity and responsibilities. There may be differences in the views held regarding the balance between state activity and private enterprise; but there is everywhere a tendency to assign to the state a wider authority and greater initiative as an agency for improving the social standards and the economic life of the community. Its competence in this respect has indeed become increasingly the test of the success with which a modern Government employs the powers committed to it. It is characteristic that among the more enlightened colonial powers this conception has now been projected from the domestic field into that of colonial policy, and a close study of social factors has become as essential in colonial administration as it has for the effective conduct of metropolitan politics.

The observations I have just made have a general bearing on the extent of the field of knowledge to which a modern colonial administration must have access. But there are circumstances which give them a special relevance to the study of systems of landholding and land rights, at all events as regards a large number of the Colonies. In a few of them, as for instance the older 'Colonies of Settlement' in the West Indies, lands have from the first been held on forms of tenure and title based on those prevailing in Great Britain. Circumstances have therefore limited the field in which their administrations may have to concern themselves with issues connected with the form of tenure or title. They may, for instance, have to legislate in order to determine the rights of surface proprietors in subsoil minerals; they may have to decide whether in the course of allotting Crown land for settlement, the title given should preferably be freehold or leasehold, or again, they may have to regulate by statute the relations of landlord and tenant. These questions may involve issues of considerable importance in the economic and social life of the community; but they have a less extended range than the issues which arise in the numerous African and Asiatic territories where the prevailing forms of land tenure are those prescribed by indigenous custom.

In this class of territories the administrations have of course been faced from an early date with the need for determining the nature of the tenure to be recognized in lands over which rights were being granted by the Crown, or acquired by concession from native authorities, especially in areas where legislation or administrative practice has made such concessions subject to official control. In such cases the responsibility of the government has been obvious, and the issues involved in determining the form of tenure to be prescribed were relatively simple. But the manner in which private lands are held by members of the native communities and the nature of the rights exercised over them give rise to a series of problems of a different character, though their significance has not always been fully appreciated.

It is true that a general understanding of the indigenous systems of landholding has been felt to be essential to those engaged in native administration, since these systems reflect in the most characteristic manner the political and social constitution of the community. A knowledge of local custom has been required on the part of those engaged in determining judicial issues regarding land, whether they have done so as officers of the Courts administering the statutory law, or as officers charged with the supervision of Native Tribunals administering the indigenous customary law where this procedure for trying issues is in force. Land has been less commonly used as the basis of taxation in the Colonies than in some other parts of the Empire, as for instance in British India, but in the few areas where this practice prevails, it has necessarily involved a study of the current system of holding land and the maintenance of a machinery for ascertaining the titles of those subject to this form of tax. But while there has been a general recognition of the need of knowledge for these particular purposes, and while there has of late years been a more active realization that existing knowledge must now be further implemented by systematic local studies, in another respect there has been some lack of recognition of the importance of the changes which economic forces produce in the customary systems of land holding, and of the extent to which a modern administration may have to take account of the bearing of these changes on the development of primary production.

Land-owning custom is an integral part of the social structure, and, as has been truly said, 'the social scene grows out of economic conditions, to much the same extent that political events in their turn grow out of social conditions'. There have of course been stages in the world's history when economic forces have had a less direct influence in modifying forms of land tenure than some other factors. Thus in the middle ages of Europe the system of land tenures was bound up with jurisdictional and governmental rights, and the changes which took place at that period were largely due to alterations in the series of duties and obligations which these rights connoted. The process was gradual; for some centuries the bulk of English legislation and the attention of English lawyers were concerned with the definition or adjustment of this class of rights. But at a later period, when the holding of land became progressively dissociated from rights and personal obligations which had their origin in political or social relations, and when economic factors exercised an increasing influence over the tenures under which land was held, the change was rapid and more clearly defined. Expressed in legal terms, the effect of economic forces has been to produce in England a gradual assimilation of the law of real property to that of personal property.

In many of the African and Asiatic Colonies, the process of change has been accelerated, and is likely to be increasingly accelerated in the future, in proportion as the more primitive systems of holding and utilizing land become adjusted to the needs of a modern economy of production and marketing. It is often possible to observe within the same territory the existence of communities which are at the different stages involved in this process of adjustment. When a pastoral is replaced by an agricultural economy, parts of the areas held in common by larger units (such as the tribe or clan) are recognized as having passed into the usufructuary occupation of smaller units, such as the family, either in its narrower or more extended sense. Where members of a group, such as an extended family or clan, cease to be members of it and proceed to farm on their own account, they acquire land as individuals. A more clearly defined change occurs when the cultivation of marketable crops takes the place of purely subsistence production. Boundaries become more clearly recognized; the units occupying the land tend to be narrowed down to the small family or even the individual; the conception of ownership gradually begins to replace that of usufruct. This is true even of areas where cultivation is, owing to the character of the climate or soil, still of the 'shifting' type; but the movement is of course even more marked where farming is of a permanent or intensive character.

A further stage arrives when, with the growing density of population and increased pressure on the land, holdings acquire a transferable value, and rights in them become more completely commercialized. It must be observed at the same time that the influence of economic factors is then seen chiefly in the manner in which rights are evolved and in the use which right-holders make of these rights, as for example by sale or transfer, or by the creation of tenancies. The manner in which rights in land pass by succession may still be regulated by tradition or social custom. This may itself have important economic consequences. A notable instance is the procedure by which holdings are subdivided among members of a family on the death of a right-holder, or are 'fragmented' in compliance with the procedure by which each of the subdivided shares is further dispersed in different localities in order to give the new holders access to lands of different quality. Many of these customs can be traced back to economic causes; the subdivision of land on succession, for instance, is possibly a relic of the time when cattle or other movable possessions were recognized as the sole form of individual property. But such practices, once firmly established, are long enduring, and tend to retain their force long after the conditions under which they were formed have ceased to exist.

In the earlier stages of development, changes in the system of land tenure due primarily to economic causes may be described as automatic, in the sense that they have consisted of a series of natural adjustments, which have seldom been the result of conscious decisions by the community or embodied in formal rules. At this stage, change in the actual form of tenure and in the rights attached to it must usually have appeared in the light of a conflict between established custom and new practices; the recognition given to a new practice meant that it in turn became a part of accepted custom. The process by which recognition has been given to the change has, in general, been through the decisions of the village elders or of the tribunals which have provided, under a variety of different forms, the means of adjusting differences arising between individuals, or between individuals and the community. The function of these tribunals was no doubt viewed by the community mainly as that of interpreting the bearing of established land custom on the particular point at issue. But since they also had to judge between the merits of previous custom and of a new practice growing up under the pressure of changing circumstances, the cumulative effect of their decisions has clearly had a wide influence in shaping the form which land rights have taken. In many Colonies, and particularly in Africa, this process is still strongly in evidence. All observers agree, for instance, as to the part which the decisions of the African Native Tribunals have taken in adapting previous custom to the requirements of more modern practices of production and marketing.

The development in recent years of the system of Native Authority Councils in many of the African Colonies may serve to give a more systematic character to this process. The Councils have powers to make rules for defining or for modifying customary law, and these rules, if endorsed by government, are binding on a Native Tribunal within their jurisdiction. There is a considerable variety in the measure to which they have availed themselves of this procedure. In the more economically advanced areas, there are some Councils which have sought to give formal recognition to transactions involving the sale by individuals of such rights as custom gives them over the lands held by them. There is ample evidence to show that the practice of sale has already become common in the areas included within the jurisdiction of these particular Councils; it is, however, noteworthy that earlier African land custom admitted only of the pledging, not of the sale, of rights in land. This followed logically on the conception that the land is the property of the community and that the rights of individuals extend only to its use. The formal recognition of the power of private sale would have the effect of giving a proprietary status to a right which by African tradition has always been treated as usufructuary, and as subject to the ultimate control of the community in pursuance of its reversionary interest in the land.

Other Councils have not sought to make a departure of so wide a character, but have confined themselves to attempts to determine the rights arising as the result of improvements effected by the occupier of a holding, as for instance by planting long term crops, such as coffee or cocoa. It must at the same time be noted that there are large areas in Africa where similar problems have not as yet presented themselves. These areas are either less closely populated or still practise the more 'extensive' methods of cultivation, and in this case the modifications of custom which have been considered by the Native Authority Councils refer chiefly to such matters as the allocation of waste lands among the members of the community or the procedure regulating succession.

There is another factor which has had a general influence in shaping the form in which systems of land tenure have developed in many of the Colonies. It has already been mentioned that in certain areas, notably in the West Indies, lands have from the first been held on forms of tenure similar to those prevailing in Great Britain; rights arising in such lands have been determined on analogies drawn from the English common or statutory law of property. In certain of these Colonies—as for instance in British Guiana, Jamaica and St. Lucia—certain features of the English law defining the relations of landlord and tenant have been reproduced by local enactments. But in the many other Colonies where the indigenous systems of land tenure prevail, the development of land rights has tended to be influenced by the fact that, side by side with lands held under native forms of tenure, there have also been considerable areas held under the forms recognized by English law.

In these Colonies, lands alienated by the Crown to settlers or industrial enterprises were at an earlier stage granted or sold on terms equivalent to freehold, though later policy has preferred a system of long leasehold. The conditions governing such transactions have frequently provided for an initial period of beneficial occupation, with a prescribed amount of expenditure on development, but these are incidents known also to English tenures. The holding of such lands has not been confined to Europeans; the extensive *mailo* lands in Uganda are, for instance, held entirely by natives of the country. But in certain of the territories holders of native lands have made a conscious effort to assimilate their own traditional forms of land rights to those under which alienated lands are held by grant from the Crown. However strongly the native may be attached to the traditions and associations which regulate his social life, it is inevitable that many individuals in the more progressive native communities should be increasingly attracted by the possibility of acquiring the more exclusive rights of possession or of transfer offered by modern English forms of tenure, in place of those which reflect in varying measure the tradition of collective landholding. There are conspicuous instances of this in the Native Reserves bordering on the Highland area occupied by Europeans in Kenya.

An influence of a somewhat similar nature has also been exercised by the existence of the British Courts of Justice and of lawyers practising the English law. The enactments under which the British Courts are constituted normally provide that they shall have regard to the customary native law where it is not repugnant to equity nor incompatible with any Colonial law for the time being in force. But the customary law in regard to the holding and use of land is not always easy of application by the British Courts. This is not due merely to the fact that in many cases, and particularly where the prevailing custom is that of a collective right in the land, the fundamental concepts on which the customary law is based necessarily differ very widely from those which regulate the modern English law of real property. There are difficulties of a more tangible nature. Where the customary law has come under the influence of a regularized system of law, such as that of Islam, the difficulties may be less apparent; but in many other cases, and particularly in Africa, the principles of the customary law and its local application are not readily recognizable.

The more primitive societies, and especially those who have not evolved for themselves the art of writing, seldom think of their institutions in precise terms or attempt to analyse the principles on which they are based. Even to the sociologist, the rights associated with the holding of land in native communities must often appear indeterminate and difficult to categorize; a judicial authority must find unusual difficulty in forming a clear view of them amid the complex of social privileges and obligations of which they form a part. His task would be facilitated were there made available to him a comprehensive study of the customary law prevailing in the Colony, or even a digest of the growing body of case law on the subject. Unfortunately he very seldom has this advantage. In the circumstances it is not unnatural that in attempting to find a logical basis for deciding the particular matter at issue, he should often tend to approach it from the more familiar standpoint of the English law of property. The difficulty encountered by British Courts in this respect has been recognized in certain of the African Colonies, where the trial of issues regarding rights in land held under the native customary law has been confined to the Native Tribunals or to officers acting in an administrative capacity. But there are notable cases to the contrary, the most striking of which is the Gold Coast Colony. There the attempt to apply the terms of English law to land rights which in many important respects are still largely those traditional in Africa, and the use by inexpert hands of conveyancing on the English model, have led to much confusion and much unprofitable litigation.

One further process which may influence the form taken by land tenures must also be noted. In many countries of the world, the system of land tenures has been given a more precise and established form by the institution of a procedure for the public registration of conveyances or for the maintenance of a public record of titles. These are not alternative processes; they serve different purposes and may exist side by side; but the maintenance of a public record of titles must inevitably have a more far-reaching effect than the mere registration of conveyances. It is unnecessary to recall here the history of the long debates in England on the merits of these systems. Proposals for the registration of conveyances date as far back as the time of Henry VIII; schemes for the general record of titles were discussed by the Commonwealth Parliament. The subsequent stages in the historyof this question are marked by the reports of the Commissions of 1829 and 1857, the Westbury Act of 1862, the Cairns Act of 1875 and the Halsbury Act of 1897. That the public record of titles has in practice been confined to two only of the English counties is probably due to the complicated nature of the settlements and 'uses' to which real property has been subjected.

The course taken by this development in England has, however, been influenced by circumstances of an exceptional nature, to which there is no analogy in most of the Colonies. It is more in point to consider the position in British India. There not only are conveyances subject to public registration, but there is, save in some areas which came under the Permanent Settlement of 1793, an officially maintained record of all titles in the lands lying outside the urban areas. This had its origin in the requirements created by the fiscal system inherited from earlier rulers, under which the state derived its chief resources from a share in the produce of the soil; the main contribution of British rule was the systematic commutation of the share of produce into a money tax and its adjustment to the ascertained production of different soils and types of cultivation. The 'land revenue', as the tax was called, was fixed for a sufficiently long period to give security to the cultivator, but was liable to periodic revision in view of changing prices or an alteration in the system of culture. This procedure involved a cadastral survey and a record, prepared after detailed local investigation, of the titles of the rightholders who became liable to the payment of land revenue. It is of the essence of the record that it should be kept continuously up-to-date, by entering all mutations due to succession, sale, mortgage or the like.

The record of titles, which was thus originally designed to meet fiscal requirements, subsequently acquired a value in clarifying private rights and in giving a sense of security to rightholders which exceeded its importance as a record of obligations to the State. For the present purpose, however, it is necessary to refer only to the influence which this process has exercised in shaping the form of land tenures. The officers who prepared the initial record set out to ascertain and describe the rights which were exercised under local custom, but they tended to define them in terms familiar to the English law of property, much perhaps as the Norman compilers of the Domesday Book tended to record in terms of feudal law certain classes of English tenures with which they were not themselves familiar. The terms of English law were admittedly more appropriate to Indian conditions than they would be to those prevailing in Africa and some other parts of Asia; but it is to this tendency that we owe the wide recognition in India of what is practically a freehold right, unrestricted in respect of the power of transfer or encumbrance.

Broadly speaking, the systematic record of titles has in the Colonies been confined to lands held under English forms of tenure, of which the greater part are to be found in the Crown lands alienated to settlers or to private enterprises. With few exceptions, the Colonial Governments have not yet contemplated the extension of the system to lands held under native forms of tenure. A record of titles, unfortunately incomplete, has been maintained in respect of the *mailo* lands in Uganda, and the system under which all lands in the Malayan States are treated as held from the Sultans on payment of quit-rent has involved the maintenance of what is in effect the basis of a record of title. But if and when circumstances require the institution of some procedure for the record of titles in native lands, the terms in which titles are described will become of great importance. In England, such a record is largely a matter of convenience, in that it can provide an authoritative and readily accessible record of individual rights, but they would be described in terms which already have a clearly established meaning in common or statute law. In the conditions of most of the Colonies, the institution of a record of native titles would have an influence in shaping the form of land rights and in defining their content which might be hardly less important than that which could be exerted by an act of legislation.

It seems clear that some form of procedure for recording titles in native lands must sooner or later be introduced by many of the Colonial governments, though doubtless it would be undertaken by stages, beginning with the more economically advanced areas. Where there is little pressure on the land or where considerable areas of waste are still available for occupation, the existence of indeterminate or ill-defined rights in land does not involve any serious disadvantage. The system of rights is well understood within the community; the differences which arise about the use of land are relatively few, and the traditional methods of adjusting them are adequate for the purpose. But a time arises when a procedure appropriate to an 'extensive' system of using land becomes unsuitable for its more intensive use; indeterminate or ill-defined rights are then a source of uncertainty and insecurity, and prejudice the development of agriculture. They are a fruitful cause of litigation, and litigation becomes all the more burdensome when the Courts have no certain standards on which to adjudicate. There are already instances quoted in Africa where persons desiring to acquire rights in land have found themselves obliged to compound with five or six parties successively claiming the right to dispose of them. The maintenance of a record of titles is unfortunately expensive, as it must be continuous if it is to serve its purpose. It is not necessary to discuss here the extent to which it must be preceded by a cadastral survey, nor which of the various forms of record adopted in different parts of the world is most suitable to Colonial conditions. The purpose for which reference has been made to the matter here is to point out that in many cases the introduction of some form of record may be unavoidable.

This survey of the processes which are liable to influence the formation of systems of land tenure in the Colonies has necessarily been somewhat cursory, but it may serve as a background for considering the significance which the results of this development may have for Colonial Administrations, and the direction in which they may suitably utilize such powers as they may possess in order to guide its progress. Its immediate results will be seen most obviously in the economic and social field, but it is clear that they must ultimately influence also the character of the elements which will be represented in the political institutions of the country. A community of self-cultivating peasant landholders will obviously present political characteristics far different from one of which the prevailing economy is of large landed proprietors and a subordinate tenantry. It is noteworthy that much of the modern agrarian legislation in Continental Europe, while primarily designed to secure a more equal distribution of landed property, has also been largely influenced by a desire to readjust the political forces resulting from the manner in which property is held.

In the extensive Colonial areas in which the system of landholding is based on the conception of a collective right in the land, the most conspicuous effect of economic development will, as has already been remarked, appear in the progressive individualization of holdings. That process will have the economic advantage of giving to the holders a greater sense of security and a greater incentive to a more intensive type of cultivation; on the other hand, its undue acceleration may hasten the disintegration of the present social structure and thus weaken the basis on which the institutions of local self-government are now being built up. Then, again, the direction which individualization may take is important. The form taken may be that of a proprietary tenure which excludes the reversionary interest of the community or the exercise of any control by it; it may, on the other hand, be that of a usufructuary occupancy which secures full enjoyment of the land to the holder and his successors during its beneficial use, but enables the community to resume possession of a holding when its beneficial use ceases, or to terminate possession on payment of equitable compensation for improvements effected.

Again, assuming that the tenure which is evolved is that of proprietorship, it will make a difference whether this carries the rights usually associated with freehold, namely, the free power of sale or of encumbrance, or whether there are any limitations to the use of such rights. They may, for example, be restricted in respect of the class of persons to whom proprietorship can be transferred, or of the type of mortgages or other encumbrances which may be effected. It is unnecessary to enlarge on the importance of this last consideration in colonial conditions. A free use of the power of transfer may facilitate the formation of large-scale holdings, and though this has an economic advantage in respect of those types of production which require the use of capital and organized management, it has other possibilities of a less desirable character. Thus it may result in the creation of a class of landlords which performs no economic function in return for the share which it receives of the produce of cultivation; it may again lead to the replacement of the self-cultivating peasant landholder by tenants who may have no security either in respect of their tenure or of the incidence of rentals. Apart from other considerations, the existence of a tenantry with insecure rights is an obstacle to the formation of co-operative organizations either for credit or for marketing purposes. The growth of a landlord system may even lead, where there is considerable density of population, to the creation of a landless class, a source of grave economic and social weakness so long as local conditions offer no alternative form of employment in industry or commerce.

There can be no question that the form of proprietorship which carries a full power of transfer or encumbrance has its value in providing the means for raising long-term credit based on the land itself, apart from the short-term credits obtainable on the security of the crops. This is an important element in obtaining capital for expanding the area of cultivation or securing the equipment necessary for a more intensive use of land. Experience has shown that there is often a difficulty in replacing this source of credit by other means, such as state or private organizations for the supply of long-term agricultural credit. Only where the co-operative credit society is very fully developed does it seem capable of providing a satisfactory substitute. But experience has also shown that credit acquired on the basis of land rights is always liable to be misused in order to provide expenditure, often on an extravagant scale, for other than agricultural purposes. It is unnecessary to enlarge on the disastrous effects which have followed on the wide misuse of agricultural credit in this manner by the ignorant and inexperienced landholders of some Asiatic and African countries. The economic serfdom of large numbers of the agricultural classes in those countries has proved a grave menace to material progress and social order, and in some cases has been the cause of serious political unsettlement.

There are further implications in the form taken by the development of the local system of land tenure and rights; if they are not of the same order, they are nevertheless of some practical importance. An undue acceleration in the growth of a system of proprietary tenures may impair the success of major schemes of irrigation, which depends largely on the holding of land in units suitable for irrigated cultivation. The establishment of exclusive rights over pastoral lands may make it difficult to adopt the regime of rotational closures necessary to prevent their deterioration. Measures necessary for soil conservation, such as contour ridging, may be rendered more difficult; if, for example, the existing rights in the 'strip' lands common in parts of the Middle East (which are often over a thousand yards in length and only one or two in breadth) were crystallized into proprietorship, there would be an additional difficulty in giving effect to measures for soil protection. Exceptional difficulties are also liable to occur in connection with the rights in certain forestal products, for example palm trees. As experience shows, such rights may be held in a manner which presents grave obstacles to the development of economic methods of processing or marketing.

It is not possible to adopt any uniform solution of the problems to which developments of this nature may give rise. The solution must lie in finding a balance between the advantages and disadvantages they present in the light of the circumstances prevailing in different localities. The powers which an administration may possess to influence or control the formation of land tenures or rights will be subsequently considered, but it is clear that if circumstances are such as to give it such powers, it should take advantage of them before rights are consolidated or vested interests are established.

The difficulty of taking action when rights are consolidated is obvious. In various parts of the world it has been found necessary, partly for economic and partly for social reasons, to undertake legislation in order to curtail the power to transfer or encumber proprietory rights; typical examples are to be found in the Punjab Act of 1900, or the Zanzibar legislation of 1939, and there are examples also in the agrarian legislation of certain European countries, such as Poland, Lithuania and Rumania. Even more numerous are the instances in which legislation has been undertaken in order to adjust the relations of landlords and tenants, either by safeguarding the security of tenancies or by making the enhancement of rentals subject to some form of judicial process. There are, again, many instances in which Governments have found it necessary to liquidate a general state of agricultural indebtedness by instituting a statutory machinery for the composition of debts or even for their compulsory reduction. It is not unnatural that Governments should often have hesitated to embark on the drastic and indeed revolutionary legislation required to effect a radical cure of the situation which has called for remedy. But even the measures which they have taken, incomplete as they have often proved to be in their results, have invariably involved much economic dislocation and have tended to raise controversial issues in political policy. It would, of course be incorrect to suggest that the circumstances which have made legislative intervention necessary have in every case arisen from the form in which the system of land tenure has developed. But where this can be clearly seen as a contributory cause, it obviously becomes a matter of public policy to take preventive action at as early a stage as possible.

The preceding considerations refer in the main to questions arising from the manner in which systems of land tenure have—to use the term previously employed—automatically adjusted themselves to new economic conditions. But it is necessary to make some reference also to the special problems which might arise from the application of certain schemes which are now the subject of much current discussion, and involve direct action by the state in order to secure the most beneficial use of the land. As has already been observed, the increase of primary production must, in the existing circumstances of the Colonies, necessarily have a high priority among the measures taken to improve the standard of living. In previous discussions of policy, this has usually been regarded as involving a choice between two methods—the development of large-scale production through the agency of organizations or individuals having command of adequate capital resources and managerial skill, or alternatively, the stimulation of a peasant economy by making available to it the technical assistance of Departments of Agriculture, and by the organization of improved systems of marketing. This issue arises in its most critical form in respect of the production of certain commodities for the export market, and especially those which require processing. The factors involved are relatively simple in respect of some products, such as sisal or sugar; they are more complex in respect of others, such as palm oil, where (as the respective experiences of Nigeria and the Netherlands East Indies show) development depends largely on the use of scientific methods in order to meet the demand in the world market for oil of a standard quality. The part which a peasant economy can play in the production of rubber is a matter on which different views are held. But these problems do not of course present a clear cut choice of economic policies, since the social issues involved in the adoption of one or other system are not less important, and indeed in the view of many are even more important, than the economic results.

There are, however, now some schools of thought which do not consider that these two alternatives exhaust the possibilities of securing a sufficiently rapid development of primary production or the full utilization of the land resources of a Colony. One school holds that this can best be achieved, or perhaps can only be achieved, by a system in which the state and the rural community would become partners in exploiting the resources available for primary production. The former would contribute capital, mechanical equipment, skilled direction, and marketing facilities; the latter would contribute the land and the labour, the produce being shared between the two partners in a ratio adjusted to the interests involved. Those who adopt this view have doubtless been influenced by the results attained by the Soviet system of collective farming, though they have also taken into account that there are many Colonial areas in which the tradition still prevails of communal land-holding and of the pooling of labour when preparing the soil for cultivation. A second school of thought does not contemplate measures so far-reaching; it favours the use of a procedure involving a tripartite partnership between the Government, private capital and the native landholder, on lines analogous to those made familiar by the Sudan Plantations Syndicate in the irrigated lands of the Gezira. There are variants to this procedure in the Alternative Livelihood Scheme of the Sudan and the Latifiyah Estates Scheme in Iraq. A third school would still further reduce the measure of Government action, and contemplates the development of primary production through public utility corporations promoted by Government, but having a considerable measure of independence in their operation.

It would be out of place to canvass here the respective merits of these schemes. But if experiments are to be made in their use, the character of the prevailing system of land tenure in any area selected for the purpose must have an important bearing on the ease with which they could be introduced. The introduction of any fully developed system of collective farming would obviously involve a control by the community over all existing rights in the land, whether they had taken the form of a proprietary or a usufructuary tenure. It is only possible to say here that the operation might present somewhat less difficulty in the case of the latter. As regards the scheme described as that of tripartite partnership, it will be recalled hat the introduction of the Gezira project involved the statutory acquisition by the Sudan Government of the leasehold throughout a prolonged period of all rights in the land, subject to the provision that existing right-holders should have a claim to any tenancies created on the lands brought under irrigation. Even the operations of a Development Corporation might involve the need for readjusting the areas occupied by individuals or groups of right-holders, in order to secure the most suitable units for cultivation. That might in particular be essential where land has been subject to a high degree of subdivision or fragmentation. It is of interest to note that the acquisition of the land recently required for an experimental farm in the Middle East involved negotiations with no less than six hundred right-holders.

Assuming, however, that the Colonial Administrations have so important an interest as has been suggested in the course taken by the formation of land tenures or rights, it still remains to consider what powers they may possess for guiding or controlling it. There is a wide diversity in the circumstances which determine these powers. Where, as in certain of the West Indies, rights over private lands are well established in forms analogous to those familiar in the English common or statute law, the Government could now only take action by means of legislation. That would in effect be also the course open in Ceylon. In certain West African territories, of which the Gold Coast Colony is the most conspicuous example, the power of the Government to affect the form of land tenures by other than legislative processes is also limited by circumstances. The form of tenures has not yet been stabilized, and customary rights are still undergoing a rapid process of development under economic influences; but long-standing policy precludes the Government from direct intervention in the rights in native lands. The theory of the 'ultimate' right of the Crown in all the lands of the Colony may doubtless prevail, as it does in English common law, but it has not been construed in this case as giving the Crown any greater degree of control over rights in private lands than would be available to the Crown in England.

Any measure designed to determine the nature or to control the exercise of such rights would therefore have to take the form of legislation; it is of interest to note that the only measure of importance so far passed by the legislature is the Concessions Ordinance, which prescribes that all concessions of lands made by private right-holders must be validated by the Supreme Court, and limits the area over which individual concessions may extend. The situation is, in broad terms, much the same in the Sierra Leone Protectorate. At the same time, there remain open two ways in which the Administration may exert some influence over the form in which land rights may develop in these two Colonies. It can bring pressure to bear on the native authorities, though the scope for action is perhaps less in the Gold Coast than in some other parts of Africa. There would be a more definite field of influence if and when the Government proceeded to introduce any machinery for the public record of titles.

But there are many Colonial territories in which the Governments are in a stronger position to take action otherwise than by legislation. The situation in the Malayan States, to which allusion has already been made, gives the Administration definite powers to determine the form which tenures or rights shall take. In certain African territories, as for instance in the Northern Territories of the Gold Coast, Northern Nigeria or Tanganyika, the Government has asserted rights which have been embodied in statutes of which the effect is to declare that all lands in the territory are native lands, to be held and administered for the use and common benefit of the natives of the territory. But all such lands are 'at the disposition' of the Government; no title to the occupation and use of lands is valid without the consent of the Governor; the Governor must in the exercise of his powers respect native law and custom. One of the main objectives in taking these powers was to secure full control over alienations by natives to non-natives. Where such alienations are made, they now normally take the form of 'occupancy' rights, for a definite term, not of freehold.

As regards the lands remaining in native occupation, which of course constitute the great majority of lands in those territories, the validity of the title of any individual or group of individuals will, in terms of the statute, depend on its recognition by Government, but it has at the same time been provided that the right of occupancy will include the title of a native or native community using or occupying land in accordance with native custom. While the purport of this provision is to afford a general safeguard for native customary rights, the law does not itself determine the form of the rights which an individual may have in the land he occupies or which may arise as between individuals and the community. These are left to be determined by custom, and in some areas custom, as interpreted by the Native Tribunals, has, in response to economic changes, begun to recognize relations which have much of the character of individual proprietorship. The manner in which customary rights are being developed within the general framework of the over-proprietorship of the Crown, is thus a matter of importance, and the administration clearly has the power to determine the form in which they shall be recognized.

There are other considerable areas in Africa where the Administration has an even more definite authority and a more direct responsibility, those, namely in which previous policy has led to the creation of 'Reserves' for native occupation. The right of the native community to occupy the lands of the Reserves is secured by statute, and this position is not affected by the fact that, in strict terms of law, the proprietorship in the lands must be held to lie in the Crown or the body which is vested by statute with the trusteeship over them. Here also the nature of the rights which may be exercised by individuals or groups of individuals, subject to the over-riding conception of the proprietorship of the Crown or the trustee body, are left to be determined by custom. In some areas, more particularly in certain of the Kenya Reserves, the growing process of individualization is leading to the recognition among the native community of rights which have a close resemblance to freehold. They are, it is understood, finding support from the decisions of the Native Tribunals, and they may therefore attain the character of established custom. But it is not clear whether the existence of rights of this nature is in accord with the views of the Administration as to the most appropriate form of tenure under which lands in the Reserves should be held by members of the native community. It would be embarrassing if a conflict should develop between established native custom and official policy. It could be avoided if the Administration were to clarify its intention in this respect and to institute the machinery necessary to give effect to it.

It seems unnecessary to labour the argument by drawing other illustrations from the many diverse units of which the Colonial

Empire is composed. I will only revert to the point made at the beginning of this Introduction. Our policy of Colonial development enlarges, perhaps to an embarrassing degree, the range of matters to which Colonial Administrations must now give their consideration. But among them the questions which arise in connection with the system of land tenures and rights must have a very strong claim on their attention. The land, and the interests of those who live on the land, must always be their first care. And as the Anglo-American Caribbean Commission justly remark in their Report of August 1943, 'the productivity of land and the social advancement of the people are dependent as much upon the evolution of sound systems of land tenure as upon the development of improved agricultural practice'.

HAILEY

CHAPTER I

The Economic, Social and Political Importance of Systems of Holding Land

The complex character of land tenure

The word tenure, from the Latin *tenere* = to hold, implies that land is 'held' under certain conditions. There are wide variations in these conditions. The occupiers may or may not be owners, and the owners may or may not be occupiers. Land may be held by landlords, leaseholders, or peasant proprietors. The landlords may be individuals, companies, or Governments. There are innumerable forms of tenancy. There may be tenants with full rights of occupancy, tenants for a fixed term of years, or tenants at will. Where there is a dual interest in the occupation of land, tenancy may take the form of the system known as *métayage*, whereby the proprietor receives a proportion of the crops; or it may take the form of labour or cash contributions. Land may belong to a kinship or local group, the individual members of which have rights of users only. It may belong legally to the State, but in practice the occupiers may enjoy all the privileges of proprietors. It may be heritable and alienable, or heritable but inalienable. It may be heritable by certain classes of relatives only. It may be held subject to rules for the prevention of subdivision and the promotion of good husbandry. There is a common saying that property is a bundle of rights, and to no form of property is this more applicable than to land.[1]

The importance of land tenures in the development of Agriculture

The conditions under which land is held are of far-reaching importance for the development of agriculture. If land is plentiful, population sparse and the people are still content with a subsistence economy, then it is possible to practise a system of shifting cultivation without doing any damage to the land, and without the necessity

[1] But land tenure cannot be studied solely from the legal standpoint. While in the narrower sense it may be described as 'the body of rules which govern the practice of cultivation and apportionment of produce', yet in its wider sense it covers, as Malinowski insists, the whole relationship of man to the soil. This relationship on the one hand transforms the land, and on the other causes human beings to live together in families and other forms of social groupings, bound together by common work and by common religious ritual and beliefs which serve as a kind of charter for the right to use the land. Thus the study of land tenure, besides being a study of agricultural economies, is also one of sociology. See *Coral Gardens and their Magic*, by B. Malinowski, Vol. I, pp. 318, 338, 376. Chapter XI of this book indicates the method of field-work which, in Malinowski's opinion, must be followed in any comprehensive investigation of systems of tenure.

of imposing rigid rules of tenure. But when the population becomes denser, or for some reason there is a marked increase in the area of cultivated land, it may become necessary to devise more settled systems of holding land. In Uganda the acreage of the more important crops increased from 1,210,722 in 1916 to 4,030,952 in 1936, a change which meant that three and a half times as much land had become necessary in 1936 as was required twenty years previously. In consequence the fallow periods have been gradually reduced, and if this process is permitted to continue, large areas must be thrown out of production.[1] In many parts of the British Colonial Empire there are clear signs that population, under the influence of new economic conditions, is fast outgrowing available land, and if existing standards of living are to be improved, or even maintained, then shifting cultivation must give way to rotational farming. In other words there will have to be extensive alterations in the methods of holding land. In Kenya recently (1937) a Government Committee pointed out that land tenure was of fundamental importance in relation to the problem of malnutrition and that, on this account, research into the methods of holding land was a matter of the utmost urgency. In some districts of Kenya the congestion had, they said, become so great, that, in the absence of regulation, the land situation would, within ten years, almost certainly become chaotic.

Factors which determine the character of tenure

The character of the crops may determine the character of the tenure. Some forms of cultivation can best be carried out on a plantation basis with the assistance of outside capital, which may demand the grant of freehold title or of leases for a lengthy period. Where there is insufficient security of title, crops which take many years to mature cannot usually be grown, nor can the funds necessary for development be raised on the land. Peasants are not usually possessed of sufficient capital, technical equipment, or the marketing organization, which would enable them to compete in world markets.[2] On the other hand, plantations, by reason of their very specialization and reliance on a single crop, are liable to collapse, with a collapse in the price of the commodity they grow, and to be broken up into small holdings, whereas the absence of any cash basis for his crop keeps the farm of the subsistence agriculturist intact.

[1] See *A Report on nineteen Surveys, etc.*, by J. D. Tothill, D.Sc., formerly Director of Agriculture in Uganda.

[2] But they are becoming increasingly enabled by the development of the Co-operative movement.

Yet many subsistence agriculturists have taken to the growing of plantation crops, with the result that land which was formerly the collective property of the group has now become the private property of individual members of the group, with new rights of transfer and new rules of inheritance. On the other hand, again, with the mechanization of agriculture and the demand for large-scale production, peasant farming is, in some countries such as Russia and Mexico, giving way to co-operative agriculture on a basis of large collective farms.[1]

A few examples will illustrate the response which tenure makes to the character of the crop. In the sugar industry the need for regular supplies of cane, coupled with technical developments, have tended both in Fiji and the West Indies towards the aggregation of individually-owned plantations into large company-owned estates.[2] But in the case of other plantation crops, where capital expenditure on a large scale for processing is less necessary, individually owned plantations have continued to predominate. Thus, most of the cocoa and coco-nut plantations of the West Indies are owned by single individuals. With these the capital cost of planting and tending, until the production period arrives, is generally met by mortgage, when personal funds are inadequate. Compared with sugar, the preparation of cocoa requires no large capital outlay. It is for this reason that it has been possible for the people of the Gold Coast to build up, on the foundation of peasant proprietorship, the most prosperous cocoa-growing industry in the world. This has been done in a single generation. Yet, since the life of a cocoa-tree is hardly more than a generation, and yields begin to decline after twenty-five years, it has become apparent that cocoa-growers on the Gold Coast are faced with the problem of having to adopt more scientific and more intensive methods of cultivation than are easily attained under a peasant system. In Nigeria, also, there is the same problem of adapting a system of peasant ownership of land, and of palms, to the production of a grade of palm-oil which will be able to hold its own with the standard products of the plantations of the East. In Kenya and Tanganyika the manner of land distribution has, to a large extent, determined the form of agricultural development pursued by Europeans on the one hand, and by native Africans on the other; so that not only may the character of the crop determine

[1] Individual holding of land, however, is not incompatible with co-operative methods of farming. In some parts of Africa it co-exists with collective holding, and this, indeed, is the system followed in Russia to-day.

[2] In Mauritius the introduction into sugar factories of the vacuum pan and large-scale central was followed by a reduction in the number of estates equipped with factories. In due course these estates ceased to function and were broken up into a series of small holdings. See Dr. Martin Leake's *Further Studies in Tropical Land Tenure* in *Tropical Agriculture*, Vol. XVI, No. 1. The writer is much indebted to these studies by Dr. Martin Leake.

the system of tenure, but the system of tenure and the character of the land may determine the character of the crop. Obsolete methods of holding land may entail obsolete systems of cultivation.

Climate, also, may have a determining effect on tenure. Northern Nigeria, for example, with its comparatively dry climate, is more suited to short season crops than to the cultivation of perennial products such as cocoa, and efforts are on this account being directed towards promoting a balanced system of 'mixed' farming, under which the fertility of the soil will be maintained by a settled population.[1] This policy, if successful, will entail revolutionary changes in the existing system of holding land. Again, where water supplies are deficient, there is usually a sparse population, and cattle may be the dominant element in the economy. Large areas may be left undeveloped as grazing grounds. In many parts of Tanganyika mixed farming on a permanent basis can only be established where the water supplies are adequate.[2] In Cyprus, drought conditions have been a main cause of agricultural debt.[3] In Antigua the frequency of drought is one of the principal reasons for basing the agricultural economy almost solely on sugar.[4] In Fiji the earliest sugar enterprises were located in the wetter regions of the islands, but experience showed that richer sugar-cane juices could be obtained from canes grown in the drier regions. And so lands which were formerly under sugar cane have now passed into pastures for stock-raising and dairying. In Ceylon, shifting cultivation is common in the dry zone, which has offered little attraction to any but subsistence agriculturists, but in the wet zone the production of tea, rubber, coco-nuts and other economic crops has led to an enormous development both of large estates and of village holdings.[5] In Malaya, also, the suitability of the climate for the cultivation of almost every form of tropical product has acted like a magnet for foreign capital and led to the establishment of countless plantation industries under company ownership. In West Africa, on the other hand, the unhealthiness of the climate has operated against European settlement and has been at least partly responsible for the differences between the West African and East African Colonies in the legal position regarding the tenure of land.

It may be pointed out, however, that many of the unfavourable conditions created by climate can now be overcome. Irrigation schemes have transformed the economic life of many countries, and

[1] By 'mixed' farming is meant the combination of arable and animal husbandry.

[2] See the 1938 report of the Director of Agriculture. C. Gillman's *Geography and Hydrography of Tanganyika*, 1943, is an instructive study of the economic effects of climatic conditions.

[3] See pp. 62 and 69.

[4] *Antigua Agricultural Report, 1938.*

[5] See the *Amalgamated General Report for Ceylon, 1929*, p. 95.

in the future may be expected to restore to cultivation immense areas of land, particularly in Africa.[1] Moreover, new methods of seed selection enable crops to be grown in regions where the shortness of the rainy season formerly precluded agriculture.[2] In China, and other parts of the world, semi-desert regions are being brought under cultivation by means of tractor methods. Machinery is, therefore, affecting tenure, and is everywhere tending to replace the small-scale methods of the individual by the large-scale methods of the co-operative group. The increased use of machinery may be expected to lead to an increase in the numbers of the landless classes, or to free large sections of the community for other forms of industry.

Systems of marketing affect systems of tenure. Where, for example, the economy is one of small peasant producers, the dependence on middlemen for the marketing of the crops may lead to conditions of 'sharing' or of debt-servitude and the wholesale loss of land. This has happened in Cyprus, Ceylon and Zanzibar. In Zanzibar the Government was obliged to intervene in order to prevent agricultural lands falling into the hands of non-agricultural moneylenders. Interlocked with the question of marketing is that of transport. In the Northern Territories of the Gold Coast the absence of suitable transport facilities has been a limiting factor in the production of crops for export, and this in turn has prevented the development of land tenure along the individualistic lines which are now characteristic of the Southern regions. In Northern Rhodesia the distinctions in the methods of alienating land to Europeans, based on distance from the railway line, have caused much dissatisfaction, while the insufficiency of access to the railway for the inhabitants of the native reserves has been one of the factors that have led to a revision of the land policy of the Protectorate.[3] In many territories ribbon development along railway lines and motor roads has created serious problems of soil erosion.

The relative merits of freehold and leasehold provide yet another example of the interdependence of land tenure conditions and of agricultural development. It has long been held that freehold is the surest method of encouraging the improvement of land. Agriculture

[1] Egypt depends almost exclusively on its irrigation system which is now in process of transformation from a 'basin' system under which the land lay fallow in summer to one in which crops can be grown continuously throughout the year.

[2] Technological investigations may lead to the discovery of grasses or other fodder plants which are able to survive the long dry seasons of tropical and subtropical regions, and this may transform the local systems of husbandry and so of tenures. Some grasses, incidentally, (e.g. elephant grass) appear to have a special potency in producing a good soil structure and their use may prove the best of all measures to prevent erosion, which is primarily due to climatic conditions.

[3] See *Report of the Commission appointed to Enquire into the Financial and Economic Position of N. Rhodesia (1938)* Colonial No. 145, Para. 164.

is a long-range industry and the conditions attaching to leases have often been found to be a hindrance to development. Recently in Kenya many of the European settlers have objected to the revisable rental conditions of their leaseholds, and demanded an inheritable estate such as freehold alone can provide. Freehold title, they maintain, belongs to the very essence of colonization. Similar demands have been made by Negro farmers in the West Indies, Indians in Fiji, and many of the peoples of Uganda. The wide demand for freehold may be regarded as part of the general development of economic individualism.[1]

Yet the indiscriminate grant of freehold title may have the most disastrous effects on the welfare of any territory, since it may effectively tie the hands of governments in all schemes of agricultural advance. Ignorant peasants armed with freehold rights may soon destroy the country's capital. An effective system of State ownership, on the other hand, assures to the community the maintenance of the fertility of the soil, as well as such incremental value as may arise, not from the efforts of the occupiers, but from the development of the country as a whole. Yet, where the cultivators are mere occupiers at the will of the Government, there may be an excess of bureaucratic control which may interfere with initiative and lead even to political unrest. There will be more to be said on this subject later.[2]

Religion often colours the attitude of peoples towards the land, and many cling to exhausted soil because their ancestors lie buried there. Indeed, in Africa, the ancestors are commonly regarded as the real owners of the land. Thus, immigrant conquerors may continue to recognize, in land administration, the traditional authority of the heads of the indigenous groups. On the other hand, magico-religious beliefs, notably in the form of the fear of witchcraft, have been a frequent cause of migration. To countless people in Africa freedom to migrate may be of paramount importance, not merely that they may escape from economic or political oppression, but from the tyranny of evil spirits. It will be seen later that elasticity is one of the characteristics of native systems of tenure, and this makes it possible for complete strangers to be given a free share of village land.

Then there are the moral or treaty rights of natives. In order to

[1] But there is now a reaction from individualism towards co-operation (e.g. in Russia, Mexico, and China).

[2] See Chapter XX (pp. 243-8). Sir Henry Rew has observed that the line of demarcation between ownership and tenancy is not so well-defined as at first sight appears. Ownership may give no more than limited control of the land, while, on the other hand, the terms of tenancy may be such (as in the case of the new class of State tenants in Denmark) that they confer practically all the rights of ownership. See Art., 'Land Tenure' in *Ency. Brit.*

protect the interests of the natives it may be necessary to maintain systems of tenure and of agriculture which do not permit of the full exploitation of the land. There are many peoples in the Colonial Empire whose social cohesion might be seriously impaired by sudden innovations in the system of holding land. All over Africa, for example, land is held and worked on a kinship or local group basis, and if an individual system were suddenly substituted in the interests, say, of mixed farming, many social values might be lost, including the break-up of the co-operative labour groups which are highly efficient units of production. On the other hand, some systems of tenure may persist long after the social conditions which called them into being have disappeared.

Bound up with the social organization are systems of inheritance. In some communities personal property passes to sons, but landed property goes to sisters' sons. This may work well under a subsistence economy, but with the introduction of plantation crops, such as cocoa or coco-nut, a farmer may be unwilling to sink his personal capital on a plantation that would pass to his sister's children. In the Gold Coast the suggestion has been made that under such circumstances sons should be allowed to inherit, on condition that a rental for the land is paid to the sister's children. This is another instance of the effect which may be produced on tenure by the introduction of commercial crops.[1] Other difficulties caused by rules of inheritance are when lands, which have been received in pledge, are inherited, not by the family heir, but by sons, on the ground that such lands were obtained by the father's personal effort and not by that of the family group. The excessive sub-division of land caused by certain systems of inheritance—notably the Muhammadan—is a major problem in almost every colony.[2] And so, too, is the excessive fragmentation that arises from the attempt to give each of several heritors a share of each of the various types of land that constitute a holding. On the other hand, rights of co-ownership may be a bar to development, and where there are a number of heritors, but only one works the land, a distinction may arise between ownership of the land and ownership of its produce.

[1] But conflict between patrilineal and matrilineal principles may be a normal state. Malinowski has shown how, in the Trobriand Islands, the father of a family and his wife's brother each tries to get as much as he can out of his legal claims and at the same time tries to weaken the legal claims which work against his influence and power. See *Coral Gardens and Their Magic*, Vol. I, p. 359.

[2] In order to prevent undue sub-division, testamentary and intestate succession may be made subject to control. But if succession is restricted to a single heir the working capital of the property may be seriously reduced, since the heir may be obliged by the social code to make provision for his younger brothers. In some dependencies, e.g. Cyprus, the land laws are complicated by the fact that there are different rules of inheritance for Christians and for Moslems.

Then, again, there are the land rights of women, a subject to which little attention has been paid. From a recent survey of a Gold Coast village the Government was surprised to find that out of 267 independent cocoa farmers, 104 were females. In Nigeria an attempt to introduce green manuring had to be abandoned in a certain area when it was found that, under the local system of tenure, women were entitled to grow their minor crops among the major crops of the men.[1] The fact, too, that in the palm-oil belts women may be entitled to the kernels of the palm-trees owned by men has created difficulties for the Government in its attempts to improve the cultivation of palms. In certain regions of Malaya no land held under customary title, or any interest therein, may be transferred to any person other than a female member of the tribe, and it was found necessary to introduce legislation whereby titles formerly assigned in error to males could be cancelled.[2]

Finally, there are the political aspects of land tenure. Land hunger has ever been a potent cause of political unrest, and empires have been destroyed through the deterioration of the soil. From the very dawn of history there has been State legislation with regard to land. In ancient Greece one of the measures that made Solon famous was his abolition of landed debt, and the limit which he placed on the purchase of land. In Rome, in 367 B.C., a limit was also placed on the amount of public land which any individual might occupy,[3] and in 342 B.C. the *lex Genucia*, by controlling interest rates and reducing the amount of landed indebtedness, prevented the rich upper classes from continuing to hold the free peasantry in subjection, by means of loan capital. In England, from the Norman Conquest to the Wars of the Roses, the maintenance of the army and the liability to serve the king were made dependent on the feudal system of holding land, and it was for this political purpose that the Domesday survey was compiled.[4] Feudalism, indeed, may be defined as at once a system of land tenure and a system of government.[5] In France, one of the principal features of the French Revolution was the redistribution of lands which transferred property from the aristocracy of the Church and State to the middle and lower classes,

[1] In many communities wives have the right of use of land, but not the right of disposal.

[2] *Laws of the Federated Malay States.* Cap. 2-5, sec. 3. See also pp. 42-43.

[3] The *leges Liciniae Sextae* of 367 B.C. provided that no one might occupy more than 500 *jugera* (about 300 acres) of the *ager publicus*, nor herd upon it more than 100 head of cattle and 500 head of small live stock.

[4] It has been said that throughout the feudal period 'what really interested the King's lawyers and the courts about land was, not its economic, but its political importance'. See *The Book of English Law*, by Dr. Edward Jenks, p. 317.

[5] See *An Historical Introduction to the Land Law*, by W. S. Holdsworth, p. 4. Prof. Holdsworth remarks that 'the tendency to split up the powers of government amongst the landholders of the country is the effect of the absence of efficient central government'.

thereby giving to the State 'a fresh and deep foundation of security in the soil'.[1] In Ireland, the unhappy relations between landlords and tenants, and the congestion on the land during the nineteenth century, created many of the political conditions which ended in the establishment of the Irish Free State.[2] In Mexico, also, it was the abuse of the landlord system that produced the revolution of 1910.[3] The Russian revolution was immediately followed by the application of the principles of socialism to agriculture and to land, and the example of Russia is having a profound influence on land tenure systems all over the world.

There is, too, a notable difference between the political 'make-up' of areas held by peasant owner-cultivators and those held under a landlord and tenant system. The grant of political representation to a large tenant class may have as its first result the absorption of all political interest in tenancy conditions, to the exclusion of every other aspect of the social or economic life.[4] Moreover, the sense of responsibility and the interest in the stability of political institutions shown by peasant owner-cultivators differ widely from those of persons whose tenure of holdings is less secure.

Taxation is one form of the State's attitude to land. In Australia, where land taxation has taken the form of taxes on the unimproved value of the land, the rates of taxes have been graduated so as to bear heavily on the large landowners. This has had the intended effect of breaking up the larger holdings. In England, heavy taxation after the 1914-18 war caused large reductions in the number and size of the old estates. Many proprietors were forced to mortgage their land and many tenant farmers bought farms from landlords who were unable to carry on. Other agricultural properties fell into the hands of speculators. In many parts of the British Commonwealth taxes have been imposed on undeveloped land,[5] and at the present time the governments of Kenya and of Tanganyika are considering the adoption of this means of bringing into the market

[1]See J. M. Thompson, *The French Revolution*, p. 164.

[2]Land problems, if not the cause, may be made the excuse for political agitation.

[3]The character of the landlord-tenant relationship has a direct effect, also, on agricultural development. Absentee landlordism and rack-renting are a hindrance to good husbandry: and on the other hand, discontented tenants may abuse the land, taking everything out and putting nothing back. In times of high prices landlords may resume the land themselves, and in times of low prices they may be unable to collect their rents. Litigation between the two groups leads, not merely to hostility and possibly to political unrest, but also to the dissipation of capital that should go to improve the land. Where the landlord is a corporation, there may be an absence of co-operation between the landlord and the tenants or employees. Or the corporation and its tenants may, as in Fiji, work in such close collaboration that the two together form one large co-operative society.

[4]In Hungary, for example, one of the political parties is 'The Small-Holders Party.'

[5]A note on the taxation of undeveloped land will be found at p. 128.

land suitable for development. Even a small tax may have its effect. In British Honduras, where there is a tax of ¾d. per acre on all classes of land, an appreciable amount of land has been relinquished to the Crown because of the inability or unwillingness of owners to meet the taxation payments. The area of privately owned land is, therefore, said to be steadily decreasing.[1] In Tonga (Friendly Islands), many young men are said to be refraining from taking up farming land because of the small tax that they would be required to pay.[2] In some parts of Africa, taxation has forced some independent farmers to become labourers on the land of others.[3] But in many areas it has stimulated subsistence farmers to grow commercial crops, and so has helped, indirectly, to raise the standard of life.

There are other political aspects of land-holding. In many parts of Africa the right to the use of land is dependent on allegiance to a chief or chiefs. The authority of chiefs, sub-chiefs and heads of clans and families is bound up with the land.[4] The grant, therefore, to individuals of absolute rights of ownership would tend to disrupt the native polity, and so, too, would the indiscriminate sale of tribal lands by chiefs. The control of alienation of land has in consequence been one of the main planks of the British system of 'Indirect Rule'.

[1] See *Agriculture in the West Indies*, Colonial No. 182, p. 239.

[2] See p. 216.

[3] The very fear that the land may be used as a basis for taxation may preclude close investigation into native systems of tenure or attempts to alter them. It may be observed, incidentally, that chiefs may oppose legislation which (e.g. by recognizing prescriptive rights) would curtail their authority and the incomes they derive from the administration of land.

[4] Among the Akan of the Gold Coast there is a proverb that 'All power lies in the land'.

CHAPTER II

Native Systems of Tenure

The need for more accurate study of Native systems

In the first chapter sufficient was said to indicate the highly complex character of systems of land-holding, and that problems of tenure are interlocked with the whole social, political and economic structure. We may now pass on to consider some of the characteristic features of the indigenous or less developed systems found in many dependencies, notably in Africa. Here it is important to note that it is only in recent years that reliable information on this subject has been obtained. Many of the early investigations were vitiated by unsound methods of approach, such as the use of abstract questions—the answers to which were often given by interested parties—instead of the concrete method of tracing the actual history of plots of land. Another frequent source of error has been the presupposition that native conceptions of ownership must be basically the same as those of Europeans.[1] English terms such as 'rent' or 'lease' have been employed to denote practices which bear only a superficial resemblance to those denoted by these terms. The gifts given to chiefs as administrators of land have been assumed to be 'rent', and the chiefs to be 'landlords'. To add to the confusion, the same English word has been used in different senses, so that, for example, (to quote Dr. Lucy Mair) those who have said that there was no such thing as 'property' in land have

[1] In a Privy Council judgement in 1921 their lordships observed that 'In interpreting the native title to land, not only in Southern Nigeria but in other parts of the British Empire, much caution is essential. There is a tendency, operating at times unconsciously, to render that title conceptually in terms which are appropriate only to systems which have grown up under English law. But this tendency has to be held in check closely. As a rule, in the various systems of native jurisprudence throughout the Empire, there is no such full division between property and possession as English lawyers are familiar with'. (Amodu Tijani *v.* The Secretary S. Nigeria. 2 A.C. 399, 1921.)

Lord Lugard has observed that the term 'ownership' when applied to land is relative, even in England, where it is qualified by the right of Parliament to expropriate the owner if the land is required for some public purpose such as a railway. In Africa the term is still more qualified. The ascription of 'ownership' of land to a chief is only accurate if the term is used in its native sense. (*Dual Mandate*, p. 316.) Professor Raymond Firth has also pointed out that the precise meaning of ownership is different in every culture, varying according to custom, tradition, and the relative social status of those who enjoy its privileges. The key to the understanding of a system of native land tenure lies, he says, in realizing the inadequacy of such terms as 'communistic' or 'individualistic' and in grasping the complex scheme of titles, claims, privileges and obligations on the part of individuals and the community with which the native himself invests the control of the soil. (See e.g., *We, The Tikopia*, pp. 406-7 and *Primitive Economics of the New Zealand Maori*, pp. 330-1, and 375.)

meant one thing, while those who have argued that there was 'property' in land have meant another. Again, the words 'in theory' or 'theoretically' have frequently been employed to square the presuppositions with the facts. Time and again there appear such contradictions as 'in theory the land belongs to the Chief, but in practice the Chief is not consulted', or 'theoretically there is no negotiable freehold . . . but in practice the effective sale of land is of frequent occurrence'. Confusion, too, is caused by loose translations of native terms, so that a word rendered as 'purchase' may not mean 'outright purchase' but 'redeemable purchase'—a very different matter. Or to take a final example, there is the common practice of distinguishing tenures as either 'communal' or 'individual'. Yet the two may exist side by side and interwoven.[1] The term 'communal' has often been applied to lands in which individuals have well-defined rights, and it has been applied constantly to useless lands over which neither individuals nor groups of individuals claim any rights at all. On the other hand, 'individual tenure' has been used to mean anything from a mere right of user which cannot be alienated, to a freehold estate with the fullest freedom of disposition.

The absence of accurate information regarding native systems of tenure has had many unfortunate effects. In the making of treaties with natives, Colonial Governments and individuals have assumed that they were being given exclusive rights over land, whereas the natives have assumed that they were merely granting the qualified rights of user which they themselves enjoyed. On the other hand, some governments have enacted laws recognizing the native rights as though they were the equivalent of freehold rights in Western countries, thus conferring on the natives an authority to dispose of lands over which, under their own law, they only had usufructuary rights.[2] Failure to understand the custom of shifting cultivation has led successive governments to under-estimate the amount of land required by native tribes, or to claim as Crown property land which they had believed to be vacant.[3] In Ceylon much land was

[1] Professor Malinowski has pointed out that 'every relationship between man *v.* soil is emphatically both individual and concerted. . . . The real problem is not the "either—or" of individualism and communism but the relation of collective and personal claims'. See *Coral Gardens and Their Magic*, Vol. I, pp., 379 and 380.

[2] See Dr. Felix M. Keesing's, *The South Seas in the Modern World*, p. 99.

[3] See p. 78, footnote 2. Also, *An African Survey*, p. 745. Dr. Felix Keesing, speaking of the Pacific communities, observes that 'A mistake frequently made by government officials and others has been to regard only those lands in active use for economic purposes as being covered by valid native titles and to classify the rest as unoccupied or waste lands. In native eyes, however, virgin or fallow territories are nearly always covered by some form of tenure, actual or potential. . . . Difficulties have likewise arisen where, in accordance with Western practice, governments have put legal restrictions upon the ownership and use of forests and their products, on water and marine resources and on minerals.' Op cit., p. 98.

appropriated under the Crown Lands Ordinance of 1840 to which the villagers had a legitimate claim,[1] and similar mistakes have been made in East Africa. It has been assumed that Chiefs were the owners of tribal lands and could sign them away as they pleased, whereas in fact the chiefs were no more than public trustees. On the same principle, chiefs and other leading personages of a tribe have obtained for themselves privileges regarding land which they would not have obtained had the local Government been instructed in the facts. Under the Uganda Agreement of 1900, 'A government which supposed itself to be confirming native rights turned the Chiefs by a stroke of the pen into landlords entitled to exact rent from their former subjects and to dispose of their land for cash,' while in the Gold Coast, 'the reckless granting of concessions by the Chiefs was allowed on the assumption that their right to make such grants followed logically from their authority over stool lands.'[2] In Kenya, the land legislation prior to 1938 proceeded on the assumption that the native reserves were commons in which private rights to land did not exist.

Pastoral Rights

The most elementary form of land occupation is where pastoral peoples range freely over large areas in search of fresh grazing and of water. Normally under such conditions there is no need for defining rights.[3] Where the pastoralists come into contact with the agriculturists they are welcomed because of the milk and butter made available. Most agriculturists, also, are aware of the value of cattle manure. Disputes arise, however, when the cattle damage the crops, and agriculturists are often on this account put to the trouble and expense of fencing in their lands. In many parts of Africa there is continual litigation, and a good deal of bloodshed, on account of trespass by cattle, and in Nigeria it is not uncommon for a man living in one village to farm on the lands of another where there is less interference from domestic animals.[4] In the Gold Coast, Sir Henry Belfield considered (in 1914) that restrictions should be placed on the grant of land for grazing, with a view to curbing the

[1] See H. M. Leake in *Tropical Agriculture*, Vol. XV, No. 11.

[2] Dr. Lucy Mair at the Oxford University Summer School on Colonial Administration, 1938. It is interesting to note, as regards the Uganda Agreement, that in a despatch of 15th June, 1900, the British Foreign Office observed that 'the introduction of the law of England in regard to land, which appears from the wording of the Agreement to be the intention of its framers, may create a very complicated system.' As indeed it did. (See pp. 132-7.)

[3] But there may be well-defined routes to definite areas which the pastoralists are allowed by custom to exploit.

[4] See, e.g., *Land Tenure in an Ibo Village*, M. M. Green, p. 30.

pernicious proclivities of pastoralists,[1] and in Cyprus farmers have held that, were it possible to eliminate indiscriminate grazing by sheep and goats, the crop production could be doubled.[2]

Where pastoral peoples are, for various reasons, confined to limited areas, more definite grazing rights may arise. Thus, in the arid regions of Tanganyika, private grazing rights have grown up in the areas around water supplies, or where the movements of cattle are restricted on account of tsetse-fly. A plot of grazing ground may be held by an individual, a family, or a group of persons who have agreed to herd their cattle together. And since the conversion of waste land into suitable grazing land, and its subsequent maintenance, may involve considerable labour, owners of grazing-grounds sometimes let them out on a rental basis. Progressive individuals may even, nowadays, obtain permission from the tribal or village authorities to construct dams or other appliances for conserving water, and so establish for themselves purely private rights over what was formerly public property. It is clear that developments of this kind must be creating many problems; private enterprise may deserve encouragement, yet any wide extension of private rights may upset the local land economy and interfere with Government schemes for the development of agriculture and the control of erosion. In many parts of Africa there is a dangerous degree of soil deterioration which can be attributed largely to overstocking, and the remedy may lie in a variety of measures such as the reduction or redistribution of herds, the introduction or extension of rotational grazing, or, where circumstances are favourable, the substitution of an agricultural for a pastoral economy. Grazing-grounds, moreover, require to be controlled if they are not to become breeding grounds for weeds and ticks; and for many other reasons grazing regulations may be necessary. These can more easily be put into practice, by Native Administrations, where rights are of a collective rather than an individual character. It has been pointed out also (by Mr. D. W. Malcolm) that in Tanganyika, wherever personal rights in grazing grounds are recognized, there is continual litigation, since the grazing-grounds form a patchwork, and the boundaries are seldom clearly marked. No such difficulties exist where the grazing-grounds are annually allocated by the village authorities.

[1] Despatch to Secretary of State, 3rd April, 1914.

[2] See B. J. Surridge, *A Survey of Rural Life in Cyprus*, 1930, p. 71. The Cypriot laws relating to malicious damage have recently been made more effective (by Laws No. 20 of 1935, 31 of 1935, and 7 of 1937). Under the Licensing of Shepherds Law a limit is placed on the size of the flock and the number of shepherds, and under the Goat Law a village can, by a majority ballot, exclude all but tethered goats from its confines.

In Kenya the Land Commission of 1933 recorded a comprehensive condemnation of large grazing commonages, 'which are frequently used as a species of bank for the storage of bride-price.' They stated that even the areas added expressly for the purpose of accommodating cattle (while over-grazed areas of the reserve were rested) should not be used as grazing commonages free to all without restriction, but should be used on an organized plan.[1] A committee recently appointed by the Government of Kenya to advise on the steps which should be taken to deal with the problem of overstocking, recommended (in 1941) that 'immediate steps should be taken to restore to grazing all areas that are unsuitable for cultivation and to encourage the return of stock to cultivated holdings in order that it may fulfil its proper function of adding milk to the dietary of the people, and of manure for use on arable land and pasture. . . . Native agriculturists should be constantly reminded that there can be no return to the old conditions which permitted shifting cultivation and the allocation of almost unlimited grazing areas for stock, and that the only place for stock in modern conditions is on the cultivated small holding, where, by means of the proper use of manure, the continuous farming of the land without loss of fertility is made possible'. The committee recommended that strict measures of grassland and soil control should be applied throughout both the pastoral and the agricultural native areas of Kenya. These recommendations have been accepted by the Government of Kenya; and similar policies are being considered, or have been accepted, by other Colonial Governments.

It should be remembered, however, that other than purely economic factors may have to be considered in dealing with grassland management. There are many tribes, such as the aboriginal peoples of British Guiana, who, if they are to avoid extermination, must be allowed adequate land in which they can continue to live the nomadic life of their forefathers.[2] There are treaty obligations, such as those with the pastoral Masai, which cannot lightly be set aside; and there is the semi-sacred character which is attached to cattle in many African dependencies.[3] The Director of Veterinary Services in Tanganyika has recently observed that obsession with the problem of soil erosion may make us forget that, after all, the soil was made for man and not man for the soil, and that when Governments interfere they must beware lest in removing one evil

[1] *Report of the Kenya Land Commission, 1933*, para. 1670. See also paras. 1980-2040.

[2] *The West India Royal Commission Report*, p. 398.

[3] Pastoral peoples may be more concerned with property rights in cattle than in land. R. H. Lowie has observed that among the Ruanda of the Belgian Congo a monarch, instead of being regarded as the owner of the land, is regarded as the owner of all the stock. Among the Rwala of Arabia there are rules governing the inheritance of camels, but none regarding the inheritance of land.

they create many others.[1] Nevertheless, it is clear that the whole problem of grassland management deserves much closer attention than it has anywhere received. Grass is no longer to be regarded as a mere cover for waste lands, but as the world's most valuable single crop. Governments will in future have to embark on large schemes of reclamation of waste lands, and schemes also of permanent pasturage let out for grazing on a controlled basis. Much more information is required regarding the nature of pastoral rights. Generally speaking, the character of the tenure must be determined by the local circumstances. In some circumstances the best remedy for overstocking will be the promotion of intelligent individual tenure and rotational grazing; in others, communage systems may accord better with native economies and modes of life, and also with Government schemes for future development.

Agricultural Rights

A more permanent relationship with land is established by agriculture. This assumes an infinite variety of forms, reflecting the use to which land is put and being related to the amount and quality of the land available,[2] to the local climate, to the character of the crops grown, and to the social and political institutions of the people.[3] When native societies are stabilised the rules of land tenure are never vague or ill-defined, and if to-day there is confusion, this must be ascribed to the introduction of new legal conceptions regarding land, and new economic conditions to which the indigenous systems have not yet had time to make the necessary accommodation.

One of the main distinctions between Native systems of holding land and those of Western societies is that the former are largely dominated by personal relationships, whereas the latter are subject to the impersonal legal conception of 'contract'. In some areas of the Empire, however, there has been a fusion, or confusion, of these two conceptions, so that in a single dependency the two principles may exist side by side, or in opposition, often with chaotic results.

[1] H. E. Hornby in an article on 'Overstocking in Tanganyika Territory', *East African Agricultural Journal*, March, 1936.

[2] Availability of land determines the type of tenure. R. H. Lowie has observed (in his article on Land Tenure in the *Encyclopædia of the Social Sciences*) that Kirghiz bands in Asiatic Russia were communists in the summer when land was abundant, but individualists in the winter when a dearth of sheltered quarters was coupled with private ownership of winter territories, which were marked out by natural or artificial boundaries and guarded against trespassers.

[3] It has been frequently pointed out (e.g. by Professor Lowie) that since property rights are correlated with other social phenomena, a study of land tenure requires a consideration of government, clan and family organization, and also of economic activity, technology and religion. All social institutions are closely concatenated, and a single institution should not be selected and treated as an isolated problem.

In many parts of Africa, for example, the holders of usufructuary rights in land are now endeavouring to convert them into indefeasible titles and are arming themselves with bogus deeds often obtained from bogus lawyers at considerable expense.[1]

In describing the land tenure systems of the South Seas communities, a distinguished American anthropologist has observed that the most typical form of tenure in pre-European times was for 'living sites and cultivations around villages to be very precisely defined as to what families or individuals had authority over them and as to who could use them; but for forest hinterlands and river or ocean frontage to be held collectively by the communities concerned. . . . Nowhere was there any complete collectivism or communism such as some theorists have postulated for the primitive world. . . . But frequently a large group of individuals had rights in some piece of property, based on kin ties or other traditional factors. Again, where a person such as a chief appeared to be an owner or landlord, he was often really more of a supervisor or trustee. He exercised authority over land rather than possessed it'.[2]

This statement would also apply generally to the indigenous tenures of Africa. These are often described as 'tribal' or 'communal ownership'. But the basis of land administration is not usually the tribe but the village, and land is not usually owned or worked by any large unit. Everywhere there are individual rights, that is to say that a single individual, or two or more close relatives, have definite rights to a particular plot of ground and to its produce. But these rights are qualified by membership of a family, clan or local group. They are limited to the period of effective occupation and restricted in respect of succession and therefore of transfer. Sale is normally forbidden and may indeed be unthinkable.[3] The rights in fact partake more of the nature of possession than of property.[4] If the holding is quitted it reverts to the holder's kindred or to the village, and may be re-allocated. In some cases all the lands of a village have been divided out among the kindreds composing the village,

[1] Lord Hailey has observed that in the Gold Coast the use of English documentary forms of transfer, coupled with the growth of land values and the use made by chiefs of their powers over 'stool' lands for the grant of concessions, has led to a break-up of the older usages. Large numbers of land cases, moreover, are brought on appeal to the Supreme Court, and although the Court maintains the customary rights of the family in succession to land, it has tended to deal with transfers in terms of English law. See *An African Survey*, p. 856. See also below, pp. 163, 179-182, and 295-7.

[2] Dr. Felix M. Keesing, op. cit., p. 98.

[3] But a family, lineage or sib may, by common consent, sell part of its ancestral lands for some necessary purpose, such as the payment of debts, the carrying on of family trade, the provision of bride-prices, the purchase of agricultural implements, the payment of the costs of litigation, or State demands. An individual may also alienate self-acquired property.

[4] R. H. Lowie observes that an individual's right may be no more than a preemptive possessory right—he has exclusive rights while he is there, but loses them if he leaves.

and all the lands of the kindreds in turn have been divided out among the extended families composing the kindred. But sometimes the villages and kindreds still hold reserves of undivided lands which are allocated as required. Or parts of them may be portioned out annually if the individual holdings are found to be insufficient.

In order to make these principles clear a number of authorities may be quoted. In their judgment in the Southern Nigerian case cited above, the Privy Councillors made the following observations: 'A very usual form of native title is that of usufructuary right, which is a mere qualification of or burden on the radical or final title of the Sovereign, where that exists. But this estate is qualified by a right of beneficial user which may not assume definite forms analogous to estates, or may, where it has assumed these, have derived them from the intrusion of the mere analogy of English jurisprudence. . . . There is yet another feature of the fundamental nature of the title to land. . . . The title, such as it is, may not be that of the individual, as in this country it nearly always is in some form, but may be that of a community. Such a community may have the possessory title to the common enjoyment of a usufruct, with customs under which its individual members are admitted to enjoyment, and even to a right of transmitting the individual enjoyment as members by assignment *inter vivos* or by succession. To ascertain how far this latter development of right has progressed involves the study of the history of the particular community and its usages in each case. Abstract principles fashioned a priori are of but little assistance and are, as often as not, misleading.'[1]

Professor Schapera, in his account of land tenure in Bechuanaland, states that the Chief controls the allocation of land and assigns a residential area and a separate arable tract to each of the wards in his capital. The holding of each ward (or small village) is controlled by the ward-head, who must provide land for all the households under his authority. He may also admit outsiders who apply to him. The head of a household assigns plots to his dependants; every family must have its own land, and, if a man has more than one wife, each is entitled to a separate dwelling and field.[2] Grazing land is not similarly divided among the households, but every owner of cattle may graze them freely within the area controlled by the ward-head. 'In every instance the possessor of land is entitled merely to its use, and not to absolute ownership. Should he go away temporarily he can take up the land again on his return. Land passes only by way of gift, inheritance or gratuitous loan. It is never treated as a com-

[1] Amodu Tijani *v.* The Secretary, S. Nigeria, 2 A.C. 399. 1921.

[2] Generally-speaking it is true to say of African tenures, as of Indian, that women have only a life interest in land.

modity that can be sold or hired out. There is, therefore, no opportunity for land speculation and no incentive to the acquisition of large holdings from which a return can be derived in the form of purchase price or rent. Tribal law moreover limits the amount of land that people may hold.'[1]

In describing the land system of the Wa-Bena of Tanganyika, Mr. and Mrs. A. T. Culwick state that: 'Land, *per se*, has no value in the eyes of the Mbena and nobody bothers about it until it is cleared. Any member of the tribe, or any stranger who has been granted permission to settle in the country, can of right take and clear as much land as he requires for his house, his fields and possibly a family burial-ground. As soon as he has done this, the position has changed. The work he has put into the plot gives it value. It is now his property and no one may encroach on it. So long as it continues to be used, it remains in the possession of him or his heirs. . . . When a man deserts exhausted ground, he no longer calls it 'my field'. He will, however, refer to it as 'my old field', indicating thereby that he still has certain proprietary rights over it, should he care to exercise them. . . . The temporary occupier of a field is thus regarded as something more than merely its user; he has rights which extend beyond the period of actual use. It is considered as his absolute property as long as he wishes to keep it. . . . His rights over it last as long as he wishes, whether it is in use or not, and further, he has the right of disposal. He can, if he wants, dispose of a field to his neighbour. Such transactions naturally take place but seldom, when every man has land and to spare for the taking, but they do sometimes occur, as, for instance, when a man has inherited a good field at some distance from his home. He may negotiate a transfer to another, usually a relative, receiving in exchange goods, cash, or services of some kind. But as land itself has no value, he is really, of course, selling the work of clearing and breaking the ground, and any crops which may be growing on it at the time of transfer; i.e. he is actually being paid for improvements, and not for land itself, though at the same time he, as the owner, is transferring his rights over the land.'

As regards grazing, in granting a man permission to take certain grazing grounds, the tribal authorities among the Wa-Bena give him both rights of use and rights of disposal over it. At his death the appropriate heir inherits the land on the same terms, and thus the

[1] I. Schapera, *Native Land Tenure in the Bechuanaland Protectorate*, 1943, pp. 44-46. It is worth observing, as Dr. Audrey Richards has pointed out with regard to the Bemba of N. Rhodesia, that, while there may be no tribal law restricting the amount of land which a man may occupy, social convention may impose a limit, according to the status of the individual. Fear of the accusation of pride or a reputation for personal ambition, so often associated with charges of witchcraft, are important factors. See *Land, Labour and Diet in Northern Rhodesia*, p. 271.

family may hold it permanently. As for the head of the village, he has not only the first claim on uncleared land but also, if he cares to exercise it, 'a rather vague power to dictate to his people where they should or should not cultivate'. Similarly, he has absolute discretion in the matter of grazing grounds. 'But let a man once clear a patch of ground and he cannot be evicted, nor can the local authorities turn men off grazing grounds of which they have taken possession.'[1]

In an Ibo village in Nigeria the following classes of land were observed by myself.[2] The first class includes lands which are sacred or taboo. These surround the shrines of public cults or are lands specially marked off for some magico-religious purpose. The ownership is regarded as vested in the deities or ancestors, and no one would normally attempt to use any fraction of such lands for farming.[3] Lands of this character are found all over Africa, and in most dependencies there are statutory provisions for their protection.[4]

The next type of land is the virgin forest, which has remained unused for farming purposes because it has not been required, or because the village authorities (that is to say the village chief or the heads of kindreds) have forbidden farming there, lest the village should lose the use of the forest as a means of defence, or as shade, or a source of supplies of wood or fibre. But if a piece of uncleared forest has no obvious public use, then anyone may clear it for farming purposes, and the land so cleared becomes his private farm. He cannot be deprived of it and he can pledge it or transmit it to his children. But should there be any uncertainty as to whether the village may require the uncleared patch, the would-be farmer must first obtain the permission of the local elders or of the special official authorised to act as administrator of lands.

The third class of land is farm-land held in common by the entire village, ward, kindred or extended-family, and is formally portioned out afresh each time it is to be farmed. Where the common land belongs to the entire village it is usually infertile soil for which there

[1] *Ubena of the Rivers,* by A. T. Culwick and Mrs. G. M. Culwick, pp. 236 *et seq.*

[2] *Law and Authority in a Nigerian Tribe,* by C. K. Meek, p. 100.

[3] But it is a sign of the times that some farmers, driven by land hunger, have recently cleared patches of taboo forest in order to plant yams. It is said that if anyone takes this step (without interference from the elders) and farms for two years in succession without suffering misfortune, he is considered to have become the owner of the patch, which ceases to be taboo.

[4] E.g. in the Gold Coast Concessions Ordinance of 1939 (No. 19), it is laid down [Sec. 12 (9)] that no Concession shall be certified as valid unless the Court is satisfied that the customary rights of natives are reasonably protected in respect of 'fetish' lands. On the other hand, in the Sierra Leone Concessions Ordinance (No. 29 of 1931), it is an offence to represent any land in respect of which a certificate of validity has been issued by the Court to be 'fetish' land, and no one may put 'fetish' on such land (Sec. 54).

is no demand. Where it belongs to a kindred or extended-family group it is parcelled out annually to members of the kindred whose private holdings may be insufficient. It can only be leased or pledged to strangers with the consent of the whole group. Similarly, if the land is to be redeemed, it should be redeemed by the group as a whole. In these days cases occur where an individual member of a group redeems group-land at his own expense and then claims it as his private property.

Finally, and most important of all, comes the land which is individually held—that is to say by a single individual or by a small working group composed of a father and sons, or a man and his younger brothers or cousins. Such land is acquired by inheritance, or by clearing virgin forest, or in return for a loan. In many villages there is no land at all which is not held by individuals. Land so held can, among the Ibo and many other African tribes, be pledged without reference to anyone, and it is common practice for a man to pledge his land in order to cancel a debt, to pay a bride-price, or even nowadays to raise the cash for his Government tax. Land which has been pledged is normally redeemable at any time, at the same rate at which it has been pledged, and in many African tribes there is a proverb which states that 'A thing which is pledged is never lost.'[1] In point of fact, however, land which has been pledged is often permanently lost. It may be pledged for a sum far in excess of that normally given, and become irredeemable, all evidence of the original transaction having been lost. In this way rich individuals have acquired land in perpetuity. There will be more to say about the pledging of land at a later stage.[2]

From these descriptions it will be evident that there is a fairly general common pattern of land tenure, associated for the most part with subsistence agriculture, which is still the prevalent form of economy.[3] But there are many variations or modifications. Thus,

[1] Compare Leviticus xxv. 23-4 (R.V.): 'And the land shall not be sold in perpetuity: for the land is mine. . . . And in all the land of your possession ye shall grant a redemption of the land.'

[2] See Chapter xxii (pp. 256-271).

[3] The semi-communal or open-field system in operation in England from Anglo-Saxon times to the nineteenth century presents many parallels to the pattern here described. 'The land of the village community was divided up into two or three open fields [*campi*], which were cultivated in a certain rotation. Each of these fields was divided into a number of strips [*seliones*], which averaged about an acre in extent: and the strips were divided from one another by turf balks. Each landowner possessed a certain number of these strips in different places in the open fields. It is probable that the strips were scattered in this way in order to give each owner a little bit of the good land, a little bit of the indifferent, and a little bit of the bad. . . . In addition each landowner had certain common rights. One and sometimes two of the common fields were left fallow each year, and over these fields there was a right of common of pasture for the cattle of the villagers. . . There were also rights of common over the extensive waste lands which adjoined the village.' See W. S. Holdsworth, op. cit., p. 39.

persons who are short of land may obtain a temporary loan or lease, in return for a proportion of the crop at harvest. This proportion may be so small that it is no more than a token of obligation and an acknowledgment that the land has been lent and not given away. Or it may be so substantial that the relationship between the grantor and grantee assumes something of the character of *métayage*. Nowadays, there is a tendency in some areas for gifts in kind to be replaced by cash, and so to become regular rental payments. In other areas, again, the grantor of land, which would formerly have been given away free or for some trifling consideration, may demand a comparatively large sum of money and argue that this is not purchase-money but compensation for the trouble of having cleared the land. There will be references to developments of this kind at a later stage.[1]

In a number of Colonial territories (e.g., Nigeria, Uganda, Tanganyika and Tonga) there were formerly feudal forms of tenure, fiefs or estates being conferred on officers of State, members of the royal families and other notables. These tenures will be described in succeeding chapters,[2] and it need only be observed here that they have developed in very different ways in the different dependencies, or sometimes even in the same dependency. In the Buganda and Bunyoro districts of Uganda, the rights of tenants have been secured by varying means, but in the Toro and Ankole areas there is little security of tenure beyond that of the goodwill of the landlord.[3] In Tanganyika the landlords are still entitled to make certain demands on the crops of their tenants.[4] In Northern Nigeria the estate system has, for the most part, disappeared, but some royal estates are still largely worked by ex-slaves, whose position has become assimilated to that of 'clients', paying an annual tithe. In the State of Nupe the amount of tithe varies with the personality of the Emir, from one or two bundles of corn annually to as much as one-third of the entire harvest.[5] In many parts of Africa chiefs have tended to become landlords, and landlords have tended to assume the rôle of chiefs.

The landlord-tenant relationship is not, however, a common feature of indigenous systems of tenure. In most of the colonies the peasant farmer is still free and independent. And although this may serve to slow down the rate of progress, it is a prime factor in the maintenance of social stability. On the other hand, the fact that

[1]The whole question of change in native land law as a result of European influence and the introduction of commercial crops is given separate treatment in Chapter XXIV.

[2] See especially pp. 132, 138 and 153.

[3] See p. 141.

[4]See p. 114.

[5] S. F. Nadel, *A Black Byzantium*, 1942, p. 199.

individual rights are exercised within the framework of the kindred organization and are qualified in many important respects, particularly as regards the right of alienation, may present serious impediments to agricultural development on modern lines, though it may continue to perform a useful function under a subsistence economy. It will be seen later that in some dependencies, notably Fiji, special legislation has been introduced in order to give greater freedom for individual enterprise.[1]

The principle that he who clears land establishes rights of a permanent character has existed all over the world from ancient times.[2] It is based on the fact that the clearing of virgin forest involves heavy work. And under all indigenous systems of tenure it is an accepted principle that the expenditure of labour creates rights. It is for this reason that economic trees which require attention are held in private ownership, and that the property is in the tree itself and not in the land on which it grows. On this account also the ownership of plantations differs from that of arable land used for growing subsistence crops; and ancestral property, which is held collectively by the kin and cannot be sold, differs from acquired property which is at the complete disposition of the person who acquired it. For the same reason also, in the Dikwa Emirate of the British Cameroons, where ordinary agricultural land has no negotiable value, the particular class of land known as *firki* is bought and sold, since its use entails heavy labour in clearing, ditching and the diversion of flood water.[3] This principle is largely, no doubt, the real explanation of the fact that the descendants of the original occupying families are considered to have a special degree of

[1] See p. 206.

[2] *The Laws of Manu* (India) declare (IX, v. 44) that 'He who clears a piece of land is the owner of it,' and 'What a brother has acquired by labour skill, without using the patrimony, he shall not give up without his assent, for it was gained by his own exertion.' 'Sages who know the past declare a field to belong to him who cut away the wood or who cleared and tilled it, and a deer to him who owned the arrow which first struck it.' Sir Paul Vinogradoff states that in the law of ancient Greece, 'there is one group of rules in which the influence of men's labour is recognized as generating real rights, although these rights do not reach the standard of full property. I mean the growth of protected tenant right. On territories reclaimed from the waste . . . special rights approximating to ownership were conceded in order to improve cultivation.' (*Outlines of Historical Jurisprudence*, Vol. II, p. 216). In Muhammadan law it is a well established principle that 'whoever cultivates waste lands does thereby acquire the property of them' (Hed. 610). For an example of the application of this principle of encouraging agricultural enterprise see p. 66. In the Dera-Ghazi-Khan district of the Punjab the person who clears jungle and brings land under cultivation is protected by statute. He cannot be ejected as long as he continues to cultivate; his occupancy right is heritable; he can cut down self-grown timber for agricultural purposes; he can build houses, though if he vacates his holding he can remove only the materials he has paid for himself; he can sink a certain type of well; and he can sublet his holding temporarily but not permanently. See Sir W. H. Rattigan, *A Digest of Civil Law for the Punjab*, p. 255.

[3] See *British Cameroons Administrative Report, 1923*. Appendix III.

ownership, and that a religious sanction is given to this view.[1]

The annual or periodic allocation, or re-allocation, of village lands is a common technique of native systems for ensuring a fair distribution of land.[2] Thus, among the Marri of Baluchistan, land was formerly redivided every ten years in order to meet the needs of strangers, who were welcomed on account of the strength they added to the tribe.[3] Among the Brahui and Lhota Naga there was also a periodic redistribution in order that each clan should have land proportionate to the numbers of the clansmen. In Fiji, the land of a clan that had died out reverted to the community, and at the present time it reverts to the Crown as 'ultimus hæres', and is redistributed among those who are short of land.[4] In many parts of Africa chiefs have the right to take away from families any of their land which is not required.[5] In Palestine, also, there is a custom, widely prevalent, by which village lands are periodically redistributed. The method of redistribution appears to vary considerably from village to village. It is obvious that a custom of this kind, while it secures a fair share of land to all, must be difficult to maintain under conditions which demand the fullest forms of security, and that it must militate also against attempts to promote an effective system of land registration.

There is one further feature of native systems of land-holding to which some reference should be made, namely, the absence from native customary law of any limitation of time within which claims over land—or indeed anything else—can be asserted or enforced.

[1] In commenting on the tradition that the Kikuyu of Kenya bought out the original occupiers, the Dorobo, the 1929 Committee on native land tenure observed that this was done (*a*) because of the great respect for the right of first use; and (*b*) in order to propitiate the ancestors who are believed to be immanent in the locality. See *Native Land Tenure in Kikuyu Province*, Report of Committee.

[2] It may be added that the practice of re-allocation is also a denial of the 'allodial', or 'free ownership', conception of land-holding.

[3] *Census of India, 1901*, Vol. V. J. D. Mayne stated in 1883 that redistribution was still practised in the Pathan communities of Peshawar and that this marked a transitional stage between joint holdings and holdings in severalty (*Hindu Law and Usage*, 9th Edition, p. 307).

[4] Among the Kikuyu of Kenya the official known as 'muramati' has powers of adjusting the land distribution in cases where one family has diminished and another has increased. (See the *Report of the Committee on Native Land Tenure in Kikuyu Province*, I, paras. 19-23.) In Cyprus if land is allowed to remain uncultivated for a period of 10 years it can be resumed by the State (see p. 64). In S. Rhodesia, under the Land Apportionment Act of 1930, grants of land may be forfeited if not beneficially used. Numerous other examples of statutory provisions of this kind could be given. See e.g. p. 129.

[5] This has led many observers to conclude that the Chiefs are the real owners of the land. But normally the Chief cannot deprive a family of any of its land without general consent, and it is almost an axiom to say that a Chief can give lands but cannot take them away. Chiefs in fact are merely trustees for the people, though many have in the past assumed the position of landlords, and many are endeavouring to do so at the present time, in areas where land has become a commercial commodity.

This may be a matter of no great consequence under a shifting system of cultivation, for if a farmer is dispossessed of one plot of land he can go to another. But where land has become valuable, or plantation crops are grown, sudden dispossession may inflict serious injustice. The absence from native law of any 'statute of limitations' has in many dependencies been considered a serious bar to security and so to development, and to be an encouragement of recurrent litigation and of many forms of fraud, such as the postponement of claims to land until the land has been extensively improved.[1]

In 1927 the Government of the Gold Coast proposed to introduce into the Colony a Statute of Limitations which would be applicable not merely in the British Courts, but also in the native courts, with a view to getting rid of some of these evils, and protecting non-natives who had acquired from natives an interest in land.[2] The proposal, however, was vetoed by a Council of Chiefs, on the ground that it was directly contrary to the native principle that long uninterrupted possession does not create an adverse title. The new measure would be opposed to the native rule which requires families to pay off their debts (in which land might be included), however long it may take them to do so:[3] and it would have the general effect of forcing the people to adopt English forms of tenure and of transfer. The Bill was accordingly dropped.[4]

Native law is not incapable of making its own accommodation to new conditions. Moreover, equity is its governing principle, and it knows very well how to deal with individuals who postpone their

[1] Sir Ernest Dowson, in speaking of land tenure conditions in Iraq, has observed that 'any dispute may be re-opened at any time if circumstances promise a more favourable consideration of a disappointed party's case'. And he added that 'One's personal status at any given time may be a determining factor.'

[2] The proposed measure was entitled 'The Civil Proceedings Limitation Bill', and the underlying principle was officially described as 'to safeguard the title to property and the fruits of individual enterprise from the assaults of those who have unreasonably delayed in asserting their claims. By ensuring security from such attacks, after the expiration of fixed periods, property may be enjoyed and developed without fear of being involved in extensive litigation and of being put to a defence which the passage of time has rendered hazardous.' The Bill proposed to impose a time limit of twelve years for the institution of proceedings to recover land or to recover money secured by any mortgage. In the case of debt, arrears of rent or interest, etc., the limit was to be six years.

[3] Property in land is often pledged for money loans, etc., and the pledgee takes possession until the loan is repaid. It was contended that under the new measure the pledgee might, after twelve years, become the permanent owner of the property. The people of the Gold Coast have a proverb that 'Debt dries but never rots'. It is interesting to note that according to the ancient custom of the Punjab the power to redeem mortgages of land lasted for ever. The limitation period introduced by the British has often been attacked by Punjabis as an unfair innovation on their customs. See *Punjab Customary Law*, by C. L. Tupper, Vol. III, p. 218.

[4] Some of the judges of the Supreme Court considered that the practical effect of a time limit would, in the case of land, increase rather than lessen litigation.

claim to land until the existing occupier has carried out extensive improvements. In the Gold Coast itself a case is on record, as long ago as 1878, in which a family tried to eject a farmer who had purchased a piece of land from the head of the family fourteen years previously. It was admitted that the family-head had conducted the sale without consulting the other members of his family. Nevertheless, it was held that, as the other members of the family had taken no action and the purchaser had improved the land, he could not be disturbed.[1]

In many parts of Africa it is an accepted principle that voluntary abandonment of the use of any land should extinguish all prescriptive claim. And there may also be a rule that no individual or group shall hold more land than can be effectually used. Yet many clans, families and individuals are in fact laying prescriptive claims to larger areas than are, or will be, required, under more settled systems of cultivation. There is a growing tendency also for prescriptive rights of user to become crystallized into rights of an exclusive proprietary character. The problem is, therefore, arising in many dependencies as to how far such claims can continue to be recognized. If land is to be regarded as a national asset, then timely steps should be taken, wherever this is still possible, to prevent excessive shareholding.[2]

Summing up the main characteristics of indigenous systems of land-holding, it may be said generally that these are devised to meet the needs of a subsistence system of agriculture and depend on a sufficiency of land to allow of a rotation which includes a long period of fallow. Land is held on (*a*) a kinship, and/or (*b*) a local group basis. Individuals have definite rights, but these are qualified by membership of a family, kindred and ward (or small village). Similarly, the individual claims of families exist concurrently with the wider claims of the clan or local group. Title, therefore, has a community character. It is also usufructuary rather than absolute.[3] Land may only be sold under conditions which do not conflict with the rights of the kin or local group. The chief is the custodian of

[1] Bayaidu *v.* Mensah, 1878. Under the Ottoman Land Code, state land can be acquired by 10 years uninterrupted possession. In the Punjab it was laid down by the Tenancy Act of 1887 (Sec. 9) that no tenant should be deemed to acquire a right of occupancy by mere lapse of time. But every tenant was deemed to have a right of occupancy who had for more than two generations been occupying the land, without paying rent, prior to the passing of the Act. The limitation for a suit to have an alienation of ancestral land declared void, or for an heir to recover possession, was (in 1920) fixed at six years. See the Punjab Limitation (Custom) Act, 1920.

[2] In South Africa no native, holding land under the Glen Grey Act of 1894, may hold more than one parcel of land.

[3] The rights are of the ancient Greek rather than the Roman pattern. Sir Paul Vinogradoff has observed that Rome developed the conception of *absolute* property, while Greece worked out a conception of *relative* property rights. *Historical Jurisprudence*, Vol. II, p. 198.

land, but not its owner. The normal unit of land ownership is the extended-family, or kindred. Land once granted to a family remains the property of that family, and the chief has no right to any say in its disposal. This constitutes a definite limitation on the conception of land as the collective property of the tribe or local group. The kinship basis of land-holding ensures social stability, but the absence of individual proprietary rights prevents the raising of money on land and so is a hindrance to development.[1] Land may be pledged and redeemed at any time. The principle of redeemability ensures that land shall not be permanently lost, but it may be an impediment to progress since no one will attempt to improve land of which he may be deprived at short notice. The restrictions on the sale of land, the limitation of possession to the period of effective use, and the periodic re-allocation of land, all ensure that land shall not be uselessly withheld from cultivation or lost to the community.

The ownership of Trees

Reference has been made to the fact that there are special rules governing property in economic trees, as distinct from the land on which they grow. The rules differ with the different kinds of trees and there are wide variations in local custom.[2] But generally it may be said that, as in the case of land, so with trees, labour creates rights. Thus, while the fruit of wild palm trees may be free to all,[3] restrictions on this freedom appear as soon as the trees are prepared for the tapping of wine. This is a laborious process, and the person who carries it out establishes a proprietary right over the tree which he has tapped. Similarly if a person *plants* a palm or any other economic tree, the tree will belong to him. Before planting he will generally summon elders as witnesses, more particularly if the land

[1] But, as Lord Hailey has pointed out, individual tenure is not the only remedy. If, for example, a clan or tribal unit were to become an economic as well as a social or political unit, 'raising capital against the value of clan or tribal lands, acting as a co-operative banking or selling organization, and taxing individuals through a rent upon their holdings, a rapid transition to individual ownership of land might possibly be avoided. But any such development assumes a roughly parallel development of all the individuals in a given community.' See *An African Survey*, p. 1430.

[2] In the case of timber, for example, local custom varies with local conditions. Where the country is heavily timbered no rules may be necessary, and it may be considered an advantage to all if the forest is cut down and land made available for cultivation. But where timber is scarce rules may be stricter.

[3] But in many areas only the inhabitants of the village owning the land on which the trees grow would have the right to collect the fruit. In the Gold Coast the right to collect forest produce on 'stool' lands may be subject to permission from the Chief and the payment to him of a proportion of the proceeds. In many parts of West Africa palms growing on house or house-farm are individually owned, while those growing on the country or 'bush' farm-lands are owned by the community. Raffia palms, which are valued as a source of palm-wine, mats, cloth and canoe poles, are usually individually owned and descend from father to son.

does not belong to himself. If he leaves his village he loses his right over his farming land, but he does not lose his rights over his trees. He may let his land, but he does not thereby let his trees. There is a saying among the Yoruba of Nigeria that 'A tenant should not raise his eyes upwards.'[1] Trees may, however, be let with the land, and after a long period a tenant may attempt to claim both as his own. But it is easier to establish a prescriptive claim to land than to trees.[2] On the other hand, trees may be let apart from the land,[3] and temporary loans of trees are often given nowadays by persons who are in need of money to pay their taxes.[4]

A lessee or temporary occupier of land may, with the owner's permission, plant a few economic trees, such as breadfruit, pear, or kola-nut, and he would retain rights over them in perpetuity. But, if he were to plant more than a specified number, a dispute would arise. In many communities custom forbids a grantee of land to plant any permanent crop such as cocoa, as this would be regarded as an attempt to acquire permanent ownership of the land. A prohibition of this kind may be necessary in communities where there are no written conditions attaching to a grant of land. In Basutoland chiefs do not encourage the planting of trees on arable land as this would give the appearance of preferring a claim to the land. In Zanzibar plots of Crown land have been successfully appropriated by being planted up with clove trees.[5] It is stated that in Zanzibar, since it was permissible to sell clove trees, so it became permissible to sell the land; it was not possible to separate thickly-growing clove trees from the land on which they grew.[6]

It is obvious that, under the circumstances described, many problems must arise. Thus, administrative difficulties may occur where, as among the Nyakyusa of Tanganyika, a man resides and farms in one chiefdom and owns bamboos in another. And these difficulties become greater if the trees are of a kind that may spread disease when left unattended. Agricultural Departments may have

[1] Where land is leased under Government ordinances there may be restrictive covenants respecting trees. Thus, in Fiji, under the Native Land Trust Ordinance of 1940, lessees may not cut down trees without the consent of the lessor, nor remove or dispose of by sale any forest produce growing upon the land.

[2] See *A Black Byzantium*, by S. F. Nadel, p. 192.

[3] In Zanzibar in 1933 the standard annual rent for a clove tree varied from Re. 1/- to Rs. 3/-, while that for a coco-nut was anything from 4 annas to one rupee.

[4] See *A Black Byzantium*, p. 191.

[5] And, vice versa, land on which mangrove trees grow has wrongly, in Pemba Island, been regarded as Crown land because of the fact that permits have to be obtained from the Government for the cutting of mangrove poles.

[6] Information of District Officer of Pemba. In 1912 the Chief Commissioner of Ashanti stated that, "We had to make a rule that when a man had properly planted a cocoa plantation it should be regarded as his own, so as to give him the fruits of his labour. This was the beginning of individual ownership (of land).' See Cmd. 6278 (1912), p. 87.

to insist that coffee trees, for example, shall either be kept clean or uprooted, and local authorities may find themselves obliged to take temporary or permanent possession of trees belonging to absentee owners. Cases of absentee ownership are less infrequent than might be supposed, since the fear of witchcraft often impels primitive peoples to move from one locality to another.[1]

Problems also arise from the practice of pledging economic trees. The head of a family may pawn some of the family trees in order to defray the funeral expenses of his predecessor. It would be the concern of all the members of the family to redeem the trees as soon as possible. But until this is done the creditor appropriates the fruit as interest on the loan. Mr. Ward Price has observed that, among the Yoruba of Nigeria, creditors often obtain from the trees more in the way of interest than the whole of the principal sum, and that in many cases the chances of repaying the loan are so small that the plantation becomes for all practical purposes the property of the creditor.[2] There are countless young men in West Africa to-day who would be the owners of economic trees if their fathers had not pledged them for a sum which they had never been able to repay, just as there are countless others who are landless because their fathers had pledged more land than the family could afford to lose.

The extent of the confusion that may arise as the result of the separate ownership of trees and of land may be illustrated by the following example. The owner of trees on land which is not his own may decide to pledge his trees, and the owner of the land may in turn decide to pledge his land. The pledgee of the land may then, with the owner's permission,[3] plant economic trees on his own account, and later he, too, may pledge his trees. It is easy to see that such a situation is almost certain to lead to disputes and litigation.[4]

Again, when a pledgee relinquishes the land, he may be compelled to relinquish also his permanent crops which cannot be harvested or removed. Or he may be allowed to retain an interest in his crops, or be given a sum of money as compensation. In some communities he is compelled to cut down his permanent crops. It is said that at Nyeri in Kenya an owner may, on resuming land which had been planted with permanent crops, allow it to lie fallow for a period, so as to avoid the charge of having resumed ownership in order to appropriate the late occupier's crop. There is a well-known trick in Africa by which the owner of uncleared land grants

[1] See e.g. G. Wilson's *Land Rights of Individuals among the Nyakyusa*, 1938, p. 31.

[2] *Land Tenure in the Yoruba Provinces*, H. L. Ward Price, 1933.

[3] An owner would not usually allow a pledgee to convert his food-producing land into a plantation of permanent crops.

[4] In Tanganyika where rights in mango and other trees may be bought and sold, some Native Authorities are considering revising this rule, owing to the friction that arises when the owners of trees enter the land of others to collect the fruit.

cultivation rights to another, and then, at the end of a single season, reclaims the cleared land for his own use.

In Zanzibar the owner of overgrown land may allow another farmer to clear the land and plant it up with clove trees. When the trees begin to bear, the landowner will formally make over half of the land to the cultivator, retaining the other half for himself. This is said (by the local District Officer) to be a regular method of obtaining 'freehold property'. In Cyprus economic trees are often situated on other people's land, and there may be many divided interests in some small field containing no more than twenty or thirty carob and olive trees. To take an example, on the land inherited by the several heirs of the deceased A, there may be trees owned by B, C, D, and E, and by the several heirs of F and G. The land itself may be under mortgage to X, and some of the trees belonging to B and E may be let to Y and Z.[1]

Under the Ottoman Land Code, which formerly governed land tenure in Cyprus, trees growing naturally on land pass with it to the purchaser or heir, without being specially mentioned. But trees grafted or planted by man are in a different category. These are held independently by a 'mulk' title.[2] The land on which 'mulk' trees (or buildings) stand is not considered to have a separate existence, but to be merged in the trees (or buildings). It is only on the disappearance of the trees (or buildings) that it reverts to its land category. There is a pre-emptive provision in the Code that 'the possessor of any land on which there are "mulk" trees or buildings, land on which the cultivation and possession are subordinate to the trees and buildings, cannot part with the land by way of gift or for a price to anyone other than the owner of the trees or buildings, if the latter claims to have it transferred to him on payment of its *tapu* value'.[3] It may be observed, also, that according to the law of Islam, 'In sales of land, the trees are included in the sale, even if it is not so specified; but [growing] corn is not so included unless so specified. In the sale of trees with fruit growing on them, the fruit [of that year] belongs to the seller unless the buyer makes it a condition of purchase, and the seller may be required to gather it and deliver the purchase.[4] In the sale of fruit [without the trees] the purchaser

[1] See *A Survey of Rural Life in Cyprus*, prepared by B. J. Surridge, p. 51. The excessive subdivision of trees is no less a problem than the excessive subdivision of land, particularly in Muhammadan areas. Plantations of coco-nuts, etc., may be rendered valueless since the trees may be owned by so many heirs that no single individual has sufficient trees to induce him to keep the plantation clean. In some parts of the Sudan where dates are the main cash crop the industry has suffered much because joint ownership of palms, or even of a single palm, has prevented the substitution of better varieties.

[2] For an explanation of 'mulk' title see p. 63.

[3] See *Ottoman Land Laws*, by Stanley Fisher, Article 44, p. 17.

[4] Commentator's note: 'Shafi'i held that the fruit should be left until it begins to mature.'

must gather the fruit immediately; if it is stipulated that the fruit is to be left on the trees, the sale is invalid.'[1]

It is clear from these data, and from the great variability in the rules relating to the ownership of trees, that many difficulties are being experienced in the attempts to adapt native systems of tenure to the requirements of plantation cultivations under modern conditions. Each district will have to hammer out its own law according to local circumstances.[2] But the native authorities have a right to expect guidance in this difficult matter, and if this is to be provided it will be necessary that much fuller information should be obtained and that there should be more pooling of information between one colony and another.

[1] This quotation is from the Hidayah. The Shafi'ite doctrine will be found in Sachau, *Muhammadanisches Recht*, Berlin, 1897, 272, § 14, 296 sq.

[2] To take an example, in Tanganyika, the Federation of Nyanza Chiefs has ruled that trees, as well as immovable property, must be considered as village estate. See *Colonial*, No. 165 (1938), p. 214. In the Punjab, prior to the passing of the Tenancy Act of 1887, a tenant was frequently restrained by custom from planting trees or making improvements without the consent of the landlord. But the Act does not appear to protect custom in this respect. See Sir W. H. Rattigan, *Digest of Civil Law for the Punjab*, pp. 297 and 300.

CHAPTER III

Malaya

Malaya comprises:

(1) The Colony of the Straits Settlements, including Singapore Island (with Christmas Island and the Cocos-Keeling group), Penang (with Province Wellesley), Malacca and Labuan. These areas are British territory and are administered as Crown Colonies.

(2) The Federated Malay States of Perak, Selangor, Negri Sembilan and Pahang.

(3) The Unfederated Malay States of Johore, Kedah, Perlis, Kelantan, Trengganu, and Brunei. The Federated and Unfederated Malay States are British-protected States under the rule of Sultans who are juridically independent, though politically dependent on the British Crown.

The total area of Malaya is 53,283 sq. miles, and the total population in 1938 was estimated to be 5,278,870. A noteworthy feature is that, whereas in 1911 the Malays constituted 54% of the population and the Chinese 34%, the latter now slightly outnumber the former.[1] Agriculture employs at least 1¼ million people, of whom 800,000 are smallholders and 400,000 are labourers on estates. The terms of employment of the latter are governed by the Labour Code (No. 6 of 1933)[2]. In this there are special provisions for the large body of immigrant labour from India, China and the Dutch East Indies. It is to be noted that of the total Indian population of 743,555, less than half are employed on estates—in contrast to Ceylon, where seven-eighths of the immigrant Indians find work in this way. A large amount of land, both rural and urban, in every part of Malaya is owned by Indians. In the Straits Settlements Indians hold land valued at $16,666,466, in Perak they hold 72,948 acres, in Selangor 41,639, in Negri Sembilan 28,000, in Pahang 15,111, in Johore 16,215, and in Kedah 40,334. These figures do not include land held indirectly by Indians as partners in firms or shareholders in registered companies, nor as owners, or part owners, of land in the names of persons belonging to other countries.[3]

[1] The figures on 30th June, 1938, were: (*a*) Malays, 2,210,867
(*b*) Chinese, 2,220,244.

[2] For some account of the status of labourers on estates, see the *1938 Annual Report of the Malayan Department of Labour*, p. 50.

[3] This information is taken from the *1938 Annual Report of the Labour Department*.

Malaya has a low density of population. Only two-fifths of the total area are inhabited, and only one-fifth is settled land. The main crops, in order of acreage, are rubber, rice, coco-nuts, oil palms, pineapples, fruits, areca nuts, tapioca, bananas, coffee, vegetables, tea, gambier and tobacco. Rubber is the dominating crop, having a planted area of over 3¼ million acres, out of a total cultivated area of about 5 million acres. The prosperity of Malaya has been almost entirely built up on rubber and tin. In 1938 there were 726,670 acres of rice under cultivation, and it is noteworthy that the country only produces one-third of its rice requirements. 613,417 acres were (in 1938) planted with coco-nuts, 72,143 acres with oil palms, and 67,394 acres with pineapples.

Of the 3,296,647 acres planted with rubber, 2,031,969 were in estates and 1,264,678 were in small holdings. The following table shows the nationality of rubber *estate* ownership:

(1)	European	1,530,420 acres
(2)	Chinese	322,641 ,,
(3)	Indians	87,795 ,,
(4)	Others	91,113 ,,
		2,031,969

This table shows a marked preponderance of European ownership of estates, but if small holdings are included the area held by Asiatics exceeds that held by Europeans. Most of the coco-nut plantations are in the form of small holdings held mainly by Asiatics.

As regards rice or 'padi', which is the staple food of 99% of the population, although special measures have been taken under the land legislation of the various Malayan governments to encourage the production of rice, 612,000 tons of rice had to be imported into Malaya in 1938. The Department of Labour stated in their 1938 Annual Report that 'it does not pay under Malayan conditions to produce, commercially, ordinary foodstuffs, and neither the capitalist nor the worker is at all tempted to turn his energies to such production. Even for the Malays in the rice-growing areas it is necessary to prescribe the methods of production and to safeguard their interests by arranging to buy their "padi" at Government mills'. The outbreak of the war emphasised the danger of relying on external sources for food, and the Government took additional steps to open up new rice lands. In Johore rice land was offered at several years' tenure, free of quit rent, and proposals were also made to relax the laws against the alienation of land to non-Malays, so as to allow Chinese and other non-indigenous peoples to acquire land for the purpose of growing rice. But even these inducements had little effect, and it is clear that Malaya is not naturally suitable for rice-growing, since irrigation is required in the planting season, at the driest time of the year. Thus, the solution of Malaya's rice problem lies largely in the provision of additional irrigation facilities. It does not appear that the extension of rubber cultivation has led, in Malaya, as it did in Ceylon, to any extensive abandonment of rice lands.

The only other food production of any importance, apart from a certain amount of fruit grown by Malays, is that done by Chinese market gardeners in the vicinity of towns, estates or mines. Chinese small growers have also turned their attention to the cultivation of derris, and it is interesting to observe that rice-milling has been developed as a business by Chinamen.

Of the total area of Malaya about 20% is forest reserve, 21% is alienated land, and the remaining 59% is unalienated or State land.

The Straits Settlements

In the Straits Settlements, with an area of only 1,357 sq. miles and a population density of 1,000 to the sq. mile, the land problems are of an urban rather than an agricultural character. After the founding of Singapore, leases were granted for a period of 999 years, but in 1838 leases for 99 years were introduced. Land in the country was also obtainable on short-term leases, but from 1845 onwards, as a result of the flourishing condition of agriculture and the consequent demand for greater security of tenure, grants in freehold were issued for lands outside the limits of the town. Insufficient allowance was made for the town's expansion, and at the present time some areas are held in the most crowded parts of the city under titles originally issued for purely agricultural land.

After the transfer of the Settlements to the control of the Colonial Office in 1867, the titles for land, both in town and country, were leases for terms of 99 or 999 years, but in 1886 an ordinance (No. 11), which is now the Crown Lands Ordinance,[1] introduced a statutory form of Crown title—the present statutory land grant, which is a grant in perpetuity, subject to a quit rent ('yielding to His Majesty, His Heirs and Successors the annual rent of dollars—') and subject also to various implied conditions and covenants which hitherto had to be expressly provided for in the document of title itself. This statutory grant became then, and until recently continued to be, the usual form of title issued; but the present policy is to restrict the issue of grants in perpetuity, substituting as far as possible leases for terms not exceeding 99 years.[2]

[1] Cap. 113 of *The Laws of the Straits Settlements*, Revised Edition, 1936.

[2] This information is taken from the *1939 Annual Report of the Social and Economic Progress of the People of the Straits Settlements*, p. 86.

The Crown Lands Ordinance also provides (in special circumstances) for grants in fee simple, and there is provision for revision of rent (after 1st January, 1915, at the end of every thirty years): but the rent payable in any term of thirty years must not exceed by more than 50% the rent which was payable in the immediately preceding term. In making the revision no improvements made by the land-holder or his predecessors in title are to be taken into account.

The premium payable for the alienation of Crown land varies with the situation. For purely agricultural land a premium of from \$50 (£6) to \$100 (£12) per acre was being charged in the years before the war, with quit rent at \$1 (2/4) to \$2 per acre.

In recent years, with the increase in rubber estates and the rise in land values, there has been a tendency for the small fruit and vegetable growers to be crowded out of the island. As a counter measure the Government has freely issued permits for the temporary occupation of Crown Land, which are renewable year after year. This has had a marked effect in keeping the small cultivators on the land. There is an Ordinance to prevent encroachment on Crown Lands.

Land in Penang and Province Wellesley, is held, as in Singapore, by grant or lease from the Crown. In the early days much misunderstanding and confusion surrounded land transactions in this area, and the attempts of succeeding Governments to cope with the situation have resulted in a great variety of tenures. It is said that at the present time there are eleven types of titles.[1] There is little unoccupied land left in the Settlement.

In Malacca, the tenure of a considerable portion of the town has remained unchanged since the days of Dutch suzerainty, and in many cases possession is evidenced by documents of title in Dutch. The remainder of the land in the town is mostly held under Crown leases for 99 years, but there are a few leases for 999 years, and also some statutory grants. In the country, alienated land is generally held under statutory grants or leases from the Crown for 99 years, but small-holdings owned by Malays are held under customary tenure, which is governed by two Ordinances, namely, 'The Malacca Land Customary Rights Ordinance' (Cap. 125) and 'The Mutations in Titles to Land Ordinance' (Cap. 126). No transfer of customary land is valid unless it is made to an individual qualified to become a customary land-holder, that is to say, a Malay domiciled in Malacca and any person holding a certificate from the Resident Councillor of Malacca that he is qualified to hold customary land. Every customary land-holder has a permanent, heritable and transferable right of use and occupancy, subject to (*a*) the

[1] *Handbook to British Malaya* (1935), p. 104. The earliest titles in Penang derive from the East India Company.

payment of rent or assessment as imposed by law; (*b*) the reservation in favour of the Crown of all minerals and of the right of making roads, etc.; (*c*) the liability to give free labour for the performance of certain customary duties 'for the common benefit of himself and the other customary land-holders' (including the duty of preparing the 'sawah' for planting and the simultaneous planting of rice); and (*d*) certain restrictions regarding the planting of crops considered to be exhausting to the soil. Customary land which has not been cultivated for a period of three years reverts to the Crown, and if it appears that the land has been used mainly for building purposes rather than for agriculture, the Governor in Council may declare that the land is no longer held under customary tenure.

The rights of a customary land-holder in Malacca are registered in the Mukim Register, that is to say the land register of the local subdivision, and every registered holder may charge his interest in the land, by way of mortgage, with the payment at the appointed time of any principal sum of money, either with or without interest.[1] But no mortgage or sale is valid unless carried out in accordance with the Enactment. Parties to a mortgage must attend at the Land Office for the registration of the mortgage, and sales of land for the payment of mortgage debts must be held at the Land Office or other convenient place specified by the Collector. All transfers have to be noted in the register, and, when transfers are made, the local headman (or two other reliable witnesses) must attend as security against impersonation or fraud. It is of interest to note that, if the landholder is a Muhammadan, his land must descend according to the rules of Muhammadan law, but that the Muhammadan law may be varied by local custom.

All transfers are supervised by the Collector of Land Revenue, who is also empowered to direct land-holders to erect boundary marks and keep them in a proper state of repair. The Collector has wide general powers under the Ordinance, and a noteworthy feature of the legislation is that there is a bar to the jurisdiction of Courts relating to claims in respect of which jurisdiction is given the Collector—except where there is express provision to the contrary.

Since the Mukim Register plays a predominant part in the recording of land rights throughout Malaya, a sample page is shown below.

[1] In Malacca there is a form of mortgage known as 'Chagar' whereby the land is redeemable by repayment of the amount advanced *without interest*. This form of mortgage is common all over Africa.

Number of the entry	Survey No.	Number and nature of former document of title	Name of proprietor	Area	Boundaries	Nature of cultivation	Express conditions	Name of kampong or place	Annual rent	Restrictions	Remarks
									$: C		
								L.S.	Signature of Collector.		

Extract issued to.................this..........day......19..

Signature of Collector.

Name of Proprietor	Subsequent dealings	Remarks	Name of Proprietor	Subsequent dealings	Remarks

It may be noted in conclusion, as regards the Straits Settlements, that the 1939 figures for land distribution (excluding Labuan, Christmas and Cocos Islands) were as follows:

Total Area	=	1,260	sq. miles
Alienated land	=	932	"
Crown or State land	=	232·8	"
Forest reserve	=	95·2	"

Alienated land constituted 74% of the total.

The Federated Malay States

The Federated Malay States embrace the States of Perak, Selangor, Negri Sembilan and Pahang. These States are not technically British territory, nor do their inhabitants rank as British subjects. They came under British protection, as a result of treaties concluded in the 'seventies and 'eighties of last century. Under these treaties the Rulers of the States agreed to accept a British Resident responsible to the Governor of the Straits Settlements, whose advice they would accept in all matters, except those relating to Malay custom and the Muhammadan religion.

The Federated Malay States have a total area of 27,540 sq. miles and of this State land represents 15,243 sq. miles or 56%, reserved forest represents 7599 sq. miles or 27%, and alienated land 4698 sq. miles or 17%. Land tenure is regulated by (*a*) The Land Code of 1926;[1] (*b*) The Mining Enactment,[2] since the Land Code does not apply to mining land; (*c*) The Land Acquisition Enactment;[3] (*d*) The Malay Reservations Enactment;[4] and (*e*) The Customary Tenure Enactment.[5] There is a Land Office in each of the twenty-four districts, and in some cases, where districts are subdivided, there may be more than one Land Office.

All land not held under title vests solely in the Ruler of the State, but State land may be converted into private ownership by the British Resident of each State, acting on behalf of the Ruler and in the manner prescribed by the Code. The Resident may acquire any land when it is needed for a public purpose. He may constitute any land a reserve, and, with the approval of the Ruler, he may acquire land for a residential or factory area, for vegetable gardens and for leasing as mining land. He may, however, delegate certain of his powers to Collectors. In most districts, for example, Collec-

[1] Cap. 138 of the 1935 Laws of the Federated Malay State.
[2] Cap. 147.
[3] Cap 140.
[4] Cap. 142.
[5] Cap. 215.

tors may alienate to Asiatics country land up to ten acres, and may also permit the temporary occupation of State land under licence or pending the registration of title.

There are five classes of land, namely: (1) Town land; (2) Village land; (3) Country land exceeding ten acres in area; (4) Country land not exceeding ten acres in area; and (5) Foreshore and sea bed. Town and village lands are generally alienated by auction, the conditions of auction and the reserve price being fixed by the Resident. The document of title is either a grant or a lease, and the word 'grant' is defined as including a lease of State land in perpetuity or for a term of not less than 999 years.

The usual form of wording in a grant is 'to hold for ever subject to the payment therefor of the annual rent of dollars—, until revision takes place'. The Code lays down that the rent of all land alienated after 31st December, 1909, is subject to periodical revision, which may result either in enhancement or reduction—the first revision being due to take place on 1st January, 1940, and subsequent revisions at intervals of not less than thirty years. In fixing the new rent the Resident may not take into account any improvements made by the proprietor or his predecessors. The revisable rent system is an obvious means of protecting the rights of the State, of enabling it to share in the increased value of land, and of preventing the excessive accumulation of land by single individuals. But the absence from the Federated Malay States' legislation of any percentage by which rents may be increased is somewhat remarkable, especially as limits are fixed elsewhere in Malaya.

In the case of country land exceeding ten acres, the document of title is also a grant or lease. Premium is at the Resident's discretion, and quit rent is at the rate of $1 per acre for the first six years, and thereafter $4 per acre. There are implied conditions regarding good husbandry, and there must be a bona fide beginning to cultivate within twelve months of the date of registration. It is thus virtually impossible for speculators to take up land and wait for a rise in value, since before this could happen the State would have intervened and resumed the land. Moreover, even although a grant may be given *in perpetuity*, this is not the equivalent of freehold, since the grant is subject to the Land Code and also to any conditions which may be set forth in the grant itself.

Coming now to land of less than ten acres, that is to say the land of the small-holders, the document of title may be an entry in the Mukim Register, or a grant or lease of State land, and there is an implied condition that the land must be continuously cultivated in a proper manner, to the extent of one-half of the total area; if this is not done over a period of three years, the proprietor loses his rights. Premium for this land varies, and the quit rent is $1·60—

$4·00 per acre for first-class land, $·80—$1·20 for second-class land, and $ ·60 for third-class land. The Resident may impose conditions specifying the particular product or class of products which, or which alone, is to be cultivated. He may also, with the approval of the High Commissioner, make a rule compelling the proprietors or occupiers of rice lands to give their labour free for the performance of such works and duties as may be for the common benefit. Incidentally, it may be observed that, under Chapter 145 of the laws, the Resident has power to declare certain areas to be irrigated areas which may not be used for any other purpose than the cultivation of rice—a necessary provision in a country where rice is the staple food, and any undue extension of other crops might lead to conditions of famine.

In the Federated Malay States the land system has not developed along the lines originally projected. As in various other dependencies, (e.g. Uganda), it was originally considered that there should be two distinct types of title, (*a*) one suited to European and commercial interests, and (*b*) the other suited to native occupiers. To meet the needs of the former a system of registration based on that of Sir Robert Torrens was introduced, and a form of registered title was provided which conferred the fullest measure of ownership considered compatible with the rights reserved to the Government. This necessitated accurate survey and the other expensive items of procedure connected with an up-to-date system of registration. In the case of native holdings no such elaborate procedure was considered to be necessary or desirable, and the only test recognized was that of occupancy. A register of land held according to native law and custom was introduced, and any person registered therein obtained a permanent right of use and occupancy in his land. This right, though transferable and transmissible, fell very far short of ownership in the English sense, and since it was no more than a right of occupancy it did not confer the right to lease or charge the land. Accurate survey was not necessary, and transfer was carried out by merely altering the name in the Collector's record. The system was simple, but quite adequate to the requirements of the country.

The development of plantation crops, however, coupled with the fact that the native system existed alongside and intermingled with one which depended on survey, tended to produce an assimilation of the customary title to that of the registered title, with the result that (writing about 1930) the Commissioner of Lands considered that the difference between the two forms of title had become negligible. The occupant of land held by native custom was now the owner of land held by entry in the Mukim Register. He possessed a document of title, he could charge or lease his land, its area was surveyed, dealings had to be executed in a statutory form duly attested, and the instrument had to be registered before it became effective. The only notable difference in the system of registering grants and that of registering native rights was that in the case of the former the registration was metropolitan, while in the case of the latter it was local.[1]

It is claimed by some that the new system has been a signal success. The early difficulties created by unsurveyed land have disappeared and it is said that not one per cent of the transactions involving registration calls for the intervention of a lawyer. But others maintain that assimilation of the native customary title to that of the European registered title has not been an unmixed blessing; it conferred on the peasant a title the value of which he did not understand, except as a means of raising cash, and so made him an easy prey to the Chinese and Indian moneylender.

Prior to 1929 there had been, throughout the Federated Malay States, an intensive campaign for explotiing the tin resources of the country and this had resulted in the formation of many companies to work suitable areas with dredges. The Government then decided that some limitation must be put to the wholesale alienation of land and that, except in special circumstances, no further applications for mining land or for the conversion of agricultural to mining title outside existing mining areas should be entertained.[2] It was laid down also that, within mining areas, alienation or conversion should not in general be approved, unless it were essential for the efficient development of existing undertakings. It is not clear how far these decisions were intended to be temporary or provisional. There are many areas held under agricultural title, or included in village and town lands, which are known to be tin-bearing, and these, no doubt, will be developed in due course. Moreover, as mining methods improve, large areas which are now of no economic value are likely to become valuable as mining land.[3]

A further measure for securing the land interests of the native population is the Malay Reservations Enactment of 1933 (Cap. 142). Under this law, which superseded an earlier Enactment of 1913, the British Resident, with the approval of the Ruler of the State in Council, may declare any area of land within the State to be a Malay

[1] See *Surveys for Title in the Federated Malay States*, by W. F. N. Bridges, p. 13, quoting the Legal Adviser and Commissioner of Lands.

[2] Under the Mining Enactment lands alienated otherwise than for mining purposes may be resumed for mining purposes, against the will of the proprietor, by the Ruler of the State in Council, upon payment of compensation. (Cap. 147, sec. 133.)

[3] See *Handbook to British Malaya*, 1935 edition, p. 44. It may be pointed out that when a mining company converts agricultural or village land into mining land it is required to make adequate provision for the dispossessed. Some villages have been rebuilt with a much improved lay-out.

Reservation. Any State land, reserved forest, land reserved for public purposes, or alienated land, may be included in such a Reservation. No State land included within a Reservation may be sold, leased or otherwise disposed of to any person other than a Malay, and there are general restrictions on transfers, charges, and leases to persons other than Malays. There are restrictions as to dealings in holdings by attorneys, and also as to caveats. No lien by deposit of the issue document of title for any Malay holding as security for a debt is capable of being created in favour of any person; no Malay holding in a Reservation may be attached in execution of a decree or order of any Court; and no Malay holding in a Reservation shall vest in the Official Assignee on the bankruptcy of the proprietor. Reservation lands may, however, be charged to the Government, and to approved co-operative societies. It is interesting to note that the definition of 'Malay' insists not merely that the person shall belong to a Malayan people speaking a Malayan language, but also that he professes the Moslem religion.

The final feature of interest in the land legislation of the Federated Malay States is the Enactment which deals with Customary Tenure (Cap. 215). This concerns the customary land law of Malays belonging to certain tribes in certain districts of Negri Sembilan. Among these tribes it would appear that land is customarily held by females, and the enactment provides, *inter alia*, for the rectification of registers in which males have in the past been wrongly entered as customary holders of land. Subject to the provisions of the Enactment, no customary land or any interest therein may be transferred, charged, transmitted or otherwise dealt with except in accordance with the custom. It is not possible, therefore, for a grant to be issued for any customary land, nor may customary land be transferred or leased to any person other than a female member of one of the tribes specified. It may be charged to any female member of any of the tribes specified, and there is a special provision permitting the charging of customary land to the Collector or to a recognized local Co-operative Society. The restrictions against leasing are also relaxed when the period of the lease does not exceed twelve months.

Another interesting provision is that the consent of the *lembaga* or headman of the tribe is required before any customary land may be transferred, charged or leased; but the Collector may over-ride the *lembaga* when the latter unreasonably refuses consent or appears to give a consent which is contrary to custom. The Collector is also empowered to give a life occupancy of land to (*a*) a son, or (*b*) a maternal uncle of a deceased holder, who, though having left a female customary heir, has left (*a*) no female issue, or (*b*) no issue nor maternal sister. The customary heir becomes the registered owner of the land, but the life-occupant and the registered owner become jointly responsible for the rent due to the State. Where the deceased has left no customary heir, the Collector may order the estate to be sold and the proceeds paid to the deceased's son or maternal brother or, in their absence, to the Muhammadan Religious Fund.

There are many interesting features about customary land-holding in Negri Sembilan and other areas of Malaya, which have been described in the works of Messrs. Parr and Mackray (*Rembau*), E. N. Taylor (*Customary Law of Rembau*) and G. A. de C. de Moubray (*Matriarchy in the Malay Peninsula*). There is a clear distinction between ancestral land and acquired land, though the latter in due course becomes ancestral land.[1] This distinction has become emphasised by the development of rubber and other plantation crops, which illustrate the principle of all native systems of land-holding that everyone should be free to dispose of the results of his own individual efforts. Rubber land has now become heritable by males as well as females, and the claims of children are preferred to those of the matrilineal kin. This is a development which has been observed also in the Gold Coast with regard to the inheritance of cocoa-lands.[2] Moreover, whereas formerly a husband had no rights in land, nowadays he has a right to a half share of rubber land which has been developed jointly by himself and his wife. This is a revolutionary change, since it makes it possible for tribal land to be held by persons who are not members of the tribe. In this connection it is worth observing that by native law the sale or mortgage of ancestral property outside the kin or tribe was strictly forbidden, and if the holder of ancestral property, to which there were no immediate heirs, wished to dispose of it, she[3] had to grant an option to her own clan or tribe before seeking a purchaser elsewhere. This rule appears to be breaking down and would not in any case apply to plantation land. Mr. de Moubray (writing in 1931) remarks that 'during the last quarter of a century it became customary for Malays to open up plantations, sell them to Chinese and then open up more land: whereby plantations became an article of commerce'.[4]

[1] G. A. de C. de Moubray states that acquired property enters the category of ancestral property when it has been inherited by the grand-daughters of the person who acquired it. Op cit., p. 126. Strict Muhammadan Law makes no distinction between ancestral and self-acquired property, nor between movable and immovable property. See Sir R. K. Wilson, *Digest of Anglo-Muhammadan Law*, fifth edition, revised by A. Yusuf Ali, p. 61.

[2] See pp. 176-7. Cf. also Sir R. K. Wilson's *Digest of Anglo-Muhammadan Law*, p. 38, where it is stated that in Bombay 'the principle was laid down [in 1913] that the Khojas were governed, in succession and inheritance, by Hindu law *as applied to separate and self-acquired property*; otherwise the general presumption was that they were governed by Muhammadan law and usage'.

[3] Ancestral property descends to daughters.

[4] Op. cit., p. 138.

CHAPTER IV

Malaya (Continued)

The Unfederated Malay States

The Unfederated Malay States consist of Johore, Kelantan, Kedah, Perlis, Trengganu, and Brunei.[1] The total area of these States is 24,483 sq. miles, and of this 16,124 sq. miles are State land, 5450 sq. miles are alienated land, and 2909 are forest reserve. Generally speaking, it may be said that land legislation in the Unfederated Malay States has been gradually assimilated to that of the Federated Malay States. But it will be useful to give some account of the land situation in each state.

Johore

Direct connection between Great Britain and Johore began in 1895 when the Sultan of Johore undertook to receive a British Agent exercising the functions of a Consular Officer. In 1910, having had an unofficial adviser for some years, the Sultan reorganized his Government with the assistance of the Governor of the Straits Settlements, and in 1914 he agreed to receive a British General Adviser whose advice must be asked and acted upon in all matters affecting the general administration of the country and in all questions other than those touching Malay religion and custom.

Johore has an area of 7330 sq. miles and in 1938 the population was estimated to be as follows:

Europeans	1080
Eurasians	440
Malaysians	308,240
Chinese	311,620
Indians	84,090
Others	4400
	709,870

Agricultural industries occupy the premier position in the economy of the State. In 1938 the area planted with rubber was 891,151 acres, of which 365,966 acres were cultivated on holdings

[1] Brunei is situated on the west coast of Borneo and need not be dealt with in this study. It has an area of 2,226 sq. miles, of which 1,364 sq. miles are State land, 594 sq. miles are forest reserve, and 265 sq. miles or 12% are alienated land.

of less than 100 acres. The area under coco-nuts was 171,733 acres. It is noteworthy that although small coco-nut holdings are mainly owned by Malays, the production of copra is largely in the hands of Chinese who either purchase the nuts or lease the holdings. Pineapples occupied 50,597 acres, and oil-palms, grown entirely on large estates, occupied 35,368 acres. Other important crops are areca nuts (38,402 acres), which are grown in mixed cultivations with other *kampong* products, coffee (9,041 acres), rice (6,268 acres), and tapioca (2,521 acres). It is said that tapioca is losing its importance owing to a State regulation that it must not be planted on virgin jungle land as a solitary crop.

In Johore, prior to 1910, small holdings were occupied byMalays and Chinese under an unwritten customary law, which conveyed a limited right of ownership. The clearing of land created for the occupier a proprietary tenant right, transferable and heritable. But this right was conditional on certain personal services, the maintenance of cultivation and the payment of a royalty on produce to the State. Large holdings were taken up as estates by Europeans, Chinese and others, under leases or permits granted by the Sultan, the conditions of tenure including reservation of mineral rights and certain powers over forest lands, provision for re-entry for public purposes, and a cultivation clause.[1] In 1910 land legislation was introduced on the lines of that followed by the Federated Malay States, and this, with numerous amendments, is consolidated as Chapter I of the 1935 revised edition of the laws of Johore.

In Johore, out of a total of 7,330 sq. miles, 1,165 sq. miles or 16% are reserved forests, 4085 sq. miles or 56% are State land, and 2,080 or 28% are alienated land.[2] State land is divided into three classes, namely, (*a*) Town or village lands; (*b*) Country lands of 100 acres and under; and (*c*) Country lands exceeding 100 acres.

The right to alienate State land is reserved to the Sultan in Council and there are the usual provisions regarding the revision of rent, although a recent enactment[3] makes it possible for the Sultan, upon the application of the proprietor of any land, to rescind any previous condition in the document of title, to impose any new condition, and to reserve a fresh rent. State land may be alienated under lease for a period not exceeding one hundred years, and there is a general provision that, after any land has been alienated for agricultural purposes under permanent title, no right to mine the land shall be granted except with the special sanction of the Sultan. There are (as in the other States) penalties for the unlawful occupation of state land or of land alienated for mining and public purposes.

[1] *Handbook of British Malaya* (1935), p. 107.
[2] These are the 1939 figures.
[3] No. 3 of 1941 (Sec. 14).

Country lands of 100 acres and under may be alienated under grant or lease or under title by entry in the Mukim Register, and no claim to land is valid unless registered—the Collector being required to keep a record of all mutations.[1] Land of this category which has been abandoned for three consecutive years is liable to forfeiture, even if quit rent has been paid. If the land has been alienated for cultivation, it is deemed to have been abandoned if not kept under cultivation to the extent of one-fourth of its area.

Country lands exceeding 100 acres may be alienated by auction or otherwise as the Sultan-in-Council may direct. There is a right of re-entry if a bona fide commencement to cultivate has not been made within twelve months of the date of grant or lease, or if the land has not been cultivated to the extent of one-fourth of the total area within five years of the date of grant.

In 1936, following the lead of the Federated Malay States, a law was enacted in Johore with a view to preventing interests in land from passing out of the hands of the Malay peoples. This law is entitled the Malay Reservations Enactment (No. 1 of 1936). Its provisions are similar to those of the corresponding act of the Federated Malay States, which has already been described. In 1938 the total area under the Reservation Enactment was estimated to be 30,125 acres. In 1936, also, provision was made under the Labour Code (Amendment) Enactment, 1936, by which employers are required to set aside land (one-sixteenth of an acre for each labourer who has dependents) suitable for use as allotments or grazing land. On the majority of estates there is adequate land for this purpose.

It may be noted in conclusion, as regards Johore, that land taxation takes the form of a premium on alienation varying from $1 to $100 an acre for agricultural or mining purposes, and from 10 cents to 50 cents a square foot for residential or commercial purposes (unless the land is auctioned) and an annual quit-rent varying from 60 cents to $4 an acre on all land (except in a few cases where titles are rent-free). In 1938, however, a waiver of part rent on lands planted with coco-nuts and areca-nuts had the effect of reducing rents on these lands from $3 to $2.

Kelantan

The State of Kelantan was formerly under the suzerainty of Siam, but in 1909 the Siamese Government transferred to Great Britain 'all rights to suzerainty, protection, administration, and control whatsoever which they possessed over the States of Kelan-

[1]Registration is governed by Part V of the Land Enactment (Cap. I) but recent important amendments are contained in Enactment No. 3 of 1941. In 1936 a law (No. 18) was enacted for the abolition (on application) of old titles and the issue of new ones in conformity with the Land Enactment.

tan, Trengganu, Kedah, Perlis and adjacent islands'. In the following year a treaty was concluded between Great Britain and the Raja of Kelantan whereby (under Article 2) the Sultan agreed to receive a British Adviser whose advice he would follow in all matters of administration other than those touching the Muhammadan religion and local Malay custom. The Raja also engaged (under Article 3) not to enter into any agreement concerning land or to grant any concession to, or by, any individual or company other than a native or natives of Kelantan, without previously obtaining the consent of His Majesty's Government; provided that, should the area of the grant or concession not exceed 5000 acres of agricultural land or 1000 acres of mining land, the written consent of the Adviser thereto should suffice.

The State of Kelantan has an area of 5,750 sq. miles, of which 4,320 are State land, 80 are forest reserves, and 1,350 are alienated land. The approximate areas under cultivation for the more important crops are as follows:

Rice	145,000 acres
Rubber	91,000 ,,
Coco-nuts	60,000 ,,
Areca-nuts	7,000 ,,

There are also about 25,000 acres under fruit trees and miscellaneous crops. With the exception of about 32,000 acres of rubber land owned by registered companies or large private owners, practically the whole of the remaining cultivated area is owned by small agriculturists.[1] A typical small holding is between three and five acres of rice land, an acre of high land on which the family house and *padi* store are built, and in many cases also another acre or so of rubber, probably at some distance from the house. It is interesting to observe that among the aboriginal inhabitants of the mountainous region of Kelantan there are groups of Negritos and Indonesians, of whom one of the most marked characteristics is the part played by co-operative endeavour in their daily life. In their planting of annual crops in forest clearings, largely by a rotation of crops and a limited period of fallow, they are said to stand at a higher level than any of the other aboriginal peoples. Each group restricts its clearings to a definite area, so that there is no wholesale destruction of the jungle.[2]

Prior to 1881 no land registers were kept in Kelantan, the dis-

[1] Less than 2% of the population can be considered as wage-earners and many of these also possess land of their own.

[2] See the *Annual Report on the Social and Economic Progress of the People of the State of Kelantan, 1939*, p. 5.

posal of land being in the hands of local headmen acting on behalf of the Sultan. But in 1881 greater security of tenure was made possible by the introduction of a system of registration of changes of tenure. In 1926 a Land Enactment was brought into force embodying the principles of the Torrens system of registration of title, but this was in 1938 superseded by a new Enactment (No. 26), though the principles of the Torrens system were retained.

The entire property in, and control of State land in Kelantan are vested in the Ruler, who may alienate it in the manner authorised by the Enactment and not otherwise, and may impose any restrictions of interest on the alienation as he considers fit. But the Sultan in Council may delegate certain powers of alienation and occupation to his Adviser on Land and Mines, and also to District Officers. He may alienate under lease any State land for mining purposes on any terms that he considers fit and, with the consent of the proprietor of any land alienated for agricultural purposes, he may alienate the whole or any part of such land under lease for mining purposes. All tin, gold, coal, petroleum and other minerals are the property of the State and no document of title other than certain specified mining titles confers any right to remove such minerals. The Sultan may also reserve any land for a public purpose.

Land is divided into the same classes as in the Federated Malay States, and there is also provision for the revision of rent. But in Kelantan revisions may take place at intervals of not less than fifteen years, and no revisions may have the effect of increasing the rent by more than 25%. In making revisions no account may be taken of improvements. There are implied cultivation conditions. For example, in the document of title for any country land not exceeding ten acres, the whole of the land must be continuously cultivated to the satisfaction of the District Officer. There are special cultivation conditions for land exceeding ten acres, but not exceeding fifty acres, and for land exceeding fifty acres. There may be express conditions enjoining the planting of rice, or prohibiting the planting of rubber. Another noteworthy feature in the Kelantan legislation is the restriction placed on the subdivision of lots. The minimum area into which a plot may be divided is one-quarter of an acre,[1] though the Sultan may, in any particular case, authorize a smaller subdivision.

All registered land-holders have the right to transfer, charge or lease their land, but leases may not (after the coming into force of the Enactment) be for a longer period than thirty years. An even more notable restriction is the stipulation (in Section 104) that 'the Land Registrar shall refuse to register any transfer, charge or lease of land by a native of Kelantan to a party who is not a native of

[1] 250 *depa*—a *depa* being 43.56 square feet.

Kelantan until such transaction has received the sanction of the Sultan in Council, subject to the imposition of such restrictions in interest and such conditions in the document of title and such terms of rent therein as he may think fit. Any such transfer, charge or lease shall be null and void unless the previous sanction of the Sultan in Council shall have been obtained'.

In the case of any breach or default in the observance of the conditions (express or implied) of any document of title, the District Officer may, on the Ruler's behalf, re-enter the land, and, upon registration of such re-entry, the land shall be forfeited to the Ruler and the title of the owner extinguished. Thus, if the owner of a holding not exceeding ten acres fails to cultivate it continuously, the District Officer may take possession. Or he may re-enter land on account of failure to pay the land rents. It is laid down (Sec. 179) that as soon as possible after the 31st of March in each year the District Officer shall cause the following notice to be posted throughout the District: 'Proprietors of land are hereby reminded that the annual quit rents on their land are now due. Unless these rents are paid soon the lands will be sold and the proprietors will lose them!'

In Kelantan there is, as in other Malay States, a Malay Reservations Enactment (No. 18 of 1930). There are the usual restrictions on the alienation of reservation land to persons other than Malays, though a Malay may grant a month-to-month lease to a non-Malay, of land which is not situated within the boundaries of a town. He may also, subject to the approval of the Sultan, grant to a non-Malay a lease for three years of land situated within the boundaries of a town. But a notable modification of the Kelantan Reservations Enactment is a recent enactment (No. 8 of 1940) which empowers the Sultan to approve of the alienation, transfer or transmission of any reservation land to any person who is not a Malay.

Kedah

The land tenure legislation of Kedah, which was enacted in 1932[1], follows so closely the principles and procedure of that of the Federated Malay States that it need not be described here in any detail. A few features only need be noted.

The entire property and control of State land in Kedah is vested in the Sultan, but certain powers of alienation may be delegated by the President of the State Council to the Land Alienation Board, the Director of Lands or any Land Officer. The Board, for example, may, if all its members agree, alienate country land up to five

[1] See Chapters LVI, LVII and LXIII of the 1934 edition of the *Laws of Kedah*.

hundred *relongs*[1] in area, and a Land Officer may be empowered to alienate land within a Malay Reservation or outside a Reservation to a person of Malay race, subject to a special condition prohibiting the cultivation of any product other than rice. No State land may be alienated until it has been surveyed.[2]

The document of title to any town land, or to any country land exceeding fifty *relongs*, is known as a Surat Putus Besar, or Lease of State Land: that to any country land not exceeding fifty *relongs* is called a Surat Putus Kechil. It is interesting to observe that the term 'Surat Putus' has long been applied to titles issued by the Sultans of Kedah. It is said that they were originally decisions of judges on land disputes, countersigned by the Sultan, which eventually developed into a system of protective certificates issued independently of any dispute.

Land alienated under grant may, subject to rental and cultivation conditions, be held in perpetuity. There may be special conditions to enforce or prohibit the cultivation of any particular product. On the other hand, in the absence of any restrictions set forth in the document of title or imposed by law, a proprietor has the right to transfer, charge, or lease his land. He may also devise hi interest, but if he is a Muhammadan he is in this respect, as in other respects, subject to the provisions of Muhammadan law.

There is in Kedah, as in the Federated Malay States, a Malay Reservations Enactment (No. 63) under which the State Council may declare any area of land to be a Malay Reservation. But, in Kedah, State land may be alienated to a Siamese as well as to a Malay, provided the Siamese is certified by the Director of Lands to be an agriculturist permanently resident in the State. No reservation land owned by a Malay may be transferred to any person who is not a Malay, and no land owned by a Siamese may be transferred to a person who is not either a Malay or a Siamese. This latter provision will presumably have the effect of increasing the holdings of the Malays at the expense of the Siamese. All documents of title (except Permits) may be charged to anyone; but, if the charger does not pay the money due, the land, if owned by a Malay, may be sold only to a Malay, and, if owned by a Siamese, may be sold only to a Malay or a Siamese. A lease may be granted by the owner to *any person* for a period of not more than three years, but *bendang* or rice land may not be leased by a Malay to any other than a Malay, or by a Siamsee to any other than a Malay or a Siamese. It is interesting to observe that the Kedah definition of a Malay has recently been revised and

[1] A *relong* = .71 of an acre.

[2] In 1939 the figures for alienated land in Kedah were stated to be 1,240 sq. miles or 32%. Reserved forest land was 1,019 or 27% and State or Crown land 1,561 sq. miles or 41%.

is now 'a person professing the Muslim religion and habitually speaking the Malay language, of whose parents one at least is a person of Malayan race or of Arab descent'.[1]

Perlis

The State of Perlis accepted a British Adviser in 1909, in consequence of a treaty concluded between Great Britain and Siam. In 1930 a treaty was signed by which the Perlis Government agreed to continue under the protection of Great Britain, which exercises the right of suzerainty. The State is governed by the Raja with the assistance of a State Council. The population in 1938 was as follows:

Malays	44,360
Chinese	8,103
Siamese	1,991
Indians	978
Europeans and Eurasians ..	14
	55,446

The State has an area of 316 sq. miles and of this 171 sq. miles or 54% were (in 1938) State land, 50 sq. miles (or 16%) were Reserved Forest, 90 sq. miles (or 28·4%) were alienated for agricultural purposes, and 5 sq. miles (or 1·6%) were held under mining titles.

Rice cultivation is the main occupation of the Malay population, and here, as elsewhere in Malaya, *padi* planters help each other by collective work, particularly for the maintenance of irrigation channels and measures against pests. Many miles of fences have been constructed under this communal system for the purpose of keeping wild pig out of the rice areas, and in the ploughing of fields and harvesting of crops neighbours help each other in large parties. It may be observed that the planting up of new *padi* lands involves much preliminary labour in clearing and bund-building, and on this account the State takes a lenient attitude to the unauthorised occupation of State land for rice cultivation, being content usually with regularising the position by granting an occupation licence or title. It is of interest to note also that *zakat* or tithe assessed on the rice crop is paid by cultivators to the local religious organization for charitable purposes, and that every householder also makes a contribution of milled rice at the end of the Muhammadan annual fast. In 1938 there were 4,388 acres under rubber, of which about 3,000 were in the form of small holdings of less than 25 acres. Coco-nuts occupied an area of 3,152 acres.

[1] See Enactment 9 of 1354, Sec. 2.

Prior to 1916, agricultural holdings were held under old grants which gave a brief statement of the facts on which the occupant based his claim, a reference to the proceedings held to verify the facts, and a statement of the law applicable to the case as expounded by the Kadi. The decision of the Raja conferring title on the holder of the deed and to his heirs and successors was set out. This was followed by a description of the land, and as a precaution against fraudulent alteration, by a reference to the number of lines of which the document consisted and the number of corrections of errors therein. A rough sketch of the land was usually given on the back of the deed.

Land alienated in 1916 and afterwards was entered in the 'Register of Milek' or register of approved applications, pending demarcation or survey. Before the outbreak of the war the old grants and the entries in the Register of Milek were being replaced (under the Land Code enacted in 1937) by entries in the Mukim Register for country land not exceeding fifty *relongs*, and by Large Grants for town-village land and for country land exceeding fifty *relongs*.

The new Land Code (No. 11 of 1356 A.H.) consolidated and amended the law relating to land, registration of title, and the collection of land revenue. It declares the entire property in and control of State land to be vested solely in the Raja. Land may be alienated by the President of the State Council, in accordance with the provisions of the enactment, but not otherwise.[1] Every document of title to land, other than a lease of State land, is deemed to be in perpetuity,[2] but in the absence of any express provision to the contrary any land alienated under the enactment is deemed to be held on the express condition that the proprietor agrees to abide by the provisions of the enactment, including any future amendments thereof.

The document of title to any town or village land or to any country land exceeding fifty *relongs* is a Large Grant or lease of State land, and the document of title to any country land not exceeding fifty *relongs* is an entry in the Mukim Register or a lease of State land.

The entire right over waters of whatever nature is vested in the Raja, and the right to all mines, minerals and jungle produce on alienated land is reserved to the Raja. There is the usual reservation also to the State of certain other rights, such as the right to make

[1] The President may delegate to the Commissioner of Lands the power to alienate country land not exceeding 15 relongs to Asiatics and to impose special conditions. He may delegate also the power to permit the temporary occupation under a licence of State land or land reserved for a public purpose.

[2] Subject to the provisions of the enactment and to any condition, restriction and obligation either expressed in the document of title or implied by the enactment.

drains, lay cables, and so on. The rent on all land is liable to periodic revision, at intervals of not less than thirty years.[1] The rates of rent fixed for any one revision period may not exceed the rates fixed for the immediately preceding period by more than 50%.

Unless the contrary appears in the document of title, all country land not exceeding 100 *relongs* alienated before the coming into force of the Enactment is deemed to have been alienated for the purpose of cultivation and, if such land is left uncultivated for three consecutive years, the proprietor is deemed to have made default. Land exceeding 100 *relongs* may also be resumed if abandoned for three consecutive years. Land alienated as *bendang* must be used for the cultivation of rice. There are various implied cultivation conditions, and there is a specific provision that tapioca may not be planted without special permission.

All land comprised in any document of title is subject to the Enactment and cannot be transferred, transmitted, leased, charged or otherwise dealt with except in accordance with the provisions of the Enactment. A proprietor has the right to devise his interest in any land, subject to the conditions of the Enactment, and in the case of Moslems subject to the Muhammadan law.

In 1938 the minimum rates of premium on alienation of State land for agricultural purposes were as follows:

A.	For rubber cultivation.	
	(1) For areas up to 15 relongs	$10 a relong
	(2) " " from 15 to 100 relongs	$15 "
	(3) " " over 100 relongs	$25 "
B.	For Bendang land (any area)	$3 "
C.	For Kampong and other cultivation.	
	(1) For areas up to 50 relongs	$5 "
	(2) " " over 50 "	$10 "

The minimum rate is usually charged. Annual rents on a relong of agricultural land were as follows:

(1) For rubber cultivation	$1
(2) For padi or kampong cultivation	50 cents to $1

Finally, it is to be noticed that in Perlis there is a Reservations Enactment (No. 7 of 1353, amended by No. 11 of 1354) similar to the Malay Reservations Enactment of Kedah (described above). But

[1] The first revision may take place on the first day of Muharram 1365 in respect of land alienated prior to the first day of Muharram 1366 and on or after the first of Muharram in respect of other land alienated prior to the coming into force of the Enactment.

there are a number of variations. It is not laid down in Perlis that a Siamese to whom State land may be alienated must be an agriculturist permanently settled in the State; and it is not permissible for Malays and Siamese to lease their land to anyone for a period of three years. No Reservation Land held under a document of title by any Malay may be mortgaged, charged or leased to any person who is not a Malay, and a Siamese holder may not mortgage, charge or lease his land to any person who is not a Malay or a Siamese. Furthermore, no Malay or Siamese holding in a Reservation may be attached in execution of a decree or other order of a Court.

Trengganu

The land legislation of Trengganu has recently been revised (by Enactment No. 3 of 1357, which came into force on the 1st of January, 1939). The most important change introduced by the new enactment is the safeguarding of Malays from loss of their land, by the provision of Mukim Register titles which cannot be transferred or charged to others than Malays. Another important change is that in future the distribution of small estates will be carried out by the Collectors and not by the Courts. In the past the failure to distribute the estates of deceased persons according to the provisions of the law has been one of the chief weaknesses of land administration in Trengganu.

The new Land Enactment follows generally the legislation of the Federated Malay States, but has many points of special interest. The entire property in, and control of State land, is vested solely in the Sultan, who, however, delegates many of his powers to the Commissioner of Lands. There are five forms of documents of title. That to any town or village land is a grant or lease of State land, that to any Mukim land is by entry in the Mukim Register, that to any country land not exceeding ten acres and not being Mukim land is a Grant Kechil (small-holding grant) or a lease of State land, that to country land exceeding ten acres is a Grant Besar (large-holding grant) or a lease of State land, while that to the foreshore or sea-bed is a lease of State land for any period not exceeding twenty years.

It will have been seen that, in Trengganu, country land under ten acres is divided into two classes, namely, Mukim land and land held under a Grant Kechil. The definition of Mukim land is of interest. It is 'country land not exceeding ten acres in area other than land wholly or mainly planted or held under conditions allowing it to be planted with a commercial crop, the proprietor of which is a person belonging to any Malayan race who habitually speaks any Malayan language and professes the Muhammadan religion or who has obtained the special permission of the Sultan in Council to be registered as a proprietor of such land'.

The proprietor of Mukim land is deemed to have a permanent, heritable and transferable right of use and occupancy, subject to certain cultivation and other conditions, but he may only transfer or lease his holding to a person or persons entitled to hold Mukim land, and in the case of a lease the period must not exceed three years. Mukim land may not be charged except with the express permission of the Sultan in Council and then only if the charge is in favour of the Government or of a person entitled to hold such land. Mukim land is not liable to attachment by order of Court, and no court may recognize or give effect to any equitable mortgage, charge or lien made by deposit of document of title in favour of any person not qualified to hold Mukim land, nor may any Court deal with or determine any matter relating to Mukim land in accordance with any principle of equity in favour of any such person.

In these provisions there are features of interest for other Colonies. In particular attention may be called to the condition that Mukim land may not be planted with commercial crops. If Mukim land is found to be planted in a manner incompatible with its definition, the Sultan in Council may cause it to be forfeited or may approve the issue of a 'grant kechil' in exchange.

There are, in Trengganu, the same general provisions as in the Federated Malay States for the revision of rent at intervals of not less than thirty years; and in fixing a new rent no improvements made are taken into account. Agricultural land is subject to a premium varying with its quality, but there is no premium in the case of rice land, and rent on rice land is remitted for the first three years.

The total area of Trengganu is 5050 sq. miles. There are no reserved forests. The area of State Land was, in 1939, given as 4635 sq. miles, and that of alienated land as 415 sq. miles. Alienated land, therefore, constituted only 8% of the total.

In conclusion, it may be permissible to quote the following summary of the land situation in Malaya made recently by a group of members of the Royal Institute of International Affairs, in an interim report dealing with the post-war problems of the Far East.[1] 'There can be no question,' they said, 'that the interests of the indigenous population and the requirements of subsistence production demanded the application of control over the alienation of land. But it is not easy to assess the adequacy of the steps taken . . . since

[1] *Problems of the Post-War Settlement in the Far East.* Interim Report by a Group of Members of The Royal Institute of International Affairs. British Malaya, Paras. 14 and 24.

the standard which must be applied is the ratio of the reserved areas to the area suitable for peasant cultivation and not to that of the total area of the country. The measures taken met with criticism from differing points of view. Indians and Chinese resented the creation of obstacles to their acquiring a larger holding of land, though it should be noted that the position they sought was for the most part that of landlords, rather than of self-cultivating proprietors. Malays objected to the curtailment of their opportunities for raising credit on their holdings. This aspect of the question is intimately linked with that of agrarian indebtedness. . . . On the whole, however, there is no reason to believe that the Malay has suffered from shortage of land; his chief difficulties were to be found in other directions. . . . Are the steps taken in regard to the alienation of land adequate to preserve a just balance between the interests of the small-holder and those of the capitalist enterprises? Is the existing system of land tenure such as will not only give stability of tenure to the small-holder but will minister to the needs of progressive farming? What further measures are required to mitigate the growing menace of agrarian indebtedness? What steps are needed to enable the indigenous community to secure the short-term finance required for agricultural purposes, without resorting to immigrant money-lenders, always a fruitful source of racial or communal differences? Do the circumstances require that members of the immigrant communities should be given larger opportunities to acquire small holdings?'

CHAPTER V

Ceylon

CEYLON provides another example of a dual agricultural economy, namely, peasant and plantation cultivation. But Ceylon has had many systems of tenure. In the days of the Dutch and Portuguese, and of the Kandyan kings, tenure bore a feudal character. Feudal dues were periodically paid to the overlords, and a record of these was kept. With the abolition of land tax these records, which were *prima facie* proof of ownership, disappeared. On the British occupation of Ceylon personal service as a condition of holding land was abolished, and all land for which proof of ownership could not be produced was presumed to be Crown Land (Ordinance No. 12 of 1840). Many villages, in consequence of this law, lost lands to which they were by customary law entitled, but on the other hand (between 1840 and 1897) large areas of Crown land, much of it forest reserve, were illegally appropriated by cultivators.[1]

In 1897 the "Waste Lands Ordinance" was passed, with the purpose of preventing further encroachment on Crown Lands. Legislation has also been passed for dealing with the claims of private persons to land to which the Crown has a presumptive title.[2] Moreover, with a view to dealing systematically with all the undeveloped land in the island, a special department—the Land Settlement Department—has recently been established.

One of the principal obstacles to land development in Ceylon has been the uncertainty of titles to land. There has been no system of registration of title. Eighty years ago an attempt was made (under Ordinance No. 8 of 1863) to introduce a system of land registration which provided for registration of deeds, as well as of title on a cadastral survey. But this proved unsuitable to the older systems of tenure and was superseded by various Ordinances, none of which has proved adequate. In 1936 the Ceylon Judicial Commission expressed surprise that the island still lacked 'that necessary feature of a civilized administration'—a cadastral survey, and observed that the absence of land disputes in Malaya was due to the fact that there was a complete cadastral survey and registration of title.[3] The block

[1] In Northern Rhodesia a recent Land Commission has recommended that the boundaries of Crown Land should be demarcated on the ground as soon as possible, since much damage had been caused to tobacco-growing land by the encroachment of natives. (See the *Report of the Land Commission on the North Charterland Concession Area, 1933*, para. 14.)

[2] See the Land Settlement Ordinance, 1931, amended by Ordinances No. 22 of 1932 and No. 31 of 1933.

[3] *Ceylon Sessional Paper*, VI, 1936, Para. 122.

survey of Ceylon was a cadastral survey, but was concerned only with the delimitation of Crown lands, and it does not appear that any general cadastral survey has yet (1944) been planned. Legislation has been prepared to provide for registration, but no substantial progress has been made towards recording the titles or rights of the vast majority of Ceylonese who hold their land under customary forms of tenure.[1]

The rules governing inheritance in Ceylon have long had a detrimental effect on tenure. In the absence of testamentary declaration, of which there is little, the property descends according to the law under which the deceased lived. There are at least six legal systems in Ceylon, namely, Roman-Dutch law, the English law, the Kandyan law, the Tesalawamai, the Mukkuwa law and Muhammadan law. This leads to constant difficulties over transfer, and since primogeniture is foreign to all the indigenous systems, inherited farms are subject to rapid subdivision. Owing to the difficulties and expense of legal partition, the inherited land may be held in undivided shares, an arrangement which may be inimical to development if the family is large. On the other hand, if the property is divided, each inheritor may be left with a unit too small for economic cultivation.[2] Thus, joint shareholders sometimes cultivate the land in turn. This avoids excessive subdivision, but is liable to lead to excessive exploitation of the land.[3]

Prior to 1918 practically all land alienated by the Crown for agricultural purposes had been sold outright. But towards the end of the last war a system of leasing was introduced, though outright sale still continued to some extent. In those localities where peasants tended to part with their holdings to larger owners, particular care was taken that small lots should be issued on leasehold or on permits which contemplated a restricted tenure preventing such alienation. In 1935, under the Land Development Ordinance, far-reaching changes were made in the tenure of land alienated by the Crown. Under this Ordinance (Cap. 320) provision is made for the systematic mapping-out of Crown land for such purposes as village expansion, village forest and pasture, indigenous systems of cultivation, the protection of the sources and courses of streams, the prevention of soil erosion, and so on. Grants and life-permits may then be given for holdings. Grants are only issued for land which

[1] The general question of registration of title is discussed in Chapter xxiii.

[2] The Ceylon Banking Commission quoted cases of 1/328th part of an acre, and 3/448th parts of one *jak* tree.

[3] A common form of tenancy in Ceylon is that known as 'andhe', in which the owner of the land supplies the cultivator with a buffalo for ploughing and half the manure, in return for half the crop. This system of *métayage* is said to be less productive than when rents are paid. (See 'Agrarian Problems of Ceylon', by H. E. Peries, in *Public Administration*, Oct. 1940.)

has been surveyed and they are subject to certain essential conditions which run with the land, and they may be made subject to certain additional conditions. The essential conditions provide for an annual payment to the Crown in perpetuity of a specified sum, for the regular cultivation or utilisation of the holding in a specified manner, and for the protection of the holding from excessive subdivision.[1] As a further protection against subdivision there are special rules governing succession. The grant may also contain a condition that the holding shall not be leased or mortgaged except to the Crown, and that no other disposition shall be made except with the prior permission in writing of the Government Agent. The holding may not be seized or sold in execution of the decrees of any court, though the Government may do so to discharge a debt to the Crown. Land held on permit is also immune from seizure or sale.

In order to encourage landless villagers in crowded areas to take up land in less congested localities, particularly in the dry zone where much of the land is Crown land, the Government has initiated colonization schemes in which the colonists are helped both with money and with land. Many difficulties have been encountered in making these schemes popular. There is the expense of converting the irrigable area into paddy fields and of purchasing cattle and erecting buildings (the Government's subsidy being partial only). The absence of facilities for marketing and obtaining subsidiary employment, the unhealthiness of the climate and the severance from the rest of the social group, are other disadvantages. It is hoped, however, that in time large tracts of the dry zone which were formerly populous and are now almost uninhabited, will be reclaimed. At the present time in the dry zone, the prevalent system of cultivation is the shifting system known as 'chena'. Under this form of tenure tracts of jungle are periodically cleared, burned, cultivated for one or two seasons and then abandoned.[2] 'Chena' lands may be held privately, or leased, or obtained by grant from the Crown.

Coming now to the plantation cultivations, most of the Ceylon tea companies are worked under joint stock management, and owned by British capital. Holdings by native companies and individuals

[1] Every grant must contain the following conditions: (1) The owner shall not dispose of a divided share of the holding less, in extent, than the unit of subdivision specified in the grant. (2) The owner shall not dispose of an undivided share in the holding less than the minimum fraction specified in the grant. (3) No person shall be the owner of an undivided share of the holding less in extent than the unit of subdivision specified in the grant. (4) No person shall be the owner of an undivided share in the holding less than the minimum fraction specified in the grant. A condition may also be imposed that the owner shall reside upon the holding.

[2] The principal 'chena' crops are Eleusine coracana, maize, Italian millet, Paspalum millet, Panicum millet, Sesamum indicum, and various pulses. Yams, sweet potatoes, plantains, vegetables and curry plants are also grown.

constitute only one-fifth of the total area under tea. In rubber, too, British capital predominates (about 45%), but in 1934 there were no fewer than 4830 native-owned estates. The higher proportion of native-owned rubber properties, as compared with tea, appears to be due to the fact that rubber cultivation imposes less exacting demands on labour, and local labour can therefore be obtained for work on rubber plantations. The Ceylon Banking Commission of 1934 observed that native capitalists had not organized themselves under joint stock principles, preferring to work their business on their own account, even when it had reached a size too big for their private resources. To the Ceylonese, possession of land is an attribute of social status, and so personal ownership is preferred, even at the cost of starving the property or of borrowing money at usurious rates.

The third great plantation crop is coco-nuts. In the village economy this takes first place and is the peasant's principal money crop. At least 50% of the total area under coco-nuts is reckoned to consist of holdings of ten acres or under. Moreover, almost the whole of the capital employed in the coco-nut industry is Ceylonese. But in 1934 there was heavy indebtedness, and much coco-nut land had passed into the hands of moneylenders, many of whom were foreigners.[1] In 1935 an Ordinance (No. 13) established a Coco-nut Board with power to hold, acquire, sell or lease property, to aid and finance associations of co-operative societies, and to foster the marketing of coco-nuts in various other ways.

The following table gives the acreages of the chief crops of Ceylon (as estimated in 1938).

Coco-nuts ..	1,100,000	Palmyra ..	50,000
Rice	850,000	Cacao ..	34,000
Rubber ..	604,111	Citronella ..	33,000
Tea	556,650	Cinnamon ..	26,000
'Chena' crops ..	140,000	Tobacco ..	14,000
Areca nuts ..	69,000	Cardamons	6,000

In conclusion, some reference should be made to the prevalence of agricultural debt in the island. This had had a long history, but came to a head as a result of the great trade depression. The establishment of a State Mortgage Bank in 1932 met a real need in the credit system of the island, but in the opinion of the Banking Commissioners its beneficial effects reached only a very small fraction of the people, largely as a result of the confusion in the titles to land. Peasant agriculturists had to resort to private financiers, and large numbers lost their lands, their homes and means of living. It

[1] *Ceylon Sessional Paper*, XXII, 1934, para. 681.

had been held that unfortunate debtors should be allowed to remain as tenants on the lands they had lost, but the Commissioners observed, with some asperity, that farmers whose incompetence had deprived them of their lands were not likely to be careful tenants, when they no longer had the incentive of ownership. In this connection it may be remarked that in some provinces of India a proprietor who has lost his lands is given the right to continue in occupation at a privileged rent. His tenancy is heritable but is not transferable, the purpose being to give the ex-proprietor a means of support which he cannot barter away.

Not all moneylenders in Ceylon are professional moneylenders. As in Cyprus, so in Ceylon, moneylenders may include almost every class of society. Retired officials commonly use their savings to make advances on mortgage, with a view to the ultimate acquisition of the debtors' land. Members of the legal profession also engage freely in mortgage finance, being well-versed in the best methods of securing their own interests.[1] Landowners, eager to add to their holdings, may be the most rapacious of all lenders. They supply their tenants freely with implements and foodstuffs, and exact heavy interest, either in cash or in the form of an increased share of the tenant's crop. All of these amateur creditors, moreover, are free from the control of the money-lending laws.[2]

In the end the Government of Ceylon found it necessary to intervene, and debt conciliation legislation was enacted in 1941 (Ordinances Nos. 39 and 40).

[1] The Ceylon law of mortgage is peculiar and involved. It was described as an ungodly jumble' by the 1936 Judicial Commissioners, who stated that in consequence of the confusion the public were becoming reluctant to lend money on the security of land. See *Ceylon Sessional Paper*, VI, 1936, paras. 123-145.

[2] *Ceylon Sessional Paper*, XXII, 1934, paras. 210-213.

CHAPTER VI

Cyprus

THE island of Cyprus has an area of 3,572 sq. miles, which is a little larger than that of Norfolk and Suffolk. Its climate is considerably varied, but the average rainfall is only 20·58 inches. Most of the rains fall in the winter months: in summer the plains become parched and a large part of the vegetation disappears. The rainfall is liable to considerable fluctuations, and the occurrence of several consecutive dry summers may have disastrous effects on the crops. Drought, indeed, is the island's greatest problem, and the extension of irrigation its greatest need.

In 1931 the population of Cyprus was 347,959, or an average density of 97·4 persons to the square mile. The native inhabitants fall roughly into two categories, (*a*) Greek-Christian, constituting 79·5% of the total population, and (*b*) Muhammadan, constituting about 18·5%. The island was under Turkish rule until 1878, when the Sultan of Turkey consented to its occupation and administration by Great Britain. In 1914, on the entry of Turkey into the war on the side of Germany, Cyprus was annexed to the British Crown.

The courts apply the local laws and certain Ottoman legislation specified in the new Courts Law (No. 19 of 1940), the common law and the rules of equity in force in England in 1914, and any statutes of the Imperial Parliament applicable to the Colonies in general or to Cyprus in particular. The family law of the various communities is expressly saved. The courts also apply the English law and rules of evidence, if there is no local provision in that respect. Land tenure was formerly governed by the Ottoman Land Code, but this code has recently (1945) been superseded by new legislation.

The main industry of the island is agriculture, the products consisting of cereals, carobs (locust-beans), olives, wines, silk, cotton, raisins, grapes, oranges, peaches and other fruits. Agriculture is largely dependent on irrigation, the water for which is obtained mainly from wells in the dry season and by flooding from streams during the rainy season. The development of agriculture has been greatly retarded by the deficient rainfall. But drilling has revealed the presence of underground water and, with the formation of a Water Supply and Irrigation Department in 1939, it is hoped not only to continue the development of underground supplies, but also to impound and put to regulated use many surface supplies which are at present running to waste.

As already observed, land tenure in Cyprus was, until 1945,

regulated by the Ottoman Law in force at the time of the British occupation of the island in 1878, though many important modifications had been introduced by later local legislation.[1] In Turkish times titles for land were issued by the fiefholders and those for buildings by the local courts. But after the reforms effected in Turkey during the reign of the Sultan Abdul Mejid all titles in Cyprus were granted by the Crown through the Land Registry Department, which had an office in each district, as well as sub-offices in some thirty villages. Land was made subject to an immovable property tax, as well as to an educational tax assessed by the Land Registry Department. The immovable property tax was fixed at the rate of two per thousand of the capital value.

Under the Ottoman system there were five categories of land: (1) *Mulk*,[2] or immovable property held in private ownership; (2) *Arazi*[3] *Mirie*, or State land; (3) *Arazi Metrouké*, or land left for the use of the public; (4) *Arazi Mevat*, or unoccupied land; and (5) *Arazi Mevkoufé*, or *vakf* land dedicated under the Sacred Law.

Mulk property was characterised by the fact that it was held in private ownership in the same way as chattels. The State had no proprietary rights in *mulk*. *Mulk* comprised houses, trees, building sites, and small plots inside towns and villages. It included *Arazi Memlouké* or (a) land which at the time of the general registration of lands in 1862 had been found, with the implied consent of the State, to have been built over or set aside to form the site of a town or village; and (b) land separated from *Arazi Mirie* and granted by patent from the Crown to be held in full ownership as *Arazi Memlouké*.[4]

Arazi Mirie, or State land, included the bulk of land in Cyprus. The term implied that the legal ownership was vested in the Crown, the possessor having only the perpetual enjoyment. Alienations had to be registered, and buildings could not be erected without the permission of the State. Yet, for all practical purposes, a possessor of *Arazi Mirie* enjoyed full rights of ownership, being able to sell or mortgage his lands without restriction.[5] But he was unable to dispose of them *by will*, and if *Arazi Mirie* became

[1] For a full description of the Ottoman system of land-holding in Cyprus see Sir Stanley Fisher, *Ottoman Land Laws* (1919). Also *The Handbook of Cyprus*, 1930 edition, pp. 125-160.

[2] *Mulk*=property.

[3] *Arazi*=land.

[4] *Memlouké*=owned as *mulk*. Other forms of *memlouké* mentioned in the Ottoman Land Code (Art. 2, items 3 and 4) existed exceptionally, if at all, in Cyprus.

[5] In Palestine, Iraq and other Ottoman territories many of the restrictions on *miri* or State lands were formally removed by an act of 1913. Permission was no longer required for alienation or mortgage, and State lands were made liable for the debts of their occupier. Trees planted and buildings erected on State lands were made subject, as regards disposal and transfer, to the laws applicable to the land on which they stood.

vacant by the failure of heirs it was offered to (1) owners of *mulk* accretions (trees[1] or buildings); (2) co-sharers of the land; (3) persons having an interest (such as an easement), and (4) inhabitants of the same village having need of land.[2] Otherwise the land escheated to the State and was regranted to the highest bidder. The holder of *miri* was under a duty to cultivate, and if he failed to discharge his duty for three consecutive years without valid excuse the land became vacant and, if he did not obtain a re-grant, was liable to be dealt with as if he had died without heirs.

Arazi Metrouké comprised (a) land left and dedicated to the public, such as public roads; and (b) land left to the inhabitants of towns or villages as a body, such as pasture lands. It included communal forests, places of worship (other than mosques) and markets. It could not be used for any other purpose than that for which it had originally been assigned.

Arazi Mevat. This term means 'dead land' and was applied to vacant land which lay at least one Turkish mile[3] from a town or village or at 'a distance beyond the power of a very loud human voice to carry' (Land Code Art. 103, and Mejelle Art. 1270). Anyone could open up and convert land of this category into arable land, provided he had obtained permission from the competent authority. He acquired a *miri*, not a *mulk*, title.[4]

Finally, there was *Arazi Mevkoufé* or *vakf* land—that which had been dedicated by persons having full ownership of the land, on condition that the income should be applied to some pious or religious object. From very early times family settlement was recognised as a pious object, subject to the rule that, as a *vakf* must be in perpetuity, there must always be a gift to some pious or charitable object in the event of the family becoming extinct.

Most *vakfs* in Cyprus are vested in, or administered by, the Delegates of Evcaf, in accordance with the provisions of the Cyprus Evcaf (Mohammedan Religious Property Administration) Order and Law of 1928 and 1934. They are divided into certain classes. One category of *vakf* property was known as *Idjaretein*. True *vakf*

[1] Under the Ottoman law trees growing naturally on *mirie* land passed with it to the purchaser or heir. But trees grafted or planted by man were held independently by a *mulk* title. In Palestine, however, under Article 5 of the Ottoman Law of Disposition the *miri* holder now receives only the *usufruct* of economic trees and buildings; i.e., he is given a right of possession in the trees and buildings similar to the right in the land. See Goadby and Doukhan, *The Land Law of Palestine*, p. 33.

[2] A note on pre-emption will be found at p. 70.

[3] A Turkish mile=the distance covered at walking pace in an hour by an animal such as a donkey.

[4] But under a law (No. 7) of 1941 it was laid down that no title could be acquired in any vacant or unoccupied lands which were not privately owned, save under a grant or disposition by the Governor, and it was made an offence for anyone to occupy, plough or sow on such lands.

could only be leased for a limited period, usually three years, but when a *vakf* fell into disrepair and was likely to disappear, the Administrator might lease it in perpetuity by collecting in cash a sum equal to the full value, and, also by charging the property with an annual charge (*idjare*). The charge was in most cases merely nominal and was imposed in order to emphasise the fact that the purchaser did not become the legal owner, but only held the property on a kind of perpetual lease. The possessor of *Idjaretein* was as free to deal with his property as the possessor of *Arazi Mirie*. But whereas the legal ownership of *Arazi Mirie* vested in the Crown that of *Idjaretein* vested in the Delegates of Evcaf.[1]

Another category of *vakf* land was known as *Arazi Mevkoufé Takhsisat*. This was not, as its name might indicate, real *vakf* property. It was land which was subject to the same provisions of the Land Code as were applicable to *Arazi Mirie*, with the exception that all Government dues were payable to the *vakf* concerned.[2]

Such, in outline, was the land system of Cyprus until the enactment in 1945 of the Immovable Property (Tenure, Registration and Valuation) Law (No. 26).[3] This law was the outcome of discussions which had been begun in 1934, when a special committee appointed for the purpose submitted a new draft land code. It had long been felt that the Ottoman Land Code was out-of-date. With its many categories of land, each subject to separate laws relating to possession, transactions, and succession, the whole system had become highly complicated, and sometimes almost unworkable. Land fell into one category, and trees and buildings into another, with the result that in thousands of cases the land belonged to one owner or group of owners, while the trees and buildings on the land belonged to other owners. The laws of inheritance were also complex and antiquated. For not only were the shares of heritors different for different categories of property, but for *mulk* property they varied according to the religion of those concerned. The separate ownership of land and trees had been a fruitful source of litigation, and the laws of inheritance had been a principal cause of the excessive fragmentation and subdivision of holdings that characterised the land tenure of Cyprus.

Under the new law of 1945 the Ottoman categories of immovable property known as *Mulk*, *Arazi Memlouké*, *Arazi Mirie*, *Arazi Metrouké* and *Arazi Mevat* have been abolished, and all immovable property is now owned, held and enjoyed subject to the simplified provisions of the new law. *Mulk* and *Arazi Memlouké* continue

[1] Information based on an official note by the Hon. Stelios Pavlides, K.C., Attorney-General, Cyprus.

[2] In theory there are two other forms of *takhsisat*, but these are unimportant.

[3] The Law was enacted in December, 1945, but was not brought into operation until September 1st, 1946.

to be owned or held as private property, while *Arazi Mirie* which was in private possession at the date of the coming into operation of the new law is also to be owned as private property and freed from the restriction on testamentary disposition. *Arazi Metrouké* continues to be the communal property of the town or village, while *Arazi Mevat* and all other vacant property not privately owned are to be owned by the Crown as Crown property. *Vakf* property will continue to be held in accordance with the *vakf* laws, but by a law (No. 14) enacted in 1944 *Idjaretein* property had been converted into *mulk*, the Evcaf being compensated for their loss of revenue from this source. Under the same law *Arazi Mevkoufé Takhsisat* had been converted into *Arazi Mirie*.

But even more important than the abolition of the Ottoman categories of land are those provisions of the new law by which trees and land can gradually be brought under one ownership. It is laid down that where trees and land belong to different persons the owner of one shall not sell his interest without giving a prior right of purchase to the owner of the other; and where a landowner has economic trees growing on his land he shall no longer be allowed to transfer or mortgage the trees without also transferring or mortgaging the land on which they stand. Furthermore, the Director of Land Registration and Surveys is empowered, on the application of any interested party, to effect re-adjustments, so that in no case shall a tree, vine or building be owned by a person other than the owner of the land. If this cannot be done by partition or re-adjustment of interests, then the owner with the greater interest may acquire the minor interest on payment of its value as estimated by the Director, any person affected thereby having a right of appeal to the Court (Secs. 22, 29). Similarly, if a co-owner of immovable property wishes to sell his share he must give an option of purchase to each or all of the other co-owners (Sec. 24).

The new law also contains important provisions designed to check excessive subdivision of holdings. It is laid down that in all cases of division or partition of immovable property, no division or partition shall be lawful if it contravenes the provisions that 'no vineyard, orchard, grove or land irrigated or capable of being irrigated from a perennial source of water shall be divided into holdings of less than one *donum* in extent' (a *donum* $=\frac{1}{3}$ of an acre), 'or, if capable of being irrigated from a seasonal source of water, into holdings of less than two *donums* in extent'; and 'no land used for agricultural purposes which is not irrigated either from a perennial or a seasonal source of water shall be divided into separate holdings of less than five *donums* in extent' (Sec. 26b and c).

As regards *vakf* immovable property it should be noted that formerly only *mulk* property could be made *vakf*; but now that the distinction between *mulk* and *Arazi Mirie* has been abolished it has become necessary to restrict the right of making *vakf* to property within the limits of towns and villages which would formerly have been classed as *mulk*. Outside these limits land can only be made *vakf* if, in the opinion of the Director of Land Registration and Surveys, it is sufficiently covered with trees or buildings as to fall within the old category of *mulk*.

Part III of the new law deals with registration. The Director of Land Registration can compel registration of unregistered property, but may no longer register trees and buildings independently of the land, unless these belong to a person other than the owner of the land. It is also laid down that proof of undisputed and uninterrupted adverse possession for a period of thirty years entitles the possessor to be deemed the owner of the property and to have it registered in his name. But no title can be acquired by adverse possession as against the Crown or any registered owner. Formerly *Arazi Mirie* could be acquired by uninterrupted possession for a period of ten years. Another important provision of the section on registration is that boundary disputes must now be determined, in the first instance, by the Director of Land Registration and Surveys, though any dissatisfied party will have a right of appeal to the courts. This provision should help to put some check on prolonged and costly litigation over boundaries.

It remains to add that in 1945 there was also enacted a new law governing wills and succession (No. 25 of 1945). One of the novel features of this law is that, unlike the former law, it brings Muhammadans within its purview.

Cyprus is a country of small landed proprietors. In 1930 the average size of a peasant holding was computed to be 25 acres.[1] But the holdings were not usually self-contained, and an owner might have to spend several hours daily walking from one of his small plots to another.[2] Economic trees, moreover, were often planted on other people's land and were seldom planted in groves where they could be properly tended. There were immense difficulties in surveying and registering these small plots, which were constantly being made smaller. In 1940 Dr. Raeburn, who was conducting investigations on the problem of water supply, found that the Government would have to compensate 250 different owners in order to take over an area of 240 acres! Such conditions are a great hindrance to schemes of development, since agreement between large numbers of people is not easily reached about

[1] See B. J. Surridge, *Survey of Rural Life in Cyprus*, p. 58. This Survey contains an immense amount of valuable information about tenure conditions in Cyprus.

[2] Registration figures in 1930 put the average size of an arable *plot* (as distinct from a *holding*) at 5.36 *donums*, or 1¾ acres, but Mr. Surridge considered this misleading as in many cases the division of plots had not been registered.

measures which may require additional capital, different agricultural methods and additional hard work. Excessive fragmentation not only entails disproportionately high costs of cultivation and great waste of time and energy in going from one plot to another, but it impedes, or precludes, the use of power implements, and the introduction of measures of irrigation and soil conservation; it may even prevent the cultivator from residing on his own land.

In Cyprus the basic cause of fragmentation and excessive fractionation is the system of inheritance, which requires property to be divided in prescribed shares among all the heirs. The new legislation makes some amendment in this respect; but laws against subdivision can easily be evaded, and even under the new inheritance law heirs may still be numerous. The real remedy would therefore be a radical change in public opinion and established custom. This applies also to schemes for the consolidation of holdings.[1]

In Cyprus, peasants whose lands are too small for their needs may obtain additional land by leasing the surplus lands of other peasants, or of religious institutions. Many of the lands owned by the Orthodox Church have been let by public tender for periods of from three to five years. The lessees have generally been prosperous peasants who cultivated as much of their property as they could, and sub-let the rest, usually the less productive plots, to men of smaller means. In this way many of the poorer peasants have been forced to pay excessive rents and fall into debt, while the lands have steadily deteriorated. The obvious remedies, which would lie with the landlords, would be longer leases and proper compensation for improvements. Proposals have been made that some of the lands of the religious institutions might be acquired for the peasants, and similar suggestions have been made regarding some of the ''Chiftliks' or large farms, particularly those belonging to absentee landlords. There is, incidentally, a long-standing

[1] These and other important questions of land tenure in Cyprus are discussed fully in the *Report of the Land Utilization Committee, 1946, Nicosia.* See also *The Proceedings of a Conference on Land Use in a Mediterranean Environment*, held in Cyprus in April, 1940, pp. 19-20. Many countries have attempted to tackle the problem of fragmentation and excessive subdivision. In Germany and Denmark legislation was introduced under which the farm could be inherited by a 'preferred heir' who would compensate the other heirs. In Denmark an Act of 1919 provided that the land should not be divided into holdings which were not sufficient to maintain a family without the help of outside labour. In Czechoslovakia and India systems of exchange between owners have been introduced so that plots may be merged in one ownership. But one of the chief difficulties of consolidation is that it may have to provide for redistribution, not into one compact holding for each cultivator, but into two, three or more holdings of varying fertility. The suggestion has been made, for Cyprus, that instead of a redistribution of village lands, subject to the agreement of the majority of landowners—the system followed in the Punjab—some villagers might wish to pool their lands and hold them henceforth in communal ownership.

grievance among the peasants of Cyprus that 'Chiftlik' proprietors own, by immemorial right, the waters of rivers, not merely while running through their own property but after they have passed by. Farmers, therefore, living lower down the river, are obliged to pay heavy dues if they wish to use the water. The existence of these rights has proved a serious hindrance to the formulation of irrigation schemes.

As might be expected under a system of peasant proprietors who had been accustomed to sell their produce to a small ring of merchant moneylenders, agricultural debt had long been one of the principal problems of Cyprus.[1] The general decline in commodity prices, which had coincided with three years of drought, brought matters to a head in 1933. In 1934 it was found necessary to pass a Reserve Price Law[2] in order to prevent farmers from selling their lands for sacrificial sums. In the same year Sir Ralph Oakden was sent to Cyprus as Financial Commissioner,[3] and as a result of his recommendations the Agricultural Bank and Co-operative Societies were reorganized with a view to helping the peasants to free themselves from dependence on moneylenders. In 1940 an Agricultural Debtors Relief Law was enacted, and under this law the Debt Settlement Board, between June 1940 and October 1945, dealt with 19,055 applications for relief, involving a total debt of £1,452,006. Settlements were effected amicably in the majority of cases and interest was reduced to 5%. By October 1945 only £258,656 remained to be paid. The Cypriot farmers have thus been freed from the moneylender. Whether they will remain free will depend on the extent to which co-operative credit, co-operative marketing and a sense of thrift can be developed. There is danger in all schemes of debt settlement by statutory action that they may encourage farmers to resort to borrowing, and to postpone repayment in the hope that the State will again intervene.

[1] Even in classical times the Cypriots seem to have had a proclivity for debt. In letters to Atticus (V^{21}, VI^{1}) Cicero describes how, on his arrival in Cilicia as governor, he had to deal with a prefect called Scaptius who had been accused of ill-treating the town councillors of Salamis in Cyprus, in a vain attempt to recover a large sum of money which he had lent at 48%. Cicero refused to make any order for payment which would carry a higher rate of interest than 12%.

[2] This law (No. 15 of 1934) was superseded by various others. Under the most recent Reserve Price Law (No. 29 of 1940) the reserved price must not exceed the assessed value of the immovable property and may be reviewed in the case of abortive sales. It should be noticed also that under the Cyprus Agricultural Relief Law of 1940 a farmer whose land is attached for debt has to be left with sufficient land for the support of himself and his family, house accommodation, wearing apparel, provisions for three months, baking and cooking utensils, farming implements not exceeding the value of £10, one pair of cattle, fodder and seed grain. Cf. the Five-feddan law of Egypt by which an indebted farmer is protected against the loss of his last five feddans of land—a feddan being about one acre.

[3] His report was published in 1934 under the title of a *Report on the Finances and Economic Resources of Cyprus.*

A NOTE ON PRE-EMPTION

Right of pre-emption is the power of buying a thing before others. This right is known to most systems of law. In Roman law contracts of sale might contain stipulations that if the purchaser subsequently proposed to part with the property he must give to the vendor a right of re-purchase on specified terms. In England the Land Clauses Consolidation Act of 1845 (sec. 128) prescribed that superfluous lands must first be offered to those from whom they had originally been taken, or else to the adjoining owners. In the United States the law of pre-emption played a prominent part between 1841 and 1873 in the alienation of the public domain. It legalized the vested interests of squatters, giving them the first opportunity of buying their claim.

Pre-emption is a well-known feature of Muhammadan law. The possible pre-emptors, in order of preference, are (a) co-sharers in the property, part of which is sold; (b) persons who own a property to which the property sold is servient in respect of an easement, such as a right of way or a right to discharge water; (c) owners of contiguous property, unless the estates are large.[1]

Under the Ottoman Land Code there are various provisions conferring a right of pre-emption. Article 4, for example, prescribes that 'If the possessor by title deed of land lying within the boundaries of a village has transferred it to an inhabitant of another village, the inhabitants of the former place who are in need of land have, for one year, the right to have the land adjudged to them at the price at which it has been sold.' The Ottoman Code also prescribes conditions (Articles 44 and 48) under which *mirie* or State land may not be sold without giving a prior right of purchase to the possessor of *mulk* trees or buildings on the land. In this connection it is important to note that there is a distinction between a prior right of purchase before sale and a right of pre-emption after sale. The former right is called *rujhan* and the latter *shufa'a*. The right of *rujhan* is a right against the vendor, and, under the Ottoman Code, applied only to *mirie* or State land. The holder of a right of *shufa'a*, on the other hand, could claim from a purchaser the right to take over his bargain and stand in his shoes.[2]

In India the Muhammadan law of pre-emption was applied by the courts of British India as 'a matter of justice, equity and good conscience'. But in the Madras Presidency the High Court refused to recognise pre-emption, since it placed a restriction on the

[1] There are variations in the Muhammadan law of pre-emption, according to the different schools. Shia law, for example, does not recognise a right of pre-emption on account of vicinage.

[2] I am indebted to Professor Vesey-Fitzgerald for drawing my attention to this distinction.

liberty to transfer property and was therefore opposed to the principle of 'justice, equity and good conscience'. In some Indian Provinces rights of pre-emption were conferred by Acts of the Indian Legislature. In the Punjab, for example, the Pre-emption Act of 1913 admitted a right of pre-emption in agricultural land and village immovable property. In the case of agricultural land no person other than a member of an agricultural tribe in the same group of agricultural tribes as the vendor could exercise the right of pre-emption. The intention here was to prevent agricultural lands from falling into the hands of urban moneylenders. But in general the purpose of pre-emption has been to prevent strangers from becoming sharers in the village. In many parts of India, therefore, rights of pre-emption have commonly been created by contract between the sharers in a village.[1]

In Ceylon and Malaya, also, rights of pre-emption are commonly exercised by members of a community with a view to keeping land within their own body,[2] and among some tribes of Tanganyika the owner of a plantation is not permitted to sell it without giving a first refusal to members of his own kindred or clan.[3] In Eritrea no one may sell, let, or give away his lands without first offering them to the other members of his kindred, and, if they decline, to his fellow villagers.[4] In the Gold Coast, if the headman and council of a village decide to sell a piece of land, the occupants of any plots on the land must be given the first refusal.[5] The right of pre-emption may thus serve to prevent the disruption of village-life, as well as to mitigate the disadvantages of the excessive sub-division of land.[6]

[1] For data regarding the law and custom of pre-emption in India, see Sir R. K. Wilson, *A Digest of Anglo-Muhammadan Law* (sixth edition by A. Yusuf Ali), Chapter XII; D. F. Mulla, *Principles of Mahomedan Law*, 11th ed., Chapter XIII; J. D. Mayne, *Hindu Law and Usage*, 9th ed., p. 319; and Sir W. H. Rattigan, *A Digest of Civil Law for the Punjab*, 7th ed., Chapter VII.

[2] See e.g., G. A. de C. de Moubray, *Matriarchy in the Malay Peninsula*, p. 85.

[3] See e.g., H. Cory and M. M. Hartnoll, *Customary Law of the Haya Tribe*, p. 138. In 1933 the tribal court of Unyanyembe (Tabora district) decided that if anyone built a substantial modern house on land held under native customary tenure and wished to offer it for sale, the tribesmen should have a right of pre-emption.

[4] S. F. Nadel, *Africa*, Jan., 1946.

[5] J. M. Sarbah, *Fanti Customary Laws*, p. 88. In ancient Babylonia there was a law by which the head of a tribe could reclaim land alienated to a stranger by repaying to the latter the amount which he had paid for the land. (See Sir W. H. Rattigan, op. cit., Chapter VII.) The ancient Hebrews were also enjoined to redeem land which had been sold to strangers. (See Leviticus XXV, 25-28, Ruth IV, 3-4, and Jeremiah XXXVI, 6-15.)

[6] But the principle of pre-emption has been opposed on economic grounds and also because it may do more to disturb the peace of communities than to preserve it. (See R. K. Wilson, op. cit., p. 68.) Sir Michael O'Dwyer in 1916 considered that in the Punjab the administration of the law of pre-emption had given rise to abuses such as blackmailing, speculative litigation and the exaggeration of prices in sale deeds. Nevertheless he refused to recommend the abolition of the law. (See the *Report of the Punjab Codification Conference*, 1914.)

CHAPTER VII

Zanzibar

ZANZIBAR has been a microcosm of all the land problems of the Colonial Empire. It provides an outstanding example of the difficulties which may overtake any territory which relies mainly on money or export crops and fails to place restrictions on the encumbrance and alienation of land. In the end the Government of Zanzibar found itself compelled to take over the accumulation of mortgage debts and to pass legislation which would ensure that the occupational use of land should not become divorced from its ownership.

The principal industry of Zanzibar is the cultivation of cloves, and there are as well numerous plantations of coco-nuts. The larger clove and coco-nut estates are owned by Arabs, the smaller by Swahili and indigenous African peoples, who also cultivate cassava, maize, rice and other ground crops and fruits. Some of the larger plantations have recently been acquired by Indians, almost invariably in satisfaction of debts.

The Arabs acquired their land in a variety of ways—by appropriation or by force, as a gift, or in consideration of some nominal sum. In due course the land was planted with cloves, and since it was permissible to buy and sell the trees, so it became permissible to buy and sell the land, it being impossible to separate thickly-planted trees from the land on which they grew. By an extension of this principle uncultivated areas also became subject to sale. Many plantations have been enlarged, or new holdings obtained, by encroachment on Crown or common lands. In Pemba island a regular method of obtaining property described as 'freehold' is for a clove cultivator to obtain the temporary use of a piece of uncleared land, and then plant it up with cloves. When the trees begin to bear, the owner of the land divides it into two equal shares, one of which he makes over to the cultivator with deeds of conveyance properly executed and duly registered. Even freed slaves have become possessors of 'freehold' obtained in this way. But in some parts of Zanzibar it is still considered shameful to part with family land, and it is said that some individuals who do so endeavour to clear their conscience by reading a passage from the Koran. Usually, however, the alienation of family land is not an easy matter, since the interests of many individuals are usually involved.

In addition to the sale of land there is, in Zanzibar, a great deal of leasing. A clove plantation may be leased for as much as 50% of the estimated crop. But for subsistence crops the demand may only be

10% or less. Walls may be built round fields to protect the crops from pigs, and this tends to establish more permanent rights. Walled enclosures are often sold, but the payment is not so much for the land itself as compensation for the building of the wall. On Zanzibar island land is commonly leased or rented to rice-growers, the owner of the land receiving as rent a share of the crop equal to twice the amount of the seed. Or rent may be paid in cash, a reduction being made if the crop is poor.

Many owners of plantations encourage the settlement of squatters in order that, by ground cultivation, the plantations may be kept clean. The owners, moreover, have, in the squatters, a ready supply of harvest labour. The squatters live rent-free and may even be given occasional gifts. But, if the land is rich, a formal rent may be demanded.

As in Cyprus, so in Zanzibar, the great slump in world prices brought the old-standing problem of agricultural debt to a head.[1] Many of the Zanzibar Arabs lost their ownership and were compelled to remain on their plantations as the serfs of absentee landlords.[2] The position of the Swahili was even worse and many Swahili were compelled to mortgage their lands or sell them altogether. The rate of alienation was greatly increased by the practice of "conditional sales"—a form of mortgage common both to Hindu and Muhammadan law.[3] By 1933 it was reckoned that half of the agricultural property of the islands had passed into the hands of the money-lending classes and that at least half the remainder was encumbered. In 1934, as a temporary expedient, the Government of Zanzibar passed an Alienation of Land Decree, which declared a moratorium on existing debts and forbade the alienation of Arab or African lands to persons not of Arab or African race, except under specific conditions. In 1938 The Land Protection (Debts Settlement) Decree enabled the Government to purchase the interests of mortgagees and other creditors on lands owned by Arabs and Africans, and in 1939 the Government proceeded to legislation which would ensure that debts would not again be accumulated on the security of the lands. A decree (No. 9 of 1939) was enacted to control the alienation of agricultural lands owned by Arabs and Africans, and to forbid the attachment of such lands (or of their

[1] Among the contributory causes of debt had been (*a*) the excessive buying of land during periods of prosperity, and (*b*) the absence of foreclosure. With regard to the latter, creditors had endeavoured to extract as much as they could from the current return, either in the form of cash or of contributions of produce or of service. Defaults in these had often been capitalized arbitrarily and added to the original debt, which became less and less redeemable.

[2] The creditors preferred to leave mortgagors on the land, partly because of the creditors' lack of interest in agriculture, and partly because of the impossibility of realizing in cash the capital value of debts nominally secured on the land.

[3] Muhammadan Law is the fundamental law of Zanzibar.

produce) for debt. In the case of leases the Alienation Board was empowered to refuse consent to a transfer which would deprive the lessor of sufficient resources for the support of himself and his dependants during the currency of the lease, or would be contrary to the best interests of the lessor. In the case of a mortgage the purpose of the loan must be for the maintenance or improvement of the land or any other purposes approved by the Board,[1] the mortgagor must be left in possession of land sufficient for his needs, the amount of the loan must not exceed two-fifths of the value of the land to be mortgaged, interest on the loan should not exceed 9% per annum, and the mortgage deed should contain provisions for the amortisation of the loan.

The new legislation in Zanzibar evoked a great deal of criticism, particularly from the Indian community, who maintained that it introduced racial discrimination by taking away land from Indians while allowing Arabs and Africans the privilege of acquiring it. Restrictions on the sale of land, they said, prevented it from passing to those who could use it best. The Indian community would be debarred from investing their savings in land, and this, in the long run, would prove an impediment to agricultural development. To these criticisms the Government of Zanzibar replied that the legislation was not directed against Indians as such, but against the dispossession of the agricultural classes, who happened to be Africans and Arabs. It had, indeed, been modelled on legislation which had been successfully applied in India itself.[2]

The passage of the Alienation of Land Decree marked the culmination of the Zanzibar Government's attempt to settle, once for all, the problem of agricultural debt. But there still remained the question of a systematic settlement of rights to land. The Registration of Documents Decree (Cap. iii) had provided for the registration of documents affecting immovable property, but there was no record of titles to land. Accordingly in 1937 a Bill was introduced for the Settlement and Registration of Rights to Land—a Survey Department having been established the previous year. The Bill provided for the appointment of Settlement officers, the formation of units of settlement and registration, the settlement of claims in a schedule of claims, the public investigation and settlement of claims (including those of the Government), the drawing up and publication of a schedule of rights, and the establishment of a new Land Register. Registered rights were alone to be valid, and no action was to lie in respect of unregistered disposition. The need for such a scheme had long seemed obvious, if only because uncertainty re-

[1] In 1933 Messrs. Bartlett & Last had stated that the proportion of agricultural debt incurred for agricultural development had been negligible.

[2] The Punjab Land Alienation Act of 1900.

garding the validity of claims had been an important factor in the excessive rates of interest charged for loans on the security of land. Moreover, the Government's proposals for the redemption of mortgage debts, involving as they did the use of public money for the purchase of the interests of mortgagees, appeared to demand that the task of investigating and registering title should be carried out as soon as possible. The Bill has not yet, however, become law, and the Government appears to be doubtful whether the benefits likely to be derived from a system of survey and registration on the lines suggested would justify the cost.

As regards the Debt legislation of 1938, it is not yet (1943) possible to say how far this is likely to have the results expected. Doubts have been expressed as to the adequacy of the security on which advances have been made and also as to the likelihood that the relief afforded will be of permanent benefit. Moreover, it would appear that the extent of the debt and dispossession was considerably less than had been represented. On the other hand, much-needed relief has been given to the agricultural industry and many farms have been saved from dispossession. The control imposed on the alienation of land by Africans and Arabs also appears to have been fully justified.

CHAPTER VIII

Kenya

KENYA provides, perhaps, the most signal of all examples of conflicting interests in land. And the conflict is not confined to the respective claims of Europeans and native Africans but extends to the various categories of natives themselves. Indians, also, whose numbers are more than double those of the Europeans, have long felt aggrieved at the privileged position accorded to Europeans in thc Highlands of Kenya.[1] Among Europeans themselves there is dissatisfaction with tenure conditions and a demand for the re-introduction of freehold, for the institution of a system of rent redemption and for the abolition of the system of rent revision. There are problems of native squatters on European estates: and of urbanized Africans who are making increasing demands for agricultural land. There are problems connected with the development of individual native holdings—a policy favoured by the Government because it leads to a more economical use of land, but which is already tending to create a landless class of Africans. In the Coastal belt there are important problems of survey and of the registration of title. There are problems of fragmentation of holdings, of subdivision and of reclaiming large areas of land which are waterless or infested with tsetse fly; and there is the persistent problem of erosion. So urgent are many of the problems of native lands in Kenya that the Government is considering the immediate establishment of a Department of Native Lands.

Politically, Kenya consists of a Colony and a Protectorate, the latter being a narrow strip of land fringing the Coast. Physiographically it consists of (1) a region poorly watered, comprising some three-fifths of the total area of the Colony; (2) a plateau raised by volcanic action to a height varying from 3000 to 9000 feet; (3) the Great Rift Valley containing Lakes Rudolf, Nakuru, Naivasha and others, and (4) a portion of the basin of the Victoria Nyanza which is 3,726 feet above sea-level.

The population of Kenya immediately before the war was as follows:—

[1] Non-Europeans have long been debarred as a matter of 'administrative convenience' (under sections 71 and 73 of the Grown Lands Ordinance of 1915) from the ownership of agricultural land in the European Highlands. There is, however, no statutory racial bar.

Europeans	20,894
Indians	44,635
Goans	3,734
Arabs	14,077
Other non-natives	1,774
Total non-natives ..	85,114
Africans	3,280,777
Grand Total	3,365,891

The total land area of Kenya is estimated to be 224,960 sq. miles. The population density is, therefore, about fifteen persons to the sq. mile. But the distribution is extremely uneven. Nearly two-thirds of the total area are inhabited at an average density of less than one person to the sq. mile. On the other hand the density figures for the Kikuyu reserves were (in 1933) 283 persons to the sq. mile, and these reserves included many waterless areas, so that in some regions the density was very much in excess of 283. Recently density figures of 1100 and even 1800 to the sq. mile have been reported.[1] In any appraisement, therefore, of the land situation in Kenya the wide variations in the quality of the soil and in the distribution of population must always be borne in mind. It should also be remembered that the basis of land valuation may be different not merely as between Europeans and natives, but between one native tribe and another—the agricultural Kikuyu, for example, and the pastoral Masai. Furthermore, this basis is continually changing with the change in agricultural and pastoral practice, and one of the problems which the Kenya Land Commissioners of 1933 had to face was whether they were to consider the value which land had had for the natives at the time of its alienation, or which it had for them now, or which it was likely to have for them in the future. In order to illustrate this point the Commissioners instanced an area which, when the alienations were made, was unfavourably regarded by the natives, since it was too cold for the crops which they had been accustomed to grow: but in later years this land had been found to be well suited for the cultivation of European potatoes and so had assumed a new value in the native estimation.[2]

In 1938 (the latest year for which full figures are available) the land distribution of Kenya was approximately as follows: Native reserve lands amounted to 51,839 sq. miles, and natives were also in occupation of 119,097 sq. miles of sparsely inhabited country

[1] See *Hansard*, Vol. 130, No. 16 (of 1st February, 1944).
[2] *Kenya Land Commission Report* (Cmd. 4556), para. 221.

comprising the Northern Frontier District, Turkana and an extension from Uganda. Alienated land amounted to 11,037 sq. miles (including 69 sq. miles in native reserves and 276 sq. miles of coast freehold), with some 1346 sq. miles which had been surveyed and were available for alienation. The balance of the land was made up of Government reserves, townships and unalienated Protectorate lands.

The European Highlands

Most of the alienated land, that is to say about one-twentieth of the whole territory, comprises the area set aside for European settlement and known as the European or White Highlands. The British Government's policy regarding the European Highlands has been consistent over a long period. In 1908 Lord Elgin laid it down that, while legal restrictions should not be placed on any section of the community, as a matter of administrative convenience grants of land in the uplands should not be made to Asiatics.[1] The Crown Lands Ordinance of 1915 stipulated that transfers between persons of different race would require the sanction of the Governor. In 1923 the Devonshire Paper declared that 'After reviewing the history of this question and taking into consideration the facts that during the last fifteen years European British subjects have been encouraged to develop the Highlands and that during that period settlers have taken up land in the Highlands on this understanding, His Majesty's Government have decided that the existing practice must be maintained as regards initial grants and transfers.' This policy has been adhered to by every subsequent Government, and the present Duke of Devonshire has recently stated in Parliament that there is no intention of altering it.[2]

When the Kenya Land Commission made its report in 1933 the

[1] *Tenure of Land in the East African Protectorate* (Cmd. 4117), 1908, pp. 25 and 33. In 1906 Lord Elgin, as Secretary of State for the Colonies, had expressed his approval of the practice then in force of limiting land holding by Indians (outside townships) to the areas east of Kiu and west of Fort Ternan (Cmd. 4556, para. 1943).

[2] *Hansard*, Vol. 30, (No. 16 of 1st February, 1944). The policy has been criticized as inconsistent with the declaration of the Devonshire White Paper that if and when the interests of the African population and those of the immigrant races conflict the former shall prevail. It is held that, while the setting apart of the Highlands interfered but little with native interests at the time, (though these seem to have been greater than was formerly supposed), it deprived the natives of a future means of relieving congestion, which has now become acute. Moreover, the European settlers have failed to make full use of the land allotted to them. For Indian criticism see footnote 1, p. 85. The racial situation regarding land in Kenya has recently been discussed by Elspeth Huxley and Margery Perham in *Race and Politics in Kenya* (Faber & Faber 1944). This contains, in the Introduction, a valuable summary by Lord Lugard. The Devonshire White Paper (*Indians in Kenya*, Cmd. 1922 of 1923) was and remains the official considered statement of inter-racial relations in Africa.

area alienated to Europeans amounted to 10,345 sq. miles and was being used as follows: 11·8% was being cultivated, 40·7% was being used for stock, 20% was occupied by native squatters and 27·5% was not in use. The Commission recommended a demarcation by which the area of the Highlands would be fixed at 16,700 sq. miles, of which 3,950 would be forest reserves, leaving a balance of 12,750 sq. miles. They also recommended that the rights of native occupiers in the Highlands should be extinguished and that those of resident labourers on European estates should be regulated. To this there will be further reference later.[1] At the present time (1944) it is reckoned that the amount of land actually alienated to Europeans is about 10,937 sq. miles (7,000,000 acres) but that of this only 2,031 sq. miles (1,300,000 acres) are suitable for cultivation, and only 1,350 sq. miles (864,000 acres) are actually under cultivation. The number of European settlers is about 2000, and the number of surveyed farms is 2700. All of these farms, except about 150, are being developed—some on a more intensive scale than others. The amount of undeveloped land is so extensive that the Government has been considering the necessity of introducing a tax on undeveloped land.[2]

Since 1915 grants of land surveyed for agricultural purposes have been for terms of 999 years. But nearly half the alienated land in the colony is held under the Crown Lands Ordinance of 1902, which provided for leases of ninety-nine years. Many grants of land, particularly in the vicinity of Nairobi, were made in freehold title under this Ordinance. Leases under the Crown Lands Ordinance of 1915 carry rentals of twenty cents per acre, revisable in 1945[3] and every thirty years thereafter.

During the period 1912 to the end of 1936 (apart from the Ex-Soldier Settlement Scheme of 1919) land grants were usually sold by auction, but in view of the diminishing amount of available land this method of alienating land was found to be unsuitable, and in 1937 a system was introduced by which direct grants of Crown land were made to approved applicants. But township plots are sold by auction, for terms not exceeding ninety-nine years.

The European settlers have long been opposed to the revisable rental conditions of the Crown Lands Ordinance of 1915, which, they declare, are inimical to settlement and a serious deterrent to the provision of capital for land development. They have also urged with determination that the redemption by capitalization of rentals payable on leaseholds from the Crown should be permitted, thereby opening the way to the conversion of leaseholds into freeholds.

[1] See p. 87.

[2] For a note on this subject, see p. 128.

[3] Revision of rents has been postponed owing to the war.

These questions were recently (1941) referred by the Government to a Land Tenure Committee which recommended that the present system of revisable rents should be abolished; that lessees from the Crown should be permitted to redeem the whole or any portion of the Crown rent payable under their leases at any time during the currency of the lease, subject to the fulfilment of prescribed development conditions; that an option be given to the holders of all existing ninety-nine leases of agricultural land under the Crown Lands Ordinance of 1902 to have their titles converted into leases for 999 years at a rent of twenty cents per acre per annum; and that every lessee should have the right, on the fulfilment of certain conditions, to obtain a grant of his land in freehold. Two members of the Committee, one of whom was the Commissioner of Lands and Settlements, issued a minority note in which they stated that they did not consider that a case had been established for the granting of freehold titles. The idea that land is held in trust by the Government for the people had been gathering strength, and any proposals now made should conform with that principle and should be in the direction of strengthening rather than weakening the relation of the State to the land. The maintenance of improvements was of first-rate importance, and the Government would be in a stronger position to enforce continuing development conditions under a leasehold system. They added that the main objections to the existing titles in the Colony had not been against leasehold as such, but against the system of revisable rents.

It appeared from the evidence submitted to the Committee, that there was a popular misconception that the term freehold meant the absolute ownership of land 'free' from all conditions and restrictions. Yet according to English law certain covenants are enforceable against all subsequent owners of freeholds, and partial restraints may be imposed on alienation. In Kenya, freeholds sold under the provisions of the Crown Lands Ordinance of 1902 were made subject to forfeiture by the Crown if they remained undeveloped without reasonable excuse. This condition was removed in 1915 (under Section 4 (3) of the Crown Lands Ordinance of 1915), though probably more as a matter of policy than because of any doubt as to its legal effectiveness.[1] There is still a notable restriction on freeholds. Under Section 73 of the Crown Lands Ordinance of 1915 it is lawful for the Governor-in-Council to veto any sale, transfer, mortgage, assignment, lease or sub-lease if the person to

[1] Doubts had, in fact, been expressed whether maintenance of development conditions could be enforced against the holders of freehold. The Land Tenure Commission of 1922 recommended that freehold title should only be granted after the land had been properly developed over a number of years. Thereafter maintenance conditions would be automatically safeguarded, since no grantee who had paid a fair market price for his land could afford to allow his asset to depreciate.

whom the land is to be transferred is of different race from the person who proposes to make the transfer. This Section applies to all land sold or leased under the Crown Lands Ordinances of 1902 and 1915, and is thus equally enforceable against leaseholds or freeholds.[1]

The general question of freehold tenure and of revisable rents in the Colonies will be reviewed separately at a later stage,[2] and it need only be observed here that the Secretary of State saw no reason for departing from present practice in Kenya. The system of rent revision might, perhaps, be made less rigid, but the principle must be maintained that substantial increases in land value should accrue to the State and not to private individuals. Some of the reasons for not abandoning the principle of regular revision of rents would also apply to the proposal that leaseholders should be permitted to redeem their rents, a proposal which, if accepted, might prove a very bad financial bargain for the Colony, in view of the steady depreciation in the value of money. It had been argued that the option of commuting rent would encourage the investment of British trust funds in Kenya, but there was little evidence that the present rental system had been a serious deterrent to investment. Similarly, as regards freehold, the interests of the State must override those of individuals, though additional forms of security might be accorded to leaseholders on the lines of the English Agricultural Holdings Act of 1923.

Squatter Labour

The European estates are worked on a basis of paid labour, and many problems have arisen in Kenya, as elsewhere in East Africa,[3] with regard to native labour-tenants on estates. Under the Resident Native Labourers Ordinance of 1925 (No. 5) the contract under which the labourers worked ensured to them a plot of land for cultivation and buildings; it also prescribed the number of stock which might be brought on to the estate, and so implied a right of pasturage. There was an obligation to work for a period of 180 days for a

[1] Since the above paragraph was written important new restrictions have been placed on dealings in lands in the Highlands by (*a*) The Land Control Ordinance (No. XXII of 1944) and (*b*) The Crown Lands (Amendment) Ordinance of 1944 (No. XXIII). Under the latter the Governor's consent is required before anyone may sell, lease, sub-lease, assign, mortgage or otherwise alienate, encumber or part with the possession of any land in the Highlands. Restrictions are also placed on dealings with shares and assets in companies owning land. For the restrictions imposed under the Land Control Ordinance see p. 85, footnote 2.

[2] See Chapters XX and XXI.

[3] In West Africa, where the plantation system is virtually non-existent, the problem of natives on European estates does not arise. But analogous problems have arisen in connection with alien natives (e.g. on the cocoa gardens of the Gold Coast).

specified wage, but the contracts were purely voluntary and very large numbers of natives availed themselves of the opportunity of living under conditions which were better than they could find in their own over-crowded reserves. In particular, on the estates, there was better grazing for their stock, which soon improved in quality and increased in numbers. In 1932 it was reckoned that in the Nzoia Province alone there was something like a quarter of a million native-owned cattle on European farms and at least as many goats and sheep. The numbers kept had far outgrown the needs of the natives, and become a serious impediment to the development of estates.[1] There were other complaints against the squatters—that many of them had failed to fulfil their contract, that their settlements had frequently become the resort of thieves, and that they were generally undisciplined, living as they did outside the restraints of tribal life.

In 1932 the Kenya Land Commission reckoned that there were 150,000 labour-tenants living on estates and observed that it was scarcely to be supposed that the European area would always afford accommodation for all the squatters and their natural increase or for their stock. In the Highlands the natives had no right to the land. But they had a right to use land temporarily while in employment. Care should, however, be taken to ensure that the essence of the contract was one of labour, the employee being allowed, for his greater comfort, to keep the number of cattle necessary for his use: but if he kept more than was necessary the character of the contract would be changed, until it became predominantly a *tenancy* contract, and this (in the opinion of the Commission) ought to be prevented, as contrary to the purpose for which the European Highlands had been reserved.

The Commission realized that the return *en masse* of all the excess squatter stock would increase the overstocking which already existed in the native reserves, but they considered that a policy of limiting the numbers on the farms to the economic requirements of the natives should be steadily pursued, concurrently with that of reducing the numbers of uneconomic stock on the reserves. As for the squatters themselves, it might become a problem of first-class magnitude how and where accommodation was to be found for those who had become surplus to the requirements of the European Highlands. The Commission recommended that the Government should arrange for the accommodation of landless natives in their own native reserves, though some might prefer to take up land on a

[1] *Kenya Land Commission Report* (Cmd. 4556), paras. 2038-9. In 1938 the Settlement Committee of Kenya observed that the abuse of the squatter stock system created grave risk of cattle disease, increased farming costs and seriously diminished the area of land available for settlement.

more individual form of tenure and should, therefore, have the alternative of taking land on lease in the areas which the Commission proposed to class as C or D (i.e. 'Native Leasehold Areas' and undefined areas in which both natives and non-natives could obtain leaseholds). But the land available in both of these classes is extremely restricted; and as for the reserves, or 'native lands' as they are now called, the Commissioners themselves observed that the return to the Kikuyu reserves of 110,000 Kikuyu squatters would augment by fifty-seven to the sq. mile a population which had already (in 1932) become so dense as to cause embarrassment.[1] The problem, therefore, of squatters or labour-tenants, who may be evicted when their European employers decide to reduce their staff, remains one of considerable complexity.

In order to remedy some of the abuses of the squatter system a new 'Resident Labourers' Ordinance was enacted in 1937, and it may be of interest to review the main provisions of this Ordinance, with its subsequent amendments.[2] A native may reside on a farm (i.e. any land held under a grant, lease or licence from the Crown) only if he is actually employed on the farm, or has entered into a contract with the owner, or is otherwise authorised. If he has entered into a contract he may be accompanied by his family.[3] The contract, which must be attested by a magistrate, may not be for a term of less than one year or more than five years; but it may be renewed or varied by the endorsement of the parties. The resident labourer and every male resident member of his family over the age of sixteen must work for the owner for not less than 180 days in the year, and the owner must provide employment for the agreed period. But the time during which the resident labourer is required to work must be arranged so as to allow him reasonable time to sow, cultivate and reap his own food crops. The owner, as well as paying a stipulated wage, must provide material for the erection of a dwelling for the labourer and must also provide him with sufficient and suitable land for the cultivation of food crops and for the grazing of a specified number of stock. But certain specified crops may not be cultivated and the labourer may not cultivate any other land than that allocated. With the consent of a magistrate the agreement may be terminated, either by the owner or the labourer giving three months' notice; but the labourer must be given time to reap his crops and the owner may demand the fulfilment of any conditions

[1] *Kenya Land Commission Report* (Cmd. 4556), paras. 498, 1498, 1859, 1860, 1867, 1976, 2038-9.

[2] See the *Ordinance to regulate the residence of labourers on farms*, No. 30 of 1937, as amended by No. 18 of 1939, and No. 38 of 1941.

[3] The word family is defined as 'the wife or wives and the unmarried children'. But a native's family often includes other relatives such as a brother, cousin or a brother's or sister's child.

in the agreement regarding the period of work. On the termination of the agreement the labourer may take away all his movable property, but he may not remove buildings, for which, however, he must be paid reasonable compensation.

A magistrate may refuse to attest a contract which does not provide for a fair remuneration, and he may also refuse to attest if he considers the native an undesirable. He may, in order to prevent a breach of the peace, or if he is satisfied that a farm is not under such occupation as to ensure the observance of the provisions of the Ordinance, order the removal of a resident labourer.

No payment may be taken from any native for the right to reside on any farm or to cultivate any land or to graze any stock, or for the use of salt-licks and fuel or water. Nor may a farm owner enter into a contract whereby he would share any profit derived by a resident labourer from his cultivation or from the increase of his stock. The Ordinance provides penalties for offences committed by resident labourers. These include drunkenness, the refusal to carry out legitimate orders, and the use of insulting language. Farm owners, on the other hand, may be punished for failure to pay wages due to their labourers, or to provide them with medical attendance during serious illness.[1]

Native Areas

In 1932 a Commission was appointed to inquire into and report upon the needs, present and prospective, of the native population in respect of land. The Commission issued in 1933 a Report which marks an epoch in the history of land rights in Kenya.[2] The Report raised two fundamental issues, namely, the method of adjusting native reserve lands to the needs of an expanding or diminishing population, and the extent to which any tribe had, by virtue of any agreement, the right to a monopoly of more land than it could use. The Commissioners observed that it is the proper function of Government to secure the development of land to the best advantage, and that, while private rights are recognized, a power of intervention is commonly preserved to the Crown by means of land acquisition acts and similar legislation, in order that it may be able to secure proper development. If, therefore, the possession of large undeveloped tracts by any tribe, person, or class is prejudicial to the welfare of a country, it would be a proper exercise of the function of Government, when it has armed itself with the necessary powers, to intervene and adjust the position.

[1] For further observations on squatter tenure in East Africa, see pp. 116-8 (Nyasaland) and 127-8 (N. Rhodesia).

[2] *Report of the Kenya Land Commission, 1933* (Cmd. 4556).

The Commissioners recommended that lands in Kenya should be grouped in the following categories: (1) European Highlands, to be defined in the same manner as tribal reserves; (2) Native Lands (Class A Lands)—the existing Native Reserves with amended boundaries; (3) Native Reserves (Class B1 lands)—additions made to native lands on economic grounds; (4) Temporary Native Reserves (Class B2 lands)—additions made for reasons of a temporary character; (5) Native Leasehold Areas (Class C lands)—where a private form of tenure suitable for detribalized natives would be made available; and (6) Areas (D lands) in which natives would have equal rights with other races in the acquisition of land.

In 1938 and 1939 legislation was enacted to implement the recommendations of the Commission and to provide legal security to the natives in the occupation of the lands allotted to their use. This legislation comprised (*a*) the Kenya (Highlands) Order in Council, 1939; (*b*) the Kenya (Native Areas) Order in Council 1939; (*c*) the Native Lands Trust Ordinance, 1938 (No. 28); and (*d*) the Crown Lands (Amendment) Ordinance 1938 (No. 27).

The Highlands Order in Council 1939 declared that the Highlands should consist of the areas set out in the Seventh Schedule to the Crown Lands Ordinance and that the boundaries should not be altered, except as provided in the Native Lands Trust Ordinance (1938), and the Crown Lands Ordinance.[1] It also made provision for the establishment of a Board whose function would be to protect the interests of the inhabitants of the Highlands and to advise the Governor in all matters relating to the disposition of land within the Highlands.[2]

The Kenya (Native Areas) Order in Council, 1939, provided for the establishment of a Native Lands Trust Board whose function would be to protect the interests of the natives of the Colony in the various native areas (Native Lands, Native Reserves, Temporary Native Reserves, and Native Leasehold Areas), and in particular to

[1] Strong exception was taken to the Highlands Order in Council by the Indian communities who considered that the Order gave statutory effect to the existing administrative policy of discrimination against non-Europeans. They regarded the Order to be an infringement of Article 4 of the Convention of St. Germain-en-Laye which precludes formal differential treatment between the nationals of the signatory powers (of which India was one). The Order, however, was framed so as to define the Highlands and does not contain any discriminatory provisions.

[2] The Board has now been established under the Land Control Ordinance (No. XXII) of 1944. This Ordinance places restrictions on dealings in land in the Highlands. No one may, without the consent of the Board, sell, lease, sub-lease, assign or mortgage his land. But this does not affect (*a*) any gift of land by way of testamentary disposition or (*b*) any transactions made by or in favour of the Crown. The Board may also, in certain circumstances, refuse to give consent to any transaction, upon the ground that the applicant already has sufficient land or that it objects to the proposed selling price, rent or other pecuniary consideration. In giving its consent to any transfer the Board may impose conditions that the transferee shall effect specified improvements.

make representations to the Governor when, in the opinion of the Trust Board, anything in relation to the administration, management, development or control of the land in the said areas was not in the best interests of the natives. The Order in Council also made the important pronouncement that 'the Native Lands shall be subject at all times to all such rights in respect of land as are or may be enjoyed by native tribes, groups, families or individuals by virtue of existing native law and custom, or any subsequent modification thereof, in so far as such rights are not repugnant to any law from time to time in force in the Colony'.[1]

Finally, the Native Areas Order in Council declared that the definition of 'Crown Lands' contained in Section 2 of the Kenya Colony Order in Council 1921 should no longer apply to the Native Lands. The Commission had pointed out that many natives objected to the application of the term 'Crown land' to native reserve land, since such land in their view belonged to themselves and not to the Crown. In point of fact the legal position had been made clear by the 'Barth Judgement' of 1921 whereby it was held that, as a result of the combined effect of the Kenya Order in Council of 1921 and the Crown Lands Ordinance of 1915, the native occupier was no more than a tenant-at-will of the Crown.[2] Nevertheless the Commissioners maintained that the native lands as a whole should not be styled 'Crown Lands' but 'Native Lands', the *nuda proprietas* being deemed to lie with the native population generally, though vested in a trust and subject to the sovereignty of the Crown and its general powers of control.[3]

The Native Lands Trust Ordinance of 1938 deals in detail with all the lands which were found by the Commission to be native lands by reason of historic right, together with other lands added in compensation for losses of area suffered through European settlement. They are divided into nine units, as defined by schedules, amalgamating into larger blocks the old Native Reserves; and these units are reserved for the use and enjoyment of the respective tribes to which they are allotted. Their total area exceeds that of the old Native Reserves by 1410 sq. miles.

The Ordinance contains detailed provisions for the control of the Native Lands by the Trust Board. It provides for the establishment in every administrative district of Local Land Boards, for the issue of inter-tribal occupation permits, for the setting apart of land for

[1] This gave effect to para. 1639 of the Commission's Report.

[2] *East African Law Reports*, Vol. IX, pp. 102-105. Lord Hailey has remarked that the use of the expression 'tenant-at-will' in this decision was 'a somewhat unfortunate instance of the application of terms of English law to a situation which had no real parallel in that law'. (*An African Survey*, p. 748.)

[3] Report op. cit. (Cmd. 4556), para. 1639.

mining or general public purposes,[1] for 'exclusions' (for public purposes or temporarily for mining),[2] and for compensation when land is set apart or excluded. The Governor may grant leases in the native lands to any persons, provided the land to which the lease relates has been formally set apart. Leases may be for any term not exceeding thirty-three years, or, with the consent of the Secretary of State, not exceeding ninety-nine years. The rents for leases must be paid over to the Local Native Council concerned, and in the assessment of rents due regard must be paid to the economic value of the land and to such conditions regarding improvements as may be contained in the lease. Licences for periods not exceeding twelve months may also be granted for the grazing of stock on native lands or for the removal of timber, forest produce, lime or other common minerals.

The Ordinance empowers the Governor to make minor adjustments to the boundaries of the native land units: and under the Ordinance there are rule-making powers for many purposes, including the regulation of matters relating to the tenure of land as between natives in the native lands. It is laid down that in the case of treason or rebellion any land in the native lands held or occupied by a tribe, group, family or individual may be forfeited and revert to His Majesty.

One of the most important of all the provisions of the Native Lands Trust Ordinance is contained in section 70 which provides for the extinguishment of all native rights in land outside the boundaries of the native areas. This does not apply to rights enjoyed by individual natives under any specific title granted to them, nor does it apply to native rights in the Protectorate of Kenya (i.e. the Coastal belt), nor to those of tribes for whom no specific native land unit is provided by the Ordinance. But it applies specially to the European Highlands. The Land Commission had established the fact that in the Highlands there were many natives living on European-owned farms, chiefly in the Kiambu and Limuru areas, who had been in occupation long before the farms had been allotted for European setttlement. The Commission had recommended that, although claims of right on the part of these natives should be admitted, it was in the best interests of the Colony as a whole that these rights should be expunged, and that the natives

[1] Land may not be set apart unless the local Native Council has been consulted and the Provincial Commissioner is satisfied that the setting apart will be for the benefit of the natives.

[2] Excluded land, unlike land set apart, ceases to be native land. But where land is temporarily excluded for mining purposes there must be added temporarily to the native lands an area of unalienated Crown Land equal in agricultural value and, so far as may be, equal in size to the area excluded.

concerned should be removed to other lands within the extended native areas.

But although the Ordinance provides for the extinguishment of native rights in the Highlands it also provides (under Section 49) that natives whose rights have been extinguished may not be removed unless the Governor is satisfied that sufficient suitable land for their accommodation is available elsewhere, and that adequate compensation for disturbance has been provided. Since it has been found that the numbers of natives with rights in the Highlands are almost ten times greater than the Commissioners supposed, the Government of Kenya has been faced with a considerable problem in finding land for those whose rights have been extinguished.[1]

The Crown Lands (Amendment) Ordinance of 1938 (No. 27) makes provision for the other areas of land which the Commission had recommended should be reserved for native tribes in satisfaction of their temporary or permanent economic needs.[2] These areas are (*a*) Native Reserves; (*b*) Temporary Native Reserves; and (*c*) Native Leasehold Areas. Their boundaries are described in the Schedule to the Ordinance, which, however, empowers the Governor to vary the boundaries of the Native Reserves and Temporary Native Reserves, when he is satisfied that, as a result of a diminution in the numbers of a tribe, or for economic reasons, any area in the reserves is no longer required. On the other hand, he may, with the approval of the Legislative Council, set aside other areas of Crown Land as native reserves or temporary native reserves. In the native leasehold areas he may grant leases to any native group, family or individual,[3] and may, with the consent of the Trust Board, sanction the transfer of leases in the native leasehold area from a native lessee to a non-native. Furthermore, he may grant, for a period not exceeding ten years, leases to non-natives of land in such areas of the native leasehold areas as, in the opinion of the Chief Native Commissioner, are surplus to the requirements of the natives. Leases not exceeding ninety-nine years may also, with the consent of the Trust Board, be granted to non-natives of land in such unalienated areas of the native leasehold areas as are available for such purpose. But in no case shall the Trust Board sanction the transfer or grant of a lease to a non-native unless it is satisfied that such transfer or grant is desirable in the interests of the natives. Where the Board withholds its consent the Governor may refer the matter to the Secretary of State, whose decision shall be final.

The Crown Lands (Amendment) Ordinance of 1938 also (in its

[1] See the *Annual Report of the Commissioner of Lands and Settlement, 1938.*

[2] I.e., the B1, B2 and C categories of the Commission's Report.

[3] The rental in the case of Native Leasehold Areas is payable to the general revenues of the Colony.

seventh Schedule) defines the boundaries of the Highlands; in its eighth schedule it defines those of the Northern Frontier District and the Turkana district, which are declared to be areas wherein the native tribes at present residing 'shall have a prior interest'.

Such is a brief summary of legislation which was intended to settle once for all the competing claims of Africans and Europeans and to remove any sense of injustice felt by the native tribes. The following table indicates the alteration in the land situation between 1937 and 1938, which followed the enactment of the new legislation.

	Area		*Difference*	
	1937	*1938*	*Minus*	*Plus*
	Sq. Miles	*Sq. Miles*	*Sq. Miles*	*Sq. Miles*
Total Area of Colony and Protectorate	224,960	224,960	—	—
1. Native Lands (previously Native Reserves)	48,345	49,755	—	1,410
Native Reserves		877	—	877
Temporary Native Reserves		507	—	507
Native Leasehold		700	—	700
2. Forest Reserves[1]	4,800	4,710	90	—
3. Alienated[2]	10,832	10,968	—	136
Townships	294	293	1	—
Government Reserves	130	124	6	—
Available	1,466	1,346	120	—
4. Unclassified	39,296	36,583	2,713	—
5. Northern Frontier Province	95,120	94,420	700	—
6. Turkana	8,818	8,818	—	—
7. Extension from Uganda	15,859	15,859	—	—
	224,960	224,960	3,630	3,630

Postscript. By a further recent amendment of the Crown Lands Ordinance (No. XIX of 1942) four areas of Crown Land have been reserved as 'Native Settlement Areas'. In these the Governor may, with the advice and consent of the Trust Board, grant a Native Settlement licence for a term not exceeding 999 years to native groups, families or individuals to occupy any Native Settlement area or any portion thereof for such period and subject to such conditions as may be prescribed. The four areas (defined in the 9th Schedule) are Olengurone, Kichuiru, Digo and Gedi.

[1] In addition there were 375 square miles of Native Forest Reserve at 31.12.1937 and 372 at 31.12.1938.

[2] In addition there were 86 square miles of alienated land in Native Reserves at 31.12.1937 and 69 square miles at 31.12.1938.

Erosion[1]

In the Native Areas of Kenya one of the outstanding problems is the steady loss of soil fertility in the more thickly populated areas. In order to combat this, steps are being taken to introduce mixed farming principles into the husbandry system. But, for the success of this, permanency of tenure is required, as well as provision against fragmentation. In some localities overstocking is a predominant cause of erosion, and where the land is held in individual tenure farmers are being encouraged to fence the outer boundaries and to control the grazing. It is reckoned that for every acre and a half under cultivation there should be sufficient grazing available on the holding for the support of one head of cattle. In due course, as fertility increases and farmers learn to stall-feed their cattle, and bed them down at night, one beast should provide sufficient manure for the upkeep of fertility on one acre of arable land. Experiments on these lines have been carried out successfully in the Machakos district where, in 1938, a loan of £23,000 was made from the Colonial Development Fund to the Machakos Local Native Council together with a free grant of £10,000 for the comprehensive treatment of 100,000 acres, as an experiment to ascertain what could be done to save the Machakos and Matungulu-Kangundo areas from destruction.[2]

Under the Native Authority Ordinance of 1937 (No. 2) Local Native Councils may make and pass resolutions[3] with regard to the use of land, and the standard resolution passed by many of the Councils all over Kenya is as follows:

1. That for the purpose of preventing soil erosion—
   (*a*) onsteeply sloping land, no person shall, except with the permission of the Headman—
      (i) for the purpose of cultivating any land cut down or destroy in any manner whatsoever, any tree, bush, or other vegetation growing therein; or
      (ii) depasture cattle, sheep or goats;
   (*b*) no person shall, except with the permission of the Headman, within ten yards of the bank of any river or stream cultivate the land, or depasture cattle, sheep or goats, or burn, cut down or destroy in any manner whatsoever any tree, bush or other vegetation;

[1] The subject of erosion in African territories as a whole is fully reviewed by Lord Hailey in Chapter XVI of *An African Survey*. The special section dealing with Kenya is at pp. 1093-99. See also Sir F. Stockdale, 'Soil Erosion in the Colonial Empire', *Empire Journal of Experimental Agriculture*, Vol. V, No. 20, 1937.

[2] *Annual Report of the Department of Agriculture, Kenya, 1938.*

[3] Resolutions, if approved by the Governor, have the force of law.

(*c*) no person shall set fire to any live grass, bush, undergrowth or forest.

2. That for the purpose of preventing soil erosion the occupier of any steeply sloping land used or intended to be used for cultivation shall, if directed by the Headman, carry out such measures with regard to terracing, strip cropping, contour ploughing, stone walling, banking, lining with plant residues, planting and maintenance of grass or plants in strips, or live wash-stops, as such Headman may, on the advice of an Agricultural Officer, direct.
3. That, in order to prevent wash being caused to land by water entering it from above, every person occupying and cultivating steeply sloping land shall leave at the upper boundary of such land, and at subsequent intervals of not more than twenty-five feet of such land parallel to such upper boundary, a strip of bush, trees, grass or crops of such a width as the Headman may, on the advice of an Agricultural Officer, direct.

The Native Authority Ordinance also empowers Headmen to require the able-bodied men to take such measures for dealing with soil erosion as may be necessary. A second standard resolution has accordingly been passed by many of the Kenya Native Councils in the following terms: (*a*) Measures dealing with soil erosion are hereby declared to be a minor communal service; and (*b*) for the purpose of preventing soil erosion all able-bodied men shall, on land other than land subject to right-holding or in private occupation, except with the consent of the occupier or right-holder thereof, carry out any of the measures specified in the Schedule hereto, and Headmen are hereby empowered to require such able-bodied men to take any of the said measures.

Schedule

(*a*) The prevention of the destruction of forest, bush or grass by fire or by any other means;
(*b*) the afforestation or planting with grass of denuded areas;
(*c*) the construction and maintenance of dams and water supplies, and the regulation of the use thereof;
(*d*) the stopping of gullies and the construction and maintenance of terraces and contour banks.

These provisions implement a recommendation of the Advisory Land Board made in 1937 that measures for soil conservation should be imposed by legislation on all land whether in native areas or in private ownership.[1] They are an example of the way in which native law is being enlarged to meet modern needs.

Tenure Problems in Kenya Protectorate

In the coastal belt of Kenya, that is to say the territory permanently leased from H.H. the Sultan of Zanzibar and administered as a Protectorate by the Government of Kenya, the land situation is in a state of confusion, partly as the result of the great variety of social conditions, and consequently of tenures, and partly because a scheme of settlement had been begun by the Government but had never been brought to completion.

In the coastal belt there are Arabs who own large private estates, on which ex-slaves and freedmen may be found living as 'tenants-at-will'. Other Arabs occupy small 'shambas' held usually on individual title. Exclusive areas were at one time assigned to the Mazrui Arabs, and these have now passed into the private ownership of individuals who may sell or lease them without distinction of race.[2] There are detribalized African natives who hold land on individual title. There are others who live in reserves of their own. In 1933 there was a special reserve for ex-slaves, and there was also a reserve for 'Mahaji' or converts to Islam. But the vast majority of the natives on the coastal belt live neither in their own land nor in reserves, but simply occupy land on sufferance wherever they can find it. Some of this land is Crown land, some private land, and some is land the ownership of which is still undetermined.

In 1897 regulations made under the Africa Order in Council authorised the grant of (*a*) ninety-nine years leases of Crown land on the basis of a plan signed by a Government surveyor, and (*b*) freehold sales within the coastal belt. In 1901 a Registration of Documents Ordinance provided for an official record of deeds purporting to create, transfer or annul interests in land. In 1902 the

[1] The Land and Water Preservation Ordinance (No. XI of 1943) empowers the Governor in Council to make rules prohibiting or controlling the breaking up or clearing of land for cultivation, the grazing or watering of live stock, and the firing, clearing or destruction of vegetation; also rules requiring or regulating the afforestation of land, the protection of slopes, the construction of contour banks, the repairing of gullies and so on. It is interesting to observe that persons required to take action under this Ordinance may, if necessary, be given advances for the purpose by the Land and Agricultural Bank.

[2] Under the Mazrui Arabs Land Trust Ordinance (No. 11 of 1931) a Board of trustees was appointed to administer the lands assigned to the Mazrui Arabs and was empowered to convey, mortgage, assign or demise any of the trust land for the benefit of the tribe on such terms and conditions as they might consider fit and might distribute any profits among the members in such manner as appeared just. They might, at the request of the majority of the tribe, sub-divide any land vested in them, and grant such land so sub-divided to such member or members of the tribe as they thought fit.

Land Regulations of 1897 were superseded by the Crown Lands Ordinance, and by 1908 it had become clear that, if this Ordinance was to function effectively, provision must be made for a settlement and record of titles throughout the whole of the coastal belt. A Land Titles Court was accordingly established under the Land Titles Ordinance (1908). This Court, under the presidency of a Recorder of Titles, was to adjudicate upon claims to land in the coastal area and to issue certificates of title to the successful claimants.[1] The certificates were to be of three kinds, (*a*) Certificates of ownership (in fee), (*b*) Certificates of mortgage, and (*c*) Certificates of interest. It was further prescribed that, in any locality to which the Ordinance should be made applicable, all land in respect of which no certificate of ownership had been granted would be considered Crown land. In 1919 the Registration of Titles Ordinance was applied to the coastal belt and this had the effect of bringing certificates of title granted after that date under provisions which entailed a rigorous survey of holdings for the issue of indefeasible titles.

The Recorder, with the assistance of a staff of surveyors and a Board of Arbitration, carried on the work of adjudication until 1922, when for reasons of economy the office of Recorder was abolished. District Officers were then appointed as Deputy Recorders, but since they had little time for this work, and there were no surveyors or demarcators available, no substantial progress was made. Moreover, although the system had been satisfactory enough for the larger and more valuable areas it had proved much too costly for the owners of small properties, many of whom had refused to take up their Certificates.[2] It had proved costly also to the Government, since in the period during which the Land Titles Ordinance had been in active operation (1908-1922) £110,000 had been expended, of which less than one-third had been recovered in fees.

In 1933 the Kenya Land Commissioners reviewed the whole position[3] and stated that they were so much impressed with the necessity of finding out, once for all, what lands in the coastal belt were at the disposal of the Crown and what lands were private, that they considered that the office of Recorder of Titles should be resumed forthwith and that the work of adjudication should proceed energetically. They observed that in the case of reserves their communal nature should not be interpreted so as to preclude the

[1] The Ordinance was thus a recognition that title could be obtained by prescription.

[2] Up to 1933 some 21,700 claims had been investigated, 9,190 certificates of registered title had been granted and 133 certificates of interest. At least 2,000 of the successful claimants had refrained from applying for their certificates.

[3] Cmd. 4556, paras. 1301-1365.

creation and recognition of private rights: this conception had already become an anachronism among the more advanced of the up-country tribes and should not be tolerated on the coast among people who claimed to have reached a more advanced degree of civilization. The general end in view should be the emergence of a regularized, though not elaborate system of private tenure, either on individual or group lines, and with a clear method of succession. The work of registering small private claims was necessarily expensive and would not be worth the money if within a few years of the issue of the title the land had become subdivided into minute fragments through inheritance. As for the detribalized natives who were living as tenants on Crown or private land, or in the six reserves which had been specially created for their use, the most practical form of assistance was not the creation of reserves, but the safeguarding of the rights of tenants, where such safeguards were found to be necessary, and the simplification of the procedure for the acquisition and transfer of land, so that the cost of acquiring small holdings should not be unduly swelled by the charges of survey and registration.

The Government of Kenya found itself in a difficult position. There was a clear necessity that Crown lands should be defined without delay, particularly as there was a possibility of fresh discoveries of mineral deposits in the coastal belt. The Government, moreover, had assumed statutory obligations both to title holders and to claimants. It had caused transactions in land, in respect of which certificates had been issued, to be illegal if not registered. Many illegal transactions had in fact been taking place; and in 1934 it had been reported that the subdivision and transfer of land in respect of which certificates had not been taken up, or in respect of which claims remained for adjudication,[1] had been proceeding, thus increasing enormously the difficulty of effecting a final settlement. The benefits of the laborious and expensive work carried out between 1908 and 1922 were being speedily dissipated.[2]

But before the Government could proceed with the recommendation of the Land Commission it had to reconsider the whole question of methods of registration and survey, since it would be useless merely to revive a system which had been shown to be unsatisfactory on account of its slowness, costliness and want of elasticity. The Government accordingly invited Sir Ernest Dowson, who had been Surveyor-General in Egypt, to visit the coastal area and formu-

[1] The claims reported to the Kenya Land Commission as awaiting adjudication when the operation of the Land Titles Ordinance was suspended in 1922 totalled 4,115.

[2] See *The Annual Report of the Commissioner of Local Government Lands and Settlement, 1934*.

late a scheme to deal with the problem. In 1938 Sir Ernest Dowson submitted a preliminary report in the course of which he observed that there would have been no need for a Land Titles Court if a determination of possessory, as distinct from absolute, title had been considered adequate. The Palestine Royal Commission had recommended the substitution of a settlement of possessory, for one of absolute, title in Palestine, owing to the great delay occasioned by the judicial proceedings necessary to obtain an immediate determination of absolute title. In this the Commissioners had based themselves on Indian experience, since in India nothing but a settlement on a possessory basis had ever been attempted. In Egypt, 1,900,000 possessory titles had been settled between the eight years of 1898-1906 and this settlement had enabled the Crown domain to be ascertained with promptitude. The determination of State domain was open to challenge in the Courts in any particular case, but since the survey and the settlement operations had been of a systematic and efficient character such challenges were rare.

But although the substitution of a possessory for an absolute title offered a means of cheapening and accelerating an initial settlement of titles, this was not a policy to be recommended unless other available means, administrative and technical, were rejected, since a settlement of possessory title was essentially not a settlement of title at all, but merely a stage towards such a settlement, which required to be brought to maturity by complementary measures if its value were not to evaporate and the whole work have to be redone, as had been recurrently necessary both in India and in Egypt.

Sir Ernest Dowson in putting forward proposals for completing the work of settlement in the coastal belt in a methodical manner, block by block (instead of by the former piecemeal method of dealing with individual property parcels), considered that the use of air photography for cadastral requirements might provide the best means of meeting the combined demands of efficiency and economy. He suggested that the aerial survey of the coastal belt might form part of a co-ordinated scheme of aerial survey for the various requirements of all the East African dependencies. This proposal was still under discussion when the war intervened. The settlement of land rights in the coastal belt remains, therefore, one of Kenya's most pressing problems.

The proposal to use air photography for cadastral purposes suggests a reference to this device as a means of detecting and mapping out areas of erosion. It is easier to ascertain by aerial photographs, than by observation on the ground, where sheet erosion is taking place. The photographs, moreover, constitute a record, so that by re-photographing any area after a year or two it is possible to say to what extent the erosion has increased or been kept in check. Aerial survey has been used in this way for several years in various parts of South Africa and is likely to play a prominent part in connection with water conservation, forest reservation, geological exploration, tsetse control, and other schemes of general development.

Recent developments in native systems of tenure

In their Report of 1933 the Kenya Land Commissioners frequently express the opinion that the development of individual tenure as opposed to group tenure was an end devoutly to be wished. But it is not always clear what they mean by individual tenure. In one paragraph they observe that 'the Kiambu district is already launched on a system of tenure quite exceptional in tribalism. It is not yet individual tenure, since the rule still seems to be that cousins separate, but brothers do not, and the group is therefore rather wider than a single family. And it is not even, in all respects, private tenure, since a right of communal pasturage remains. But these restrictions are disappearing and individual tenure is well in sight'.[1]

This passage is somewhat misleading, since all over Africa every married man is commonly entitled to a plot of land for cultivation, and it is not necessary to envisage the break-up of the African family system in order that its members may exercise individual rights. But under the native African system land cannot simply be treated as a private personal possession which may be bought and sold—it can only pass from one person to another by way of inheritance, gift or loan. There is no opportunity, therefore, for speculation nor for the acquisition of large holdings by which their owners may derive profits in the form of purchase price or rent. Landlords are not rentiers, and tenants are not tenants in the English sense, but dependents or friends to whom the land has been lent for a purely nominal sum. Native customary law limits the amount of land that anyone may hold to the amount that he requires for the subsistence of himself and his family. Land may not, therefore, be held by absentee owners. Nor is it held in compact estates, since shifting cultivation is the normal rule and, by the rules of inheritance, good and bad land must be divided out equally. A man's holdings therefore do not constitute a single farm, but are rather a series of fragments scattered over a wide area.

But in Kenya, as elsewhere in Africa, native customary law has been affected by the introduction of commercial crops and a money economy, and by the pressure of population on the land. In some areas, particularly in the Kiambu district, family lands have been converted into private individual holdings, with complete freedom

[1] Cmd. 4556 (1934), para. 522.

of transfer. Farms in fact are being bought and sold: they are often sold to pay off debts, and cases have even occurred when a farmer has been forced to sell his holding in order to pay his Government tax. Fenced-in holdings are also appearing, and even pasture lands are being enclosed. The introduction of the plough[1] has led in places to a new disparity in the division of land. Wealthy natives have been buying ploughs, breaking up large areas, and planting them with wheat, maize and wattle. These new capitalists, if unchecked, may acquire, as their own, land which is now the public domain. In some cases the members of the local Native Councils are said to be partners in this form of exploitation.[2]

These developments are being regarded with concern by the Administration, since they may foreshadow the rise of agricultural debt, the creation of a landless pauper class, and all the other evils that accompany the freedom to traffic in land. Consideration has therefore been given to the desirability of legislation to control the sale and mortgage of land, to prohibit its acquisition by absentees, to limit the maximum and minimum acreage of native holdings, to limit the amount of rent, and to give greater security to tenants.

There are dangers, however, in devising legislation of general application, since local custom displays great variation and it is considered important that land administration should be left as far as possible in the hands of the local authorities and that tenure should be allowed to evolve in a manner suited to the local needs and acceptable to the people. The imposition of a new system from the top is liable to disrupt the social organization.

In most areas of Kenya the sale of land is still contrary to native custom, and it would be unnecessary to introduce rules forbidding it. But such rules may be necessary as a preventive measure, though, where this is so, concomitant steps should be taken to provide a suitable system of agricultural credit. The mortgaging of land is also uncommon, except in the form of pledging with a right of redemption.[3] There are difficulties in fixing maximum and minimum acreages of holdings on account of the varying quality of the soil, the varying requirements of crops, the practice of shifting cultivation, and the fact that family and individual rights over land may already be well established. Many of the Kikuyu would resent

[1] In the Nyanza Province ploughing has become a trade, the owner hiring out his plough and team, with a driver, at a charge of 5/- per acre.

[2] In Nyasaland, Tanganyika and the Gold Coast, many of the wealthier natives are said to be obtaining more than a fair share of land. See pp. 119, 111, 303, and 176. In S. Rhodesia the Commission on Natural Resources reported (in 1939) that detribalized natives were acquiring land which they did not intend to occupy. In Nigeria the same phenomenon was noted by Lord Lugard nearly a quarter of a century ago. (See *The Dual Mandate*, p. 296.) For Ceylon, see pp. 60-61, and for Bechuanaland and Basutoland, see p. 304.

[3] The subject of pledging land is discussed in Chapter XXII.

a restriction of acreage as an unjust impediment to enterprise which would not be imposed on their European neighbours. The imposition of a minimum acreage would deprive many peasants of their only means of existence, although in many parts of Africa, even in Muhammadan areas where the Muhammadan law allows subdivision to the most minute fraction, Native authorities have found it necessary to impose a minimum limit.

The control of the acquisition of land by absentees is again a matter which each local authority may well settle for itself, since in some areas it may be necessary to safeguard the land interests of those who have sought temporary employment away from their homes. Rental conditions (apart from those of resident labourers on European estates) do not seem to have created, as yet, any serious problem in Kenya. Native landowners are generally averse to receiving regular rent, since this might be interpreted as pledging their interest in the land.

Consideration has also been given to the question of instituting local systems for recording transactions in land, whether by way of sale, mortgage or other method. The Kiambu Local Native Council has passed a resolution in favour of registration of titles, the South Nyeri Council in favour of registering all transactions including outright purchases,[1] the Fort Hall and Meru Councils in favour of registering transactions other than outright purchases, and the Embu Native Council in favour of regulations covering the relationship of landlords and tenants.

While full play must be allowed to local initiative, there is nevertheless a need for caution in leaving such questions as the institution of systems of records to Local Native Authorties, since the form of record adopted may decide the form that landholding shall take.[2] The whole question of native tenures would seem to require the most careful co-ordinated study. The Kenya Government is alive to this necessity and has been anxious for some time to obtain the services of trained anthropologists who would provide the necessary factual material. This is all the more urgent in view of the Government's decision that native systems of tenure must, in the interests of land economy, be guided progressively in the direction of compact permanent private holdings. The Government's policy in this matter was well summarised in 1936 by the Governor in the following statement made in the Legislative Council:—'The essential elements,' he said, 'of the new system include the replacement of shifting agriculture by a fixed agriculture which will maintain continuous production from a smaller area, leading to a more balanced

[1] In Nyeri district a system of voluntary registration of land transactions was initiated in 1942.

[2] Lord Hailey has drawn attention to this danger. See *An African Survey*, p. 878.

dietary; the prevention of soil erosion; and the reconditioning of the eroded lands. . . . Small holdings organized within the native system of land tenure, of a size to provide a reasonable return and run on up-to-date rotational lines, provide the method by which the progressive cultivator can go forward himself and at the same time demonstrate to others the proper use of land.'

CHAPTER IX

Tanganyika[1]

TANGANYIKA is mandated territory, which formerly comprised the major part of German East Africa. It has an area of 365,000[2] sq. miles and is therefore the largest territory under British Colonial administration. The population at the end of 1938 was estimated to be as follows:

Europeans	..	9,345
Asiatics ..	..	33,784[3]
Native Africans	..	5,214,800
		5,257,929

The sparsity of population is largely due to the arid conditions that prevail over wide areas of the Territory. The prolonged seasonal drought which occurs between May and October over the greater part of the central region is a serious handicap to the development of agriculture and to a fuller use of land in this area. Famine conditions occur at frequent intervals, and soil erosion is widespread. On the other hand there is a wide range of climate conditions, varying from the cool atmosphere of the Northern and Southern Highlands to the humid heat of the coastal belt, and this

[1] Considerable use has been made in this chapter of the account of land tenure given in *The Handbook of Tanganyika*, by G. F. Sayers. Other works dealing with land tenure in Tanganyika are B. Gutmann's *Recht der Dschagga* (1926), A. T. and G. M. Culwick's *Ubena of the Rivers* (1935), G. Brown and B. Hutt's *Anthropology in Action* (1935), E. C. Baker's *Report on Social and Economic Conditions in the Tanga Province* (1934), Godfrey Wilson's *The Land Rights of Individuals among the Nyakyusa* (1938), and H. Cory and M. M. Hartnoll's *Customary Law of the Haya Tribe* (1945).

[2] This includes 20,000 sq. miles of water.

[3] The 1931 Census figures for Asiatics were:

Indians	..	..	23,422
Goans	..	..	1,722
Arabs	..	..	7,059
Ceylonese	..	..	15
			32,218

The economic influence of Indians in Tanganyika is even more pronounced than in Kenya. To a large extent they control both wholesale and retail business, including the marketing of native agricultural products. They have large interests in sisal production and the ginning of cotton.

permits of the production of a great variety of crops, tropical and sub-tropical. Sisal, cotton, coffee, rice, copra, sesame, and groundnuts are important exports, and tea, sugar and tobacco are also grown for foreign markets. Native food-crops include millets, maize, rice, wheat, many varieties of beans, groundnuts, simsim, cassava, sweet potatoes, yams, taro, various gourds, onions, sugar cane, ochra, bananas, mango, pineapples and coco-nuts.

During the German occupation of Tanganyika all land was declared to be Crown land and the ownership to be vested in the Empire.[1] But the right of the Crown was made subject to the rights of private persons and of chiefs and native communities. Land Commissions were appointed for the purpose of ascertaining what lands were free for disposal as Crown land, and for setting aside, as reserves, areas which would be sufficient both for the present and future needs of the natives.[2] In view of the native practice of shifting cultivation the commissions were required to reserve at least four times the amount of land which was actually under cultivation. But in spite of these precautions, and the fact that some 175 areas in the North-Eastern Highlands were declared as reserves, nearly 2,000,000 acres of the best land were alienated, and the Germans themselves considered that in some localities insufficient allowance had been made for native needs.

Non-native tenure under German rule took the form either of leasehold or of conditional freehold. The leases were for an indefinite period. The lessee could terminate his lease by giving three months' notice, but the Government could not terminate a lease until the end of a period of twenty-five years from the commencement of the lease. A lessee also had the option of purchasing the freehold of his farm, on the fulfilment of certain development conditions.[3] In addition to these two forms of tenure a third was recognized, namely, the acquisition of title by prescription. 'This,' says Mr. Sayers, 'applied in the coastal belt where, through contact with Arabs and Indians and ideas of western civilization, natives had advanced to a recognition of individual ownership, as opposed to the communal tenure which prevails amongst most African tribes.'[4]

[1] By an Imperial Decree of 26th November, 1895.

[2] Ordinance of 4th December, 1896, *Landesgesetzgebung*. Various local ordinances were consolidated in 1902 into a single ordinance which remained in force until the British occupation.

[3] Under conversion measures recently adopted by the Tanganyika Government 369 German leaseholds were converted into freehold between 1936 and 1938. Up to the end of 1938 eighty-five German leaseholds, representing 99,336 acres, had been surrendered or terminated for non-fulfilment of development conditions.

[4] See *The Handbook of Tanganyika*, by G. F. Sayers (1930), p. 243. It may be observed, however, that this form of title does not appear to be fundamentally different from that held by innumerable African natives who are still living under tribal conditions.

Between 1918 and the enactment of the Land Ordinance of 1923 the only alienation of land to non-natives was in the form of yearly licences for the growing of annual crops—cotton as a rule. And during these years the Government set about the task of unravelling the tangle of such German records as could be found. In 1923 the Land Tenure Ordinance (Cap. 68 of the Laws) was enacted. This ordinance laid down for Tanganyika a land policy modelled on that of Northern Nigeria.[1] The Ordinance begins by declaring that 'the existing customary rights of the natives to use and enjoy the land and the natural fruits thereof in sufficient quantity to enable them to provide for the sustenance of themselves, their families, and their posterity, should be assured, protected and preserved'; and that 'the existing native customs with regard to the use and occupation of land should, as far as possible, be preserved'. The whole of the lands of the Territory, whether occupied or unoccupied, are then declared to be public lands, but with the proviso that nothing in the Ordinance shall affect the validity of any title to land or any interest therein lawfully acquired before the date of the commencement of the Ordinance and that all such titles shall have the same effects and validity as they had before.[2] Subject to this proviso all public lands and all rights over them are declared to be under the control and subject to the disposition of the Governor and shall be held for the use and common benefit, direct and indirect, of the natives of the Territory, and no title to the occupation and use of any such lands shall be valid without the consent of the Governor. The Governor, however, in the exercise of these powers over land, must have regard to the native laws and customs existing in the district in which the land is situated.

The Ordinance authorises the Governor to grant rights of occupancy both to natives and to non-natives, for terms not exceeding ninety-nine years, to demand a rental, and to revise the rental at intervals of not more than thirty-three years.[3] Rights of occupancy

[1] Under the terms of the Mandate (Article 6) the mandatory must, in the framing of laws relating to the holding or transfer of land, take into consideration native laws and customs, and respect the rights and safeguard the interests of the native population; no rights may be created in favour of non-natives without the previous consent of the public authorities. These principles had long been characteristic of the land legislation of Northern Nigeria.

[2] This proviso of Section 3 of the Ordinance is ambiguous. Its obvious intention was to protect non-native titles granted by the German Government, but by its wording it would appear to be applicable also to land held by native customary title.

[3] But should the rental be raised the occupier may surrender his rights and in that case is entitled to compensation from the Governor for his unexhausted improvements. The upset rental of agricultural land varies from 20 cents to 2/- per acre per annum. The present practice regarding revision is that this takes place at intervals of twenty years, but there are special stipulations for earlier revision in the event of the opening of a railway within a certain distance of the land.

may not be alienated by natives to non-natives and may be revoked for attempted alienation.[1] They may be revoked for various other reasons, among which is abandonment or non-use of land for a period of five years. It is noteworthy that the devolution of the rights of an occupier is governed in the case of a native by the Deceased Natives Estates Ordinance (Cap. 16), but that where a native is using or occupying land in accordance with native law or custom and without having otherwise obtained a right of occupancy under the Ordinance, the devolution of his rights upon death is regulated by the native law or custom existing in the locality in which the land is situated. This suggests that a native who is given a formal Right of Occupancy ceases to hold his land according to native custom—at least as regards the devolution of his rights. But the Deceased Natives Estates Ordinance itself prescribes that the estate of a member of a native tribe must be administered according to the law of that tribe. Incidentally, the Ordinance also prescribes that if the Governor is satisfied that the disposition of property by will is repugnant to the law of any native tribe he may declare that the will shall not be recognized.

Among other provisions of the Land Tenure Ordinance there is an implied condition in every certificate of occupancy that the occupier binds himself to pay to the Governor on behalf of the previous occupier, if any, the amount found to be payable in respect of any unexhausted improvements existing on the land at the date of entering into occupation.[2] It is also laid down that, except with the approval of the Secretary of State, no single right of occupancy shall be granted to a non-native in respect of any area exceeding 5000 acres. Finally, under the Land Regulations it is declared to be unlawful for any occupier to alienate his right of occupancy by sale, mortgage, charge, transfer, sub-lease, bequest or otherwise, without the consent of the Governor. But this regulation does not apply to transfers between natives. Furthermore, except where expressly varied or excepted, there is implied in every Right of Occupancy a covenant that for holdings of 300 acres or under permanent improvements of a minimum value of twenty shillings per acre (subject to a minimum total of 600 shillings) shall be effected within the first three years of the term, and that additional improvements of the value of ten shillings per acre (subject to a minimum total of 300 shillings) shall be effected within the first five years. For holdings over 300 acres the rates are respectively shillings 6,000 and in addition shillings 4 per acre in respect of every acre over 300 acres,

[1] Under the Law of Property and Conveyancing Ordinance (Sec. 11) there is a general restriction on the transfer to a non-native of land belonging to a native.

[2] There are implied covenants regarding improvements in every Right of Occupancy. These are specified in the Land Regulations of 1926 (Sec. 3).

and (for additional improvements) shillings 3,000 and in addition shillings 2 per acre in respect of every acre over 300 acres.

It will be observed that, under the Land Ordinance just described, freehold is not granted, and the only method of obtaining land is by way of lease, in the form of a Right of Occupancy for a period which may not exceed ninety-nine years. This system has evoked much criticism from non-native settlers, and in Tanganyika, as in Kenya, there has been a demand that land alienation policy should be based on freehold title. In considering this question the Tanganyika Central Development Committee of 1938 observed that, while the alienation of a freehold interest entails the prior extinction of community rights, a ninety-nine lease does not, since at the end of that term, or any succeeding term, the Governor can restore the land to the community. At the same time the Committee considered that a land settlement policy under which the best title obtainable to agricultural land was a right of occupancy for ninety-nine years left much to be desired. The difficulty could, they thought, be overcome by an active application of the principle of compensation for unexhausted improvements, either from the State, if the land is to become public land, or from the incoming tenant, if alienation for the succeeding term is to another party. Elsewhere in their report the Committee observed that precautions taken to safeguard the interests of future generations might be carried to excess and be a deterrent to development.[1]

Another factor affecting land titles in Tanganyika under the present law was mentioned by the Committee. Under the provisions of the Land Acquisition Ordinance (Cap. 71) the term 'public purposes' (for which the State may acquire any land) is defined as including acquisition 'for the use of the native inhabitants of the Territory'. This enlargement of the formal powers of land acquisition imported into titles an element of uncertainty which was neither desirable nor necessary. If, in spite of the investigations made before alienation, it were found during the ninety-nine years that the land was in fact required for the use of the natives, then the method of transfer by private treaty was still available. Under existing conditions the indefeasibility of the titles of non-native land-holders in Tanganyika was undermined by the provisions of the Land Acquisition Ordinance.

The Development Committee also considered that the system of rent revision reduced the value of the leasehold title as a security; that the system of alienating land by auction was open to objection, since the person who made the highest bid was not necessarily the person to whom the land might most usefully be granted; and that

[1] *Report of the Central Development Committee*, paras. 225 and 48. The question of freehold versus leasehold is discussed in Chapter XX.

precise surveys should not be required where adequate identifiable descriptions of the boundaries are possible without survey. To these subjects there will be references at a later stage.[1]

The present policy of the Government of Tanganyika with regard to non-native settlement is to encourage this in every way, provided there is sound reason for believing that settlement will assist in the task of promoting the prosperity and well-being of the community.[2] But many areas are regarded as unsuitable for non-native settlement, and applications for the alienation of land in these areas are not entertained, except in special circumstances. The whole of the Central, Southern, Western and Lake Provinces are closed to non-natives for agricultural and pastoral purposes, except in the case of applicants who are in a position to undertake operations on a large scale, especially in connection with water supplies. This policy has been adopted as the result of (*a*) the recommendations of the Land Development Survey which worked from 1928-32, and (*b*) a proposal by the late Governor, Sir Donald Cameron, in 1929, that large blocks of the territory should be declared to be primarily native areas—a proposal which received the cordial approval of the Secretary of State.[3] At the beginning of 1939 there were 2,069 non-native holdings of alienated agricultural and pastoral land, with a total area of 2,094,197 acres. Of this 888,910 acres were freehold, and 1,205,287 were leasehold. 766,725 acres were held by British subjects (other than British Indians and South African Dutch), 470,781 by Germans, 269,118 by British Indians, 204,039 by Greeks, and 56,818 by South African Dutch. Missionary societies held 92,348 acres.

Coming now to the consideration of native rights and the native systems of tenure, it has been indicated already that theTanganyika Land Tenure Ordinance is a confused piece of legislation. It sets out to protect and preserve native customary rights, and in order to do so declares all occupied (as well as unoccupied) lands to be 'public lands'—not 'native lands' as in the Northern Nigerian legislation.[4] But at the same time it declares that previously existing

[1] See Chapters XXI and XXIII.

[2] This statement of policy was made in Legislative Council, with the addendum that 'Non-native settlement is not to be regarded as inimical to the interests of the native population: on the contrary it is an integral part of the policy whereby Government plans to advance the general prosperity'. See the *Annual Report of the Department of Agriculture, 1938*, p. 8.

[3] Details of the steps by which land came to be closed to alienation to non-natives will be found in Appendix III of the *1938 Report to the Council of the League of Nations on the Administration of Tanganyika Territory* (Colonial No. 165). The account given, however, fails to bring out the fact that the Tanganyika Government had followed precedents set by the former German Government.

[4] It is not clear what exactly is the legal connotation of the term 'public lands'. The Ordinance clearly envisages an administrative relation by which these lands are placed under public control in order to protect native interests without

titles and interests are to have the same effect as before—a provision which would seem to exclude lands held by native customary title from the operation of the succeeding clause whereby all public lands and all rights thereto are stated to be subject to the control and disposition of the Governor, without whose consent no title shall be valid. Yet the intention of the Ordinance is quite clearly that lands held by native customary title shall be regarded as 'public lands', and if this is so then no native customary title would have any inherent validity, apart from the Governor's consent.

Section 5 of the Ordinance, however, requires the Governor, in the exercise of his powers, to pay regard to native custom. Yet he is authorised to grant to natives Rights of Occupancy the conditions of which are foreign to native custom. The holder of a Right of Occupancy is required to improve his land according to rules unknown to native law. He may be called on to pay a rent subject to revision, and his right may be revoked for a variety of reasons, most of which are foreign to native conceptions of holding land.[1] The term Right of Occupancy is defined in the Ordinance so as to 'include the title of a native or a native community lawfully using or occupying land in accordance with native law and custom', yet when the Permanent Mandates Commission expressed the opinion that the Governor's powers to revoke a Right of Occupancy might conflict with the rights derived from native customary occupation, the Tanganyika Government replied that the Governor's powers of revocability did not apply to land held under native customary title.[2]

Nevertheless, the actual working of legislation is of more importance than the form in which it is expressed, and the Land Tenure Ordinance seems to have served its purpose of ensuring general security to natives in the occupation of their lands, while at the same time making it possible for individuals to acquire private rights through the formal grant of Certificates of Occupancy. So far there have been few, if any, applications by natives for a Right of Occupancy over agricultural or pastoral land,[3] and Lord Hailey

prejudicing rights already acquired. But are 'public lands' to be regarded as State property? Or is the whole of Tanganyika Territory to be so regarded? In this connection see Annex 2 to the minutes of the Third Session of the Permanent Mandates Commission; also Annex 13, 1924 (VI), and Annex 13, 1926.

[1] When proposals were made in 1912 to apply to Southern Nigeria the land legislation of Northern Nigeria there was strong opposition on the part of the people of Southern Nigeria. Sir William Geary observed that 'to turn an occupier who, under native law, holds his land rent free in perpetuity into a rent-paying short term lessee on a precarious tenure is, bluntly, confiscation'. See Lord Lugard, *The Dual Mandate*, p. 292.

[2] See *P.M.C.* (22), November 1932, p. 157; *Tanganyika Report*, 1932, App. XIII, p. 146, and *P.M.C.* (34), 1938, p. 157.

[3] But natives occupying plots in the vicinity of townships have applied for permission to rent houses to non-natives for trading purposes and have been required to take out a Right of Occupancy and to pay rent.

has observed that a wide concession of individual titles over native lands, even if accepted as desirable in point of policy, could not be made effective without a land survey and the provision of machinery for registration.[1]

In Tanganyika individual ownership of land by natives was formerly confined to the coast regions, but the development of plantation crops, such as coffee, has led to a wide extension of the conception of private proprietary rights. The Government regards this tendency as inevitable, and in 1938 one senior official observed that 'either we must withdraw the land from the disposal of the tribal authorities and parcel out holdings in the name of Government, or we must persuade tribal authorities to recognize the rights of individuals in fixed portions of land within their jurisdiction. By the latter method land would not be taken out of the tribal area and would still be subject to native law and custom, which would consequently require amendment'.

In this connection it may be noted that individual peasant holdings have been demonstrated in Tanganyika since 1933. A holding represents an economic and compact unit of land, with improved house and cattle homestead. The object of the scheme is to show that by crop rotation and the use of cattle manure a unit of land sufficient to maintain a family can be permanently cultivated, with soil fertility unimpaired, if not increased. Nevertheless, the Director of Agriculture has expressed the opinion that the form of tenure suitable for organized peasant settlement need not necessarily be of an individual character. The view that only by the individual ownership of the land can sound agricultural progress be achieved is just as erroneous as the view that tribal ownership of land should, under no circumstances, be permitted to give way to individualism. Local conditions must determine the character of the tenure. Thus, while in the Kingolwira settlement[2] the necessity for clearing the tsetse bush, providing cattle dips, and encouraging the selected peasant holders to adopt as early as possible all the improved methods of mixed farming, has dictated the form of layout on individual rather than on communal lines, a different line of policy has been pursued in the densely cultivated and strongly tribalized

[1] *An African Survey*, p. 848.

[2] The Kingolwira Peasant Settlement Scheme is described in Sessional Paper No. 1, 1938. The area of each holding is 14 acres. Of these 4 acres are set aside for grazing and timber (for fuel and building poles). The remaining 10 acres are given over to arable crops, the main rotation being sorghum, cotton, maize and groundnuts, with subsidiaries of cassava, sweet potatoes, vegetables and fruit. Holdings are so arranged that anti-erosion measures are comprehensive with those of the whole settlement: for example, the grazing strips of the holdings run one to the other through the settlement. As more holdings are developed the tsetse fly area is pushed back and the peasant holders can then with safety purchase cattle from the herd maintained by the Agricultural Department.

country of Sukuma. Here the chiefs would not look favourably on the layout of ideal peasant-holdings, which they would regard as an inroad on native custom, and in particular on their own rights of allocating native lands. Nor do the conditions of cultivated steppe call for the same measure of organized settlement as at Kingolwira. So, in Sukuma, it was decided to extend the principles of mixed farming by propaganda through the native authorities. In this way the support of the Chiefs was quickly secured, with the result that (in 1938) 100,000 cattle-owning natives were utilizing cattle manure for crop production—the first step towards a static system of agriculture.[1]

Tanganyika has been fortunate in having a number of Administrative officers who have taken a keen interest in native systems of tenure and have produced very valuable reports. Among these are Messrs. A. T. Culwick, J. L. Fairclough and D. W. Malcolm. It may be of interest to record here some of the salient features reported by these officers.

In dealing with tenure conditions in the Bukoba District Mr. A. T. Culwick observes that there are two classes of lands (1) open lands and (2) plantation lands (banana and coffee). The open lands consist of (*a*) grazing lands on which anyone may pasture his stock, and (*b*) plots for use under a shifting system of cultivation. The latter are obtainable by applying to the local representative of the chief, in return for a gift of corn at harvest. Once a plot has been conferred the occupier has a lien on its use against all comers.

Banana and coffee plantations are in a different category, since they may take seven years or more to create. A plantation may be acquired in various ways: (1) by inheritance; (2) by allocation from the Chief on payment of a land fee of ten shillings to the Native Treasury; (3) by private purchase; (4) in satisfaction of a Native Court judgement; or (5) by obtaining from the Native Authorities (on payment of five shillings to the Native Treasury) a plot of virgin land and making it into a plantation.

With the exception of land acquired by inheritance[2] the rights in a plantation are little short of freehold. The owner may pawn or mortgage his plantation, or dispose of it by sale, gift, or bequest to any other native. But if he abandons it or dies without heirs it

[1] *Report of the Director of Agriculture, Tanganyika, 1938*. Elsewhere the Director of Agriculture has observed that cash advances made by the Government or Native Administrations to *individuals* may be a serious impediment to progress. They not only create a load of debt, which experience in the Union and in Nigeria indicates to be irrecoverable without inflicting serious hardship in periods of depressed produce prices, but they also create the impression of an endless source of supply.

[2] In most native societies there is freedom of disposition in the case of acquired property, but restrictions are imposed in the case of inherited property.

reverts to the Chief for re-allocation.[1] Many plantations have plots known as 'mbuga' attached to them for special cultivations. These have still more of the character of freehold, since, even if they are left untended, they do not revert to the Chief for redistribution.

The tenure thus described is known as 'kibanja' (plantation), but there is another tenure known as 'nyarubanja' (large plantation) under which the farmer owns a number of plantations, keeping the central one for himself and letting out the others. He pays an annual peppercorn rent to the Government[2] (in recognition of the Government's title to the land), and he receives from each of his tenants a proportion of the crop. He may be deprived of the plantation occupied by a tenant for certain offences against the tenant; he may not pledge the plantation of a tenant; nor may a tenant's plantation be attached and sold to satisfy a creditor of the owner. He may not terminate the occupancy of a tenant except for certain offences, and must allow the sons of tenants to continue the occupancy. These rules have been made under Section 15 of the Native Authority Ordinance. The evolution of this form of tenure is of considerable interest, and a separate note on the subject is attached. Here it need only be remarked that the 'nyarubanja' system is being gradually extinguished by the Government of Tanganyika, a policy long ago adopted by the Government of Uganda in connection with a similar form of tenure in Bunyoro.[3]

Mr. Culwick considered that the native law of land afforded general security of tenure and was well able to modify itself in order to meet new agricultural conditions. But greater control was required in certain directions, and Mr. Culwick proposed that rules should be passed under the Native Authority Ordinance that:—

(1) No native should be allowed to sell, mortgage or pledge any land or rights in land without the consent of the Native Authority.

(2) The Native Authority should withhold its consent unless it could be shown that the land in question was not essential to the maintenance of the holder's dependants.

(3) All transfers of land or rights in land should be registered by the Native Authority.

Mr. Culwick considered that only rights in developed land should be capable of sale, and that undeveloped land should remain, as at present, at the disposal of the community. This would discourage

[1] Ownership is not therefore absolute. The farmer enjoys a perpetual right of usufruct so long as he exercises the right.

[2] The rent is collected by the Native Authorities on behalf of the Government who then remit half the rents collected to the Native Treasury.

[3] See pp. 138 et seq.

land-hoarding and speculation, but would encourage the enterprising farmer. Unrestricted right of sale was bound to lead to the creation of a landless class, and the danger would be greatest in times of drought, floods, or locusts, when peasant cultivators would be tempted to part with their rights for immediate payments of money or of food. Land should not be used as a means of paying debts unless it were surplus land, or surplus to the debtor's subsistence requirements.

Mr. D. W. Malcolm, in a valuable study on land utilization in Sukuma, agrees with Mr. Culwick that the traditional native system of land-holding does not involve insecurity of tenure for the cultivator.[1] In fact it gives greater security than is usually co-existent with a proprietary régime. It avoids the dangers which normally flow from the unrestricted rights of encumbering or transferring land, but at the same time it is capable of modification to meet the needs of changing economic conditions. Nevertheless, there is no reason to suppose that individualization of tenure is necessary or desirable within measurable time and Mr. Malcolm considered that individual sales of immovable property should not be recognized. The German authorities had prohibited the system of land sales which had evolved in some areas during periods of extreme congestion, and recently the Federation of Nyanza chiefs had ruled that trees, as well as other immovable property, should be considered as village estate.

In Sukuma there are five methods by which land may be acquired: (1) by inheritance; (2) by the renting of personal grazing reserves; (3) by borrowing plots for a season or term of years; (4) by allocation (to new settlers); and (5) by clearing virgin land.

Land once granted cannot be taken away, so long as it is being used. The only reason for which a village headman may take away a field is in order to adjust a cattle track leading to grazing or water. This he may only do after harvest, and he must then provide a new field of equal value. If a farmer goes off on a journey, leaving his wife and family, these remain in possession of his land. If he leaves no one at home, but his food stores and household goods are there as evidence of his intention to return, then his holding may not be re-allocated, though some of his fields may be lent to another. Eventually, if he had failed to return, his possessions would be handed

[1] Mr. Malcolm gives an excellent definition of the traditional African system based on the village-group of occupier cultivators. The essence of the system, he says, consists of individual land-rights limited usually to the period of effective occupation, controlled as regards rights of transfer, restricted in relation to succession, and collectively forming the village unit of occupancy. Proprietary rights of the European pattern, on the other hand, are individual rights which are not limited by conditions of effective occupation, and the holder is free to encumber or alienate.

over to relatives, and his farm would be assigned to some new comer.[1]

In some parts of Sukuma individuals have established rights over grazing areas and demand rents from cattle-owners for their use.[2] In other areas, however, grazing grounds are lent without any rental charge. Disputes over grazing boundaries are a frequent cause of litigation, particularly where individuals have sought to reserve areas with a view to producing short, sweet herbage. Personally-owned grazing grounds may form a patchwork, the boundaries of which are not easily distinguished.

With the development of animal husbandry and schemes for water conservation, there is a likelihood of considerable change in the local land laws. If, for example, private individuals were to build dams on their own account, they would clearly establish private rights. At present, however, schemes for improving the water supplies are carried out collectively by the villagers.[3] Again, the clashing of interests between cattle-owners and farmers may necessitate the construction of more permanent boundaries, thus crystallizing private rights. As progress is made in mixed farming there will be a reduction in the seasonal movements of stock, and a greater pressure on the available arable land.

Among other changes noted by Mr. Malcolm are that, whereas formerly all houses were regarded as village property, since they were constructed by the collective efforts of the villagers, nowadays it is not uncommon for a man to build his own house with bricks purchased by himself, so that houses may now become private property which the owners are free to sell. Again, by buying ploughs, many farmers are increasing the area of the land they can farm, and this has led to an increase in the practice of borrowing land. Many are getting rich at the expense of their neighbours. Moreover, as it has become usual in Sukuma to pay for agricultural assistance, the rich man who can spare an ox to pay for collective

[1] But, in many parts of Africa, rights in ancestral lands are not lost by absence, however prolonged. In the Punjab 'The ancient custom of the country permits an absentee co-sharer in a village community to recover possession of his original holding upon his return to the village and the payment of losses, irrespective of the length of his dispossession. This customary right, however, may be controlled by express agreement.' See W. H. Rattigan, op. cit., p. 315.

[2] The conversion of bush lands into well-demarcated grazing-grounds involves a good deal of labour. Private grazing-grounds kept in good condition have become necessary in many localities owing to the proximity of tsetse fly belts which restrict the range of pasturage. A man may own a grazing ground without owning any cattle, and so may lease the grazing for a season or longer.

[3] In Bechuanaland people making dams for themselves, or deepening pans acquire private rights over the water. Some boreholes are owned by small groups of men described as 'companies'. Some wells are owned in common by all the members of the ward, others by a number of families. See I. Schapera, op. cit., p. 210.

labour is tending to become richer, while the poorer classes, with few cattle or goats, are descending lower on the economic ladder.[1]

Generally, Mr. Malcolm considers that the existing forms of collectivism should be maintained and developed as far as possible. They are eminently suitable for furthering government schemes connected with agricultural development, soil erosion, water conservation, and the redistribution of cattle. As an example of collective ownership Mr. Malcolm cites the communal grain fields found in many villages which are worked by all the villagers to provide grain for the poor or for those who have been called away from their homes on Government or Native Administration work. On the other hand, the formal creation of individual title on an extensive scale would not only be premature in existing economic circumstances but would also impugn the validity of existing forms of customary tenure.

In Tanganyika the Native Authorities have shown considerable initiative in introducing modifications into the native land law. Thus, in Bukoba, they have recently drafted rules limiting the sale, mortgage and pawning of land held in individual ownership. The Chagga Council have enacted Soil Erosion Rules, and Rules for the Conservation of Water, which impose severe limitations on tenure. Thus it is prescribed that 'the occupier of any existing land under cultivation which in the opinion of the Native Authority is insufficiently protected from erosion shall take such measures to stop soil erosion as the Native Authority, with the advice of the District Agricultural Officer, may prescribe'. In another area the Soil Erosion Rules include the general provision that 'no person shall open up or cultivate new land except upon such terms and conditions as the tribal authorities may lay down in regard to any particular area or in relation to any particular plot'.

This chapter may be concluded by an account of the procedure recently laid down by the Tanganyika Government for dealing with the rights of natives occupying lands for which non-natives have applied, or which are required by the Government for public purposes. If the Governor decides that the alienation of the land in question can be considered at all, then an Administrative Officer is required to prepare a report. In doing so he must bear in mind that, although the land for which application is made may not be immediately required for the present needs of the tribe, it may be required

[1] The growth of the squatter system is to some extent an indication of the loss of land rights. Mr. Cory and Mrs. Hartnoll state that among the Haya of Tanganyika there are many squatters on plantations. These have little security of tenure, being liable to eviction without compensation for improvements either to house or land. Some squatters, however, are business partners of the owner, with whom they may have written contracts defining their share in the cash crop of the plantation. See *Customary Law of the Haya Tribe*, pp. 145 *et seq.*

at some future date. There should be appended therefore to the report a certificate, if this can be properly given, to the effect that the land is not now required and as far as can be foreseen will not be required.

If the land is not required, any natives resident on it may continue to reside as independent occupiers, or else remove to another area. If they remain they must be allowed a generous extent of land, rent free, and without being required to obtain any documentary title. If they remove to another area they must be given compensation for the loss of their hut (at so much per room), for the loss of their land (at so much for each acre of land cultivated) and for the loss of grazing (at so much per head of cattle). In addition there must be an allowance of 50% as compensation for the general inconvenience of moving. Where the land is close to a railway or motor road the amount of the compensation would be greater. Natives not actually residing on the land, but using it as grazing ground, must also be treated according to these general principles.

These rules are laid down in a government circular (No. 12 of 1941). It would be interesting to know the procedure followed in other dependencies, under similar circumstances.

A NOTE ON *NYARUBANJA* TENURE IN THE BUKOBA DISTRICT[1]

The ancestors of the present ruling chiefs (Bakama) migrated from Bunyoro in Uganda some two or three hundred years ago. After deposing the local rulers they assumed despotic powers, and complete control of the disposition of all lands. They exacted tribute from all their subjects in the form of cowries, goats and one month's labour in each year. They were also accustomed to grant fiefs or *nyarubanja* (i.e. estates) to (*a*) their sons and daughters, (*b*) successful leaders in war, and (*c*) advisers, favourites, and those who had rendered signal services. The fief was an arbitrary assignment of lands occupied by peasants who were compelled either to resign their holdings or remain as tenants or serfs of the fiefholder, paying to him the dues and services formerly rendered to the central chief.

In 1922 Mr. D. L. Baines, a Senior Commissioner who had had experience of the abuses of similar forms of tenure in Uganda, directed that all dealings in *nyarubanja* should cease and all *nyarubanja* should be registered, with the names of their owners ad tenants. These instructions were only partially carried out. In 1926 Sir Donald Cameron, the Governor, gave general directions for the

[1] This note is based on a report by Mr. J. L. Fairclough and also on Appendix VI of the *1938 Report to the Council of the League of Nations* (Colonial No. 165).

commutation of all native forms of tribute and service, and this had the automatic effect of transforming the character of *nyarubanja* tenure. The landlords, deprived of the services of their tenants, demanded that their title to the land should be formally recognized by the Government, but the terms of the Land Ordinance precluded the grant of this concession. In 1929, however, the Government agreed that the Bukoba chiefs should be allowed to pass rules (under Section 15 of the Native Authority Ordinance) whereby

(*a*) the fiefholder or landlord should, in recognition of the Government's title to the land, pay a rent of five shillings per annum for 1–9 holdings, ten shillings for 10–19 holdings, fifteen shillings for 20–29 holdings, and twenty shillings for more than 29 holdings;

(*b*) the landlord should be allowed to harvest a certain number of bunches of bananas every year in the holding of each of his tenants, together with the crop of one coffee tree in every fifty, with a maximum of five trees, which should be specially chosen and marked. He should also be entitled to the produce of bark-cloth trees, where such existed.

These provisions are still in force, and tenants of *nyarubanja* are no longer serfs. The only evidence that their holdings are not their own property is the annual collection of rent in kind, which is now carefully regulated by law.

The evolution of *nyarubanja* tenure in Tanganyika should be compared with that of the *kibanja* tenure in Bunyoro (see p. 138).

CHAPTER X

Nyasaland

IN Nyasaland the land policy of the Government has been assimilated to that of Tanganyika. The prosperity of the Protectorate is held to depend upon the development of its agricultural resources. In this development a limited number of European planters may play, as they have already played, a leading part: but in the main the task must be carried out by the natives themselves, under European guidance. The whole of the unalienated land of the Protectorate has, therefore, (by the Native Land Trust Order in Council of 1936) been declared to be Native Trust Land, to be administered for the benefit of the natives. The significance of this declaration will be appreciated when it is stated that at the present time less than 5% of the territory is alienated land.

As early as 1884 European companies and settlers had begun to acquire land by purchasing it from native chiefs, and when a protectorate was declared in 1891 these transactions were regularized by the issue of 'Certificates of Claim', although Sir Harry Johnston, who issued the certificates, was doubtful whether chiefs had in fact any right to alienate tribal lands in perpetuity.[1] 15% of the Protectorate had been alienated in this way, the major part being held by the British South Africa Company.[2] It is noteworthy that although the rights derived from the 'Certificates of Claim' were freehold rights they were limited by a clause which provided that no native village or plantation existing on the estate at the date of the certificate was to be disturbed without the consent of Her Majesty's Commissioner, but that if such consent were given the site of the village would revert to the proprietor of the estate. New villages or plantations were not to be made on the estate without the consent of the proprietor. These provisions had important consequences which will be described presently.

When the various claims to title had been settled, the government concluded agreements with all the chiefs in the Protectorate, by which the power of further alienation was withdrawn from the chiefs and vested in the Crown. The Crown itself subsequently alienated a further 143,000 acres in freehold, but in 1936 it obtained from the British South Africa Company surface rights over 2,731,700 acres in the North Nyasa district, in return for confirming the Company's claim to the mineral rights in the area.

[1]See *British Central Africa*, 1898, p. 13.

[2] A commission appointed in 1921 found the total area of the Protectorate to be 25,162,000 acres of which 3,705,300 were held under Certificates of Claim. The share of the British South Africa Company was estimated at 2,731,700 acres.

In 1936 the land policy of Nyasaland was stabilized by the enactment of the Native Trust Land Order in Council. Under this the land of the Protectorate was divided into three classes: (*a*) Crown Lands, (*b*) Reserved Lands, and (*c*) Native Trust Lands. Crown lands are all lands and interests in land acquired on behalf of His Majesty, and include all Government sites. Reserved lands comprise land, other than Crown lands, within the boundaries of a township, reserves at Government stations, forest reserves, and all lands and interests in land (other than yearly tenancies) alienated prior to the enactment of the Order in Council.[1] Included in the reserved lands are the freehold estates, which in 1938 amounted to 1,214,493 acres.[2]

Native Trust Land is all the land in the Protectorate other than Crown and Reserved Lands. It constitutes 95% of the land of the Protectorate. It is vested in the Secretary of State for the Colonies and is administered for the use and benefit of the natives. Rights of occupancy may be granted for a erm not exceeding ninety-nine years at a rent revisable at intervals of not more than thirty-three years, but before any such grant can be made the Native Authority of the area must be consulted, and if the grant is made the proceeds must be paid into the Native Treasury. Development conditions are imposed, and all mineral, oil and timber rights are reserved.

It will be observed that in Nyasaland there is no system of native reserves as in Kenya. Nor is there any settler problem. Freehold rights are no longer accorded, and the only method of obtaining freehold is by private purchase from those who are already in possession of freehold property. The interests of the native majority have in fact been made paramount, a policy which, it must be admitted, was facilitated by the fact that, following the world slump of 1930 onwards, there was little demand for land on the part of Europeans.

Problems have, however, arisen in connection with the rights of natives living on European estates. Under their Certificates of Claim the European estate-owners were required to respect the rights of villagers already settled on the estates. But the owners failed to make any register of these villagers, and this led to endless complications when in course of time it became necessary to distinguish the original settlers from the many immigrants who had subsequently arrived. At an early stage the landlords demanded rent from all resident natives, but a High Court judgement in 1903 made it clear that rent could not legally be exacted from the original villagers. Other landlords, as the successors of chiefs, claimed to be

[1] But the alienation of mineral rights only does not constitute an interest in land.

[2] Excluding yearly tenancies the area held under leases was (in 1938) about 88,220 acres.

entitled to 'customary' labour from resident natives, and as labour soon became more important than rent a system known as 'tangata' grew up, by which tenants could pay their rent either in the form of labour or by giving the landlord a pre-emptive claim to their crops.[1] But here again difficulties occurred in distinguishing original residents from later immigrants, and also in arranging conditions of living and of cultivation which would be satisfactory to all resident natives and at the same time would allow the landlords to make the best use of their land.

Various attempts were made to deal by legislation with the many problems involved, and in 1928 a comprehensive measure known as 'The Natives on Private Estates Ordinance' was enacted. This is one of the most interesting attempts to deal with native rental conditions in Africa and may be compared with the 'Busulu and Envujo law' which was enacted by the native government of Buganda in 1927.[2] The Ordinance provides that all estate owners must keep a register of all natives resident on their estates and may not allow any but one of the following categories to take up residence:

(*a*) Resident natives (i.e. those who own or reside in huts with the knowledge of the estate-owner; or who have been in residence for a period of three years).

(*b*) Exempted natives (domestic servants or temporary labourers).

(*c*) Natives under special agreement (i.e. those given permission to reside subject to a written contract, approved by a magistrate, that they will work for the landlord for a period of not more than six months in any one year).

Under the Ordinance every resident native is entitled to a site for his hut and to such cultivable land, within a reasonable distance from his hut, as may be sufficient for growing his subsistence crops. But he may only grow commercial crops with the landlord's consent. He is permitted to take, from undeveloped land on the estate, grass and other material for the erection and maintenance of his hut. If he is required to move his hut or his farm he is entitled to compensation. He is liable to pay rent to the landlord at a rate fixed by the District Rent Board, subject to a maximum approved by the

[1] For an interesting parallel (and contrast) compare the evolution of rental conditions on the native-owned 'mailo' estates of Uganda (pp. 132-5). See also footnote (1) at p. 128.

[2] See Chapter XII, p. 135. Since many of the European estates provide their native tenants with an agricultural supervisory service and credit facilities, the Nyasaland system may also be compared with that of the Colonial Sugar Refining Company of Fiji or the Gezira Cotton Scheme in the Sudan (see pp. 204 et seq. and the Appendix).

Governor.[1] But, if he prefers to do so, he may work for wages in lieu, or in abatement, of rent. Under this arrangement a rebate of rent due may be earned (in addition to wages) at the rate of one-third for each month's work between October and February, and one-sixth for each month's work between March and September. Proportionate rebates may be earned in respect of shorter periods than a month.

The wages must be at the prevailing market rate, and if the owner is unable to offer work he must allow the resident native to grow and sell to the landlord such economic crops as will be the equivalent of the rent. If the landlord neither offers work nor allows the resident native to grow and sell economic crops, then he loses all claim to rent. No landlord may order a resident native to quit his estate without giving six months notice prior to the end of a quinquennial period. The order to quit must be served by the District Commissioner, who must first be satisfied that less than 10% of the resident natives have been given notice to quit at the end of the quinquennial period. But resident natives may be summarily ejected if the District Commissioner is satisfied that they have been guilty of misconduct or failed to pay any rent due within one month of its being recoverable. If a native is ordered to quit, or is summarily removed, it is laid down by an amending Ordinance (No. 16 of 1938) that the Government must provide for his settlement on Native Trust Land.

There are two further important provisions in this Ordinance. The first is that nothing in the Ordinance shall prevent an estate owner from leasing any particular plot to an individual tenant, provided the agreement is in writing. And the second makes it lawful for the Governor in Council to acquire compulsorily for native settlements an area not exceeding one-tenth of the area of any private estate which exceeds ten thousand acres, by giving in exchange Crown land of equivalent value elsewhere. But the Goverment's power to take land in this way from any particular estate may only be exercised once.

It will be seen that this Ordinance is an attempt to give equal treatment all round. If an estate cannot offer employment and refuses to allow the growing of economic crops, no demand for rent is made: while in the case of unworked estates with absentee owners the resident natives are free to do as they please. But the Ordinance has been criticized because of its failure to make any distinction between original villagers and later immigrants. All alike must work for the estate owner or grow economic crops for him or else pay rent. In 1934 a Select Committee of the Legislative Council suggested

[1] In 1938 the amount of rent payable in the Blantyre district varied from 10/- to £1.

steps by which any surviving rights of the original villagers might be equitably extinguished; but no action was taken on this proposal. In 1938, Sir Robert Bell considered that conditions which had become stabilized might well be left alone, though if it were still possible to distinguish between original settlers and later immigrants then full rights of occupancy might be accorded to the former over defined areas of land to be selected by agreement.[1]

Before leaving the subject of land tenure in Nyasaland it may be observed that in 1939 the Native Welfare Committee suggested that, in order to relieve congestion in certain areas, the Government might have to buy back blocks of freehold land and also impose some limitation on the amount of land which might be held by any single farmer. It appeared that many of the wealthier natives had obtained more than their fair share of land and were using it to cultivate cash crops by means of paid labour, much of which was immigrant. Owing to the absence of supervision no attempt was being made by the labourers to follow sound methods of husbandry. Moreover, many of the poorer farmers in these congested areas had been left with insufficient land to meet the requirements of a meagre subsistence.[2]

[1] See the Report of the Commission appointed to enquire into the financial position and further development of Nyasaland, 1938 (Colonial No. 152), pp. 36 and 37.

[2] Postscript. It has recently (March 1944) been announced that the Nyasaland Government has acquired an estate of 3200 acres in the Blantyre district with a view to settling natives there under a controlled scheme having an educational basis to demonstrate the best use of land.

CHAPTER XI

Northern Rhodesia

IN 1923 the British Government came to an agreement with the British South Africa Company by which the Company, in return for the confirmation of its rights over all minerals in Northern Rhodesia (Barotseland excepted), surrendered its rights over land. It was agreed, however, that the Company should retain its title to certain freehold areas in North-Eastern Rhodesia which it held under 'Certificates of Claim' granted in 1893 by the Commissioner and Consul-General in British Central Africa. A concession of 10,000 sq. miles in North-Eastern Rhodesia given by the Company in 1895 to the North Charterland Company would also be maintained, and the Company would be given half the proceeds of all sales or leases of land in North-Western Rhodesia until the year 1965.

By this agreement the Crown obtained unfettered control over all the other land of the territory, with the exception of Barotseland, in which native rights in land had long been secured by treaties.[1] The Crown forthwith proceeded to set up native reserves, wherever local circumstances appeared to make these necessary, and when the scheme had been completed (*c.* 1930) the land situation in Northern Rhodesia was found to be as follows:

	Acres
Area alienated in freehold and individual titles	8,794,775[2]
Game and Forest Reserves	5,011,690
Barotseland	36,819,200
Native Reserves	34,712,800[3]
Crown Land	100,499,800
Total	185,838,265

The policy of establishing native reserves was an attempt to im-

[1] But the alienation of land in Barotseland was forbidden by the Barotse-North-Western Rhodesia Order in Council, 1899. An important study on land tenure in Barotseland has recently been made by Dr. Max Gluckman and published under the title of *Essays on Lozi Land Tenure* (Rhodes-Livingstone Institute 1943). This was not available at the time this chapter was written.

[2] In 1942 it was reckoned that only 3,000,000 acres were alienated to non-natives, not including 410,000 acres sold or retained by the North Charterland Company for alienation.

[3] In 1942 the amount of land allotted to Native Reserves was estimated to be 31,000,000 acres.

plement the principle laid down by the British Government in 1900 that sufficient land should, from time to time, be assigned in Northern Rhodesia for native occupation.[1] But the policy when put into practice did not prove to be satisfactory. Many native communities objected to being removed from Crown lands, and many European farmers found themselves unable to obtain labour. Some of the reserves had insufficient access to the railway, others became overcrowded, and in many much damage had been done by the injudicious use of the plough, as well as by over-grazing and wanton destruction of timber. Large areas of the reserves proved to be uninhabitable owing to the absence of water supplies or presence of tsetse fly; and at the same time many areas from which the natives had been removed were left without inhabitants. A policy of segregation, if it was to be successful at all, should have been accompanied by a systematic programme of development.[2]

The unsatisfactory condition of the native reserves, coupled with the fact that European settlement in Northern Rhodesia had proved to be very much smaller than was at one time anticipated,[3] led the Government in 1938 to formulate a new land policy modelled on that adopted by the Nyasaland Government in 1936. But instead of declaring the whole of the unalienated land to be Native Trust land (as in Nyasaland) it was decided that areas of unalienated land which were shown by ecological survey to be suited for non-native settlement, and by geological survey to contain workable mineral deposits, should be retained as Crown Land. Special provision should also be made for settled populations of urbanized and detribalized natives who, in Northern Rhodesia, as elsewhere in Africa, are becoming an increasingly important section of the community.

The Government's new policy was announced in July 1942 and may be summarized as follows:[4]

> *Crown Land* will be available for non-native settlement and for mining development. It will include land certified to be suitable for European development and all land known to contain mineral resources. It may also include areas the final allocation of which

[1] Under the North-Eastern Rhodesia Order in Council of 1900.

[2] A full discussion of the origin and development of the Native Reserves will be found in the *Report of the Commission to enquire into the financial and economic position of Northern Rhodesia 1938* (Colonial No. 145), pp. 56-73. See also the reports of Major Orde Browne, Adviser to the Colonial Office on Native Labour, (Colonial No. 150/1938), and of the 1938 Royal Commission under Lord Bledisloe.

[3] In 1938 the European population was 13,000. The African population was 1,366,425, of whom 550,000 were in Barotseland. There was thus only one European for every 105 Africans.

[4] See the *Northern Rhodesia Government Gazette* of July 31st, 1942, General Notice No. 16. Also Cmd. 6023/1939.

cannot at present be determined. *Native Trust Land* will be vested in the Secretary of State for the Colonies and will be set apart for the exclusive use of the natives of Northern Rhodesia. But provision will be made for the alienation of land for specific periods to (*a*) individual natives; (*b*) for the purpose of establishing townships; and (*c*) to non-natives in special cases and for limited areas, where it can be shown that alienation will be for the benefit of the natives and the land will not be required for direct occupation; and provided also that in such special cases not more than 6000 acres are alienated in each of the existing Provinces. It is mainly in respect of these three provisions for alienation that Native Trust Land will differ from the existing system of Native Reserves. For it is not intended that the establishment of Native Trust Lands shall stand in the way of the development of railways or of mineralized areas; and any areas which are known to contain minerals of economic value will be excluded from the Native Trust Lands. The Native Reserves may eventually be merged in the Native Trust Lands, should this appear to be desirable and in accordance with the wishes of the people. In the meantime the establishment of Native Trust Land will provide fully for the agricultural requirements of the natives and will also allow ready access to existing and prospective railway lines and to all-weather roads.

The new policy has not yet (1944) been implemented by legislation but it is anticipated that, when this has been done, Native Trust Land will embrace the following areas: (*a*) the whole of North-Eastern Rhodesia, apart from the British South Africa Company's old freehold estates in the extreme North round Abercorn, and the North Charterland Company's concession in the extreme east round Fort Jameson; (*b*) the whole of North-Western Rhodesia outside the Railway belt, with the exception of a small area in the extreme North-West, which is thought to be suitable for European farming; and (*c*) the majority of the available unalienated Crown land in the British South Africa Company's old estates in the North, in the North Charterland Company's concession in the East and in the Railway belt, leaving comparatively small areas in the three last named parts of the country as Crown land available for settlement or mineral developments.

As a preliminary to the carrying out of the new policy the Governor of Northern Rhodesia appointed, in 1943, three commissions to make recommendations regarding the division of land into Crown Land and Native Trust land in (*a*) the North Charterland Concession area; (*b*) the Railway belt and the Mwinilunga district, and (*c*) the Abercorn area. The first of these commissions, that dealing with the North Charterland area, has already issued its report and it may be of interest to record some of its recommendations. The Concession area of 6,400,000 acres had formerly been a private freehold estate owned by the North Charterland Exploration Company. In this a number of native reserves had, in 1924 and onwards, been established, but, owing to an under-estimate of the land requirements of the natives and of the probable rate of increase of population, considerable congestion had resulted, with consequent deterioration of the soil.[1] In order to remedy this state of affairs the Government took power to acquire compulsorily from the Company further land, with the result that in 1940 it purchased all the available land in the Concession, excluding the native reserves and an area of 429,945 acres already alienated or retained for alienation by the Company.

The acreage of land which the Commission was asked to apportion amounted to 3,743,055. and the recommendation was that this should be divided as follows:

Native Trust Land			
Valley land ..	2,554,000		
Plateau land ..	1,068,729	Total =	3,622,729
Crown Land			
Sasare Mining area	39,226		
European farming	81,100	Total =	120,326
			3,743,055

Under this resettlement scheme, which has been provisionally accepted by the Government, immediate relief will be given to the Native Reserves by the parcelling out (under the direction of Agricultural Officers) of village blocks in the newly formed Native Trust Land areas. Water supplies will be provided by the sinking of wells. The carrying capacity of each block will be estimated and the figure given to the District Commissioner, who will then allow a village of suitable numbers to move in.

Measures will be taken to control soil erosion and the cultivation of 'dambos', and also to ensure that each unit shall have sufficient land for the requisite periods of fallow. But the Commission emphasised the necessity of close and continuous supervision of the new settlements for a considerable number of years. 163 villages have already been moved out of the Native Reserves, but the

[1] The estimate (by the Commission of 1924) of cultivable land was (in the absence of expert agricultural advice) much too high, and that of the grazing requirements of cattle much too low. It was assumed, moreover, that the native population figures would remain stable, whereas they had increased by 33% in 18 years.

Commission stated that, in spite of their proposals, the Fort Jameson Reserves would still have 56,000 natives in excess of their carrying capacity.[1]

The Commission also recommended that a portion of Native Trust Land should be set aside for alienation to Africans in individual tenure. There are, for example, many educated natives, who, having been employed as teachers or clerks, may not wish to return to their villages but would be glad to have land of their own upon which they can establish homes and support themselves in the manner to which they have become accustomed. It was also suggested that a number of so-called 'coloured' people who had not the means to acquire land on the usual terms, and had nowhere to live, should be assigned a special area of 1,500 acres.[2]

As regards European interests, these would be secured by the constitution of four areas aggregating 81,100 acres and by the retention as Crown Land (for mineral development) of the Sasare mining area of 39,226 acres. The mineral area at Sasare is of little use for native settlement, and as for the four areas which would become Crown Land it is the intention of the Government that these shall remain so until it has been established (within a period of ten years) that the land is in fact necessary for the security and development of the tobacco industry. It had been represented that the European tobacco industry could not be established on a stable footing if the annual output were less than 5,000,000 lbs. The Government considered that if this end could be achieved by the reservation of 81,000 acres for European occupation the resultant benefit to the native population (for whom the industry provides large-scale employment) would far outweigh the advantage that would be gained by settling some 1700 natives on the land in question. More-

[1] Swaziland provides an interesting parallel to N. Rhodesia in the matter of re-settlement. There, two-thirds of the 4½ million acres had been alienated to Europeans, 40% of whom were (in 1936) absentees, while close on 1,000,000 acres were being used for grazing sheep in winter. The remaining third was insufficient for the needs of the 153,270 Swazis. 27,000 Swazis were (in 1942) landless squatters on the estates of Europeans, with no security of tenure. They had to pay a rent up to £1 per hut, or offer labour service for periods up to 6 months. But by a grant of £250,000 from the Colonial Development and Welfare Fund enough land was bought to settle all these squatters and to provide roads and houses, water supplies and schools. Officers were appointed to supervise the methods of cultivation and grazing and to see that the land was not misused. (See C. W. W. Greenidge in *Land Hunger in the Colonies*, p. 15.)

[2] It is not clear how widespread is the demand for fuller forms of individual tenure. But there is evidence that some progressive Africans advocate purely private tenure as one means of escaping from the authority of chiefs. In Northern Rhodesia natives have been required, for administrative convenience, to live in villages consisting of not less than ten taxpayers, spread over an area of not more than one square mile. This restriction has proved irksome to many and has been opposed as inimical to better methods of agriculture. The substitution of a 'parish' for a village as an administrative unit has been suggested as one solution.

over, if the area reserved were eventually alienated, it might be possible to assign for native settlement an equivalent area of unoccupied alienated land elsewhere. The Commission had drawn attention to the fact that in the Concession area nearly 80,000 acres of land alienated to Europeans were lying idle, and they had suggested that the Government should seriously consider the introduction of a tax on undeveloped land.[1] This is a matter which is still being considered by the Government. The introduction of a tax on undeveloped land is also being considered by the Government of Kenya. A note on the subject is appended to this chapter.

It is recognized by the Government of Northern Rhodesia that although the action taken, or contemplated, in accordance with the Commission's report will greatly relieve the congestion of the native areas, there will still, as the Commission points out, continue to be serious congestion in the Fort Jameson area, so long as present methods of native cultivation are followed. This position may be relieved if further land is made available through the imposition of a tax on undeveloped land or by other means, such as the use of compulsory purchasing powers. But the ultimate solution here, as elsewhere in Africa, must be the adoption of more intensive methods of cultivation, coupled with systematic measures to prevent erosion.[2] These will no doubt form part of Northern Rhodesia's programme of post-war development. It is also the intention of the Government of Northern Rhodesia to make a thorough investigation of native systems of land tenure, as soon as suitable machinery for this purpose can be devised.[3]

Coming now to the conditions of non-native tenure,[4] in the settled areas along the main railway line from Livingstone to Ndola, farms are granted under freehold title, subject to a preliminary leasehold period of five years, during which personal occupation is obligatory and a certain minimum amount of development must be carried out. Applicants must have a capital of from £1500 to £2000. 10% of the purchase price is payable on issue of the lease, and the

[1] In 1925 the Land Commission of Southern Rhodesia drew attention to the fact that syndicates and large landowners were making a revenue by way of rents from natives, out of land which they were not developing but holding up with a view to ultimate sale to settlers at enhanced prices.

[2] For the subject of erosion in N. Rhodesia the reader is referred to C. G. Trapnell and J. N. Clothier, *The Soils, Vegetation, and Agricultural Systems of North Western Rhodesia, Report of the Ecological Survey, 1937*.

[3] An excellent foundation for this comprehensive investigation already exists in Dr. Audrey Richard's economic study of the Bemba tribe entitled *Land, Labour and Diet in Northern Rhodesia* (1939), and in *The Ila-Speaking Peoples of Northern Rhodesia*, by E. W. Smith and A. M. Dale. See also Dr. Max Gluckman's recently published *Essays on Lozi Land and Royal Property* (Rhodes-Livingstone Institute, 1943).

[4] European farms in 1938 numbered about 350, falling roughly into 3 groups: (*a*) mixed farming along the railway strip from Kalomo to Chisamba; (b) tobacco in the Fort Jameson region; and (*c*) coffee in the vicinity of Abercorn.

annual rent payable in arrear amounts to 6% of the balance of the purchase price. At the termination of the leasehold period the tenant, on payment of the survey fees, has the option of (*a*) taking out freehold title on payment of the balance of the purchase price, or (*b*) taking out a further lease for fifteen years, the balance of the purchase price being payable in fifteen equal annual instalments, rent as before amounting to 6% of the purchase price outstanding, and being payable in arrear. Applicants for a lease with option to purchase, who have not the necessary capital, may, at the discretion of the Commissioner of Lands, be granted a short term lease, on the understanding that an application for greater security of title at the end of the lease will be considered on its merits, particular regard being paid to the amount of development carried out.

In the rest of North-Western Rhodesia grants of agricultural land are in leasehold for 999 years with a rent revisable after thirty years, the revision being based on the unimproved value of the land. In North-Eastern Rhodesia leasehold is for ninety-nine years with rent revisable after thirty-three years. Occupational clauses insist on personal residence for the first five years' tenancy, within which a minimum amount of development must be carried out. No premium is payable. No assignment or sub-letting is permitted except with the consent of the Crown in writing, and the land may not be used for any purpose other than agriculture. In the case of small holdings the applicant must possess £500 in cash, and leases are for periods not exceeding ninety-nine years. A premium equivalent to one-tenth of the valuation of the land is payable in advance, a good habitable house must be built, and no sub-division of the land is permitted.

Ranching land, when the acreage is greater than 6000 acres, is only granted under lease for a period of thirty years, renewable at a revised rental. Smaller holdings from 10 to 250 acres, mostly in the proximity of towns, are also only granted under leasehold, except in the neighbourhood of Broken Hill. In mining areas leasehold tenures are for periods varying from thirty to ninety-nine years. Ninety-nine year leases are also given for residential and business plots in all new townships, but in the established townships of Livingstone, Broken Hill, Ndola and Fort Jameson freehold tenure has been continued, subject to certain building conditions.

In 1943 a Committee was appointed by the Governor of Northern Rhodesia to examine the conditions under which Crown land was being alienated and to advise whether, and if so, in what respect, these conditions should be altered. This Committee issued its Report in July 1943 and expressed the opinion that under the existing system of freehold there was no control over sub-division or transfer, and although a certain amount of development was required before a freehold title was issued, once the title had been obtained all control ceased. One effect of this was that some three-quarters of a million acres of alienated land were lying idle in the territory, while there were many areas where the land was being so misused that its total destruction was merely a matter of time.

The Committee, however, went on to say that, since security of tenure is necessary to the farmer, they considered that the form of lease to be adopted should approximate as closely as possible to freehold title, that is to say, the term should be long, the annual rent-charge small and non revisable, and consequently the premium payable approximately equivalent to the value of the land. Conditions imposed should be such as would prevent the abuses associated with freehold title. The Committee therefore recommended that the term should be for 999 years, the annual rent charged being one penny per acre and the premium amounting to the valuation of the land, less a sum equivalent to twenty times the annual rent charge. Sub-division and assignment (including mortgage and sub-letting) should all be made subject to the consent of the Crown, which should have the right to terminate a lease for absenteeism or non-compliance with the conditions.

The adoption of the long-term lease, with a high premium and low rental should not, however, preclude the issue of leases for a shorter term, with a lower premium and a lease rent based on the difference between the premium paid and the valuation of the land. The premium suggested was one-tenth of the valuation of the land, with an annual rental of 6% of the balance of the valuation. The term should be thirty years, with the option of renewal for a further period of thirty years on the same rent and conditions.

In the case of small holdings these should be situated within reasonable distance of a market, the term should be for ninety-nine years, and there should be strict development and occupational clauses. Since a great deal of work would be necessary to render and keep these small holdings profitably productive, the Committee did not consider that rents should be revisable. Indeed they were opposed to the whole principle of revisable rents. This is a subject which will be discussed separately at a later stage (Chapter XXI). The subject of Freehold versus Leasehold is also discussed in a later Chapter (XX), and there it is pointed out that many of the arguments against freehold tenure apply also to very long leasehold.

The difficulties experienced in Nyasaland regarding the rights of natives on European estates do not appear to have arisen to the same extent in Northern Rhodesia. An ordinance regulating the rights of natives was enacted in 1929[1] but was never put into operation,

[1] *The Natives on Private Estates Ordinance* (Cap. 61).

and was replaced in 1939 by a 'Private Locations Ordinance' (No. 15). This regularizes the establishment of locations on estates, and requires landlords to take out licences for locations and to enter into written agreements with every person (other than a labourer) resident in a location on their land, stating concisely the terms of occupation. The agreements must be attested by the District Commissioner and approved by the Provincial Commissioner. The District Commissioner and Medical Officer of Health have a right of entry to any location for purposes of inspection, and the District Commissioner has powers of removal in the case of breaches of conditions. But nothing in the Ordinance prevents a land holder from allowing persons approved by the Governor to reside in a location on his land, provided no burden is imposed either by way of payment of rent, supply of labour below the ordinary rate of wages, or otherwise. The ordinance applies only to such areas as the Governor may from time to time specify, and it is not known to what extent it has been used.[1]

A NOTE ON THE TAXATION OF UNDEVELOPED LAND

1. Some African governments have recently been considering the possibility of introducing a tax on undeveloped land, or alternatively of using or taking powers to acquire compulsorily land suitable for settlement purposes.[2]

[1] In speaking of the connection between land tenure and the political organization of the Bemba people, and in particular of the tribute-labour given to the Chief—a custom common all over Africa and branded by Europeans as 'forced labour'—Dr. Audrey Richards observes that 'as far as abstract justice is concerned there would seem to be little to choose between black and white conceptions. The European attitude to unpaid service prevents the Government from approving the *umulasa* (tribute labour) system, and also makes it impossible for the Administration to accept service in lieu of money during an economic slump. . . . European concern at an institution which binds natives to work for their chief in return for the right of cultivation seems also inconsistent, since the squatter system of land tenure is the only means by which a large portion of the native inhabitants of South Africa claim any right to land to cultivate at all, and, in the latter case, the natives work a legal minimum, varying from ninety days to six months a year in return for the right to settle. Added to which the Bemba is free to go where he pleases without reference to his Chief, whereas the South African squatter cannot leave a farm without permission from his owner, and in some districts the native who breaks his contract with his landlord is convicted under a penal code'. See *Land, Labour and Diet in Northern Rhodesia*, p. 265, footnote 2.

[2] The Kenya Land Settlement Committee appointed by the Kenya Legislative Council in 1937 urged that pressure should be brought to bear on lessees who had failed to fulfil the development conditions implied or expressed in the Crown leases. They should be made to develop their holdings or dispose of them at reasonable prices to new settlers. Otherwise the land should be recovered for the Crown. The Committee recognized that in many instances large sums of money had been spent on development, which could not be continued during the period of depression, and that in other cases the existing holders were mortgagees who had been compelled to foreclose in order to preserve the security for their loans. But, under

2. A tax on undeveloped land would be unnecessary (except as a means of raising revenue) wherever there are covenants in the grant that the land should be beneficially used and these covenants are enforced. As an example of such covenants it is provided in the Perlis land legislation, in the case of grants in perpetuity, that if the land has been abandoned for three consecutive years it may be resumed by the State. (No. 2 of 1328.)[1]
3. In British Columbia a Wild Land Tax was first imposed in 1873. The rate in 1919 was 5% on the assessed value. There is no evidence that the tax had any notable influence in stimulating development. In Alberta the Wild Land Tax Act of 1914 imposed a rate of 10% of the assessed value on all land, subject to various important exemptions. During 1915–1917 there was a continuous decline in the acreage liable to the tax. This was partly due to the tax, but the principal cause was the high price of wheat. In Manitoba an Unoccupied Lands Tax Act was enacted in 1918, with the object of checking speculation in land values. It was repealed in 1939. There is a difference of opinion as to the effect of the legislation, but the general view appears to be that, while it forced some lands in Manitoba into production, it (combined with high municipal taxation) caused many owners to lose their land because of failure to pay their taxes. In New Brunswick the Taxation of Wild Lands Act seems to have been enacted, not for the purpose of bringing undeveloped lands on to the market, but as a means of raising revenue. In Saskatchewan the Wild Lands Tax was repealed in 1936 when rural municipalities were empowered to levy the tax as a municipal tax. But out of 302 municipalities only three or four have taken advantage of the right to impose the tax. Its imposition during the period of land booms is considered to have curbed the tendency to hold land for speculative purposes.
4. In South Africa no taxation of undeveloped land has ever been imposed in the Union. But in 1937 a Union 'Unbeneficial Occupation of Farms Act' provided for the taking over of land which

the changed conditions of 1937-1939, the Government should no longer allow large areas suitable for development to remain idle. These recommendations have recently been implemented by the Land Control Ordinance of 1944 (Part IV). Under this Ordinance a Board has been established which is empowered to place restrictions on dealings in lands in the Highlands and may, in certain circumstances, refuse to give its consent to any transaction, upon the ground that that the applicant already has sufficient land or that it objects to the proposed selling price or rent or any other pecuniary consideration. Procedure is also laid down in cases of forfeiture for non-compliance with development conditions and also for the compulsory acquisition of land by the Crown.

[1] This rule applied under Turkish law in Palestine, where it received the approval of Lord Samuel when Governor in 1924. *P.M.C.* (5), 1924, p. 57. Compare also the provisions of the Ottoman Land Code in Cyprus (p. 64). For recent legislation in Kenya see Ordinance XXII of 1944, Secs. 13 and 14.

had not been satisfactorily occupied. In Southern Rhodesia also (under the Land Apportionment Act of 1930) land may be forfeited if not beneficially used.

5. In Australia the Commonwealth Land Tax Act of 1910 was a definite attempt to break up big holdings. It provided for a tax on the unimproved value of land (with an exemption up to £5000 for residents). The Act resulted in large holders subdividing estates. Whatever expansion there has been in the acreage under cultivation since the 1914-18 war must be attributed to the repurchase of arable land by the State governments from owners who were under-using the land.

CHAPTER XII

Uganda[1]

UGANDA provides one of the most interesting examples of the evolution of land tenure as a result of recent political and economic changes. Politically, modern Uganda dates from the conclusion, in 1900, of the Uganda Agreement between the British Government and the rulers and peoples of Buganda;[2] economically it owes its origin to the development of the cotton industry. Cotton is not indigenous to Uganda, and its cultivation as a commercial crop falls entirely within the period of British administration. In 1906 the cotton production was 500 bales; in 1937–38 it was 418,000 bales, and the lint exported was valued at £3,427,948. Cotton has become in fact the mainstay of Uganda's economic life, and it is upon the foundation of cotton that the remarkable material achievements of the past quarter of a century have been reared. Almost the whole of the cotton of Uganda is produced by native enterprise and occupies close on two million acres of land.[3]

But the Government of Uganda has recognized that dependence on a single crop, however valuable, is an unstable basis on which to build the whole prosperity of a people, and for this reason it has sought to develop other profitable crops, notably coffee and tobacco, the cultivation of both of which is largely in native hands. The tea industry is also developing rapidly, though exclusively as a non-native plantation crop, and it is interesting to note that the natives are fast acquiring the tea-drinking habit. There are over 2½ million cattle in Uganda, but these are not yet being used as part of the agricultural system.

Land Tenures in Buganda Province

In the following account of land conditions in Uganda,[4] attention will be confined for the most part to the area known as Buganda,

[1] In the preparation of this Chapter, the writer has had the advantage of the advice and assistance of Mr. H. B. Thomas, O.B.E., lately Director of Surveys, and Land Officer, Uganda.

[2] Buganda is one of the three provinces of which the present Protectorate consists.

[3] An interesting feature of Uganda agriculture is that ground-nuts are commonly grown together with cotton, to the great benefit of the land, since this leguminous crop is able to increase the soil nitrogen content.

[4] This account is based largely on Dr. Lucy Mair's article on Buganda Land Tenure in *Africa*, Vol. VI, 1933, and on Messrs. Thomas and Spencer's standard work *Uganda Land and Surveys*, 1938.

since it is in this area that the most striking changes have occurred. But it will be well to remember that Buganda comprises only about one-fourth of the total area and population of the Protectorate of Uganda. In Buganda, in pre-British times, certain peoples of Hamitic origin, now usually referred to as Ba-Hima, had established themselves as rulers over the indigenous Negro inhabitants, and set up a system of land administration which had many of the features of feudalism. The King, or 'Kabaka', was the supreme authority over land, but there were as well three classes of persons who exercised local control. There were: (*a*) the Bakungu or chiefs appointed by the Kabaka to govern the administrative areas into which the country was divided; (*b*) the Batongole or particular individuals to whom land had been allotted by the Kabaka in return for services rendered; and (*c*) the Bataka or heads of the indigenous clans who exercised their authority by immemorial right. The remainder of the people were 'bakopi' or peasants, who appear to have held their land by prescription.[1] They had to carry out certain obligations towards their chief, such as building the huts and fences of the Chief's enclosure, sending him a gourd of beer every time beer was brewed, supplying him with food, and turning out to weed roads. But these were political duties and had nothing to do with land ownership.[2] A peasant could not, normally, be disturbed, and the only two cases in which a chief could exercise authority over a plot, once it had been allotted, were, (*a*) if it included a large uncultivated area (this might be re-allotted), and (*b*) if it had been abandoned. The claim of a person who had first cleared a patch of land was universally recognized, so long as any traces of cultivation remained.

A fundamental change in this system was brought about by the Agreement of the British and Buganda Governments in 1900. This Agreement defined the legislative, judicial and administrative functions of the Kabaka and his council, and provided also for a general settlement of land. The British Administration acquired the right to levy taxes, and acquired also, as its share of the land settlement, the unrestricted ownership of about half[3] the area of Buganda; but this was classified for the most part as waste and uncultivated lands

[1] A newcomer could obtain land by applying to the local chief. Anyone short of land might obtain a temporary loan from a friend for growing seasonal crops. No payment was expected, but custom prescribed some small gift at harvest from each class of crop grown. The lender of the land could resume it when he pleased.

[2] It cannot be too strongly emphasised that the practice, general all over Africa, of paying 'tribute' to chiefs in the form of annual gifts of agricultural produce must not be interpreted in terms of 'rent' or of 'feudalism'. The gifts are part of a series of mutual obligations between a chief and his people, of which the right to the undisturbed use of an allotted piece of land is merely incidental. Cf. B. Malinowski, *Coral Gardens and their Magic*, Vol. I, p. 372.

[3] The actual area proved, on survey, to be 8,307 sq. miles.

and forests. The remaining half, which included the most fertile tracts and proved on survey to have an area of 9,003 sq. miles, was assigned to the Kabaka and his family, and to the county chiefs and other notables.[1] No mention was made in the Agreement of the rights of the Bataka or clan heads, and no provision was made for the protection of the peasants and for the needs of a shifting system of cultivation, which was little understood at this period.[2] And thus there was established a small landed aristocracy who became quasi-freehold proprietors of practically the whole of the settled areas of the country.[3] Land now assumed a new character. It became a private possession at the complete disposal of individual owners. And, with the simultaneous introduction of a money economy, it also came to be regarded as a source of profit through leasing and sale. The new system of tenure became known as 'mailo'—a native method of expressing the English term 'square *mile*'.

The next important stage in the evolution of tenure was the Land Law of 1908. This defined the new form of ownership, and was enacted by the Kabaka of Buganda, since 'mailo' land was held to be vested, not in the Crown, but in the native ruler. This law provided that 'mailo' land should be freely transferable and disposable by will or customary succession to natives, but should not be transferable either in perpetuity or by lease (other than temporary annual tenancies) to non-natives, except with the consent of the Governor.[4] The area which might be held by any one individual was limited to thirty square miles. The protectorate or English law of easements was made generally applicable to 'mailo' lands, and provision was made for the resumption of land for public purposes. Land falling into escheat was to be dealt with by the Governor and the Native Council as trustees for the Buganda people. It was also laid down that the owner of a 'mailo' might dispose of his 'mailo' by will in

[1] 1,000 sq. miles were assigned to the Kabaka and his family and to the county chiefs and others. One thousand chiefs and private individuals were to receive the estates of which they were presumed to be in possession, to the extent of some 8,000 sq. miles. Included in the total of 9003 sq. miles were 573 sq. miles of official estates, i.e. land attached as an inalienable endowment to certain offices or chieftainships, the use of which is enjoyed by the office-holder for the time being. The remainder was purely private land.

[2] Even to-day the failure to distinguish between unclaimed land and land lying fallow under a shifting system of cultivation may lead to injustice, in cases where the Government takes land for public purposes and only pays compensation for land actually under cultivation.

[3] There is a striking analogy here with Bengal where 'English ideas of proprietorship were applied. The *talukdars* received title deeds and were given rights resembling those of English landlords, including the right of bequest by will, a right unknown to Hindu law'. See *Modern India and the West*, edited by L. S. S. O'Malley, p. 714.

[4] *The Land Transfer Ordinance of 1933* provides, for the whole of Uganda, effective protection against imprudent alienation of land to non-natives.

writing to any native of the Protectorate, including even children *in utero*. But it was forbidden to will 'mailo' lands to persons who were not natives of the Protectorate, or to religious bodies. Succession need not, therefore, be to an eldest son, nor even to any other member of the family—a very significant innovation. But, if a landowner died intestate, a successor would be appointed according to the customs of the Buganda.

Among other provisions it was enacted that the owner of 'mailo' lands would not be compelled to give to a chief any portion of the produce of his land, either in kind or in cash; and all transactions concerning 'mailo' land were to be written in duplicate, one copy being stored by the Government and the other held by the owner of the 'mailo'.

This law constitutes to-day the fundamental authority governing this unique form of tenure. It may be noted, however, that in spite of the limitations imposed on the alienation of 'mailo' lands to non-natives, alienations did in fact occur, first in the form of freehold and later (after 1916) of leasehold. And although each case was closely scrutinized by the Government, there were occasions on which clan lands, with their tenants, passed under the control of European planters. In some cases the Protectorate Government itself was unwittingly responsible for the sale of clan lands which, not having been claimed as 'mailo' land, had become Crown land. Many native landowners began to derive considerable incomes from the rentals of plantation land, from cotton ginnery sites, or from tenancies given to Indian petty traders, who tended to congregate in considerable settlements on native lands.

The commutation into money of the traditional service due by a peasant to his overlord, developed naturally into a regular system of rent, and by 1918 this had generally been fixed at ten shillings a year for a plot of from one to two acres. Some landlords became entitled to rent from several thousand tenants. Yet there was no security of tenure, nor indeed any formal recognition at all of the rights of tenants. Moreover, the small customary gifts of the peasantry to their chiefs had become magnified into substantial demands on the peasants' crops, so that a cotton cultivator might be called on to hand over as much as one bag of seed cotton in every three harvested.[1] These demands were additional to the month's customary labour required by the Native Government, and to the poll tax imposed by the British Government.

The discontent that had long been felt came to a head in 1921, in a demand by the clan heads and many of the peasants for a return to the ancient system of clan control of land. But as the freehold system had by now become firmly established, and over ten

[1] Compare the *abusa* system in the Gold Coast (p. 176).

thousand persons had obtained individual rights (many of the estates having been broken up into small holdings), it was clearly impossible to accede to this demand. Nevertheless, the British Government insisted on the enactment by the Buganda Government of legislation which would guarantee security of tenure to native occupiers and regulate the payment of tribute and of rents. And thus, in 1927, there was enacted the native law known as the 'Busulu and Envujo law', which was probably the first legislative enactment in Africa dealing with native rental conditions. Under this law tenants, in return for a prescribed rent, obtained for themselves and their successors a right of occupancy in their small holdings, revocable only for good and sufficient reasons and after reference to the Native Courts. Their rights to their improvements were acknowledged, and it was laid down that no sale, exchange or gift of 'mailo' land should affect either the status or duties of the peasant tenants. But tenants were obliged to continue to render to the 'mailo' owner all customary respect and obedience and to take good care of the land. They were prohibited from sub-letting their holdings, or any part of them, for profit.

In 1932 a Land Tax Law[1] was enacted by the Native Government of Buganda, and among other things this established the principle that landowners should not be entitled to the whole incremental value of their land. An even more important enactment was 'The Land (Agreements) Law' of 1939 which prohibits all dealings in unregistered 'mailo' lands. This law is likely to have far-reaching repercussions, since it sets aside native custom and extinguishes equitable as well as legal rights arising from unregistered documents. It was enacted as a result of a report by Mr. V. L. O. Sheppard, who had drawn attention to many unsatisfactory features of the local system of land registration and survey.[2] In consequence of this report a new Survey Ordinance has been enacted by the Protectorate Government, and a stop has been put to the practice by the Buganda Native Government of issuing documents which purported to be authentic instruments of land transfer. The plane-table traversing of boundaries has been re-organized and a training school has been opened for African surveyors. In this way it is hoped to provide an inexpensive method of controlled survey. An even cheaper method would be an uncontrolled sketch survey by a village agency, but this would be suitable only for a presumptive title. The issue between a guaranteed title and a presumptive title, and also that between fixed and general boundaries, has still to be fought out in Uganda, as in other parts of Africa.

[1] This law was revised in 1939.

[2] Further reference to registration reforms in Uganda will be found in Chapter XXIII.

Before leaving the subject of Buganda land tenure, it may be of interest to record some of the views held regarding the provisions of the 1900 Agreement and their consequences. They have an interest which is not confined to Uganda. It is generally admitted that the Agreement did not accurately interpret the existing system of tenure, and Messrs. Thomas & Spencer go so far as to say that 'it perpetrated a grave injustice upon the overwhelming majority of the Buganda people.'[1] Nevertheless, it has been maintained that out of evil good has come, since the original division of land among the privileged few has, by the natural process of sale and inheritance, given way to one of peasant proprietorship on a widespread scale. Originally there were 3,700 allottees. In 1936 there were no less than 18,000 registered titles to land in private ownership. Writing in 1933, Dr. Lucy Mair, who had made a special study of land tenure in Buganda, expressed the opinion that the object of the Uganda Agreement had been to provide a perpetual safeguard for existing native rights and that this object had been achieved.[2] Messrs. Thomas and Spencer also stated that it would probably be admitted that the injustice of the Agreement had hastened, as could no other means, the attainment of the goal of individual ownership.[3] On the other hand, it may be contended that the peasants would have attained a comparable position had there been no Agreement, and that the Government would have been better able to take measures for maintaining the fertility of the soil and for promoting schemes of agricultural development. It is noteworthy that the Government of Uganda has steadily refused to extend the Buganda system to the other provinces.[4] In these provinces there is hardly any land which is not classified as Crown land. It has been suggested that the policy of 'indirect rule', based as it was on the authority of chiefs, was largely responsible for the excessive land privileges given to the ruling classes of Buganda. But in Northern Nigeria, where indirect rule was also the keystone of British administration, the hold of the Fulani overlords over the land was not increased at the expense of the cultivators. On the contrary, a system of serfdom and slavery was immediately converted into one of independent peasant proprietors. This difference was largely due to the fact that in Northern Nigeria adequate financial provision was made for the maintenance of chiefs, whereas in Buganda the

[1] *Uganda Land and Surveys*, p. 33.
[2] *An African People in the Twentieth Century*, p. 165.
[3] *Uganda Land and Surveys*, p. 72.
[4] Here again there is a parallel with India. Dr. Anstey says that 'Although a landlord class was created in Bengal, in pursuance of English theories of ownership and of the value of such a class, these theories were not applied to Madras and Bombay where . . . the actual cultivators of the soil were regarded as proprietors and there were no intermediaries between them and the government'. See *Modern India and the West*, p. 281.

Government regarded the allotment of estates as a means by which the chiefs could supplement their incomes, from the rents paid by the peasantry.[1]

Land Tenures in other provinces of Uganda

Coming now to the other provinces of Uganda, under the Toro and Ankole Agreements of 1900 and 1901, a small number of chiefs in the Western Province received Crown grants of freehold, with restrictions on alienation to non-natives but without any obligations to the peasant occupiers. The area so granted amounted to 376 sq. miles for Toro and 334 sq. miles for Ankole. This represents no more than 6% of the total area of these districts, though it includes the best settled land and a great part of the native population. The rest of the Western Province and the whole of the Eastern Province are (apart from the very small area alienated to non-natives or held for 'township' or government purposes) reserved as 'Crown land'[2] for the use of the native peoples, who are at liberty to settle anywhere, subject to the tribal rules of tenure. Native occupiers of unallotted Crown lands have no legal rights against the Government, but disputes among themselves regarding occupancy rights are settled by native law or custom. Native occupiers are seldom disturbed, except to make way for public projects, and in all such cases adequate compensation is paid. Even when unalienated Crown land is unoccupied, the needs of the natives, present and future, are carefully studied before grants are made to non-natives.

The native systems of tenure in these provinces are less consolidated and more varied than in Buganda. There are various forms of clan or kinship control. In many localities land has from time immemorial been held by a particular family, and even if the area of the holding is greater than is required by the family under a shifting system of cultivation, none of it can be occupied without the family's consent. Then again, in a few crowded areas, native cultivators exercise individual rights of a proprietary character on land which is nominally and legally Crown land. This occurs, e.g. among the Bagishu on the Western slopes of Mount Elgon. Here the formal recognition and regularization under tribal control of these individual 'proprietary' rights have engaged the attention of the Government, and it is thought that the establishment of a village record book, with possibly some adaptation of the certificate of occupancy scheme, may prove suitable.

[1] In some areas of the Gold Coast the claims of Chiefs to rents in cash or kind have recently been commuted for a fixed salary, the rents being made payable to the Native or Stool Treasury.

[2] The precise significance of the term 'Crown Land' has not yet, in Uganda, been determined by formal definition.

But it is in connection with the systems of fiefs, or estates conferred on individuals by the paramount chiefs, that most of the land problems of the Eastern and Western Provinces have occurred, and in order to obtain a clear view of the character of these problems it will be necessary to give a summary of the findings of a Committee which was appointed in 1931 by the Government of Uganda to inquire into the land system of Bunyoro.[1]

As elsewhere in Uganda, the governing classes in Bunyoro claimed descent from an original stock of pastoral Ba-Hima. The king, or Mukama, who was regarded as a divine being, was the 'owner' of the country, and the sole distributor of grazing areas—the only form of land ownership which mattered to the cattle-keeping aristocracy. The aboriginal agriculturists were free to occupy any lands they required, but usually attached themselves to a cattle-owner who had been given local grazing rights by the Mukama. There were no formal taxes, but the peasants were required by custom to supply the king and local chiefs with annual gifts of corn, and to perform certain services, such as the repair of the royal enclosure. Attached to certain offices of State were 'bwesenegze' or official fiefs, and in due course there grew up also a system of smaller fiefs or private estates known as 'kibanja', by grants of which the Mukama was able to satisfy the claims of ex-officials, members of his own family and other notables. Both in the case of 'bwesengeze' and of 'kibanja' the status of the peasant occupiers was that of serfs, and they were required to pay an annual tribute or 'busulu' to their overlords.

When the British took over the Administration in the first years of this century, an attempt was made to establish a system of indirect rule based on chiefs. An annual hut tax of three rupees was payable by the people, but this could be, and was in fact, almost universally rendered in the form of one month's labour. There were practically no funds for the payment of the ruling classes, who had already been deprived of a main source of revenue through the Government's ivory regulations. Chiefs, indeed, could only recoup themselves from the labour tribute of the peasantry—a system which was permitted by the Government, and indeed, under the name of 'Luharo', was eventually given statutory authority.[2]

But with the example of Buganda before them, and having a growing consciousness of the economic possibilities of private plantations, the Mukama and chiefs in 1906 submitted to the Governor a demand for the free grant to them of private 'kibanja', with full

[1] *Enquiry into Land Tenure and the Kibanja system in Bunyoro, 1931: Report of the Committee 1932*. The members of the Committee were Messrs. J. G. Rubie, a Provincial Commissioner, and H. B. Thomas, O.B.E., who was then Deputy Director of Surveys.

[2] Under the Native Authority Ordinance of 1919.

security for the growing of economic crops. The Government was at this time anxious to promote the production of plantation crops, and considered that the Unyoro chiefs should be encouraged to establish plantations of permanent crops, such as rubber, cocoa and coffee. They could hardly be expected to do this on land which was not definitely their own. They should accordingly be allowed to purchase, at specially low rates, blocks not exceeding 1000 acres. In the case of 'saza' or county chiefs, 'bwesengeze' might be granted at moderate rates.

But the question of the allotment of land remained dormant until 1910, when the Mukama again submitted a request for the grant of private estates. In 1911 the Governor (Sir Frederick Jackson) recorded his concurrence in the principle of a grant of private and official 'mailos' to the Mukama and county chiefs and to others who had done good service to the Government. But it was not until 1915 that a definite scheme was submitted to the Secretary of State. This scheme, which followed recommendations of the Native Land Settlement Committee, presided over by Sir William Morris Carter, suggested the extension of the Buganda 'mailo' system to other areas of Uganda. In so far as Bunyoro was concerned, it was proposed to award to the Mukama and principal chiefs 511 sq. miles of land which would be partly official and partly private. In addition there would be 150 sq. miles for minor chiefs.

This proposal was negatived (in 1916) by the Secretary of State, who preferred a scheme under which all land would be held in tenancy from the Crown, the chiefs being fully provided for by way of salaries. But in 1921 the Secretary of State agreed to give way to the local government and to sanction the grant of private freehold estates. By this time, however, the local government was beginning to change its own views, as the consequences of the Buganda 'mailo' system were now becoming more apparent. And from 1922 onwards the proposal to extend the system of freehold grants to chiefs ceased to receive any official support, either in Uganda or in England. Nevertheless, it was still proposed that official chieftainships should have assigned to them areas to be approved by the Government, the occupiers of which would render regulated tribute or rents to the holder of the chieftainship; moreover, similar areas, with the appendant tribute, might be assigned for life to certain selected persons, not in official employment. Tribute from natives living on areas not assigned as aforesaid would be credited as revenue of the Native Government.

The attempt to give legislative form to these proposals soon made it clear that a settlement by which chiefs would be guaranteed 'spheres of influence', in lieu of fixed and adequate salaries, would be contrary to public policy. The upper classes would be receiving favoured treatment at the expense of the poorer, and the public treasury would be deprived of a proper source of revenue. The weaknesses of such a scheme had already been exposed in the Ankole district where certain areas in charge of the local Native Administration had been allotted to retired chiefs for life, with a right to collect rent from the peasant occupiers. Such chiefs, having merely a life tenancy, could establish no permanent ties with the occupiers, and would, in fact, have been better off with a certificate of occupancy for a personal holding on Crown land, coupled with a pension from native treasury funds.

The Bunyoro Land Tenure Committee accordingly recommended (*a*) that all tribute should be collected as a tribal due and expended upon tribal administration, terminable compensation being granted to the beneficiaries of the existing system; and (*b*) that the rejection of any landlord-and-tenant system based upon freehold grants to chiefs should be reaffirmed and that the interests of the actual cultivators—that is to say the peasants—should predominate.

It followed, therefore, that the connection between 'busulu' and land should cease, and that 'busulu' must henceforth be regarded as tribal tribute paid by the taxpayer to meet the cost of the local government. Furthermore, instead of attempting to confer security by means of the complicated, expensive and inequitable method which had been followed in Buganda, it would be sufficient in Bunyoro to issue Certificates of Occupancy which would confer all the security of tenure which was required under a shifting system of cultivation. When native farmers had progressed so far as to be ready to develop lands on European lines, and to desire to borrow money for improvements by way of mortgage, then a lease under the Crown Lands Ordinance would be available. But there was not yet even a remote indication of such a demand arising in Bunyoro.

The recommendations of the Bunyoro Committee were brought into force in 1933, and cultivators can now obtain Certificates of Occupancy which safeguard the occupier from all exactions in respect of his land, and confer on him individual rights to the undisturbed enjoyment of his holding. The occupier is not permitted to sell, transfer or sublet any portion of the land covered by the Certificate, but, on giving notice, he may sell the buildings, crops, or any improvements. He may dispose of his rights by will, and, in the absence of a will, his heir (by native custom) inherits the holding. The rights under the certificate are cancelled if the holder discontinues cultivation or occupation.

Difficulties similar to those of Bunyoro were experienced in some other districts. In the Busoga district, land originally belonged to the clan, whose leader stood to it in the relation of a trustee on behalf of his fellow clansmen. But, following the advent of European ideas and administration, there was developed in the leading classes a striving for freehold estates in which the ancient communal and subsequent feudal control would receive a modern interpretation on lines practically identical with the European conception of landlord and tenant. The Government steadily resisted this demand. In 1928 it decided to put a stop to the personal payment of 'busulu' by the peasant to the chief, and arranged that it should be embodied in the poll-tax. The chiefs strongly opposed this step, on the ground that acceptance would imply the surrender of their claims to freehold grants. Similarly, they declined to accept the offer to their leading families of eighty-five sq. miles of freehold estate which the Government made in the following year, with a view to securing an amicable settlement of this vexed question. This offer, which was withdrawn in 1935, was made, not in recognition of the justice of any claim to freehold estates, but merely as a gesture of appreciation of the loyal services of the leading Soga families.[1]

In the Toro district of the Western Province the whole of the country had, in the early days of British occupation, been parcelled out among a limited number of chiefs or 'bataka', and among kinsmen of the ruler, who was here also known as the Mukama. These fiefs were held solely by gift from the Mukama, and, since they were not hereditary, there was little security of tenure. Their value lay in the tribute of labour, food or beer which was paid by the occupying peasants. Peasants could not afford to be independent and were compelled to seek the protection of some chief. For the Mukama the grant of these estates was the only available method of rewarding services rendered, of endowing chieftainships, and of pensioning old retainers. From the outset the British Government acquiesced in the system, and continued to do so after it had become aware of the abuses to which it had given rise. It was not until 1923 that a scheme of fixed salaries was introduced and the peasant protected from exploitation. The delay of nearly a quarter of a century in arriving at a settlement in this area is said to have been attended with unfortunate results.[2]

Thus, at the present time, all land in the Western Province which has not been allocated under the Toro and Ankole Agreements of 1900 and 1901, and all land in the Eastern Province, is reserved for the people as 'Crown land',[3] and on this land any peasant is at liberty to settle. Such settlers may, in the Bunyoro district, and in the non-Agreement areas of Toro and Ankole, receive Certificates of Occupancy, and this arrangement will possibly be extended to

[1] D. W. Robertson, *The Historical Considerations Contributing to the Soga System of Land Tenure.*

[2] *Enquiry into the Grievances of the Mukama and People of Toro*, para. 17.

[3] Excepting a small area alienated in townships and for non-native plantations.

other districts. The Certificates state that, with the approval of the Governor, the local Native Authority recognizes the right of so-and-so to the undisturbed occupancy of the garden cultivated by him at such-and-such a place; that so-and-so is the absolute owner of all buildings, trees and crops which he has erected or planted; that he cannot sell the land, but may, on giving notice to the Native Authority, sell his buildings, trees and crops to another native; that he may leave his rights to an heir determined by native custom; that no rent may be collected from any other native living on the land; and that the rights are cancelled by a discontinuance of cultivation or occupation. It appears to be the view of the Government that the conditions of these certificates should not be over-elaborate, a flexible régime being worked out on the basis of local custom. But it would seem to be a matter for consideration whether, if Certificates of Occupancy are in fact necessary, they should not be given some form of statutory authority (e.g. under the proposed new Land Ordinance). Their holders pay no rent, but, like all other native taxpayers in the extra-Buganda provinces, they pay a consolidated poll-tax in which is compounded the earlier 'busulu' obligation of four shillings to six shillings annually. In actual practice, native occupiers of Crown land enjoy precisely the same security of tenure whether they sit with, or without, a Certificate of Occupancy. And, so long as the Government adheres to its present peasant policy, the value of the Certificates will be largely sentimental.[1] There has been little effort by the occupiers to obtain Certificates, save in Bunyoro, where the Native Authorities have attached importance to their issue.

On the other hand, as already observed, tenants on land held under the Toro and Ankole Agreements of 1900 and 1901 have little security of tenure beyond that of the goodwill of their landlord. Until recently each landlord was repaid from the tax collections a sum of four shillings for each taxpayer on his land. But in 1937 these refunds ceased and the landlord was permitted to collect an annual rent of four shillings from each tenant. As peasants can obtain holdings on surrounding Crown lands without making this payment, they are likely to drift away altogether from these privately owned estates.

Non-Natives

The Crown Lands Ordinance of 1903 permits the grant of land in freehold, but as long ago as 1916 sales in freehold were suspended

[1] It is stated, however, that in some districts (e.g. Busoga) the Chiefs have endeavoured to create a feeling of insecurity among the peasants, as part of their propaganda for obtaining 'mailo' land of the Buganda pattern.

by order of the Secretary of State, when only some 100 sq. miles of agricultural land and a few dozen town plots had been sold. But the legal power to create freehold remains, and although policy has dictated restraint in its exercise, this has proved useful since it has enabled the Government to make exchanges of land when expropriations have been necessary. The most effective weapon, however, for the protection of the natives against the imprudent alienation of land to non-natives is the Land Transfer Ordinance of 1906. Under this Ordinance no land occupied or held by any native, or any right, title or interest therein, shall be transferred, either *inter vivos* or by will, either in perpetuity or for a term of years, to any non-native without the consent of the Governor. This executive discretion of the Governor embraces and may, if necessary, override the consent of the Buganda Native Government, conferred by the Buganda Land Law of 1908, in respect of 'mailo' land. In practice the Governor would not approve of a mortgage of 'mailo' land to a non-native, unless the right of foreclosure and power of sale (except to other natives) were excluded. The Governor's consent has not, however, been considered necessary[1] for the grant of year-to-year tenancies of native-owned land to non-natives, and this absence of control of temporary occupation by non-natives has had some regrettable results.[2]

With regard to leases of land to non-natives in Uganda, the present practice is to limit the term of agricultural leases to ninety-nine years at an initial rent of one shilling per acre a year, with revision of rent, which shall not exceed 5% of the value of the land at the time of reassessment, at intervals of thirty-three years. Inferior or grazing land is obtainable at lower rates, but the Government's view has been that any normal agricultural undertaking which cannot bear this rent is not worth while. In the past many lessees have burdened themselves with more land than they could utilize. About 300 sq. miles are now held on lease from the Crown, while a further fifty sq. miles have been leased by 'mailo' owners. In all, both under freehold and leasehold, less than 10% of the area of Uganda is held by non-natives.

There are also special terms for special purposes, without recourse to legal regulation. Thus agricultural land in the vicinity of townships may be leased for short terms of seven, twelve, twenty-one or thirty-three years. Year-to-year temporary licences have proved a convenient form of tenure both for the tenant and the Crown. A mining company, for example, may wish to grow maize for its labourers on poor land which, though at present unoccupied, must be

[1] This point has apparently not been raised or tested in the Courts.

[2] Many of the Indian settlements are said to be objectionable on sanitary grounds. But this is an administrative matter rather than one of land policy.

kept in reserve for native expansion. Neither party would be ready to commit itself to a long-term agricultural lease.

Summary

Summing-up the main features of land administration in Uganda, it may be said that radical tenure falls into two classes, namely, (*a*) Crown Land; and (*b*) Mailo Land. By the Crown Land (Declaration) Ordinance of 1922 it is laid down that all land is Crown Land except such as is held by documentary title. The main exception is the 9,003 sq. miles of 'mailo' land in Buganda.

Mailo land can only be held by natives of Buganda Province. The titles are not Crown grants drawn under the 1903 Ordinance, but state that the ownership of an 'absolute mailo estate' is recognized by His Majesty's Government. The lease of 'mailo' land to non-natives is subject to the veto of the British Government and is very sparingly permitted. Its sale has been completely disallowed.

The major proportion of land in Uganda is unallotted Crown land. Here the legal position is that, by virtue of the Crown Lands (Declaration) Ordinance of 1922, the Crown has unfettered control. This Ordinance, however, has always been regarded as a preliminary to a formal declaration of the rights of native occupiers settled on the land. Since 1923 drafts of a Land Ordinance have been under consideration, and it would seem that the final form may follow the model of the Land and Native Rights Ordinance of Northern Nigeria.

CHAPTER XIII

Nigeria[1]

A. *General*

Nigeria with a population of over twenty millions[2] is the largest unit, numerically, of the British Colonial Empire. It is also the largest in area, if the portion of the Cameroons under British Mandate is included—the area of the whole territory being 372,674 sq. miles.[3] It consists of a Colony and Protectorate. The Colony is a small strip of land running round the coast on either side of Lagos, the capital of Nigeria and the principal port of West Africa. The Protectorate falls into three main divisions: the Northern Provinces, coinciding with the former Protectorate of Northern Nigeria, and the Eastern and Western Provinces, coinciding with the former Protectorate of Southern Nigeria. For the purposes of this chapter the Eastern and Western Provinces will be classed together as 'the Southern provinces' or 'Southern Nigeria'.

There are more than 300 distinct tribes in Nigeria, at various stages of social and economic development. This means that there is great variety in the systems of land tenure. There are, also, marked climatic differences between Northern and Southern Nigeria. At Hadeija in the North the average annual rainfall is 23·93 inches. At Forcados in the South it is 150·95 inches. Debundscha in Cameroons Province has an average rainfall of 358 inches. In the Northern Provinces millets and maize are the staple food crops, and the export crops are ground-nuts, cotton and benniseed. In the Southern Provinces yams are the principal food crops, and the export products are palm oil and palm kernels, and cocoa. In the Northern Provinces there are three million cattle, but in the Southern Provinces cattle keeping is not possible owing to the presence of tsetse fly. This means that 'mixed' farming can be used in the North but not in the South, as a means of establishing more settled systems of tenure. In the Kano area of Northern Nigeria the use of cattle manure enables the land to support a density of 430 persons to the sq. mile under a fixed system of cultivation, whereas

[1] Further data on land tenure in Nigeria will be found in Chapter II, pp. 20-1 (*Native Systems of Tenure*), Chapter XXII (*The Pledging of Land*), Chapter XXIII (*Registration*) and Chapter XXIV (*Changes in Native Land Law*). There are two valuable chapters on Land Administration in Lord Lugard's *Dual Mandate* (Chapters XIV and XV). See also Lord Hailey's *An African Survey*, pp. 768-774 and 853-856.

[2] The 1931 census returns for Nigeria showed a total population of 19,928,171. But the Government Statistician's estimate was 21,902,000. The present population is unlikely to be less than 23,000,000.

[3] The area of the mandated territory is 34,081 sq. miles.

over large areas of the Southern Provinces the only means of avoiding overcrowding is by shortening the period of bush-fallow, a process which progressively reduces the productivity of the soil.[1] In certain areas of the Southern provinces, also, the acid condition of the soil precludes the use of any other than a shifting system of cultivation.

Historical conditions have also had important differentiating effects on tenure in Nigeria. In the Colony of Nigeria, as a result of cession to the Crown by former chiefs, the radical title to land is now in the British sovereign, but this title is throughout qualified by the usufructuary rights of communities. 'Even when machinery has been established for defining, as far as possible, the rights of individuals by introducing Crown grants as evidence of title, such machinery has apparently not been directed to the modification of substantive rights, but rather to the definition of those already in existence.'[2] The native title, in fact, is so complete that the radical right of the Crown is reduced to one of limited rights of administrative interference.[3]

This freedom to deal with land, coupled with a close association with Europeans, has in the Colony of Nigeria led to the adoption of English conceptions of tenure and the partition of family holdings into freeholds by individual heirs. Squatters on communal lands have also obtained freehold rights by prescription. And although transfer follows the forms of English law it is (in the words of Lord Hailey) subject to all the vagaries of inexpert conveyance.[4]

In the Southern provinces, also, the greater part of the land is held under rights which, by long occupation, have matured into family rights. The authority of the Crown has generally been limited to the control of the alienation of land to non-natives,[5] who are now only able to obtain land in the form of leases for ninety-nine years, with the approval of the Governor, under the Native Lands

[1] It is reckoned that 150 persons per sq. mile are the maximum number that can obtain satisfactory yields by shifting cultivation (without the use of manure). In many parts of Southern Nigeria the land is cropped for two years and rested for one, an intensity which makes high yields impossible. The average density of population over the whole of Nigeria at the present time is probably about 68 to the sq. mile. The main land problem of Nigeria as a whole is not, therefore, one of shortage of land, but of how to effect a redistribution of population.

[2] This quotation is from the Privy Council decision in Amodu Tijani *v.* The Secretary, Southern Nigeria, 1921, 2 A.C. 399.

[3] It is interesting to note that according to the Ta'limu Radthi or land law of the Sokoto Empire of Northern Nigeria 'the Imam cannot assign ownership of cultivated land captured in war or ceded by treaty. He can assign ownership of deserted lands, but lands still in cultivation by the ancient inhabitants belong to them and to no one else'. See Lord Lugard's *The Dual Mandate*, p. 288 (footnote).

[4] *An African Survey*, p. 768.

[5] In Benin, after its conquest in 1896, the Crown assumed authority over lands and issued leases. But in 1917 the Oba or Chief was allowed to resume control over lands occupied by his Bini subjects.

Acquisition Ordinance. They are no longer able to obtain freehold rights, although acquisitions of this kind in the past have in some cases been recognized. After the 1914–18 war, Lord Leverhulme made strenuous attempts to obtain freehold areas in the Southern Provinces for the development of oil-palm plantations, but the Government resisted these proposals, both on the ground of protecting native rights in land and also because it favoured the maintenance and development of a peasant, as opposed to a plantation, economy. As regards the latter, it may be remarked that the problem of obtaining, under peasant conditions of tenure, a quality of oil which can compete with the standard products of the plantations of the East, is one of the principal problems of Nigeria. But considerable progress in this direction has been made, and the history of the cocoa industry, both in Nigeria and on the Gold Coast, has shown that local systems of tenure are not incapable of making adjustment to plantation requirements.[1]

It may be added that in the Southern Provinces Crown lands may be leased to natives for a definite or indefinite period and for a specified purpose. Such leases are held under English law, but may only be transferred to natives and then only with the consent of the Government.

In the Northern Provinces of Nigeria, partly as the result of conquest and succession to the authority of the Muhammadan rulers, and partly owing to the late incorporation of this vast territory and the adoption of a more progressive policy regarding land, all lands are declared by Ordinance[2] to be under the control and subject to the disposition of the Governor. No title to the occupation and use of any lands is valid without the Governor's consent. Nevertheless, all lands (whether occupied or unoccupied) are declared to be native lands; and they must be held and administered by the Governor for the use and common benefit of the natives. In his administration the Governor must have regard to the native laws and customs existing in the district in which the land is situated. It would seem, therefore, that even in the Northern Provinces the position assumed by the State is one of trusteeship, rather than of the ownership of lands.[3]

[1] But in the Gold Coast, owing to the risks attending the purchase and conveyance of land by native methods, it has become increasingly the practice to employ the forms of conveyancing recognized by the law of England, after a careful scrutiny of the title of the grantor. There is a Concessions Court which investigates claims and issues Certificates of Validity.

[2] *The Land and Native Rights Ordinance* (Cap. 85 of the Laws of Nigeria). This legislation was based on the report of a Committee appointed by the Secretary of State in 1908 to investigate the whole position regarding land tenure in Northern Nigeria. The Committee's report is contained in Cmd. 5102 of 1910.

[3] The Northern Nigerian land legislation has been characterized as 'expropriation' and criticized also on the ground that, if titles are only valid with the Governor's consent, then native customary titles must be invalid. But the lands are

The Governor may grant rights of occupancy to natives and to non-natives, and may demand a rental for the use of any native lands granted to any native or non-native. He may revise the rental in the case of land granted specifically for building purposes, at intervals of not more than twenty years, and in the case of all other land at intervals of not more than seven years. In making a revision the Governor is debarred by statute from taking into consideration any improvements made upon a site by the lessee, and from charging more than the amount which is obtainable as rent for sites similarly situated and of equal area. If the rent is raised on revision the lessee may appeal to the Courts or to the Governor, who will appoint an arbitrator. If the occupier is dissatisfied he may surrender his lease, and the Governor may award such compensation for unexhausted improvements as he may think fit. Under certain regulations the Resident of a Province may grant temporary occupation certificates for a period not exceeding twelve months.

Certificates of Occupancy may be granted for a definite or indefinite term, but in the case of non-natives the period is limited, and their holdings may not exceed 1,200 acres if granted for agricultural purposes, or 2,500 if granted for grazing.[1] The alienation of land to non-natives without the Governor's permission is prohibited. Very little land has, in fact, been alienated, and then only in connection with the development of the tin fields. Nor are Certificates of Occupancy normally issued to natives, or rent demanded from them.[2] Indeed all transactions in land between natives, as well as the settlement of their disputes, are left to the native authorities, though the decisions of the native courts are subject to revision, and approval is also required for the transfer of land to a native who is not indigenous to the district.

definitely declared to be 'native lands' and in any event, as the Privy Council pointed out in the case cited above, a mere change of sovereignty is not to be presumed as meant to disturb the rights of private owners. As for the Governor's consent, this is given automatically. He is in fact bound to give it where lands are held in accordance with native law and custom, since he is (by the Ordinance) bound to have regard to native law and custom. This, incidentally, raises interesting possibilities, in view of the fact that native law and custom are not static.

[1] An important condition of agricultural and grazing leases granted to non-natives in Nigeria is that natives resident on the land do not become tenants of the lessee, nor may any rent be changed to them. This is in striking contrast to East African practice.

[2] Lord Hailey has observed that although there have been few applications for Certificates of Occupancy, and those mostly in respect of urban lands, 'it is clear that in the northern emirates an exclusive right of user, which has now lost most of the aspects of a communal right, is being built up beneath the ultimate right of the Crown.' (*An African Survey*, p. 854.) But it has been no part of the Government's general policy regarding land in Northern Nigeria to introduce an exclusive right of user which did not exist before. Lord Lugard has expressly stated that the Government deliberately refrained from issuing Certificates of Occupancy to natives and that the land law remains a dead letter as far as native occupiers were concerned. See *The Dual Mandate*, p. 292.

It is of interest to recall that in 1912 a letter was addressed to *The Times* by Messrs. E. D. Morel, Noel Buxton and Ramsay MacDonald, inviting the Colonial Office to consider the extension of the Northern Nigerian system to the Southern territories of West Africa, 'with the threefold aim of legalizing the rights of the natives to the occupancy and use of the soil, preventing the creation of monopolies in the soil's produce whether natural or cultivated, and reserving the value of the land and freedom of access to it for future generations'. In response to this letter the West African Lands Committee was appointed. This Committee never issued its Report.[1] But the land legislation of Northern Nigeria has been used as a model in many other regions of Africa. For this reason a supplementary Note is appended to this chapter, giving the preamble and some of the main provisions of the Northern Nigerian Ordinance (The Land and Native Rights Ordinance—Cap. 85), together with the Regulations relating to Certificates of Occupancy, made under Section 24 of the Ordinance.

B. *The Native Systems of Tenure*

It may now be of interest to give some account of the native systems of tenure in (*a*) the Northern Provinces of Nigeria, and (*b*) the Southern areas. In the Northern Provinces the general principle governing the tenure of native lands is that title to land is based on a communal usufructuary right, and whatever radical right the chief may have in legal theory it does not amount in practice to anything more than an administrative control over vacant lands in the interests of the whole community. The chief is bound to assign land, when available, without rental charge, to anyone who requires it. Sometimes, however, the administration of vacant lands is vested, not in the chief, but in the head of the kindred which first settled in the area.

Individuals and families acquire rights by applying to the chief (or in some cases to the head of the oldest family). These rights are usufructuary. The grant may be in perpetuity, but the land is inalienable. It may be let, but it may not be sold. It cannot be reassigned to a stranger without the consent of the chief, who is also authorised to demand the return of land which is in excess of a grantee's requirements. The usufructuary grant confers rights over all trees, stones and pools and wells on the land, but there may be reservations in favour of the planters of trees and there may also be rules that certain trees may not be destroyed without the permission of the chief.

In 1921 the present writer observed[2] that in crowded areas

[1] See p. 177.

[2] See *The Northern Tribes of Nigeria*, by C. K. Meek, Vol. I, pp. 277-80.

applicants for land were inclined to offer, and chiefs to accept, more than the modest presents which are normally given, not as rent, but as an acknowledgment of the chief's political authority, which includes the authority to dispose of vacant lands. In virtue of these larger payments there was a growing tendency for the occupier to regard his farm as alienable property. The same might be said of house property in the larger towns. Formerly the site was regarded as the common property of the community, but this principle was giving place to one of a proprietary character.[1] Moreover, in the fertile regions around Lake Chad land had long been bought and sold, and among many of the pagan or non-Moslem tribes there had been complete freedom of alienation to other members of the tribe. Virgin land might be occupied by anyone on his own initiative, without reference to a chief or anyone else, and new occupiers of old farms obtained permission to do so, not from the local Native Authority, but from the former occupiers. Even among some of the Moslem tribes when grantees of land emigrated, their descendants, returning long afterwards, might reclaim the land.

It is clear, therefore, that, in some areas at least, occupation conferred more than a mere usufructuary right. And this conception would seem to have received some sanction from Moslem law; for although the Maliki code does not regard a grant of land as conferring absolute ownership, it does seem to consider that a chief loses his rights for all time over lands which he has once conferred. On the other hand, it is to be remembered that chiefs could, for a sufficient (and often for an insufficient) reason, banish a man from the community and confiscate his property.[2] In many areas also of Northern Nigeria it is clearly the rule that abandoned land reverts to the community and that, if an emigrant returns home, he can only resume his land if it happens to be vacant.

[1] I. Schapera notes that in Bechuanaland the sale of huts is not sanctioned by native law, and that the power of a chief to move people without compensation discourages the building of good houses. (*Land Tenure in the Bechuanaland Protectorate*, p. 111.) In the Yoruba Provinces of Nigeria an evicted person may usually take his house improvements with him. In many areas (e.g. the Ondo Division) the freedom to sell house property in the towns has led to an improvement in the standard of building. See H. L. Ward Price, *Land Tenure in the Yoruba Provinces*. Secs. 97 and 233.

[2] In Nigeria banishment did not necessarily entail the confiscation of the culprit's land. In certain cases the land was allowed to pass to the heir. But in others the entire property of the family became forfeit, and their land was given to others. In Bechuanaland, chiefs, even after the establishment of the British Protectorate, freely exercised their right of banishment. Proclamation No. 1 of 1919, however, made provision for appeal from the decisions of chiefs. The Native Tribunals Proclamation of 1934 also prohibits native courts from ordering a man to be forcibly removed from his lands and residence. But the chief is still entitled to remove people from one part of his territory to another, or even banish them altogether, provided that he does so in his administrative capacity and not as judge of the Native Court. I. Schapera, op. cit., p. 109.

The whole system of land-holding in Northern Nigeria indeed is highly elastic. This was well demonstrated at the 1939 conference of Chiefs, when certain land problems came up for discussion. The Emir of Zaria stated that in his Emirate the sale of farms was contrary to local custom. The Sultan of Sokoto, the recognized leader of all the Muhammadans of Northern Nigeria, stated that, in his Sultanate, sale was only permissible in certain areas, and he considered that it should not be permitted without the consent of the local Native Authority, and then only for exceptional reasons. In the end the Council agreed that in cases where the Muhammadan law of inheritance resulted in uneconomic subdivision, or insanitary conditions, farms might be sold and the proceeds divided among the legatees. In the following year (1940) the Conference also agreed that the Muhammadan law of inheritance might be modified to the extent of allowing local Native Authorities to determine the minimum area into which any estate might be divisible.

The elasticity of the native rules regarding transactions in land is implicitly recognized in the Regulations made under the Land and Native Rights Ordinance. These stipulate that, subject to any native law or custom to the contrary, an occupier may sell, transfer or bequeath his title to any other native of the district, with the consent of the district headman and the approval of the head chief; and that he may sell, transfer or bequeath his title to a stranger native with the consent of the head chief and the approval of the British Resident. These regulations may seem to give to district headmen an excessive authority, but it is noteworthy that when a district headman refuses to give his consent to a transfer there is a right of appeal to a Native Court, and that when a head chief refuses his consent an appeal lies to the Supreme Court.

It may be of interest now to give a brief description of the system of tenure in one of the non-Moslem tribes of Northern Nigeria, and for this purpose we may select the Jukun—a tribe distinguished by the institution of 'divine kingship'.[1] Among the Jukun all unoccupied land is free to any person to farm without reference to anyone—not even the king. A farmer may occupy virgin land in the bush, or he may farm on land which had formerly been farmed by someone else and subsequently abandoned. The only occasion on which he asks permission to farm land formerly farmed by another is when the abandoned farm includes the site of the other's former house. In this case the new farmer would ask the permission of the other, or of his descendants, for the religious reason that the spot is sacred to the previous owner, as it contains the graves, or as the Jukun

[1] The king is regarded as the source of the soil's fertility and its spiritual owner. Cf. *The Ila-Speaking Peoples of N. Rhodesia*, by E. W. Smith and A. M. Dale, Vol. I, p. 388. Also *Land, Labour and Diet in N. Rhodesia*, by Audrey I. Richards, p. 249.

would express it, the 'umbilical cords' of the former owner's forefathers.

In the larger villages, 'wards' or subsections of the village may agree to farm each in a certain direction, but there is at present no hard-and-fast rule. Members of the same household, however, generally endeavour to farm in one locality. When a farmer decides to take up a piece of virgin land he stakes his claim by raising one or two mounds round the chosen site and by cutting down a few trees. If he has a number of friends in the ward he will go to them and point out the advantages of the new locality, in order to induce some of them to take up adjoining land. This is done with the object of co-operation against farm pests. But there is no general collectivism as regards the working of farms. A farmer may work his farm with the help of a younger brother or son; but normally every married man has a farm of his own. There is, however, a definite system of co-operation among farmers at certain periods of the agricultural year. Farmers also obtain the help of relatives and friends for the preliminary work of clearing the new farm of grass, cutting down trees and digging up roots. It is hardly necessary to add that this system of tenure is designed to meet the needs of subsistence agriculture and that among the Jukun there is no plantation cultivation such as is found in the cocoa regions further south.[1] Nor is there any pressure of population on the land.[2]

Within the limits of a single tribe there may be several systems of tenure. This is well illustrated among the Nupe of Northern Nigeria where, for historical and economic reasons, there are striking differences between the tenures of the groups East and West of the Kaduna River.[3] On the Eastern side, owing to the dominance of the Fulani system of State government, land-holding assumes many complex forms and there are many methods of transfer, reflecting the attempts of the people to counteract the pressure on the land. But even in areas where there is no pressure there may still be keen competition for small pockets of rich lands, like the groves known as 'kurmi', which are a characteristic feature of Northern Nigeria. Land may be acquired in the ordinary way by a man as a member, or an adopted member, of a land-owning family: or an applicant may obtain from the village head a free grant of virgin forest or of

[1] Among the Yoruba of S. Nigeria the introduction of cocoa cultivation, and consequently of large sums of money, has in many areas put a stop to the co-operative system of free labour. Those who formerly contributed free labour in their own persons now prefer to send money contributions by which hired labourers may be employed as proxies. See W. R. Bascom, '*The Sociological Role of the Yoruba Cult-Group*' in *The American Anthropologist*, Vol. 46, No. 1, Part II, p. 63.

[2] Further details of the Jukun system of farming will be found in C. K. Meek's *A Sudanese Kingdom*, Chapter X, from which this account is taken.

[3] For these details regarding the Nupe the writer is indebted to Dr. S. F. Nadel's recent work, *A Black Byzantium*, pp. 180-201.

land formerly cultivated but now no longer required by its former occupant: or he may obtain a grant or lease by an arrangement which recognizes the new money value of land, though generally speaking in Nupe-land there is as yet no commercial utilization of land. Many, however, hold land as clients of wealthy men, to whom they make annual gifts of produce;[1] and others have obtained grants direct from the Etsu or King, in return for political services rendered. Much of the Cis-Kaduna territory is held, through the hierarchy of a feudal nobility, from one or other of the three royal houses of Nupe-land. Then there are also royal estates. These can be claimed only by the titled heads of the dynasties. They are absolutely owned and not simply administered. On each of these estates there is a small hamlet where in former times the royal slaves lived and worked—providing the king with produce; the king in turn providing the slaves with food and clothing and a plot of land for their own use. Nowadays, the position of these slaves has been assimilated to that of clients who only pay an annual tithe.[2]

Then again, land may be borrowed for a limited period, generally three to five years, as a means of relieving a temporary shortage. Landowners with sufficient land are always ready to help others less fortunate. In the Trans-Kaduna region the borrower pays a fixed rent[3] in kind, consisting of a bundle of corn. In Cis-Kaduna he pays cash down—anything from eightpence to six shillings per acre, according to the quality of the soil—plus an annual bundle of corn. But labour-service may replace the cash payments. When the grantor dies the grantee may go on working the land, as though it were his own. But one day the grantor's heir may reclaim the land. Nevertheless, if the grantor allows 'rent' [*sic*] to lapse without calling in the lease, it is assumed that he has abandoned his rights. In other words an occupier may establish rights by prescription. This is supposed to be contrary to native law, but (as has already been remarked) long occupation does in fact constitute a very strong claim, and Dr. Nadel quotes a land case in 1935 in which the Emir declared that 'We do not agree that a man should be evicted from the place which he has been working for a long time'.[4] It appears also to be a rule among the Nupe that the period of time during which the land of emigrants continues to be recognized as theirs is limited to three years. After that time the chief may reapportion the land.

In most districts of Nupe-land the local chief has special rights over certain classes of economic trees, whether they are growing on

[1] These gifts are voluntary and would not be enforced in any Native Court.

[2] But Dr. Nadel states that the demands of the different Emirs have varied, and that one recently demanded as much as one-third of the annual produce.

[3] 'Rent' is hardly the right word here. The gift of corn is (*a*) a token of gratitude, and (*b*) an acknowledgement that the occupier is not the owner.

[4] Op. cit., p. 191.

communal or on private land. Sometimes family heads exercise restricted rights to 'chiefs' trees' growing on their land, paying two-fifths of the crop to the chief and keeping the rest. But sometimes the chief may grant the full possession over these trees as a separate right. Recently the Government of Nigeria purchased one of the royal estates from the Emir of Bida, but although the land became Crown land the Emir has not parted with his rights over the fruit trees growing on the land.

Dr. Nadel makes some interesting general remarks on the land policy in Northern Nigeria. He observes that while there has been a general levelling up of the rights of the peasants, the upper classes complain that theirs have been levelled down to those of the peasants. Even the position of the peasants and craftsmen has not improved to the extent of enabling them to accumulate reserves and increase their resources to any considerable extent. The introduction of commercial crops, the cultivation of which is officially encouraged, may seem to point the way to economic betterment, yet the insecurity of these new resources may defeat their own ends.

A more recent attempt to improve the lot of farmers has been the introduction of mixed farming—a policy designed to transform the whole of Northern Nigeria into arable land cultivated on Western lines, on a basis of individual holdings. The two acres per head, which have hitherto been the average amount of land worked by a single individual, would become extended to twelve acres and ultimately to twenty. The manure gained from the draught cattle would obviate the need for shifting cultivation and would allow the almost unlimited cultivation of the same area of land.

But under this scheme, also, there are obvious dangers, since a single individual would be able to take over the whole of the holdings of the family group. The other members of the group would either have to acquire new land or else give up farming altogether. The projected increase in holdings would lead to an acute shortage of land and consequently to acute competition for its possession. The increased agricultural production, moreover, of which half would be for internal consumption, would lower the price of food crops all over the country, so that the small farmer who relies on food crops more than on commercial crops, would be compelled to sell his produce at prices insufficient to enable him to maintain his labour costs and meet the Government tax. Dr. Nadel considers that these dangers might be met by slowing up the process of transforming the agricultural system, until there was a corresponding transformation of the labour organization, the increase in the cost of the means of production being met by widening the basis of the co-operative unit. Co-operative societies, which would buy the new means of production from common funds, and would jointly own ploughs and cattle, would enable the poorer peasants to profit from the technical improvements. A co-operative society which would include all the owners of adjacent fields would be able to utilize ploughing to the greatest advantage, without incurring the danger of large-scale land exchange.[1]

In this connection it is interesting to note that a number of the Native Authorities in Northern Nigeria have introduced schemes whereby farmers may obtain small loans on easy terms to meet the initial outlay on cattle and implements. Moreover, various experiments have been made in land settlement. One of these has recently been described by Mr. C. B. Taylor in the issue of *Tropical Agriculture* for April 1943.[2] The Government of Nigeria has acquired an estate at Dandawa from the Empire Cotton Growing Corporation and here suitable settlers are, on an initial payment of thirty shillings, given a cleared fifteen acre holding, a compound consisting of two round houses and a cattle pen, four cattle and a plough. The cost of clearing the land and erecting the buildings is about £25, but this amount is not debited to the farmer since he is required by the Government to grow eight or nine acres of cotton annually. But the farmer must pay to the local Native Administration the value of the cattle and implements, as well as an interest charge of 5% on annual outstanding balances. In this way he is insured against cattle losses. He has complete security of tenure, provided he continues to farm satisfactorily. Settlers sell their crops and fat cattle to the fund, and in return are issued with cattle, implements, spare parts, seed, cash (if in credit) and even clothes. At present the Government is making no charge for the amenities provided, which in time will probably include a school and a medical clinic. It is claimed that the scheme is economically sound, but this claim would appear to be premature.

In the Kano Emirate of Northern Nigeria there is a remarkable form of tenure under which the annual taxes of the Government are assessed on the farm rather than on the farmer.[3] Here, in a densely populated region (430 to the sq. mile over an area of 488 sq. miles) the soil is relatively poor and there is no room for the normal system of shifting cultivation. Extensive use is made of manure, and, with an elaborate system of intersowing and rotation, the farmer is able to crop the same plots year after year with little fallowing.

Formerly grants of lands were made to families by the Emir. The land could not be permanently alienated, but the right to cultivate

[1] *A Black Byzantium*, p. 369.

[2] Reprinted from *Farm and Forest*.

[3] This description is taken from an article *Land Survey in Kano Emirate*, by D. F. H. MacBride in the *Journal of the Royal African Society*, April 1938.

might be assigned with or without consideration for any period, or pledged as security for a loan. The person to whom it was assigned was not allowed to erect any permanent buildings, lest this should prejudice the reversion of the land to the original holder. The sale of land was forbidden, and if the Emir heard of any case of sale he would direct the seller to refund the money paid and allow the buyer to remain in possession. At the present time, however, the negotiability of user is fully recognized and the assignment of this right for an unlimited period is hardly to be distinguished from outright sale. Captain MacBride observes that, with a rising population, freedom for such transactions is important as a check on the disruption of plots by inheritance, and that records over ten years indicate that subdivisions have been counterbalanced by mergers, so that there has been no serious diminution in the size of holdings, which appear to average some three or four acres.

Prior to the British occupation of Kano in 1903, the Fulani government imposed a farm tax which was additional to the Muhammadan tithe on harvested grain and on cattle. It consisted of a basic assessment on cultivated land, plus a surtax on crops other than cereals.[1] The basic rate was about sixpence an acre. The assessment was made by a commission consisting of the Emir's representative, the fiefholder's bailiff and the village head. It was recorded on rosaries, and after one-third of the tax had been paid to the village head the balance was divided between the fief-holder and the Emir.

The British Government decided to continue this system and in 1909 introduced a method of measurement known as 'Taki' or pacing. The farm was treated as a trapezoid, the surveyor selecting the two approximately parallel straight lines which most justly expressed the relative sectors of the actual boundary; these were paced, and half the sum of their lengths, multiplied by the length of their common perpendicular, was taken as the area of the farm. In case of doubt two perpendiculars set at extremes of the shorter parallel were paced and half the sum of the lengths was taken as the second factor. There was no plotting, the area being calculated direct from the surveyor's figures. The advantages of the 'Taki' system of survey were its extreme simplicity, neither instruments nor highly trained staff being needed. The drawbacks were the liability to error, the absence of checks, and the opportunities for dishonesty on the part of the field staff.

In 1914 a survey school was opened, and in 1916 a simple form of cadastral survey of several village areas was begun. The method

[1] Lord Lugard's statements in *The Dual Mandate* (pp. 294 and 300) that 'rentals are opposed to native law' and 'no land rent is demanded, as being contrary to native custom', while generally true, require qualification as regards the Kano area.

followed was to traverse the outer boundary with compass and steel tape; the component units were then determined by interior traverses running between previously fixed points marked by metal beacons. This framework was plotted to a scale of 1/12,500 and sections of suitable size were enlarged to a scale of 1/2500 on separate sheets of squared paper. These were subdivided by further traverses into blocks suitable for detailed work, which were sketched into a field book. The surveyor then observed the farm boundaries with reference to these sketches, the results were plotted on the large-scale plans and the areas obtained by planimeter.

In 1921 the Government Surveys had connected a base near Kano City with their main triangulation, and thereafter the fixed points used in the farm survey were tied to this by means of theodolite triangulation and traverses. At the present time the system of farm survey and measurement is substantially the same as that introduced in 1916, but theodolite is replacing compass for the initial traverse of the village boundary, chain is used instead of steel tape, and all primary work is tied to topographical beacons. The survey is a Native Administration department and the staff (in 1938) consisted of thirty-two surveyors, twenty-five draughtsmen and six computators. As it is economically practicable only in the densely populated areas where intensive cultivation is practised and boundaries are relatively stable, it is not likely to be extended beyond an area of about 2000 sq. miles round Kano city, that is to say about one-sixth of the Kano Emirate. In this area the Revenue Survey system is held to be preferable to the village income tax system which obtains in the rest of Nigeria. The farmer's tax liability is clearly defined and he can limit it by decreasing his holding. Nor are his efforts to improve his land penalised, as they may be under the income tax system. The land assessment system is, moreover, the one to which he has been accustomed from time immemorial.

Coming now to the Southern regions of Nigeria, there are important studies on land tenure among the Yoruba by Mr. H. L. Ward Price,[1] an Administrative Officer of great experience, among the Yakö by Professor Daryll Forde,[2] and among the Ibo by Miss Margaret Green[3] and Dr. J. S. Harris.[4]

Among the Yakö, Professor Forde found that each patrilineal kin group has collective rights to (*a*) a delimited dwelling area in the village, and (*b*) a number of tracts of farming land. But it is on the basis of wards, or subsections of a village, that the village territory

[1] *Land Tenure in the Yoruba Provinces* (1932). (Government Publication.)

[2] *Land and Labour in a Cross River Village*, by C. Daryll Forde. (*Geographical Journal*, July 1937.)

[3] *Land Tenure in an Ibo Village*, M. M. Green (1941). (Percy Lund, Humphries & Co., Ltd.)

[4] See footnote 2 overpage.

is primarily divided. Within the wards, the lands of the kin groups may be considerably intermingled.

The control of the land by men of a particular kin group is subject to slow but continual change by processes of piecemeal accumulation or abandonment. Over each area used by a clan there is an elder who is expected to know the established rights of all individuals of his clan, to mediate in any disputes between these individuals, and to act as spokesman in disputes with other clans.

The kinship basis of tenure does not, however, completely circumscribe the farming rights of the individual. Individuals, or small groups of relatives, of one clan may be given farming sites on the lands of another clan. Or temporary rights may be given. This occurs when a man's own clan is short of land. The petitioner for rights must accompany his request with the gift, to the land administrator of the other clan, of a gourd of palm-wine. Great importance is attached to this formal recognition of the other clan's rights.[1]

Within the clan itself there is marked individualism; and except on ceremonial occasions few effective demands can be made on the individual for the benefit of the clan, outside his own particular lineage or extended-family. The farms are held by adult men individually and most men of middle age have well established rights to perhaps half a dozen sets of plots.

Among the Ozuitem Ibo[2] the component lineages (or extended-families) of a clan hold tracts of land, often several each, which are regularly cultivated, after intervals of fallow which vary from four to sixteen years. After each fallow period the farming plots are shared out afresh, in order of seniority.

The largest land-owning unit is usually a lineage of some twenty to thirty men, but land may also be held in common by smaller groups of close kin, such as a group of brothers who have inherited the land from their father, or a group of brothers and cousins who have inherited it from their common grandfather. In this class of land the usufruct is permanently assigned to single individuals, but the commonalty of the land is preserved by the fact (*a*) that none of the land may be alienated without the collective assent of all the members of the family group, and (*b*) there may be a re-allocation of the land as a whole on the death of any member.

[1] Grantees of the usufruct of land are generally in Nigeria expected to give gifts in kind at harvest to the grantor. These gifts are not equivalent to rent, but are a reminder that the occupier is not the owner. To withhold them would be tantamount to claiming the land, and the grantor would be entitled to evict the grantee, giving him time only to reap his crops. All over Africa the 'borrowing' of land is common. Even a chief may be driven to borrow land from one of his subjects and be obliged to present the owner at harvest with a portion of his crop. See e.g. *Land, Labour and Diet in Northern Rhodesia*, by Audrey I. Richards, p. 247.

[2] This information is based on unpublished studies by Dr. J. S. Harris of Columbia University. See also his *Papers on the Economic Aspect of Life among the Ozuitem Ibo* published in *Africa*, January, 1943.

Individual rights have been acquired in the past when individual household heads have, on their own initiative, made clearings in virgin forest. But at the present time most individual rights have been acquired by purchase or in return for a loan.[1] Purchase is frankly recognized, and the purchase price is normally twice the amount of that which would be received if the land were merely pledged. In 1938 plots capable of growing 2,000 yams[2] were being pledged for 30/–; if they were sold outright the price was £3. It is not quite clear from the data whether the sales are in fact outright sales or merely conditional, i.e. whether, if the purchase price were repaid, the land could be reclaimed. In any case the sale of land is still regarded with some disfavour and only resorted to in order to meet urgent needs, such as the provision of a bride-price, funeral feast, a court fine or a bribe. Land is not sold in order to obtain liquid capital for other economic needs.

The pledging of land, on the other hand, is a custom long established among the South-Eastern Ibo. Rights to pledged land are inherited, as are any other rights, but pledged land may be repledged to a third person, and so on. If pledged land is not redeemed by the third generation the rights of the pledgor's descendants cannot usually be substantiated.[3] And thus pledged land is continually passing out of the category of individual land into that of lineage land.

While sales and pledge effect permanent or long-term transfers of control over land, transfers for shorter periods are effected by temporary leases. Between members of the same hamlet the rent may be half of that demanded from outsiders, and may not even be specified but may be paid in kind at harvest. Many rent their lands in order to meet temporary cash requirements, and land is often improvidently used for this purpose when it should be lying fallow.

Women have no direct rights over land, but wives are entitled to the usufruct of land for their personal crops. A woman may secure a measure of control over land by providing (through a male proxy) money for the purchase of land or for acquiring it in return for a loan. Women, also, may rent land, directly or indirectly. Land held by a woman passes on her death into the control of her husband, as trustee for her children.[4]

[1] This means that cultivators can extend their holdings outside the dominant system of kinship rights. A single individual may in fact have rights in several group-holding units.

[2] In Southern Nigeria the normal method of measuring land is to calculate the number of yam heaps it can contain.

[3] Dr. Harris adds that in any case the Native Courts generally hold that the rightful occupiers are those who have been in occupation for a generation or more. The writer considers this statement too sweeping.

[4] Mr. Ward Price observes that among the Yoruba it is unusual to give women grants of land, but if a woman is well off and able to build and cultivate, she may be given land like a man. *Land Tenure in the Yoruba Provinces*, Section 99. Among

The effect of all of these regulations among the Ozuitem Ibo is that the reversion of group holdings into commonalty for redistribution after three or four generations tends to restore equality of distribution within lineages, while arrangements for renting and pledging land also compensate for inequalities. But a large land inheritance confers a permanent benefit on a lineage or village, which receives fees or the use of cash for surplus lands offered for rent or in pledge. The sale of land tends to alter the proportion of ancestral land held, as between the lineages and their subdivisions, the thrifty accumulating land at the expense of the spendthrift and litigious. The failure to redeem pledged land has the same effect. Altogether, the variety of the means of obtaining the usufruct of land, whether for a single season, for life, or until the land is redeemed, ensures a sufficiency of land for every grown-up male, provided he has the support of his kinsmen to meet pledge or rental charges. Through the pledging, renting and granting of land to neighbours and strangers, pressure of population at any point can be considerably relieved.

In the Yoruba Provinces of Nigeria the native system of tenure has in many areas been transformed, partly as a result of the intrusion of English ideas of real property, but principally because of the development of the cocoa industry. The following account is based on the report submitted to the Nigerian Government in 1932 by Mr. H. L. Ward Price—a report which must be considered one of the most authoritative documents dealing with tenure conditions in the Colonies.

In the district of Ife (Oyo Province) no services or payments of any kind are exacted by chiefs on account of holding land.[1] Such gifts as are rendered to the Oba are given as an acknowledgment of his administrative authority and not as the owner of the land. There is a Yoruba proverb that 'the king has power over persons but not over land'. If strangers are allowed to occupy land, that land becomes their family property in perpetuity. Even if the land granted is not being fully used, there may be difficulty in recovering it for the community, since the rules on this point are extremely vague.[2]

All land used, or available, for growing food crops, however apportioned out, remains the collective property of the family. But

the Ekpeya of S.E. Nigeria, according to Mr. G. I. Jones, the men do no farming at all, beyond clearing the land for their wives. The men concentrate on hunting and the production of palm-oil.

[1] When a person appropriates unclaimed land he reports the fact to the Oba, not because he regards the land as the Oba's, but rather to advertise the fact that the land is henceforth his.

[2] See section 50 of the Report. But in section 88 it is said that the head chief has no right to recover and re-allocate land granted to a family, even if it is not being fully used.

the collective spirit is stronger in some families than in others, and at the present time the tendency is to regard each allocation of land to individual members as a permanent settlement. No one, however, may give away his share without the consent of the whole family, though any one may allow a tenant to occupy temporarily part of his holding for the purpose of growing food crops.

The presence of economic trees, and the particular species to which they belong, affect the system of tenure and of transfer. Thus, if the trees are cocoa and kola trees, the land becomes completely identified with the trees, as both these types of trees are planted so closely together that it would be impossible to separate the land from the trees.[1] But between palm trees there is often sufficient space to grow food crops and therefore palms may be inherited apart from the land on which they grow. Again, the cultivation of cocoa trees requires a particular type of soil, and on this account a cocoa-grower may own groups of trees in different localities.

When the head of a family dies, his successor may appropriate for his own use the major part of the deceased's cocoa trees. But, if he is already well-provided, he may be content with a small share, out of which he may give some to his full brothers and sisters. He may not, however, re-allocate trees formerly apportioned. The remainder of the trees are divided equally between each branch of the deceased's family—into the same number of parts as there are wives with children. Each branch then re-divides its share among the children. The share of the first-born son may be larger than that of the others. The widows of the deceased are not given any trees, but they are given pecuniary help from their proceeds. All these provisions illustrate the interplay of inheritance and land tenure. It is said, also, that nowadays some heads of extended families or lineages use unallocated land of the lineage for planting cocoa trees on their own account, and that the inheritance of this land is restricted to the children of the deceased. In this way tracts of lineage land pass into individual ownership.[2]

Mr. Ward Price gives some interesting examples of the ceremony which usually accompanies a grant of land. Gin, and various viands,

[1] Compare *Zanzibar*, p. 72.

[2] On this point the Governor (Sir Donald Cameron) minuted that when the head of the family plants common family land with economic crops the children should not inherit it as if it were parcelled land, and any such claims should be stoutly resisted on the revision of Native Court proceedings. It may be observed, however that everything would depend on circumstances, e.g. the nature of the agreement made with the members of the family when the head was authorized to plant economic crops, and so on. Sir Donald elsewhere admits that in many regions of Southern Nigeria (e.g. among the Ibo and Efik) the family system of holding land is proving a serious impediment to progress, since no one will plant economic crops unless he can get a share of land for his own exclusive use. In this connection local Development Committees have recently (1945) been considering the possibility of introducing palm plantation systems on the basis of individual or village ownership, with a view to obtaining more and better oil with the help of machinery.

brought by the grantee, are consumed together by the parties and the witnesses to the transaction. The grantee also splits some kola nuts and offers them to the grantor. Petitions are offered to the ancestors and spirits for the peaceful occupation of the land and for its fertility. Before this ceremony the conditions of the grant, whether temporary or permanent, and whether economic trees may or may not be planted, have been determined, and the parties, accompanied by the witnesses, have also visited the land and made a careful note of the boundaries.

In some parts of Yoruba-land, when land is conveyed outright, a meeting is arranged on the site and is attended by representatives of the Oba, of the Ogboni Society, and of the townspeople in general. Kola nuts, palm-oil and cowrie shells are placed in a pot which is covered and fixed firmly on the ground. Close to this spot four species of trees are then planted, a sheep is killed, kola nuts are split and exchanged, and petitions are offered for the peaceful and prosperous occupation of the land. The religious rites are in honour of Orisha Oko, the farm god, and the whole ceremony seals the conveyance.

Among the Yoruba generally, as indeed among all the peoples of Nigeria, there is a religious attitude towards arable land, which is regarded as the gift of Providence. Land which produces food is something sacred, which should not be bought and sold like some chattel, but kept intact for succeeding generations. The same feeling is not felt towards town land, or land which is used for the production of commercial crops. Thus, in the towns, land is commonly bought and sold. And whereas, formerly, forest land could be obtained for nothing, it is now being eagerly sought for cocoa cultivation in return for money payments, either in the form of rent or outright purchase.[1]

In 1903 a notice was published by the Bale and Council of Ibadan, and countersigned by the British Commissioner, to the effect that all land in the town of Ibadan was vested in the chiefs. Such land could not, however, be alienated from the native owners, though it might be leased for a term of years on payment of a fair annual rent. But leases could only be issued by the Bale and Council, to whom the rent would be payable. Mr. Ward Price observes that this declaration, which still had effect at the time of his enquiry, was contrary to native custom, and he adds elsewhere that, although the Bale and Council are entitled under native law to make declarations stating or modifying native law, they are only entitled to do so if the declaration is in agreement with public

[1] Mr. Ward Price gives an instance of two land-owning lineages giving grants of the same tract of forest to different people, with the result that disputes, false claims and eviction have been going on for years, involving hundreds of cocoa cultivators and creating much factional ill-feeling in the city of Ibadan (Sec. 198).

opinion and practice. They are not entitled to demand rent for land held in private ownership.

In 1918 a Native Court Rule was promulgated in Ibadan, to the effect that strangers who occupy communal land should obtain a lease of such land from the Court, with the approval of the British Resident. This rule was issued with the authority of the Governor-General, and communal land was defined as 'any land the occupation of which is, under native law and custom, controlled by the head of a native community'. Mr. Ward Price gave instances to show that the rule had been misapplied to land held in private ownership, and added that there was no longer any communal land at Ibadan.

In some parts of Yorubaland presents to Chiefs on account of grants of land have been discontinued, but in others the present may be so substantial as to raise the presumption that the land has been bought outright. An instance is quoted of a man paying to the Chiefs of Ijebu-Ode £16 for a piece of land, on which he proceeded to build a house. The man subsequently got into debt and by an order of the Provincial Court the house and the land on which it stood were sold. This case raised a good deal of discussion. Whether or not the Court was entitled to order the sale of the land depended no doubt on the nature of the agreement originally concluded with the Chiefs. But the case illustrates the difficulties of the present fluid state of the land law. This is further emphasised by many examples of inconsistent decisions in the Native Courts.[1] The data obtained by Mr. Ward Price for the Ijebu-Remo area are conflicting —due partly, no doubt, to the proximity of this area to Lagos Colony[2] and the influence of English law. Cases have occurred there of land being sold under writs of *Fi. fa.* emanating from the Supreme Court and executed by the local Native Courts. In one of these cases an interpleader was entered that the land was family land and could not therefore be sold. The Court then ordered that the house built on the land should be sold, as that was purely private property. But no one would buy the house, owing to the uncertainty of the family's claims over the site. This is another example of the uncertain character of the native land law in the more progressive areas.[3]

[1] There is, for example, great uncertainty as to the extent of an individual's rights over his family allotment. If he lets out a portion does the rent go to himself or to the family group? Mr. Ward Price cites a case where the Native Court declared that it was contrary to native law for a family to divide its land. Yet the same court in another case declared that a man might sell his allotment, provided he obtained the consent of the other members of the family.

[2] Part of the Ijebu-Remo area was formerly included in the Colony of Lagos.

[3] All over Yorubaland land-holders attempt to obtain greater security by means of written agreements drawn up by ignorant letter writers. These documents often purport to be signed by persons who subsequently deny all knowledge of their contents. (See Mr. Ward Price's Report, Secs. 202, 210 and 257.)

Mr. Ward Price states (para. 334) that in the Ife and Oyo Divisions of Oyo Province no sales of land have been discovered, despite the amount of cocoa planted in the Ife and Ilesha districts and despite the better-class houses that have been built there. It is hardly credible, however, that sales have not in fact occurred. In Benin the owner of permanent crops has complete freedom to sell them to any other native of the district. In Abeokuta and its neighbourhood sales of land have been common for the last seventy years or more. By 1928 the right to alienate had become so generally recognized that sales of farm land were regularly advertised, and as many as one hundred auctions have been held in a single year.[1] In 1933 Mr. Ward Price reported that there was always good cocoa land for sale in the Southern regions of Abeokuta division, and that on the borders of the Colony the normal price for an acre of cocoa land was £3 and two bottles of gin.

Many interesting problems of land have arisen at various times in the Province of Abeokuta. In 1903 Sir William Macgregor persuaded the Egba United Government to limit the sale of land to transactions between Egbas, and in due course an Order-in-Council was promulgated to the effect that 'it shall not be lawful for any person seised of land within the territories of Egbaland to sell, mortgage, assign or in any way encumber the whole or any part of such land to any person who shall not be a native of Egbaland, and any sale, mortgage, assignment or encumbrance made contrary to this provision shall be absolutely null and void'. The Order also made it illegal to give a lease of property to a non-native without the consent of the Alake-in-Council. In 1933 Mr. Ward Price stated that, although this Order had been strictly administered, there had nevertheless been numerous sales to non-Egbas, since the definition of the term 'non-Egba' had not proved watertight.[2]

In 1922 an influential group of natives of Abeokuta protested to the Alake and Council against the practice of dismantling roofs and removing other materials from houses in order to satisfy judgement debts, and they made a formal demand that everyone in Egbaland—individuals, families and larger social groups—should be given the facility of obtaining a written title to their property. They should also be given the freedom to mortgage, lease, or sell their properties as they pleased.

The Alake and Council, in forwarding this petition, recommended that, in view of the large amounts invested in houses and stores, the law forbidding sale, mortgage or lease to non-Egbas should be relaxed in Abeokuta town, but they did not recommend that the same right should be conceded outside the town. They felt

[1] *An African Survey*, p. 854.
[2] *Land Tenure in the Yoruba Provinces*, Section 251.

it to be a sacred duty to protect family property and communal land, and unless the existing safeguards were maintained whole family properties would soon pass into the hands of European capitalists, and their people become landless or labourers on farms, which had once been ancestral possessions.

Sir Hugh Clifford, the Governor, supported these views, observing that a progressive trading community naturally demanded the right to raise money, when necessary, on what was for them their capital investments. If it could be shown that a property was the personal property of an individual it would be arbitrary to preclude him from raising money upon it by mortgage from the safest, most economical and most reliable quarter, namely a European Bank. To prevent a prudent man from entering into legitimate financial transactions upon which the safety and expansion of his business might depend would be an unwarranted interference with freedom.

The argument of the Governor that anyone who held land (e.g. a cocoa plantation) as his personal property should be allowed to deal with it as he liked, went beyond the recommendation of the Alake and his Council, who were opposed (apparently) to free dealings in any kind of agricultural land.[1] The Lieutenant-Governor of the Southern Provinces also pointed out, as regards town land, that if the right to foreclose were conceded then European firms who exercised it would violate Section 3 (*a*) of the Native Lands Acquisition Ordinance, unless the agreement or mortgage had received the special approval of the Governor. If freedom of foreclosure were allowed, the Banks, although they would give the natives the fairest loan terms, would obtain land rights of a freehold character.

In the end the Secretary of State agreed (in 1925) that while no agricultural land in the Egba Division should be sold, leased or mortgaged, the mortgaging of crops should be allowed. But no land included in a compound (apart from that on which the house stands) might be mortgaged. Within the confines of Abeokuta, however, house property might be mortgaged, but in the event of foreclosure only Egbas would be allowed to buy. Every mortgage or sale should be made subject to the condition that the Alake and Council, with the British Resident, should be satisfied that the

[1] Lord Lugard had already laid it down that 'If a native cultivator sells or mortgages his permanent improvements, e.g. a plantation of cocoa trees, to an alien (which for practical purposes involves the transfer of the land) the transaction should require the sanction of the Governor equally with a sale of the land, and a definite period for the duration of the transaction should be fixed. If the purchaser or mortgagor has the sole use of the land the right of the native ruler to demand a ground rent should be recognized.' (See *The Dual Mandate*, p. 307.) In another passage he states that 'it should be the duty of Government to withhold from native chiefs the power of allowing sales to persons not subject to their jurisdiction, and to enact that mortgages and sales of permanent improvements to such persons should have no legal recognition.'

seller or mortgagor was the real owner of the property. It would be advisable also that a small Registration Office should be established at Akeokuta, so that transfers (past and future) could be recorded.[1]

In 1933, the Governor, Sir Donald Cameron, in commenting on Mr. Ward Price's Report, observed that a man who cleared new land for himself, or acquired land by purchase, was free to sell it and could devise it to any other native of Nigeria under English law which was of general application in Nigeria, if he pleased, instead of under native law and custom.[2] The suggestion that an Egba should only be allowed to sell to an Egba would not be effective unless special legislation were introduced to the effect that, without exception, all land should be devised in accordance with native law and custom—an impossible proposition in Nigeria in the twentieth century. Natives should be allowed to deal freely with all their land, farming or non-farming, provided that on no account should farming land become attachable for debt. Crops, however, might be mortgaged. He would also allow natives to mortgage non-farming land to aliens, but only on the condition that if the mortgagee had to foreclose he would receive (whatever the title of the mortgagor might be—leasehold or other) no more than a lease for a reasonable term, just as he would receive a lease (with the approval of the Governor) under the Native Lands Acquisition Ordinance. Natives should not be allowed to mortgage farming land to aliens, and, as indicated above in the case of transactions between natives, farming land should not be attachable for debt. Non-farming land attached for debt and disposed of to an alien should also be the subject of a lease.

Some of these recommendations would have required new legislation and Sir Donald Cameron prepared a Bill for an Ordinance to empower the Governor-in-Council to impose certain restrictions on the alienation of land in the Yoruba Provinces. But the framing of

[1] The Alake and Council passed some rules in 1929 to enable landowners to have their holdings registered in a local registry, after survey and after the Council had confirmed their titles. The Government, however, did not approve the rules. In 1938 Native Authority rules were drafted for Abeokuta, but these were postponed pending the arrival of an expert from India.

[2] This is doubtful and would depend on the particular circumstances and on local practice. Local custom may or may not permit testamentary disposition. The right to clear land is obtained under native law. If members of the family had helped in the clearing they could dispute a will which excluded them from succession. Normally individually-owned land becomes family land on the death of the owner. The community, also, may, under their local law, have an over-riding right which would enable them to dispute a will under which the land had e.g. been left to a member of another tribe. The Supreme Court is empowered to enforce the observance of native law as between natives. In the Punjab, however, 'no person shall contest any alienation of non-ancestral immovable property or any appointment of an heir to such property on the ground that such alienation or appointment is contrary to custom'. See 'The Punjab Custom (Power to Contest) Act' 1920, Section 7.

satisfactory provisions was found to be extremely difficult, and in common with other problems of land tenure was postponed until the conclusion of the war, and an adequate staff made it possible for the inquiries to be resumed.[1]

SUPPLEMENTARY NOTE

The Land and Native Rights Ordinance (Northern Provinces of Nigeria)

A. Preamble and main provisions.

'Whereas it is expedient that the customary rights of the natives of the Northern Provinces to use and enjoy the land of the Protectorate and the natural fruits thereof in sufficient quantity to enable them to provide for the sustenance of themselves and their families[2] should be assured, protected, and preserved; And whereas it is expedient that native customs with regard to the use and occupation of land should, as far as possible, be preserved; And whereas it is expedient that the rights and obligations of the Government in regard to the whole of the lands within the boundaries of the Northern Provinces of the Protectorate and also the rights and obligations of cultivators or other persons claiming to have an interest in such lands should be defined by law:

Be it enacted by the Governor of the Protectorate of Nigeria as follows:

(3) 'The whole of the lands of the Northern Provinces, whether occupied or unoccupied on the date of the commencement of this Ordinance, are hereby declared to be native lands: Provided that nothing in this Ordinance contained shall affect the rights of the Governor or of the Niger Company in, to or over the lands specified or referred to in the Second and Third Schedules, or either of them, to the Niger Lands Trust Ordinance. (Cap. 86.)

(4) All native lands and all rights over the same are hereby declared to be under the control and subject to the disposition of the Governor, and shall be held and administered for the use and common benefit of the natives; and no title

[1] A recent Ordinance (No. 73 of 1945) empowers Native Authorities to make rules, subject to the Governor's approval, relating to the use and alienation of lands within their jurisdiction. See p. 301, footnote 2.

[2] This wording seems to envisage a purely subsistence agricultural economy.

to the occupation and use of any such lands shall be valid without the consent of the Governor.

(5) The Governor, in the exercise of the powers conferred upon him by this Ordinance with respect to any land, shall have regard to the native laws and customs existing in the district in which such land is situated.

(6) A title to the use and occupancy of land shall be termed a right of occupancy, and the grantee thereof shall be termed the occupier.

(7) It shall be lawful for the Governor—

(*a*) to grant rights of occupancy to natives and to non-natives;

(*b*) to demand a rental for the use of any native lands granted to any native or non-native; and

(*c*) to revise the said rental in the case of land granted specifically for building purposes at intervals of not more than twenty years, and in the case of all other land at intervals of not more than seven years.

B. Regulations made under Section 24 of the Ordinance stipulate that:

(1) 'It shall not be lawful for any native holding a Certificate of Occupancy to sell, transfer possession, bequeath or otherwise alienate his title to a non-native except with the consent of the Governor.

(2) Subject to any native law or custom to the contrary an occupier, being a native, may sell, transfer possession or bequeath his title to a blood relation, being a native: provided that the transaction shall be null and void unless the change of title is duly registered within a period of six months.

(3) Subject to any native law or custom to the contrary, an occupier, being a native, may sell, transfer possession or bequeath his title to any other native permanently resident in the same district, with the consent of the district headman and the approval of the head chief, subject to registration.

(4) An occupier, being a native, may sell, transfer possession or bequeath his title to a native not resident in the district only with the consent of the head chief and the approval of the Resident, subject to registration.

(5) If the district headman under regulation 3 refuses consent, an occupier may appeal to the native court; and if the head chief refuses consent under regulation 4, he may appeal to the Supreme Court.'

CHAPTER XIV

The Gold Coast[1]

I

THE Gold Coast resembles Nigeria in that there are two distinct systems of land administration. In the South, that is to say in the Colony and Ashanti, the control of land is vested in the native communities; whereas in the Northern Territories it is vested in the Crown. In the Colony and Ashanti, with the exception of (*a*) a very limited area which the Government has acquired for public purposes, and (*b*) forest reserves, all land is claimed by the 'Stools' or tribal authorities or else by families or private individuals. There is now no land which is not so claimed. The grant, therefore, or 'concession' of any interest or property in or over the land, with respect to minerals, precious stones, rubber or other products of the soil, is negotiated directly between the native owners and the concessionaires. But in order to safeguard native rights and interests, and to give protection to non-natives seeking a sound title, these transactions are, by the Concessions Ordinance, subject to validation by a Divisional Court. The control over the grant of 'concessions' is, therefore, exercised by a Judicial body and not by the Executive Authority—an unusual feature of land administration, and one which has met with considerable criticism.

Thus, in the South, the Crown has assumed no general rights over land. If it requires land for public purposes it may have to purchase it, on full consideration. All unoccupied land is at the disposal of the local or paramount native authority ('stool'). But in the Northern Territories the Government found it possible to assume a general control. Here there were large areas of unclaimed land which could be preserved for the benefit of the community,

[1] For the study of native systems of land tenure in the Gold Coast there is an extensive literature which includes (*a*) an official report on *Customs Relating to the Tenure of Land* (1895); (*b*) *Fanti Customary Laws*, by J. M. Sarbah (1904); (*c*) *Gold Coast Native Institutions* and *The Truth about the West African Land Question*, by J. E. Casely Hayford; (*d*) *Comments on Gold Coast Ordinances*, by H. W. Hayes Redwar; (*e*) the various works on Ashanti, by R. S. Rattray (1923-32); (*f*) *Akan Laws and Customs*, by J. B. Danquah (1928); (*g*) *The Natives of the Northern Territories of the Gold Coast* (1921) and *The Gold Coast* (1931), by A. W. Cardinall; (*h*) various articles by M. Fortes on the Tallensi of the Northern Territories; (*i*) M. J. Field's *Social Organization of the Gâ People*; (*j*) W. H. Beckett's *Akokoaso—a Survey of a Gold Coast Village* (1943); (*k*) Sir H. C. Belfield's Report on Gold Coast land legislation (Cmd. 6278)—1912. The West African Lands Committee, appointed in 1912, issued a draft Report in 1916, with minutes of evidence, and correspondence and papers laid before the Committee, but neither the Report nor the accompanying papers have been made public.

and in 1927 a 'Land and Native Rights Ordinance' was enacted, on the model of the Northern Nigerian legislation. All lands were declared to be 'public' lands; with the qualification that the validity of existing titles would be recognized. Provision was made for the granting of Rights of Occupancy, and it was laid down that no native could alienate his land to a non-native without the consent of the Governor. In 1931 this Ordinance was revised (by No. 8), the term 'native' was substituted for 'public' lands, and a declaration was added that these native lands were at the disposal of the Governor 'for the use and common benefit of the natives'. In consequence of this legislation there are no serious land problems in the Northern Territories; nor are any likely to arise which would be beyond the competence of the Government to solve.

But in the South the position is very different. Here, in the words of Professor Hancock, 'the relations which ensued between concession-hunters, Chiefs and the Government illustrate very forcibly the paradox that a government which wished to dispossess a native people could hardly do better than proclaim the principle of absolute ownership by the native communities.'[1] In 1897, it is true, an effort was made to establish the right of the Crown to all land in the Colony which was not being beneficially occupied, but owing to the opposition of some chiefs and other persons the measure (The Public Lands Bill) was dropped.[2] In 1912 the position had become so crystallized that Sir H. C. Belfield considered that any endeavour

[1] *Survey of British Commonwealth Affairs*, Vol. II, p. 182. Lord Lugard observes in *The Dual Mandate* (p. 309) that 'A civilized power in Africa, while recognizing the rights of the native Chiefs to dispose of tribal lands on behalf of their people, cannot escape responsibility for seeing that those powers are rightly exercised'.

[2] In 1894 Sir W. B. Griffith had, with the approval of the Secretary of State, introduced into the Legislative Council a Bill for an Ordinance to vest waste lands, forest lands and minerals in the Crown. All existing native rights of occupation and the right of chiefs and headmen to grant to natives free farming rights were to be protected. This Bill was deferred and replaced in 1897 by the Public Lands Bill, which declared that public land might be administered by the Government and defined the powers of native chiefs over such land. A native chief or head of a family was to be precluded from creating, except with the consent of the Governor, any private right in any land under his control, except as follows:—He might authorize a native to occupy land as a site for a habitation or for agricultural, industrial or trading purposes, or he might allot land for shifting cultivation. Furthermore, the customary rights of natives to take timber and forest produce, and also to get minerals on public land, were expressly recognized. The transmutation of tribal and family holdings into individual rights was to be promoted by conferring a 'settler's right' upon any native in possession by native tenure, at the commencement of the Ordinance, of land which he used as the site of a habitation or for non-shifting cultivation, and also upon any native who, after the commencement of the Ordinance, occupied public land under the authority of his Chief for three consecutive years. The possessor of a settler's right was to have a permanent and heritable right of occupancy. It was also to be transferable, with this limitation, that no assignment could be made, without the consent of the Governor, to a person not a native. The Governor was to be empowered to convert a settler's right into a 'land certificate', which was to be valid as against the world and would allow land to devolve according to English law.

on the part of the Government to extend the rights of the Crown would amount to a breach of faith with the people.[1] In Ashanti the failure of the Government to take early steps to acquire proprietary rights had less reason, since here Great Britain was in the position of a conquering power and was entitled to proclaim the lands of Ashanti as the property of the Crown.[2] This claim was waived at the time, and could not subsequently be asserted.

Until recent times the position of the chiefs or 'stools' in regard to land was generally the same as in other African communities. The people looked to the chief and elders to administer the land on their behalf. The chief allotted such areas as were sufficient for each subdivision, and held the remainder in reserve against the further needs of the future. But the demand for gold-mining concessions, which began about 1880, led to wholesale alienations by chiefs at the expense of native occupiers.[3] With the development of the cocoa industry at the beginning of the present century the demand for land became greater, and this, coupled with the spread of English principles of conveyancing, led to a rapid growth of private or individual forms of ownership. At the present time it is said that the Gold Coast farmer of the South is so land-conscious that it is becoming the rule rather than the exception that he should obtain his farm by way of absolute grant, evidenced by a written instrument.[4] No indefeasible title based on a Government survey can, in fact, be obtained,[5] but many landowners nevertheless waste their money on private surveys which are usually merely ground plans unrelated to the triangulation of the Colony. These worthless surveys are often regarded by their possessors as title deeds, and unscrupulous claimants to land use them to overawe less sophisticated occupiers whom they wish to dispossess. In his report on the legislation governing the alienation of native lands in the Gold Coast Colony and Ashanti[6] Sir H. C. Belfield in 1912 recommended that the control of alienation should be transferred from the Judicial Court to the Executive government, though he insisted that nothing

[1] Cmd. 6278.

[2] The Order in Council of 26th September, 1901, after reciting that the territories hitherto known as Ashanti had been conquered by H.M.'s forces, declared the annexation of those territories.

[3] Chief Mate Kole of Manyo Krobo stated in 1912 that he had personal knowledge of a case in which a Chief granted 32 concessions of 4 sq. miles each, at a rental of only £50 each, 'thereby depriving the people of permanent cultivation over the whole of this extensive area'. See Cmd. 6278, p. 59.

[4] *Annual Report of the Social and Economic Progress of the People of the Gold Coast*, 1938-39.

[5] There is a Lands Registry for the registration of deeds in the Colony and Ashanti, but registration of title has not yet been introduced. In the former Crown estate of Kumasi a compulsory system of registration has been established by agreement.

[6] Cmd. 6278, paras. 84-141 and para. 37.

should be done to suggest that the people were to be deprived of 'their inherent right of disposition of their lands'.[1] Mr. F. H. Gough, the Senior Puisne Judge of the Gold Coast at that time also favoured this proposal, observing that it was quite impossible for a Judge to have such exact knowledge of land matters as an executive officer on the spot. Sir Hugh Clifford (Governor from 1914–1920) also favoured control by the Executive. In 1926 Lord Harlech (then Mr. Ormsby-Gore) drew attention to the prevalence in the Gold Coast of litigation over land, which he described as the curse of the country. Boundary disputes had become increasingly frequent and the result was that many stools had been seriously impoverished, while some had been reduced to a condition of bankruptcy. The subjects of the stools had been subjected to heavy levies to pay lawyers' fees, and this was one of the chief causes of discontent among the poorer peasantry.[2] Mr. Ormsby-Gore did not, however, consider that at that time any radical change in the general policy of the Government in regard to land was either practicable or desirable. But in the following year the Governor (Sir Gordon Guggisberg) recommended the institution of a separate Land Court, with two new Judges, as one of the steps essential to the setting up of a satisfactory system of land tenure in the Gold Coast,[3] the other most important steps being the enactment of a Statute of Limitations and the adoption of a system of Registration of Title. Reference has already been made to the proposal for a Statute of Limitations, and its rejection by the chiefs on the ground that it was directly contrary to the native principle that long uninterrupted possession does not create an adverse title.[4] A general system of Registration of Title would also have been premature in 1927, since it would have presupposed well-defined titles to land which did not in fact exist at that time, and do not exist to-day. In 1931 Sir Ransford Slater considered that the creation of a Court or Commission

[1] The West African Lands Commission considered that such questions as the proper limitation of boundaries, the amount of the consideration of the grant, the settling of the terms of the transfer, and the adequate protection of the natives were matters which could only be properly regulated by the executive, subject to a reference to the Court in matters of title. The proper time for arranging these matters was before and not after the concession had been granted. Sir W. B. Griffith, a Chief Justice with great experience of land cases in the Gold Coast, shared this view. (Para. 163 of Draft Report.)

[2] Cmd. 2744, p. 147.

[3] In 1943 a Committee appointed to enquire (*inter alia*) into the procedure for dealing with land disputes considered that native tribunals were the most suitable courts to try disputes about land held under native customary tenure, both because of the members' knowledge of native customary law and because they can more easily detect false testimony on the subject. But in cases in which the value of the land was £50 or over, appeal should lie to a Land Court constituted by a Land Judge and if of £300 or over, a further appeal should be to the West African Court of Appeal. Effect is being given to these recommendations.

[4] See p. 25.

to deal specifically with claims to land would encourage litigation and also encourage subordinate chiefs to try to cut adrift from their paramount chiefs. The development of questions relating to land tenure should, he considered, be allowed to evolve from within. With these views the Secretary of State concurred, and the recent new Concessions Ordinance (No. 19 of 1939) has proceeded on the assumption that the previous Ordinances (No. 14 of 1900 and No. 3 of 1903) had been found suitable to local requirements. Few changes of importance have been introduced. Section 3 provides that grants of rights in land by a 'native' to a 'non-native' shall be void unless made in writing, and section 21 (2) reduces the area of concessions, other than mining concessions, which may be held by one person or company, from forty to twenty sq. miles, though the Governor may authorize holdings in excess of twenty sq. miles. This modification has been made in view of the possibility of the development of the timber industry. Section 11 provides for the maintenance in Ashanti of the procedure whereby concessions may not be granted by a chief without reference to an Administrative Officer—a form of procedure which does not apply to the Colony.[1] Section 26 provides that the mining rent in respect of a mining concession shall become payable after three years from the date of the certificate of validity, but enables the Governor-in-Council to exempt any particular concession from the operation of this section. It is anticipated that this provision will discourage persons from obtaining concessions for speculative purposes, without taking adequate action for their development within a reasonable period. By Section 31 security of title under a certificate of validity is strengthened by rendering such a certificate unassailable on any ground save that of fraud.

But the general position regarding land tenure in the Gold Coast is very far from satisfactory. The cocoa industry dominates the country. In 1936 it represented 63% of the total exports, and 98% of all agricultural products. It is a new industry.[2] The introduction of a tree-borne crop which may occupy the same land for twenty-forty years has destroyed the balance of a system based on rotational occupation by short-term cultivations. Yet the effects on tenure have received little study. According to Professor W. M. Macmillan, who carried out investigations on cocoa-growing conditions in the Gold Coast in 1939, 'The most elementary facts are still unknown and undiscoverable. It is said, for example, that the

[1] The West African Lands Committee considered (in 1916) that native land law had been little modified in Ashanti and that this was due to the fact that the action of the Courts had been restricted and the influence of the Executive had remained supreme.

[2] In 1897 the Gold Coast exported 71 tons of cocoa or .085% of the world's production; in 1936 it exported 307,000 tons or 43.2% of the world's production.

number of individual producers may be in the neighbourhood of 300,000. Any such figure is a worthless guess and no one, perhaps least of all a Government official, has any precise knowledge of how the total is made up—what proportion, for example, really are still peasant cultivators on some part of their original tribal holdings, how many are individual owners (and it may be absent and multiple landlords), who and how many are tenants, and whose tenants. It is only very lately that the Government has made public its awareness of an immense volume of wage-labour employed on cocoa-farms.'[1] Professor Macmillan concluded that 'neither the people nor Government can know how to act till the facts are understandably presented'. In 1938 the Commission on the Marketing of West African Cocoa stated that 'Land has been in great demand. Strangers . . . have been willing to pay large sums for land on which to establish farms. The custodians of tribal, stool and family lands . . . have welcomed the opportunity of easy money. With a complete ignorance of mensuration, and with no more than an oral indication of boundaries based on impermanent marks, land has been allotted to all comers who had money to offer. Cases are not infrequent of the same land, or parts of it, being sold twice over, and land titles are a most fruitful source of highly expensive litigation. The position of these immigrants in relation to tribal discipline is a subject which is still under dispute: the firmness of the footing they have established on the land seems not to be in question'.[2]

The most valuable contribution to the knowledge of cocoa-growing conditions in the Gold Coast is Professor Shephard's *Report on the Economics of Peasant Agriculture in the Gold Coast*, (1936).[3] In this attention is drawn both to the need of investigating tenure conditions and for a greater measure of government control over land. Native communities do not look ahead, and in the Gold Coast will not, without guidance, think even of the future of their own cocoa farms, or take any of the necessary long-range measures such as spacing, pruning, draining, 'supplying', manuring, and so on. Dr. Martin Leake has also observed that the trees in the Gold Coast are already beginning to decline and that, unless the decrease is counter-balanced by the opening-up of new areas, production will decline. The alternative is to maintain production on a permanent basis of a much higher degree of technical skill than is being shown at the present time.[4] In the official *Gold Coast Handbook* for 1937 it is stated (p. 37) that, 'Improvement in the quality of the farmer's work has not kept pace with his increased

[1] *Europe and West Africa* (Meek, Macmillan and Hussey), p. 82.

[2] Cmd. 5845. *Report of the Commission on the Marketing of West African Cocoa*, para. 58.

[3] *Sessional Paper* No. 1, 1936.

[4] *Tropical Agriculture*, Vol. XV, No. 12.

out-turn. Questions of tillage, cultivation drainage, shade, protection from wind, pruning, manuring, control of pests and diseases, receive practically no attention from him, and his methods of preparation of the cocoa-bean and of palm-oil are defective. A notable and serious defect of the local agricultural system is the absence of any provision for financing the farmer's work. In the event of a serious epidemic of disease in the major crops, or of a depression of prices of export produce, there would be no machinery for financing new enterprises.'

Land tenure is closely bound up with methods of cultivation, and a government policy of *laisser-faire* regarding either is (in the words of Professor Shephard) just as reprehensible as the improvident use of land by an individual farmer. If peasant agriculture is to be maintained on a sound basis it must be combined with scientific cultivation and a scientific use of land. As things are, the methods of cultivation are defective and there is widespread insecurity of title. The credit system is inadequate to the agricultural needs, indebtedness is rife, and land is falling more and more under the control of moneylenders and absentee landlords.[1]

A survey made in Ashanti some years ago by the Agricultural Department on farms of 1,250 farmers showed an average area per farmer of two and a half acres only. Professor Shephard stated that in the Colony the average cocoa farm was four acres, and that this was too small to yield sufficient ripe pods to ensure proper fermentation of the wet cocoa. Ten years ago some interesting statistics on tenure were collected by an Agricultural Officer (Mr. W. H. Beckett) for a single cocoa-growing village, called Akokoaso. The village lands comprised thirty-eight sq. miles. Of this two and a half sq. miles were forest reserve, two and a half sq. miles were occupied by village compounds, and three sq. miles were under cocoa cultivation, (two of the three sq. miles were planted with trees which had not yet come into bearing, and it was here that the food crops of the village were grown). The village had thus a balance in hand of some thirty sq. miles. This balance of 'stool' land was vested in the chief as trustee for the community. Nevertheless, individual members of the community were not required to obtain permission before clearing a piece of reserve land for farming. And once they had established their farms they could hold them in permanent right and transmit them to their heirs.[2] Even

[1] A Moneylenders Ordinance was enacted in 1941 but it is unlikely to be more effective than such ordinances are elsewhere. Debtors will not deprive themselves of their only source of credit.

[2] In 1912 Chief Mate Kole stated that 'in the case of private ownership, which is possible in some instances, the land is quite out of the control of the chief. The sale of such land is subject to the consent of the owner's family'. 'Most of the plantations (palm-oil trees, cocoa and rubber) are the individual property of the owners and can be sold without reference to anyone but members of the owner's family.

strangers could, by purchase, secure full rights of possession for themselves and their descendants. If they could not pay the purchase price they could still, by application to the chief, obtain rights of a less permanent character. Of the 354 cocoa-farmers, 267 were independent, while 87 were dependent, working on the crop-sharing system known as 'abusa'.[1] Many of the independent farmers were multiple owners and employed bailiffs. There were also 24 regular wage-earning labourers.

The existence of these 'bailiffs', most of whom appeared to have been at one time independent farmers who had later fallen into debt and mortgaged their property, and the continuous increase in the numbers of agricultural labourers, must be considered one of the most disconcerting features of the present land situation in the Gold Coast. It would seem that the small peasant cultivators are losing their independence to the wealthy few. The Cocoa Commission in 1938 formed the opinion that peasant cultivators owned only a minority of the farms and those of the smallest size.[2] They instanced a case of one wealthy farmer who owned no less than 79 widely scattered farms, and they stated that the employment of labour had become a regular feature of the industry—a fact which in itself constitutes a revolutionary change.

Another remarkable feature in Mr. Beckett's figures for Akokoaso was the number of female owners. Of the 267 independent farmers 104 were females. How far this was due to attempts to avoid the customary rules of matrilineal succession did not appear. But it was

In the case of those plantations which are situated on Stool land, the rights of the owner are limited to culture and usufruct. There is no right of alienation. So far as individual property is concerned, the owner has also the power to mortgage the land, but in the case of Stool property only with the consent of the occupier of the Stool'. The Chief Commissioner of Ashanti (F. C. Fuller) also stated that 'When family land is leased it is customary to inform the Chief, but this is purely an act of courtesy, as the latter has no right to interfere in family matters.' He added that in Ashanti 'we had to make a rule that where a man had properly planted a cocoa plantation it should be regarded as his own, so as to give him the fruits of his labour. That was the beginning of individual ownership.' Cmd. 6278, pp. 58, 59 and 87.

[1] Under the *abusa* system the owner of the land receives from the tenant one-third of the crop. When the crop to be grown is a permanent crop, like cocoa, the use of the land is given on the understanding that it will pass to the tenant's heirs, provided the payments are maintained. Though a tenant has no right of alienation, he may transfer his interest to a third party. See J. B. Danquah, *Akan Laws and Customs*, p. 220. Nowadays the *abusa* payments are frequently made in cash as an annual rent, which may be fixed or may vary with the prices obtained for the crop. A cocoa-farmer who employs a labourer may do so on the *abusa* basis of payment, i.e. of one-third of the crop or its equivalent in cash. A recent development in some areas of the Gold Coast is for the grantor of land for cocoa cultivation to be paid outright by a third share of the plantation when the trees have begun to bear. The grantee then, presumably, becomes absolute owner of the remaining area. If the grantor is a chief he may have to hand over one-third of his annual share to his paramount chief. A Stool or Native Authority which leases land for cocoa cultivation may demand a nominal rental only until the plantation has begun to bear.

[2] Cmd. 5845, para. 59.

stated that many farmers had made over their farms to their wives in order that their sons, and not their sisters' sons, should succeed. If this is so, then it would seem that in the Gold Coast a close study of the rules of inheritance is required as an integral part of the general study of land tenure.[1]

The Gold Coast

II

A Note on the West African Lands Committee of 1912

IN 1912 a Committee was appointed by the Secretary of State for the Colonies to consider the laws in force in the West African Colonies and Protectorates—other than Northern Nigeria—regulating the conditions under which rights over land or the produce thereof might be transferred, and to report whether any and if so what amendments of the law were required, either on the lines of the Northern Nigeria Land Proclamation or otherwise. This Committee sat on fifty-two occasions for the purpose of taking oral evidence, and in addition a great deal of evidence was taken on commission in West Africa. But the outbreak of war in 1914 interfered with the completion of the work and a draft report only was issued, as a confidential document, in 1916.

The Committee began its report by observing that it was one of the fundamental principles of Colonial legislation that, in countries acquired by cession or by conquest, private property, whether of individuals or communities, existing at the time of the cession should be respected. This did not, however, derogate from the right of the Supreme Legislature to regulate in the public interest the use to which an owner might put his lands, or to prevent him from using his lands in a manner calculated to prejudice the welfare of the community. The exercise of such rights, while restricting the

[1] Some further remarks on the subject of inheritance will be found at p. 180, footnote 2. It may be pointed out also that if a Gold Coast native marries under the Marriage Ordinance (Cap. 105), instead of under native law, then his legal status is altered and the native law of succession is abrogated. But in the case of intestacy there is no escheat to the Crown, and real property, the succession to which cannot by the native customary law be affected by testamentary disposition, must descend in accordance with the provisions of native customary law. But the native customary law is itself being modified in some areas, especially where matrilineal principles were formerly followed. Thus the Akim Abuakwa State Council has recently passed a law that in cases of intestacy one-third of a man's private property, which may include a cocoa plantation, shall pass to his children, the remaining two-thirds being divided between his widows and his matrilineal kin.

powers of owners, did not imply any claim to ownership on the part of the Crown. All European legislation was full of such restrictions, and to represent legislation of this character as inconsistent with private rights of ownership, and still more as an attempt by the Government to appropriate the ownership, was opposed alike to reason and experience.

The Committee then proceeded to summarize some of the principles which, according to the evidence, characterized the indigenous systems of tenure in West Africa. In the native conception land is God-given like air and water, and every single individual is entitled to a share. But land is not simply the property of the living—it belongs also to the ancestors and to future generations. As a Nigerian chief had put it, 'I conceive that land belongs to a vast family of whom many are dead, few are living, and countless members are still unborn.'[1] The common native expression that no land is without an owner is a symbolic expression of this conception, which is wholly opposed to the European view that 'unoccupied' or 'vacant' or 'waste' lands are unowned.

The individual who first clears land and cultivates it establishes for himself definite rights over the land and over the improvements which his labour has effected, and these rights are shared by his family and descendants. But normally individuals only enjoy rights as members of their family or village, and there can be no true understanding of native land customs without a realization of the corporate character of African social life. By virtue of this the ultimate ownership of land vests in the community, so that the 'stool' or the family has what would be described in English law as a right of reversion—a right which cannot be lost by prescription. The ownership of land, therefore, by a family is not analogous to that of tenancy in common under English law, but is rather a joint and indivisible ownership, no part of which is capable of being alienated voluntarily or involuntarily by any individual occupant of a portion of the land. Every grown-up male has a right to an individual share of land and as long as he behaves himself he enjoys perpetuity of tenure. But he cannot sell the land. Nor is it permissible to alienate land permanently to strangers. Where there is an abundance of land members of foreign communities may be granted a temporary use of land and may in time, through inter-

[1] Dr. R. S. Rattray, the distinguished Gold Coast anthropologist, has somewhere said that 'land can never be the subject of individual testamentary disposition, because everyone is from birth a beneficiary under a kind of universal succession'. But it is necessary to distinguish between ancestral land, which may not ordinarily be alienated, and self-acquired land, which may. As regards ancestral property there is, in the words of Sir W. H. Rattigan, 'a residuary interest in all the descendants of the first owner, however remote and contingent may be the probability of some among such descendants ever having the enjoyment of the property'. (See *A Digest of Civil Law for the Punjab*, p. 72.)

marriage, be absorbed into the community. If the stranger uses the land for shifting cultivation he is not usually required to make any contribution from his crops, but if he intends to grow cocoa or some other permanent crop he is usually called upon to pay a proportion of his crops to the Native Authorities. This is a natural development seeing that the extension of permanent cultivation within a community must often trench upon the area available for the cultivation of foodstuffs.

Such is a description of what the Committee described as 'pure native tenure', the form of tenure which is still practised over the greater part of West Africa. But in certain areas of the West Coast, European influences of various kinds connected with gold-mining enterprise, and with the exploitation of tropical produce, and perhaps most of all the introduction of English legal ideas and the conception of freehold and mortgage, had tended to act as a solvent to the native law of land. In the Gold Coast this process had been accelerated by the rapid development of permanent cultivation in the form of cocoa,[1] and also by the policy of non-intervention pursued by the Government—a policy of which the chiefs and certain classes of educated natives had taken full advantage. Sales of land by the Native Authorities, alienation of large areas for prolonged periods to strangers, and the growth within the community of a species of individual ownership, were among the changes which these influences had brought about.

The Committee used the term 'individual ownership' in the sense that it was ownership by an individual as opposed to a community or family, and that its distinguishing feature was a power of alienation as wide as that of a tenant in fee simple in England. The owner could sell or mortgage during his lifetime. His power of testamentary disposition appeared to depend on custom, as did devolution after death when there was no will, but the general rule was that native individually-owned land became family land on the death of the owner intestate. The Committee indeed, in several passages, (e.g. para. 99), drew attention to the very important fact that land which had once passed under English tenure did not necessarily remain under English tenure. It frequently reverted to

[1] Elsewhere in their report the Committee argued that the introduction of a crop having a commercial value for export purposes need not necessarily affect the character of the native tenure, and they cited the case of cotton in Nigeria and ground-nuts in the Gambia. But there is all the difference between the effects on tenure of *permanent* as against seasonal crops. The Committee added that in Ashanti there was no evidence to show that the native conception of tenure had been modified by the introduction of cocoa; but if this was so, it was due (as the Committee themselves suggested) to the intervention of the Executive who insisted that strangers, while being given adequate security of tenure, should not be given the power to dispose of the land. Strangers were required to pay a proportion of their crops to the Native Authorities, and the land remained vested in the community.

the native category. If, for example, a piece of land had, by native customary methods, been transferred by a native to a European, it would cease to be held by native tenure and would pass from one European to another by the ordinary methods of English conveyance. But if the land were again sold to a native, who had been assisted by his family to buy it, then quite clearly that land would again become subject to native law. And so, as Sir W. B. Griffith, a former Chief Justice of the Gold Coast, had remarked, 'The tenure under which land is held can vary with the status of the owner, and no owner impresses on the land any permanent form of tenure.'[1] This is a principle of first-rate importance and one which should be borne in mind when fresh land legislation is being considered.[2]

When the use of land for residence or for the production of agricultural produce for export or sale acquired an economic value, the right of possession of land also acquired a saleable value, and judicial decision began (perhaps in the sixties of last century or earlier)[3] to establish side by side with the 'communal' system a system of individual ownership in the sense described above. The Legislature did nothing to discourage the course of judicial decision in this respect, and in fact the provisions of the Supreme Court Ordinance with regard to the enforcement of judgements, and of the Land Registry Ordinance with regard to the registration of instru-

[1] See the *West African Lands Committee Correspondence* (No. 1048), p. 306.

[2] With regard to the rights arising out of private, individual ownership, Mr. Justice Smith (Gold Coast) stated in 1891 that, 'Family property can be traced to individual ownership. A person being the absolute owner of land—that is land that he has himself acquired—has every right to dispose of it, verbally or by writing, the latter mode formerly in one or two cases, but now frequently resorted to. Failing this the land descends according to the native law of inheritance, and then becomes family property, and the mode of alienation is the same as that of the stool property of the chief or king.' This is quoted by J. M. Sarbah op. cit., p. 273. Sarbah also observes (p. 61) that, 'In the Coast towns a member of a family may make separate or private acquisitions and dispose of them as he pleases in his lifetime, provided none of his family nor any part or portion of his ancestral or family property contributed to the acquisition of such property. But any property of his that remains undisposed of at his death descends to his successors as ancestral property.' See also H. W. H. Redwar, op. cit., p. 80 and the comment by Sir Donald Cameron quoted at p. 166, together with my footnote. It may be added that many attempts have been made in the Gold Coast courts and also in Nigeria to argue that lands which have been dealt with by written documents between natives are no longer lands held under native tenure. But the mere fact of using an English form of conveyance does not create an English form of tenure.

[3] Sir W. B. Griffith, who was Chief Justice of the Gold Coast from 1895 to 1911, controverted the view that in former times land in the Gold Coast could not be sold. All his judicial experience had proved that the buying and selling of land had been common. Witnesses had constantly declared that the land in dispute had been bought by their ancestors. In Akwakim and the Twi-speaking countries there was an old-standing native procedure in selling land known as 'cutting the *guaha*', (described in the *Journal of Comparative Legislation* in 1906—Vol. VII). Under the *guaha* custom the vendor agreed that if he ever wished to redeem the land he would pay double the amount which he had received for it—a native method of admitting that the transfer was an out-and-out sale. (For a similar custom in Nigeria see C. K. Meek, *Law and Authority in a Nigerian Tribe*, p. 104.)

ments affecting land, presupposed that land could be held by natives as individual owners.

In 1907 Sir W. B. Griffith gave a judgment which carried the conversion of 'stool' or community property into private property a step further than had been previously recognized. In this case (Lokko *v.* Konklofi) Lokko had lent Konklofi a sum of money, receiving the latter's land as security for the debt. The money was not repaid, and so Lokko took out a writ of *fi. fa.*, and Konklofi's hamlet, together with his cocoa and sugar farms, were attached in execution. The local chief put in an interpleader that the stool had a reversionary right to the land which had been granted to Konklofi's father about forty years previously. The Chief Justice held that the occupation had been of such continuance and of such a character that the land must now be deemed to be the property of Konklofi and therefore seizable in execution.

It might have been supposed that since Konklofi had been so long in occupation, and had inherited the land from his father, the land had entered the category of 'family' land. The judge, however, held that the land was not family land, but stool land, and then went on to make the important observation that, 'The decisions as to family land, which reach far back, show that the English courts will not, other than in exceptional cases, permit family property to be seized in execution. In this way the family reaps the advantage both of the native and English law, without the disabilities of either system. By native law the family property could not be seized for the debt of one of the members, but any member of the family might be *panyarred*[1] until the family paid the debt and expenses; the English law put an end to the *panyarring* but allowed the family to retain the advantage of non-seizure for a private debt. Had section 19 of the Supreme Court Ordinance 1876 been in force at the date of the first decision, it is possible that the courts might have invoked the aid of the concluding words of that section,[2] and have required the family to pay, and in default have allowed the property to be sold. That course, however, was not adopted and the law is now settled in favour of family property.'[1]

[1] *Panyarring* = kidnapping individuals in order to obtain restitution of debts—a typical feature of native law in Africa. See e.g. J. M. Sarbah, op. cit., p. 282.

[2] Section 19 provided for the recognition of native law or custom, and the concluding words were, 'In cases where no express rule is applicable to any matter in controversy the Court shall be governed by the principles of justice, equity and good conscience.'

[3] Land in the Gold Coast is frequently sold in execution, and many purchasers have believed that they had acquired an indefeasible title, the land having been sold through the Court. But a purchaser only acquires the right, title and interest of the judgment debtor, and he may be confronted by a third party claim—that of the family. It is easy for a family to prove that some of them had assisted the debtor in building or repairing the house attached, or in acquiring the land, and the court

The West African Lands Committee criticized the decision of Sir W. B. Griffith on the ground that the case had been treated by the Court exactly as a similar question would have been dealt with in an English court. In England the way in which the right to the land had devolved, the tacit recognition of the possession by the defendant and his father, the exercise of the right of building and planting on the land, the absence of all evidence of the payment of rent or rendering other services to the original owner of the land, would have raised a very strong presumption that the occupant was tenant in fee simple of the land; and though it might be an admitted fact that the land was originally the property of the stool the operation of the Statute of Limitation would, under the circumstances of this case, have practically converted the right, which was originally only a tenancy at will, into an estate in fee simple.

When, however, the facts relied on were looked upon from the point of view of native custom, their consideration led to a very different result. It was a leading principle of Gold Coast customary law that stool land was inalienable by the occupier. It cannot by any act of the occupier be converted by gift or sale into private property in the hands of another person. The occupant can use the land as he pleases, build on it, plant trees, cultivate cocoa and dispose of the produce. At his death it devolves according to local custom. But what he cannot do, consistently with native custom, is to alienate it, whether by sale or mortgage, so as to give the purchaser or mortgageee a right over-riding that of the stool.[1]

The West African Lands Committee considered that the Lokko decision might have far-reaching results in transferring stool property into private property, and in order to put some limit on this practice they recommended that there should be legislation (applicable not only in the Gold Coast but in Southern Nigeria, Sierra Leone and the Gambia) by which the powers of Native Authorities in respect of community lands, and of heads of families in respect of family lands, should be declared to extend only to

(1) leases or licences under statutory provisions, and
(2) customary transfers for occupation and cultivation, subject to the rendering of any customary dues and services, a

is then compelled to release the house or plot from attachment. An immense amount of fraud has been practised in connection with these family claims both in the Gold Coast and in Nigeria. And this can ultimately be attributed to the misapplication to native tenures of English legal procedures.

[1] In his judgment Sir W. B. Griffith said, 'If by native law a pledge of such land for a debt was valid, how can it be said that the land cannot be attached under a writ of *fi. fa.*?' But under native law pledged land remains permanently redeemable. He also said, 'there has been no express alienation by the stool, but there has been recognition of the exclusive occupation'. But exclusive occupation does not, or at any rate did not, under native law confer a right of permanent alienation.

proviso being added that no such transfer should operate to deprive the community or family of the land itself.

As regards the right of a native occupant to transfer the land he occupies, the Committee considered that there should be a statutory declaration—

(1) that it should be presumed that all land of which a native is in beneficial occupation belongs to the family or the community of which he is a member; and

(2) that the native occupier of family or community land holds the land on behalf of the whole family or community and has no separate or individual interest in the land, though he has in the crops. He is, therefore, only entitled to sell or mortgage the latter; consequently he has no interest in the land which can validly be taken in execution or sold.

These proposals seem open to the criticism that they do not take account of the fluidity of native custom, or of the cycle by which stool land becomes individual land, and individual land in turn becomes family land. They would interfere also with the native techniques for relieving congestion on land, through the practice of pledging and sale. The right of communities and families to sell their lands—surplus lands maybe—had long been recognized by the Government Courts both in the Gold Coast and in Southern Nigeria.[1] Moreover, the proposals would severely restrict the development of individual tenure, which is considered by many African governments and most Agricultural Departments to be an essential condition of progress.[2]

The Committee considered that security of tenure for the individual cultivator could best be attained by the careful supervision of the native tribunals. Special supervision would be necessary where permanent crops were concerned, since these affected the area available to the community as a whole for the planting of food crops. There might be a simple form of registration through the Native Courts, or alternatively the permanent cultivator should be entitled to apply for a lease in the same way as a non-native. The disadvantage of the leasehold system would be that it would create

[1] The conditions under which village and family land could be sold under customary law in the Gold Coast are clearly stated in J. M. Sarbah's *Fanti Customary Laws*, pp. 88-92. See also H. W. Hayes Redwar, *Comments on Gold Coast Ordinances*, pp. 76-81.

[2] The West African Lands Committee gave it as their considered opinion that in the country districts 'legislation should have as its aim the checking of the progress of individual tenure and the strengthening of native custom' (para. 315). The Kenya Land Commission, on the other hand, considered that tenure should be 'progressively guided in the direction of private tenure, proceeding through the group and the family towards the individual holding' (para. 1650). See also p. 107.

a dual form of tenure and tend to lessen the powers of the Native Authorities.[1]

The Committee did not propose to interfere with the vested rights of persons who had become individual owners. They would have wished the holding of an inquiry into the claims of all persons alleging themselves to be individual owners, with a view to registering them and establishing a registry of title applicable to them. But this, they thought, would result in a flood of litigation which would gravely aggravate the existing evil. They considered, therefore, that the question as to whether a person was entitled to sell or mortgage a particular piece of land should be decided by an intending purchaser or mortgagee, subject to any recourse he might have to the Courts by law.

But it may be objected that these suggestions are a shelving of the whole problem and that they set aside one of the Committee's first principles, namely the duty of the Supreme Legislature to regulate in the public interest the utilization of land. Moreover, they would throw upon the courts the making of land policy, another principle to which the Committee had expressed the strongest opposition.

In view of the fact that conditions in some of the urban districts of the Gold Coast (and also of the other West African dependencies) had become so changed by contact with Europeans, and that native customary tenure had been to a large extent superseded by a form bearing striking resemblances to English land tenure, the Committee considered that each dependency should have the power to declare that any district subject to these conditions should be exempt from the operation of the customary rules of tenure and that tenure on English lines should be recognized. The Ordinance giving effect to this suggestion might declare the law to be administered as follows:

(*a*) Communities or families should be empowered to sell or mortgage their land.

(*b*) The presumption that all land of which a native was in beneficial occupation belonged to the community or family should not apply, but the contrary presumption should be made.

(*c*) Individual owners should have the power to lease, sell, or dispose by will of their land and it should be liable to seizure in execution for debt.

(*d*) Assurances should be by simple document in writing.

[1] But a leasehold system administered by the Native Authorities would increase rather than lessen their authority, and in the case of 'strangers' would be more effective than exacting a proportion of the crop—a system which the Committee had described as 'a natural development' (see p. 179).

(*e*) Upon the death of an individual owner, probate or letters of administration should be requisite to perfect the legal title of the successor. But with regard to the devolution of the beneficial interest in default of testamentary disposition a strict adherence to the rules of English law should not be required.

(*f*) When not otherwise provided the rules of English law should apply to land unless injustice would be the result.

This suggestion of determining by statute the areas in which English and Native land law should respectively apply has not been adopted in any of the West African dependencies, but the principle received the approval of Lord Lugard, whose observations on the subject in *The Dual Mandate* are of such interest that they may be quoted in full. 'In all these dependencies,' he says, 'English law is largely if not exclusively applied in the big cities and to a varying degree beyond them. No doubt European concessionaires, holding land devised to them in deeds drawn by native barristers in English, and other native aliens, probably have their own ideas as to the tenure of their holdings. And it seems clear that the grantors themselves have only the vaguest conceptions as to the conditions of the grants. How the Courts—bound by Ordinance to take cognisance of native custom—can in these circumstances determine suits is to the layman a mystery.

'The first and most urgent step would seem, therefore, to be the determination by Ordinance of the area in which English law applies. This might be limited in the first instance to the urban and suburban districts on the Coast and fixed by the Legislative Councils of the respective colonies, to be extended if need be by resolution of the Council. Within that area all land titles would of course be registered.

'Outside these districts it would seem to be desirable to enforce registration (within a prescribed period) of all holdings not already registered, in which individual ownership is claimed, whether by aliens or by natives. The remainder of the land should be declared to be subject to native tribal tenure and (except for Government purposes) alienable only in accordance with the principles of native law—e.g. the freehold could not be granted. If at any time it were desired to extend the application of English law to any transfer of land in such areas, the consent of the Governor would be required to ensure that the grantor fully understood the transaction. The conditions applicable to individual ownership might be laid down by Ordinance in simple language, viz. that the land could be sold or taken in execution, with a correspondingly simple form of lease. A similar form for tribal land alienated on leasehold might be added.

'This procedure,' said Lord Lugard, 'would not arrest natural evolution, or perpetuate by legislation a system which is in course of development, but it would ensure that native tenure could only be modified to accord with changing circumstances after due consideration and with the assent of the Government. It would in no way interfere with the right of native owners (subject to conditions) to dispose of their lands, and to make their own bargains, and if so desired, to include special terms in the lease. It would assure to the grantee the clean title he desires, and a clear understanding of the law to which it is subject.'[1]

There are, however, certain obvious objections to the proposal to demarcate areas in which English and Native law should respectively apply. It has been shown already that a plot of land held under native tenure may pass under English tenure and again revert to native tenure. Moreover, systems of tenure are interlocked with systems of social organization, and to issue a decree that English land tenure shall apply in a particular area will not alter the fact that in that area there may be many living under the extended-family system and consequently holding land in a community form of tenure. On the other hand, if cocoa cultivation is begun in some remote region of the interior it will create conditions there unknown to native law and to which native law will have to make its own adjustment. To prescribe English law for one area and native law for another would create water-tight conditions which would stand in the way of any gradual synthesis of the two systems of law. Not merely would it hinder the accommodation of native law to English law, but would hinder also the modification which English law should itself undergo in order to meet the conditions of a West African dependency. Law should be a living institution, not a fossil.

The Gold Coast

III

A Note on Litigation and Registration

THE West African Lands Committee aimed at the establishment of complete control by the Government over the transfer of land in favour of non-natives, and at the discouragement of litigation between natives—litigation which, by the

[1] *The Dual Mandate*, pp. 304 *et seq.*

great expense incurred, was a source of grave danger to the country. They agreed with the view of Sir H. Belfield that, for the settlement of land disputes between natives, executive control should as far as possible be substituted for judicial.

As regards transfers to non-natives, since native customary law is inapplicable in such transactions, it should be a cardinal principle that no transfer of any interest in land by a native community to a non-native should be valid unless it were by lease for a term of years and were made with the consent of the Governor.[1] They further recommended the creation of a system of registration of title to be applicable to the proposed leases. This system should be of the Torrens type,[2] and all leases granted in future under the Committee's scheme would be placed upon the register. As to the other grants to be so placed, only those which bore the signature of a Government official would be received by the Registrar. Thus a Crown grant in any dependency would be accepted, whilst in the Gold Coast every certified concession, and in Southern Nigeria every grant approved under the Native Lands Acquisition Ordinance, would be entitled to a place on the register. The register would contain a succinct statement of the interest of the person registered and of any limitations on his interest, and a reference to the instrument creating the interest. A copy of the instrument would be deposited in the registry and it would be necessary to provide that no transfer of any interest on the register would be valid unless registered. The rules of English law would, under the Supreme Court Ordinance, be applicable in respect of interests entered upon the register.

As regards transfer in favour of natives, the committee would have wished to hold an inquiry into the claims of all persons alleging themselves to be individual owners, with a view to registering them, and establishing a register of title applicable to them; but this, they thought, would result in a flood of litigation which would aggravate the existing evil. In the districts, however, which they proposed to exempt from the operation of native land law and where tenure on English lines would be recognized, they considered that a system of registration of title should be introduced wherever circumstances were favourable. But such a system could not be satisfactorily introduced until a proper survey had been provided. It would be

[1] The Governor would, they suggested, only give his consent when he had received a report from the District Commissioner showing the area and boundaries of the proposed grant, whether the title properly belonged to the community proposing to grant it, whether the community fully assented, whether the consideration offered was adequate, and that the grant would not materially interfere with the community's requirements in the matter of agriculture, fishing, hunting and the collection of natural products.

[2] See the chapter on Registration, p. 212 *et seq.*

necessary also to retain the existing system of registration of deeds in any area until a system of registration of title had been brought into force.

In 1924 the Surveyor-General of the Gold Coast (Colonel Rowe) advocated a thorough-going system of registration, though only of absolute titles. He was opposed to the registration of unguaranteed possessory titles. He proposed, therefore, to apply his system only to (*a*) land held under English forms of tenure, and (*b*) land held under native custom which had been gradually modified so as to approximate to or combine with European methods of tenure. Colonel Rowe's proposals were not accepted by the Government.

In 1926, as already observed, Mr. Ormsby-Gore, after a visit to the Gold Coast, stated that 'litigation about land is a curse to the country. It arises from disputes not only over boundaries between tribes and chiefdoms, but also between families and individuals. Boundary disputes have become increasingly frequent and the result is that many of the stools have become increasingly impoverished, while some of them have been reduced to a condition of bankruptcy.[1] The subjects of the stools are submitted to levies to pay lawyers' fees, and this is one of the chief causes of discontent among the poorer peasantry.' Mr. Ormsby-Gore considered that, as far as possible, there should be an endeavour to build up a system of registration of title based on the compulsory production of all relevant documents and evidence.

In so far as the acquisition of land by non-natives is concerned, it had long been a cause of complaint in the Gold Coast that it was difficult to get a good title to land, freehold or leasehold, because of the difficulty of ascertaining whether the land was held under individual or community ownership and, if the latter, what members of the community were entitled to give a conveyance. Moreover, in the absence of any law corresponding to the Statute of Limitations it was possible for a third party, after a long interval, to claim the land. Many cases had occurred of non-natives who had acquired land in good faith being obliged to pay several times over to different parties in respect of the same piece of land. The Lands Registry Ordinance provided no adequate protection since two irreconcilable documents might be, and had been, registered on the same day. Under the Ordinance it was difficult to trace the various conveyances and difficult therefore to compile any clear record of title. On all these accounts it was suggested, in 1926, that there should be legislation which would protect non-natives who had acquired an interest in land from natives, provided that reasonable steps had been taken to ascertain

[1] It is of interest to note that at the present time (1944) Native Authorities in Ashanti are not allowed to spend money on litigation. Their annual estimates have to receive the approval of the British Commissioner.

(e.g. by a certificate from the Native Authorities) that the person conveying the land was competent to do so.[1]

As regards land transactions between natives, the absence of any general settlement of titles was also held to be the prime cause of the excessive, and often ruinous, litigation. There was no finality in native law and the fact that an area of land had figured once in a court of law was no guarantee that it would not figure again in the same court, or another. A case had even occurred when a Commissioner who had concluded the hearing of an appeal from a native tribunal, and was inspecting the land before giving his judgment, met a Judge of the Supreme Court inspecting the very same area. The whole position was complicated by the difficulty of ascertaining what the native law of tenure in any area was, a difficulty which had been greatly increased by the introduction of commercial crops and the alienation of large areas of land to stranger natives—factors which were creating many new varieties of tenure.[2] An additional complication was the conflict of laws and the fact that native law was now using English terms of conveyancing which might, or might not, correspond with those of English law. Under native law land might be assigned to a family and that family would be secure against dispossession. Yet such an assignment might not, under native law, carry with it any right to re-assign.

In view of all these complications there was an urgent need for a general system of registration of titles. In a new country the capital required for the development of private enterprise could only be obtained on one security, namely land; and the existing defective nature of the titles to land was a serious impediment to commercial progress. Every form of tenure could be admitted to the Register, and every Stool, Native Authority, kindred, family or individual should be able to know with certainty what it was that they owned, and the rest of the world should be able to know also, so that anyone engaging in any transaction in land could do so with a full sense of security.

Others have opposed the institution of any general system of registration of title, or at least of indefeasible title, as this would be striking a final blow at the roots of native institutions. The registration of lands held under native systems of tenure would lead to a scramble by everyone who had acquired land by native customary methods to register an absolute title to what, under the law which

[1] The Concessions Ordinance does in fact protect the lessees of concessions from natives attempting to pass bad titles, but the Ordinance is not applicable to land within the boundaries of towns.

[2] Farmers of one chiefdom now commonly obtain land for cocoa cultivation in another chiefdom, and villages have sprung up in which the houses and inhabitants belong to one chiefdom while the land on which the houses stand belongs to another. Cf. Sierra Leone, p. 200.

alone had put him in possession of a valuable asset, could never have become his freehold property. It would lead to the more rapid alienation of native lands, which would tend to fall more and more into the hands of capitalists, Africans as well as Europeans. Under the existing native system there was sufficient security of tenure. The native occupier enjoyed what was in fact a perpetual leasehold, which not even the most powerful chief could terminate from mere caprice. But tribal and sub-divisional boundaries should be demarcated, and also family lands. These could then be given formal title and vested in a trust. A land tax might also be imposed.

Others again have advocated a middle course. Any general system of registration would require a large and costly staff, and the people interested in land would find themselves involved in heavy costs. In the more remote areas they would lose their lands from sheer ignorance. But as regards lands held in private ownership—that is to say lands held by individuals or families which could be alienated without the sanction of any public authority—there was need for some form of registration, even though there might be difficulties in proving title and a large proportion of the landowners were illiterate. It would be a comparatively simple matter to register possessory titles, and these would automatically mature into absolute titles under the operation of a reasonably brief time limit.[1] It might not be necessary to register all lands held in private ownership, but only those held in urban areas. Family land in urban areas could be registered in the name of trustees.[2]

These are some of the views which have been expressed regarding registration of title to land in the Gold Coast. There would not appear to be any insuperable difficulties in applying a system of registration of title to the following classes of land:

(*a*) land held under the Concessions Ordinance;
(*b*) land acquired by the Government (including lands leased by the Government);
(*c*) lands that have been the subject of final decision in Courts of Record; and
(*d*) lands held under European forms of tenure.

As regards class (*c*) it may be observed that if the proposed new Land Court were instituted as a Court of Appeal its decisions would serve as a centralising authority. As regards lands held under European forms of tenure, there would be difficulties in defining 'European forms of tenure', and it has already been pointed out

[1] Under Section 77 of the British Land Registration Act of 1925 a registered possessory title matures after 15 years into an absolute title.

[2] It is not quite clear what is the difference in the Gold Coast between family lands held under customary law and family lands held in private ownership.

that lands held under European tenure may cease to be so held when the owner dies. Any partial system of registration of title may create more difficulties than it sets out to solve.

On the other hand, there are many strong objections to any general system of registration.

These have been stated as follows:

(i) the vague and informal way in which natives deal, at least with some classes of land;
(ii) the difficulty of ascertaining the native customary law;
(iii) the absence from native law of any idea of limitation of time within which claims can be asserted and enforced in court;
(iv) individual ownership tends to become family ownership on the death of the individual;
(v) if registered, individual ownership would tend to become ownership in the English sense;
(vi) registration would lead to an increase of litigation;
(vii) registration would facilitate alienation by sale, lease or mortgage.

Other objections have been noted already, or will be stated in the Chapter dealing with registration (Chapter XXIII).

The necessity, however, of clearing up the whole position regarding titles to lands in the Gold Coast is obvious, and this issue should not be confused by the supposition that the only form of registration of title must be that of absolute title in the European sense. Nor should the argument that any attempt to clear up the situation would result in a flood of litigation be allowed to deter the Government from embarking on an obvious duty. The mere fact that a flood of litigation would be let loose is only an additional proof of the need of a general settlement. But before any attempt is made to introduce a system, or systems, of registration there is need for much more factual knowledge of the existing state of tenure conditions. It is not clear, for example, what are the changes that can be regarded as a valid development of native land law, what are the bodies entitled to declare whether any particular practice is, or is not, native law or custom,[1] what is the precise relation of family ownership of land *vis-à-vis* the community or 'stool', and what is the legal position regarding land when a 'stool' is replaced by a new statutory Native Authority. The land rights of Native Authorities clearly require to be defined, and when this has been done it may be possible for the more advanced Native Authorities to institute some form of Domesday Book or system of registration—possibly of

[1] In Ashanti the Confederacy Council has recently been empowered to declare what is native custom.

possessory title. Where the community title has been impaired it may be possible to strengthen it by authorizing Native Authorities to buy back land as the opportunity occurs—a policy which is being followed in some areas of Southern Nigeria.[1]

Gold Coast

IV

Summary

TO sum up some of the main points of this review of land tenure conditions in the Gold Coast, it would appear that the complexity of these conditions is due firstly to the rapid commercialization of land as a result of the development of mining and of the cultivation of cocoa; secondly to the native claim of ownership of every acre of land; thirdly to the Government's acceptance of a policy of non-intervention, its failure to make itself acquainted with tenure conditions, to control alienation and to exercise general forms of control which would ensure that land would be used to the best advantage of the people as a whole. This policy of *laisser-faire* left the development of land law largely to English and African lawyers trained to regard land ownership, and indeed all forms of transactions in land, from the point of view of European rather than of African law. Much confusion has been caused by the ambiguous use of the term 'individual ownership', by the failure to recognize that self-acquired property may become family property on the death of the owner, and that land alienated to Europeans and held under English law may, on returning to native ownership, again become subject to native customary law. Confusion has also been caused by applying the term 'chiefs' and 'stool lands' to heads of extended families and family lands, as well as to the recognized public authorities and State lands. On the other hand, confusion has been caused by the supposition that the sale of land was a new-fangled idea unknown to native customary law. It has also been assumed that native law is necessarily ancient custom and is therefore incapable of providing the security of tenure demanded by modern conditions.

[1] In Ashanti under the Stool Property Protection Ordinance of 1940 (No. 22) Native Authorities may no longer alienate, pledge or mortgage any Stool property (which includes land) without the consent of the Chief Commissioner. Nor may any Stool property be seized in execution or sold in pursuance of any pledge or mortgage unless the property had been pledged or mortgaged with the consent of the Chief Commissioner.

Much more knowledge is required of the native rules of inheritance. These have been undergoing change in important respects. It has been suggested that greater security might be given to individual holders if they were given a declaration that their holdings were their own private property. But this would only have a temporary effect unless the entire systems of inheritance were altered. Yet systems of inheritance are part and parcel of the social structure and rules of inheritance cannot be altered without altering also the social system of which they are an expression.

Much litigation and debt have occurred owing to the alienation of land by chiefs, but this is less likely to occur nowadays since the authority of chiefs in this respect is better understood. In Ashanti chiefs refer applications by non-natives for land to the British Administrative Officers, and in the Gold Coast as a whole land may now be regarded as safe from exploitation by Europeans.

There is, however, the danger that more and more land will fall into the hands of African capitalists. There is ample evidence already of this process and of the necessity of restricting the right of transfer among natives. The European view of land-holding, or it might be truer to say the view held in Europe yesterday, has led to the conception that a man's land is his own to do with as he pleases, and that there is no longer a necessity to offer acknowledgement to chiefs in respect of land-holding. There is a political danger in allowing individuals to become owners of 'freeholds', without owing any allegiance to the local Native Authorities. This danger has become emphasised by the arrival in many districts of large bodies of cocoa cultivators from foreign territory. If 'indirect rule' is to continue to be a cardinal principle of British policy in tropical Africa, it would appear to be essential that the local Native Authorities should remain the ultimate 'owners' of as much land as possible, since the 'ownership' or control of land lies at the root of all African conceptions of government. The freedom accorded to chiefs in the past to sell stool or community lands outright had as its natural corollary the disruption of the native polity. It should be regarded as a fixed principle that no stool or Native Authority should be allowed to grant any interest in land for a period exceeding ninety-nine years.

The precise position of family and individual ownership in relation to public or community ownership has not been sufficiently studied. While the heads of the community (i.e. the 'stool', chiefs, or Native Authorities) may not be entitled to interfere in the usage or enjoyment of lands once allotted, or in the occupation of specific families or individuals, they yet remain the general guardians of the community's interests, the chief of which is the fair distribution and proper utilization of land. With a view to exercising this control Native Authorities may find it necessary to institute local land offices with registers or Domesday Books. But the first essential preliminary to all reform would be a scientific survey of existing forms of tenure. This would include a study of the rights of the stool or state, the extent to which land in each district has passed into private ownership, the nature of the rights of private owners (e.g. whether there is a right of assignment), the extent to which land has been accumulated in the hands of individual capitalists, the relations of landlords and tenants, the rights accorded to strangers and the relations of strangers to the local Native Authorities.

CHAPTER XV

Sierra Leone

SIERRA LEONE consists of a Colony and Protectorate. In the former all land is the absolute property of the Crown, though a number of areas have been alienated by Crown grant to commercial firms and private individuals, as well as by lease to the Imperial Government for military purposes. In the Protectorate, on the other hand, all land is vested in the tribal authorities, who are declared 'to hold such land for and on behalf of the native communities concerned'.[1] But the freedom of the tribal authorities is restricted by two important laws, (*a*) The Concessions Ordinance (No. 29 of 1931) which applies both to the Colony and Protectorate and regulates the concession of land rights by natives; and (*b*) The Protectorate Land Ordinance (No. 16 of 1927) which prescribes the conditions under which land in the Protectorate may be held by non-natives.[2]

Alienation

The Concessions Ordinance lays it down that no tribal authority or any other native shall have the power to alienate land for the purpose of cultivation except under the provisions of the Concessions Ordinance or of the Protectorate Land Ordinance, and that no grant or other disposition may be made without the consent of the Governor. The Governor may only sanction concessions up to 1,000 acres if he is satisfied that the grant will be for the benefit of the local Chiefdom, or for larger areas if for the benefit of the whole country. For a grant or disposition in excess of 5,000 acres, the consent of the Secretary of State is required, and there is a remarkable provision that grants are subject to any future conditions which the legislature may see fit to impose. It is also laid down that under no circumstances may a tribal authority or any native alienate land exceeding fifty acres for any longer term than ninety-nine years, unless it is to the Colonial Government for a public purpose. The Ordinance provides for the establishment of a Court to deal with all matters relating to concessions and this Court may only certify a concession as valid if (*inter alia*) it is satisfied that the customary rights of natives are reasonably protected in respect of shifting

[1] Preamble to the *Protectorate Land Ordinance* (No. 16 of 1927).

[2] The term 'native' is defined in the Concessions Ordinance as including 'all persons of African birth who are entitled by native customs to rights in land in the Colony or Protectorate'. The term non-native, therefore, presumably includes alien natives.

cultivation, pasturage, collection of firewood, and the hunting and snaring of game. A concession may not be certified if it grants or purports to grant rights by which natives may be removed from their habitations. On the other hand, there is a provision, amusing to a European, that if anyone attempts to invalidate a concession by putting 'fetish' on the land, he shall be liable to a fine of £50 or to imprisonment for six months.

The Protectorate Land Ordinance enacts that no land in the Protectorate may be occupied by a non-native unless he has first obtained the consent of the tribal authority, and that any non-native who occupies land in the Protectorate without the approval of the District Commissioner becomes a mere tenant at will, that is to say, his tenancy may be determined by the lessor without notice. But if the consent of the tribal authority and the approval of the District Commissioner have been obtained, a memorandum of the terms of the occupation must be drawn up in a prescribed form. A non-native may not, however, acquire a greater interest in land than a lease for fifty years; and it is laid down that the rent he pays shall be subject to revision by the District Commissioner every seven years. Year to year tenancies are determinable by either party giving three months' notice. There are provisions also regarding fixtures. In the case of tenants at will, or tenants on sufferance,[1] the reversion in all fixtures, buildings and economic trees is in the tribal authorities; but in the case of a tenancy created by lease, the fixtures and buildings may (with certain provisions) be removed by the tenant, or sold to the tribal authorities, who in any case are required to pay to the tenant the fair value (to an incoming tenant) of any economic trees which had been planted by the tenant. These provisions by which improvements are paid for by the tribal authorities instead of being sold direct to the new tenant, involve the important principle of preserving to the community the ultimate control over land.

There is one further provision of interest in the Protectorate Land Ordinance. It is laid down that every non-native settler who does not hold a lease of land and is not employed by a person holding a lease, must pay a settler's fee to the paramount chief, in lieu of the customary presents or contribution of labour sanctioned by native law. But this payment, or part of it, may be remitted in the case of a non-native who by his knowledge of any special trade or calling is considered by the chief to be conferring a benefit on the chiefdom. It may be remitted also in the case of any non-native who is employed by a person engaged in any industrial undertaking.[2]

[1] A tenant on sufferance is one who, having originally come into possession of land by a lawful title, holds such possession after the determination of his title. His tenancy may be determined without notice by the lessor.

[2] See the *Protectorate Land Amendment Ordinance*, No. 1 of 1935.

The Native System of Tenure[1]

In Sierra Leone the staple food of all tribes is rice, though cassava, Indian corn, ground-nuts and millets are also grown. The ground is prepared by cutting down the timber, allowing this to dry and then burning it. At the beginning of the rainy season the surface is hoed, but the stumps are not removed and the ground is then planted. There is no system of manuring or of artificial irrigation. It is possible to use some of the swamp land and the land fringing the rivers for several years, but usually two continuous crops of rice are not taken off the same plot. Cassava may be planted among the rice and taken in the second year. The ground is then allowed to lie fallow and it soon becomes covered again with bush and scrub. The fallow period is normally five years, after which it is again cleared, burned and replanted. This system necessitates large reserves of land, and it will be seen presently that one of the major problems of Sierra Leone is the over-farmed condition of the uplands.

The Protectorate of Sierra Leone is divided into chiefdoms, each of which has well-defined boundaries. The chiefs are territorial rulers and have jurisdiction over all natives living within the limits of the chiefdom. The fundamental unit is the town, with its surrounding band of cultivable land. Each town has the tradition that it was founded by one man or one family, and all over the Protectorate, if natives are asked to state the conditions under which land is held, they will reply that the land belongs to the man who first brought it under cultivation, or, if he is dead, to his descendants. All the chiefs are agreed on this, and no custom is more clearly or explicitly stated.

But a farmer rarely settles on land by himself. He comes with his brothers, wives, children and dependents, including in the olden days his slaves: and the land is cultivated with the help of all. By working the land all acquire an interest, which soon takes the form of rights. Even slaves acquired rights, which many still retain, even though the status of slavery has long been abolished. Nevertheless, the head of the family does not lose his right of allocating the land, and he may parcel it out afresh provided he does not deprive any of the others of all their interests. On the death of the head of the family, the land over which he had exercised control may be cultivated, for a time at least, as one holding. Or his children, as they found families of their own, may divide the land among themselves, in most cases according to the original apportionment by the deceased head. The fundamental basis of land

[1] This account of the native system of tenure in Sierra Leone is based on a memorandum by the late Sir J. C. Maxwell, formerly Colonial Secretary of Sierra Leone. The memorandum (adapted) is included in *The Handbook of Sierra Leone*, by T. N. Goddard, M.B.E., 1925, pp. 82-93.

ownership is thus individual ownership, passing as the family grows up into family ownership, which in time reverts to individual ownership.

The land belonging to a town is the aggregate of the lands owned and cultivated by the individuals or families living in that town, and the land in a chiefdom is the aggregate of the lands in the different towns in that chiefdom. But it should be noted—and this is a point of first-class importance for the understanding of native rights in land—that individuals, male or female, always retain membership of their family and even if they have been absent from their village or chiefdom for many years, they are still entitled, on their return, to a share of the family land.

Transfers of land between natives have always been common,[1] and when anyone wishes to settle in another part of the country than his own, he goes to some landowner there and asks for a piece of land on which to build a house and grow his crops. He gives the landowner a gift, the value of which bears no relation to the value of the land, but is dependent rather on the social position of the newcomer. The gift is a token and may consist merely of a few 'heads' of tobacco or a few pieces of cloth. It would be incumbent on the landowner, however, to introduce the settler to his paramount chief, who would also receive a gift. If the chief were not informed of the settlement of a stranger in his chiefdom, he would have a right to fine both the stranger and his host.

The settler is required to pay a regular rent for his holding; but on the other hand he is not entitled to dispose of it as he pleases. The original owner would always claim that the land was ultimately his, though he would not normally attempt to dispossess the settler. But in course of time the claims of the original owner become vague and the descendants of the settler gradually establish rights indistinguishable from those of the original owner. Those rights, however, are only established by the newcomers as adopted members of the chiefdom, and are lost if the newcomers return to the chiefdom from which they had originally come. This is an important principle since it has frequently happened in the past, and happens still to-day, that settlers on the borders of one chiefdom attempt to transfer not merely their allegiance, but also their land to a neighbouring chiefdom in which they had formerly resided. Under such circumstances the original landowner or his heir would be encouraged by his chief to revive his claim to the land, and to dispossess, without compensation, the disloyal settler or his descendants. Many faction fights between chiefdoms have in the past occurred on this

[1] Evidence taken by the Select Committee on 'The West Coast of Africa' in 1842 showed that sales of land to Europeans by individual natives were a common occurrence.

account, and it will be seen presently that in recent years many difficulties have risen because single individuals have acquired land interests in more than one chiefdom.

The lending of land is a common practice and it is often a matter of dispute whether a piece of land had originally been given outright or merely lent. In Sierra Leone, as in other regions of Africa, there is usually no limitation of time within which a suit may be brought, though some chiefs hold that if a farmer has cultivated his land five or six times, i.e. has been in possession for twenty-five or thirty years, he cannot be dispossessed.[1] However this may be, there is general agreement that if a farmer is dispossessed after long occupation, he must be provided with land elsewhere.

It is said that the sale and pledging of land was formerly unusual in Sierra Leone.[2] There was no market for land, as there was sufficient land for all. Moreover, land could not be sold since the owner's rights were limited. A man's children, as they grow up, acquire rights in his land and would object to any permanent alienation;[3] and the chief and his people would not sanction a custom by which the land of the chiefdom might be diminished. The practice of pledging land has, however, become one of considerable importance in recent years. With the advent of permanent swamp cultivation of rice and the establishment of permanent tree crops in certain areas, holdings have come into existence on which money lenders are ready to advance money, accepting the land as security and its use as interest. To this there will be further reference in Chapter XXII, where the subject of pledging land is dealt with as a whole.

The most important problems of land tenure in recent years have arisen in connection with the extension of the cultivation of swamp rice to the mangrove belts which fringe the rivers—a method of farming which has been fostered by the Government as a means not only of relieving pressure on the impoverished uplands, but of securing the people's food and establishing a much needed addition to the export trade. Many agriculturists from the congested upland areas have already been successfully established in the swamp lands and provided with productive farms, but the process of settling a high proportion of immigrants in alien chiefdoms in a short space of time has presented many difficulties, the chief of which has been security of tenure.

In the swamps, as in the uplands, the cultivator who clears the swamp, and his family after him, own the exclusive right of using

[1] His case is very much strengthened if he can show that the graves of his ancestors are on his land.

[2] See *The Handbook of Sierra Leone*, p. 87.

[3] It is unthinkable in native law for a man to disinherit the whole of his family.

the land, but in the Scarcies area there is a notable departure from normal practice in that strangers from neighbouring chiefdoms have been allowed to clear plots for themselves, while still residing in their own homes. In this way, a single individual may, and often does in fact, own farms in two chiefdoms and is subject to two distinct Native Authorities. The Director of Agriculture (Mr. F. J. Martin) has observed that if strangers can obtain a sound title to the undisturbed use of land, there appears to be little wrong in the method of land tenure, and nothing to retard development. But if the authorities in the swamp area were to become reluctant to allow the infiltration of immigrants, a serious position might arise, since the over-farmed uplands cannot support their present population. Many of the upland peoples have been driven to the towns and mining centres in the hope of obtaining better conditions of living, thus forming nuclei of unemployment. The systematic development of the swamp areas is, therefore, essential to the welfare of Sierra Leone, and although the right of a chiefdom in the swamp area to reserve adequate living space for its own people is fully recognized, yet any attitude which would prevent the development of the large areas of potentially rich, but at present waste, swamp would have to be overcome. Already it would seem that the customary gift to the paramount chief for permission to clear a piece of swamp has become abnormally high.[1]

[1] Official Report by F. J. Martin, Director of Agriculture.

CHAPTER XVI

Mauritius and Fiji[1]

MAURITIUS. The island of Mauritius was discovered, or rediscovered, by the Portuguese in 1507, annexed by the Dutch in 1598, by the French in 1715, and by the British in 1810. It has an area of 720 sq. miles. The population in 1939 was estimated to be 419,059, of whom 271,687 were Indians. The density of 582 persons to the square mile is very high for an agricultural community. The climate is relatively free from extremes, but tropical cyclones at times cause heavy damage to the crops, and occasional droughts have also led to much distress.

The land distribution in 1940 was as follows:

Lands under sugar cane	150,845	acres
Lands under secondary crops ..	24,196	,,
Crown lands and reserves ..	80,733	,,
Township lands	18,240	,,
Other lands	186,786	,,
Total ..	460,800	,,

The amount of alienated land constitutes about 83% of the total area. Most of it became private property as a result of concessions made during the period of French occupation, but the large areas held by Indians were acquired under systems of 'métayage' or 'morcellement', whereby many large estates were parcelled out among the tenants. These systems are still practised, though on a much reduced scale.[2]

In Mauritius land tenure, like the whole of the economic life of the island, is subject to the dominance of the sugar industry. 80% of the cultivable area of Mauritius is under sugar-cane, 80% of its essential foodstuffs are imported, and 98% of its exports take the form of sugar. There are about seventy sugar estates, of which rather more than half are equipped with factories, and there are some 20,000 small planters, whose holdings constitute about 43% of the total area under cane. Most of these small planters are

[1] This Chapter is, by permission of the Society of Comparative Legislation, reprinted from the *Journal of Comparative Legislation*, Third Series, Vol. XXVI, Parts II and IV, p. 42, 'Land Tenure in Mauritius and Fiji', by C. K. Meek.

[2] It is interesting to note that among the qualifications for the franchise in Mauritius are (*a*) ownership of immovable property of the annual value of at least Rs. 300, or (*b*) tenancy at the rental rate of at least Rs. 25 a month.

Indians, or the descendants of Indians who came to Mauritius as indentured labour, and when freed from their indenture became independent growers, though many still supplement their incomes by working as part-time labourers on the estates.[1] Mauritius thus presents a striking parallel to Fiji, where 43% of the population are descendants of East Indians who came to Fiji as indentured labour for the sugar estates. But in Fiji the East Indians have become partners with the Colonial Sugar Refining Company, which relies almost entirely for its supply of sugar on the efforts of small growers, and provides them with technical guidance and other assistance; in Mauritius the small growers have regarded the factories merely as a market.

In 1937 the grievances of the small planters led to considerable unrest. A Commission appointed to inquire into these grievances found that the causes were the excessive rates charged by the factories for crushing canes, the cuts made in the prices offered for a particular species of cane, the absence of control over weigh-bridges, the necessity of having to sell their produce through particular dealers, and the general lack of credit facilities.

As a result of recommendations made by the Commission, the 'Cane Planters and Sugar Millers Control Ordinance' was enacted in 1939. This provides for the establishment of a Central Board, with a regional committee in each of the nine districts of the island. Each committee consists of two representatives of millers and four of the planters, of whom two must be small planters, i.e. producing less than 1000 tons per annum. The regional committee is empowered to deal with disputes between planters and millers, and any dispute which cannot be settled by the regional committee is referred to the Central Board. Planters growing cane in a particular factory area must send their canes to that factory, and the miller is bound to purchase all canes inside that area and to refuse canes grown outside.

With regard to middlemen, the view of the Government is that the middleman still serves a useful purpose by supplying credit to small planters. But his activities must be controlled. Under the Ordinance, therefore, every middleman must obtain a permit from the Registrar; this permit may be cancelled if the Central Board has reason to believe that the holder is not a fit and proper person to

[1] In 1940 the figures for Indian cultivation of cane were as follows:

On estates	10,895	acres
Off estates	38,258	,,
Estate ownership ..	5,515	,,
Total ..	54,668	,,

This total represented 36.2% of the total cane cultivation.

continue to hold a permit. The prices to be paid by a middleman for canes must be fixed by the miller in consultation with the planter.

Furthermore, in 1939, a 'Small-Planters Association' was formed under the Industrial Associations Ordinance (No. 7 of 1938). This will keep a close watch on all contracts between millers and small planters. With the establishment of the principle of free negotiation between the miller and the small planter, and of a right of appeal to the Central Board, it may be expected that the position of small-holders will be considerably improved.

Dr. Martin Leake has expressed the opinion that the larger estates would profit by dividing up their lands into small holdings and leasing these, thereby reducing their direct labour bill and so solving the problem of the wage-paid labourer. He added, also that Mauritius might soon be faced with the problem of how to use the excess land. The increase of local production of food would seem to be linked up with that of the extension of small holdings. With these systematically organized on a basis of family cultivation, partly planted with cane and partly with food crops, and with access to grazing areas, the local food supplies could be substantially increased.[1] Mauritius is a good example of the doctrine that the character of the tenure must depend on the type of rural economy which it is proposed to promote.

Fiji. The Fiji Islands provide an interesting illustration of a plural society. The small European population (slightly over 2%) is mainly concerned with the management of the sugar and copra industries; the East Indian (43%) with the cultivation of sugar-cane and rice; and the Fijian (50%) with the cultivation of foodstuffs and cocoa-nuts. The reconciliation of the interests of the three groups has not been easy, but it has been achieved to a remarkable degree. Most of the Indians in Fiji are Fiji-born and regard themselves, and are regarded by the Government, as an integral part of the community. They have done good service to the indigenous Fijians by teaching them the art of field agriculture.[2] The Fijians, on the other hand, have been generous to the Indians. Their recent surrender of the control of their excess lands has enabled the Government to place the relations of Indians and Fijians on a sound foundation of goodwill.

In the early days the sugar canes of Fiji were grown by the various

[1] Dr. Martin Leake 'Further Studies in Tropical Land Tenure', in *Tropical Agriculture,* Vol. XVI, No. 1.

[2] The indigenous system of land holding was largely one of service-tenures. The Chief could call for the labour of any district and use it for planting, house-building, etc. In times of famine the Chief would declare the produce of plantations to be common property.

companies with hired labour indentured from India.[1] But in 1913 experiments were begun by the Colonial Sugar Refining Company, with a view to converting the estate system into one of small holdings, and establishing thereby a contented peasantry with a direct interest in the land. These experiments proved so successful that the Company now relies almost solely for its supplies of cane on peasant farmers who are either tenants of the Company or lessees of lands owned by Fijians.[2] The Company's tenants are given a ten years' lease which is readily renewable and contains clauses to ensure proper cultivation. The holdings are of ten acres and are cultivated in four sections—two and a half acres planted with sugar cane, two and a half acres of ratoon crop, two and a half acres of Mauritius beans ploughed under for fertilization, and two and a half acres of young cane plants. The farms are so arranged that the sections similarly used adjoin, thus making for economy in the large-scale harvest operations which are carried out co-operatively. Payment is made according to the sugar content, and this itself is an inducement to good husbandry. The Company also provides transport, which has always been one of the main problems of peasant agriculture. But an even more important service is the system of estate overseers who act as the advisers and friends of the farmer, and form an essential link between the field and the factory. Tenants are not permitted to grow any other crops except sugar cane and green manures, but they are encouraged to establish gardens round their homesteads. If need be, they are given cash advances on easy terms.

This partnership between a Company holding a monopoly, and a peasant population, has been one of the most remarkable developments of Colonial agriculture in recent times, and may prove to be one of the solutions of the difficulty of adapting local peasant proprietorship to the large-scale operations of international trade.[3] Its success is evident from the keen competition to become tenants of the Company. If it can be criticized at all, it must be from the point of view of the danger of excessive reliance on a single crop. Mixed farming is nowadays held to be the best form of insurance for

[1] Indian labour was first introduced in 1878, when the cultivation of sugar began to pass into the hands of large companies working with modern machinery.

[2] Tenant farms leased by Indians from Fijians vary in size from about 2½ acres to 12. The average yield per acre produced by non-tenants of the Company is 20 tons as compared with the 23 of tenants. Not all Indian farmers grow sugar cane. Some practise mixed farming, raising rice and corn and keeping cattle and goats. The total area farmed by Indians was (in 1939) about 110,000 acres of which some 33,000 acres were held as cane-growing tenants of the Company. Some 2,000 or 3,000 acres are held by Indians as freehold.

[3] Among parallel large-scale developments elsewhere are (*a*) The Latifiyha Estates in Iraq, (*b*) The Gezira Scheme in the Sudan, and (*c*) The Alternative Livelihood Scheme, also in the Sudan. Notes on these schemes will be found in the Appendix.

peasant agriculture. Yet, if production and distribution can be controlled by international action, then it would seem to be a sound principle that every colony should concentrate on the crop which it can most profitably produce.

The Fiji Islands were ceded to the British Crown in 1874, and by article 4 of the deed of cession, the absolute proprietorship of all Fijian country not shown to be already alienated, or in actual use or occupation by some tribe or chief, or not actually required for the probable future support or maintenance of some chief or tribe, was declared to be vested in Queen Victoria and her successors.[1] Since then there have been various land ordinances, but until 1940 the ordinance of 1905 governed the tenure of land. This ordinance enabled natives to lease their land to anyone they pleased, provided that the consent of the Governor-in-Council had first been obtained. Arrangements for such leases had to be made through the Commissioner of Lands, and the leases to be duly registered. Fijian lessees were forbidden to transfer or otherwise embarrass their interests without permission, but other lessees were allowed to do so. The leases carried certain conditions requiring the improvement of land. When a lessee wished to renew a lease he applied to the Commissioner of Lands. If an owner refused renewal he had to pay the value of improvement unless it could be shown that the land was genuinely required for his own use. Otherwise the lease was compulsorily extended. The usual term for agricultural leases was twenty-one years, and for extensions ten years. Rents were paid through the Treasurer, 10% being payable to the Government, 40% to the chiefs, and 50% to the 'mataqali' or land-owning group. The land legislation also prohibited the alienation of native land by sale, grant, or exchange, except to the Crown, and it was laid down that when a 'mataqali' or land-owning group became extinct its land automatically became the property of the Crown as *ultimus haeres*. Finally, it was made an offence for anyone to be a party to any contract or arrangement relating to the tenure of any native lands, except with the written consent of the Governor-in-Council.

Such was the general situation until 1940, and it could be claimed that, in so far as alienation of land was concerned, the British Government had done its duty by the Fijians. After sixty-five years of British rule native owners remained possessed of some 3,770,000 acres out of a total of 4,500,000, or 83%. Of the area lost to them more than half (415,000 acres) had been alienated as a result of sales prior to the Act of Cession. As regards the area alienated to the Crown, 118,336 acres had been acquired as *ultimus haeres* and 82,215 acres as vacant lands for which no claim had been made.

[1] But ownership was later restored to the Fijians.

Yet the land policy failed to meet the complex situation, caused in the main by the permanent settlement of Indians in the Colony. Although the Fijians owned all the agricultural land and derived good incomes from the leasing of their lands, they looked with envy on the wealth derived by Indians from their leased sugar cane holdings. But cane cultivation is highly specialised work and was formerly considered to be beyond the competence of Fijians, the form of whose social organization was not conducive to the development of the individual enterprise which cane-production seemed to demand. Yet, through the encouragement of the Government and the co-operation of the Colonial Sugar Refining Company, Fijians began, about 1933, to engage increasingly in sugar-cane cultivation. In that year the Government enacted a Native Lands (Occupation) Ordinance which enabled an individual Fijian cultivator to obtain security of tenure over a portion of tribal land and to enjoy the proceeds of his labour without interference from other members of his social group.[1]

This development caused anxiety among the East Indians. The area on which cane could be grown was limited and competition keen. Moreover the Government, in order to protect the Fijians from their own improvidence, had (in 1930) initiated a policy of reserving permanently, for the exclusive use of Fijian communities, areas of their own unleased land in the vicinity of their villages. But quite apart from that, it was open to Fijians, on the expiration of a lease, to take back the land of their Indian tenants, on payment of compensation for growing crops and improvements. Many Fijians, who were eager to obtain for themselves the profits made by the former tenants, resumed the land and embarked on cane cultivation, but soon abandoned it, as they had not yet learned the necessary technique. In this way much good agricultural land was thrown out of cultivation, the sugar industry suffered, the dispossessed Indians had to find new homes, and their Fijian supplanters lost their rents.

The question of the length of lease was one that had long rankled with the Indians. Before 1930, Indians could not hold a lease for more than twenty-one years—a period which they considered insufficient for the recovery of capital spent on housing, equipment and general development. This discrimination against Indians was eventually removed and extensions, under certain circumstances, were granted for a further period of nine years. But many Indians still objected to the leasehold conditions. Abuses had also arisen. Although the rents charged on leases of native land were fixed by the Government, yet, owing to the keen competition for cane and other lands, Indian leaseholders frequently sublet their holdings at

[1] This Ordinance (No. 35 of 1933) later became unnecessary and was repealed.

increased rents or transferred their leases for a heavy premium. High premiums were also charged by Fijian owners for consent to a lease on renewal. On all these accounts, many of which were of their own creation, the Indians attacked the entire system of tenure, and there was a general demand for freehold grants, or failing that, for leases of the longest possible duration.

By 1936 the Government had come to the conclusion that a greater measure of control over lands was necessary, if the interests of the Indians and Fijians were to be co-ordinated, if continuity of agricultural policy and security of tenure were to be attained, and if the existing wasteful system of agriculture[1] was to be replaced by a planned economy. The Fijian leaders freely shared this opinion of the Government, and in 1940 the Native Land Trust Ordinance (No. 12 of 1940) was enacted—an Ordinance which is likely to have an influence far beyond the confines of Fiji. Under this Ordinance the control of all native land[2] is vested in a Board. Although it is provided that the Board shall administer the native lands for the benefit of the native owners, it is clearly the intention of the legislation that the interests of other sections of the community shall also be considered. The Board is to have the assistance of local committees which will advise it on questions of land tenure. This is an important innovation. There is an obvious need in all colonies for local agencies to deal with problems of land. In Fiji the local committees will provide an opportunity for the representation of Indian interests, which will not be directly represented on the Board itself.

The Ordinance further prescribes that native land shall not be alienated by native owners, whether by sale, grant, transfer, or exchange, except to the Crown, and shall not be charged or encumbered by native owners. All instruments, therefore, which purport to transfer or encumber any native land, without the consent of the Board, are declared to be null and void. The Board is empowered to grant leases and licences of portions of native land not included in a Native Reserve, provided it is satisfied that the land is not beneficially occupied, or likely to be required by the native owners. But all dealings in leases are subject to control.[3] The Board's

[1] The Director of Agriculture considered that leases should be capable of extension to periods varying between forty to sixty years. Under the short-term and haphazard system of leasing, many Indians had used the land wastefully, picking out the good soil and leaving the bad, obtaining the utmost yield for a brief period and then surrendering the impoverished land.

[2] Native land is defined as land which is neither Crown land nor the subject of a Crown grant or native grant (i.e. grant of land by native owners), but includes land granted to a 'mataqali' under Section 19 of the Ordinance.

[3] But permission is not required for the mortgage of a lease—a dangerous practice in the case of illiterate peoples. It is not clear if consent is required for a transfer to a foreclosing mortgagee. If it is, the resulting uncertainty may lead to confusion and the exaction of exorbitant rates of interest.

sanction is required for sub-leases—an important provision which will enable the Board to see that the rentals charged to sub-lessees are not unduly high, and that the general conditions of sub-leases are not harsh, as they had often been in the past. It is to be observed that licences, as distinct from leases, are issued in respect of the tenure of land as between natives on native lands, and also in respect of grazing rights and the removal of timber and forest produce. Licences are not subject to 'The Land (Transfer and Registration) Ordinance'.

The Board may set aside any portion of native land as a Reserve, and no land in any Reserve shall be leased or otherwise disposed of except to a Fijian. Thus, while all land not included in a Reserve will be available for leasing to applicants of any race, within a Reserve no one but a Fijian will be entitled to hold land. In cases in which the original area reserved appears to be too large for the present or future requirements of Fijians, the Board may exclude any portion of land from a Reserve, permanently or temporarily—but only with the consent of the native owners.[1] On the other hand, the Governor is empowered to set aside land for a 'mataqali' or land-owning unit, whose land is, or may be, insufficient for its maintenance. Where a 'mataqali' dies out, the Crown retains its right to become the 'ultimate heir'.

Finally, under the new Ordinance, very wide powers are given to the Governor-in-Council to make regulations for such general purposes as controlling the occupation or the use of native land, regulating the conservation of the soil, and any matters relating to the tenure of land as between natives on native land, regulating the grant and form of leases, and so on. The regulations relating to leases have already been promulgated,[2] and it has been laid down that for leases in properly designed areas in which due provision has been made for roading, commercial and school sites, etc., the maximum term for a lease shall be ninety-nine years. For leases of isolated unplanned areas the maximum term is fifty years, provided that, if during such term the land becomes part of a properly designed area, the lessee shall surrender the lease and shall be entitled to a lease for ninety-nine years. The maximum term for a grazing lease is fifty years, but the Board has power at the expiration of each ten-yearly period to resume any portion of the lease, not exceeding one-fifth of the original area, without payment of compensation. For leases in settled areas requiring replanning and reparcelling, the Board is to divide the leases into zones and fix the

[1] In Kenya the Governor is (by the Crown Land Amendment Ordinance of 1938) empowered to vary the boundaries of native reserves, without obtaining the permission of the natives. But he must first obtain the consent of the Land Trust Board or (in the event of the Board's refusal) of the Secretary of State.

[2] *The Native Land (Leases and Licences) Regulations, 1940.* Council paper No. 31.

term in each zone. But the term must not exceed thirty years after the coming into force of the Regulations. Leases (of whatever kind) for a longer period than twenty-five years are subject to reassessment of the rent at the twenty-fifth, fiftieth and seventy-fifth year of the lease.

The special conditions attaching to agricultural leases are as follows. If the area exceeds fifty acres and the period of the lease exceeds thirty years, the lessee must expend a stipulated sum in permanent improvements within the first five years. Moreover, every agricultural lessee must plant with crops, in a good and husbandlike manner, within the first five years, at least one-fifth of the land suitable for cultivation; at least two-fifths within the first ten years; at least three-fourths within the first twenty years, and for the remainder of the lease. He must manure the land planted, and not allow any part to become impoverished, and he must take such measures to check erosion as may be required by the lessor.

The Native Agricultural Licences (which are issued to Fijians wishing to utilize native lands within a Reserve) grant the sole right of cultivation and residence for a period not exceeding ten years and they prohibit the transfer, assignment or encumbrance of the estate, or any crops growing on it or the proceeds of any such crops, except with the consent of the Board. These are stringent provisions and the prohibition of the mortgage of crops would seem to render the Crop Liens Ordinance *ultra vires*. It is to be observed that these licences allow for the continuation of cultivation on individual as opposed to communal lines—a policy which, as already noted, was initiated by the Native Lands (Occupation) Ordinance in 1933.[1]

As regards improvements, the absence from the Ordinance of general provision for compensation is unusual and has given the appearance of being a concession to the Fijians in return for their surrender of control and of the right to charge premiums for consent. The payment of compensation as a condition of regaining control of their lands has long been one of the chief grievances of the Fijians. There are, however, a number of important provisions for improvements in the Regulations made under the Ordinance. It is laid down (in Reg. 10) that, if a lease is to be sold by public auction, so much of the upset price as is based on the unexhausted

[1] A Fijian who wishes to take up peasant farming can, on application to the district council, obtain a certificate of exemption from communal duties, provided he pays to the Chief an annual commutation fee of 10/-. An approved applicant is granted rights over a ten-acre farm for a period of ten years. He may be given a small loan from his province and he receives advice from an Agricultural Officer. Some of these individual farmers are established in new settlements of their own and have started their own co-operative societies. But most of them have remained in close association with their villages. Some of the Chiefs have opposed the grant of rights to independent farmers, since these confer legal immunity from communal obligations. See J. W. Coulter, *Fiji* (1941).

improvements[1] made by an outgoing lessee shall be payable to the outgoing lessee. On the expiration of a lease any building erected by the lessee may (by Reg. 34) be removed by him within three months. The lessor, however, has a right of pre-emption over any building and must pay to the outgoing lessee the fair value thereof to any incoming lessee—any difference of opinion being settled by arbitration.[2] Again, when a lease is surrendered, any improvements on the land are deemed to be vested in the Board (by Reg. 36), though the Board may, at its discretion, allow the removal or sale of such improvements by the lessee within a specified period. Finally, it is laid down [in Reg. 21 (4)] that if the lessee does not wish to continue in possession of the lease . . . the value of any unexhausted improvements (including buildings not removed) shall be payable by the incoming tenant (if any) to the lessee. The amount so payable shall be assessed by the Board and shall be based on the value of the improvements to the incoming tenant at the date when his tenancy begins. If within twelve months of the determination of the lease no tenant is willing to lease the land with the improvements, the outgoing lessee shall thereupon surrender all claim to the improvements.

These provisions have been stated in some detail, since the question of compensation for improvements is becoming one of increasing importance in many of the dependencies.[3] It is clearly in the interest of good husbandry that farmers should be encouraged to build comfortable and sanitary homesteads and improve their farms in every possible way. How far the Fijian provisions will work out fairly for Indian lessees remains to be seen.

In conclusion, the main features of land administration in Fiji may be summarised as follows:

[1] The word 'improvements' is defined as follows: buildings of all descriptions, fencing, furrows, planting trees or live hedges, walls, wells, draining land or reclamation of swamps, road-making, bridges, tramways, laying-out and cultivating gardens and nurseries, waterworks, sheep or cattle dips, embankments or protective works, irrigation works, water tanks, plantings of long-lived crops, and clearing of land for agricultural purposes.

[2] Regulation No. 14 prescribes that 'upon a reassessment of rent or upon the assessment by the Board of the value of unexhausted improvements on any leasehold, the lessee, if dissatisfied with the calculation of the unimproved value of the land upon which the rent is assessed, or with the assessment of the value of unexhausted improvements, shall be entitled to submit the matter to arbitration.

[3] Some interesting provisions regarding improvements to land in Sierra Leone will be found in the *Sierra Leone Protectorate Land Ordinance* (No. 16 of 1927). See p. 196. In the Punjab it is laid down (by Sec. 63 of the Tenancy Act) that a tenant having a right of occupancy has also a right to make improvements. This right cannot be taken away by agreement, but the improvement must be suitable to the tenancy and consistent with the conditions on which it is held. In Section 72 of the Act general principles are laid down for determining the amount of compensation which should be paid for improvements. The problem of improvements is one of the most urgent of Colonial land problems, particularly in Africa.

(*a*) The comparatively successful reconciliation of the conflicting interests of the three distinct racial groups;
(*b*) Government intervention to prevent tribes from alienating more land than they can afford to lose;
(*c*) Government intervention to prevent tribes holding up more land than they can beneficially use;
(*d*) Government intervention to prevent native owners from trafficking in land among themselves;
(*e*) The redistribution of land according to the increase or decrease of land-owning groups;
(*f*) The assumption by Government of measures of controlling monies payable to native owners, in respect of their leased lands (under Section 15 of the Ordinance);
(*g*) The principle of granting sole rights of agriculture and residence to inidviduals, as distinct from their land-owning group;
(*h*) The subordination of private rights in land to schemes of rural development and the maintenance of soil fertility; and
(*i*) The establishment of local agencies to deal with the administration of land.

The new legislation enables the Government of Fiji to embark forthwith on a long-range scheme of rural development. At the same time it ensures for the native owners the provision of ample lands for their present and future needs, and adequate rents for such of their land as is leased. It should ensure also ample land for settlement, whether by East Indians or Fijians, with security of tenure and guarantees against wasteful cultivation. East Indians will be encouraged to remain on the land and ultimately, when the scheme of development has been put into practice, the length of leases may be extended to ninety-nine years. By placing the administration of land in a Trust Board, instead of leaving it largely to numerous tribes holding varying views, and frequently ill-equipped to make decisions, the legislation should ensure continuity of policy. If it appears to take from the Fijians much of the management of their own land affairs, it should be remembered that, by the creation of local committees, considerable scope will be given to Fijians to take an active part in the local administration of land.

CHAPTER XVII

Tong

THE Tongan or Friendly Islands, though their population is only 33,795, are of interest from the point of view of land tenure.[1] All land of the kingdom is the property of the Crown (i.e. of Tonga not Great Britain). There are three classes of land, namely, hereditary estates (*tofia*) held by royalty and nobles, tax allotments (*abi tukuhau*) and town allotments (*abi kolo*). The interest of the holders in each class is a life interest, and every estate or allotment is hereditary according to the prescribed rules. Every male Tongan over 16 years old is entitled to receive a grant of eight and a quarter acres of land as a tax allotment and a grant of an area not exceeding one rood twenty-four perches in a town as a town allotment.[2] If he resides on an hereditary estate the grant may be made from the lands of the estate, and if he resides on Crown Land the grant is made from Crown land. No person may hold more than one tax allotment and one town allotment.

No landholder may sell or attempt to sell, out-and-out, any land to any other person; and every verbal or documentary disposition by a holder of any estate or allotment which purports to effect a voluntary conveyance, an out-and-out sale, or a devise by will of such estate or allotment is null and void. It is also an offence for any landholder to enter into any agreement for profit or benefit relating to the use or occupation of his holding, or a part thereof, other than in the manner prescribed by the Land Act. An alien may not hold, reside upon or occupy any land except in accordance with the provisions of the Act, and a landholder may not permit an alien to reside on his holding unless the alien has been granted a lease or permit. Finally, it is unlawful for any Tongan to make any mortgage agreement or other document pledging or charging or selling his growing crops of coco-nuts, yams or other produce.[3]

There is a Minister of Lands and it is his duty to grant allotments,

[1] Land tenure in Tonga is governed by the Land Act of 1927 (Chapter XXVII of *The Law of Tonga*), the Land Act (Amendment) Act 1934 (No. 19), and the Leases (Renewal) Act (No. 15 of 1934).

[2] If he forgoes his town allotment he may receive a parcel of agricultural bush land of 12⅜ acres at an annual rent of 4/-. Moreover, under the Land Act Amendment of 1934 (No. 19), an allottee on an hereditary estate may, if there is a sufficiency of land, receive (*a*) a tax allotment of 8¼ acres (*b*) a town allotment of 1¾ acres and (*c*) 5 acres of leasehold land—a total of 15 acres.

[3] It is difficult to reconcile these restrictions, excellent though they may be, with Article I of *The Tonga Declaration of Rights* (para. 2) which reads as follows: 'And all men may use their lives and persons and time to acquire and possess property and to dispose of their labour and the fruit of their hands and to use their own property as they will.'

leases and permits, to act as Registrar-General of all land-titles, direct surveys in case of disputes, define boundaries, and collect rents.

The holders of hereditary estates receive a rent of eight shillings from the holders of tax allotments on their estates, and in the case of a lease they receive 90% of the rent reserved. They must keep a rent roll. They are not permitted to dispossess allotment holders other than in a manner prescribed[1] and they may not withhold land from any person who has been granted an allotment by the Minister of Lands, provided such person does not belong to another locality[2] or hold land elsewhere. Holders of hereditary estates who have been convicted of a felony or certified as insane lose all rights to their estate.

Every allotment holder must, within one year from the date of his grant, have growing on his allotment 200 coco-nut trees planted in rows and so arranged that the trees are thirty feet apart. And he must keep his allotment free from weeds.

Inheritance

The rules of inheritance are interesting.[3] In the case of hereditary estates the inheritance descends in the first place to the issue of the deceased holder *in infinitum*. If the holder leaves several sons the eldest son succeeds. Females may succeed, but male issue is preferred to female of the same degree. No person not born in wedlock may succeed, but if marriage precedes the birth of a child, however short the interval between the parents' marriage and its birth, the child is regarded as legitimate. In the case of tax allotments there are similar rules. The inheritance descends in the first place to the eldest son or, if such son is dead, to the eldest male heir of such son. If the eldest son has died without leaving any male heir then the succession devolves upon the next eldest son, and if such son is dead to the eldest male heir of such son. If the holder dies without leaving any male heir then an unmarried daughter may inherit for her life, and if there are two or more unmarried daughters they may inherit jointly for their lives. There is a remarkable provision that the life estate of an unmarried daughter shall terminate upon proof in the Land Court that she has committed fornication or adultery. It is also laid down that a widow (who is entitled to a life interest in her late husband's allotment) loses her right if, in legal proceedings, she is proved to have

[1] Ejectment may be for failure to pay rent or maintain the allotment in an average state of cultivation. But the Minister of Lands must first be informed.

[2] But special provision is made for school teachers who may not belong to the locality. There is also provision for those who wish to move from one locality to another.

[3] See Sections 41 and 71 of the Land Act.

committed fornication or adultery. A widow loses her life interest on remarriage.

Leases

A Tongan subject who does not hold a tax allotment may apply to the Minister of Lands for a lease of a parcel of bush land. The Minister submits this application to the Cabinet, which may authorize the lease, upon such conditions and for such term and rent as it considers fit. It is not permissible for any Tongan landholder to lease land without the consent of the Cabinet. A registered holder of a tax allotment may also be granted a lease of a parcel of bush land, but the area so granted must not exceed that of the allotment already held by him. Leases may not be granted for a longer period than fifty years and are renewable upon such conditions as to rent and methods of cultivation as may be ordered by regulations made under the Land Act.[1] But no lease is granted until a report has been received from the Director of Agriculture. It should be noticed also that, under the Land Law Amendment Act of 1934, it is now possible for allotment holders on hereditary estates to receive in addition to their allotments a lease of five acres of leased land at a nominal rental for a period of fifty years. But this addition is only granted when, in the opinion of the Cabinet, there is a sufficiency of land to meet all the needs of applicants for tax allotments.

Registration of Title

Successors to hereditary estates are required to be registered in the Register of 'tofias' kept by the Minister. The 'tofia' certificate contains, in addition to the words of grant, a description and diagram of the lands comprised in the estate, together with a schedule of leases and allotments granted. A register of allotments is also kept and there is provision for the registration of leases, subleases, transfers and permits, as well as of all documents affecting leaseholds. There are rules governing the lodging of caveats.

It may be noted, finally, that the Tonga Land Act provides for a Land Court with jurisdiction to hear all disputes, claims and questions of title affecting any piece of land. There is a time limit of ten years for bringing an action before this Court.

Summing up the system of land tenure in Tonga, we note the following characteristics: (*a*) All land is the property of the Crown and all dealings in land are controlled by the Crown; (*b*) Every

[1] The Leases (Renewal) Act (No. 15 of 1934) empowers the Minister of Lands to renew a lease when a landholder has failed to agree to a renewal.

male Tongan subject over the age of 16 is entitled to a minimum of eight and a quarter acres of farming land and one rood twenty-five perches of town land; (*c*) Allotments held by any one person may not exceed fifteen acres; (*d*) An allottee must plant his farming land with coco-nut trees and keep it in good order; (*e*) No landholder may sell his land or enter into any agreement for profit or benefit relating to the use or occupation of his holding, other than in the manner prescribed; (*f*) He may not allow an alien to reside on his holding without a permit; (*g*) He may not make any mortgage agreement or other document pledging or charging or selling his growing crops; (*h*) Rents are at a standard rate fixed by the State; (*i*) Allotment holders may not be dispossessed without reference to the Minister of Lands; (*j*) The interest of holders in every class of land is a life interest; (*k*) All land is heritable according to prescribed rules; (*l*) It is not permissible for any landholder to lease his land without the consent of the State; (*m*) The State may renew a lease if a landholder has refused to do so; (*n*) All transactions in land are subject to registration.

The land system of Tonga is a signal example of a successful readjustment, carried out voluntarily by the people of Tonga with the advice and assistance of the British. The principle that the ultimate title in land vests in the person of the ruler is a logical development of the older principle that the chief holds the land in trusteeship for the people. The setting aside of hereditary estates for the use of the royal family and members of the aristocracy or lesser chiefs follows closely the development that occurred in Buganda, as a result of the Uganda Agreement of 1900.[1] But whereas in Buganda the estates assigned to the chiefs or aristocracy became purely private property, which their owners could treat as they pleased, in Tonga a life interest only was conferred. Moreover, in Tonga, unlike Buganda, care was taken at the outset to prevent the dispossession of the peasant. By the grant to every grown-up male of a holding of his own, the Tongan has been enabled to pursue the path of economic individualism. But since his holding is no more than a 'usehold' (to borrow an expression of Dr. Keesing) both he and the land are protected from the abuses incidental to the fuller forms of individual rights. The Tongan system is, therefore, one which may commend itself to African governments, for application in areas where private rights have not yet crystallized into proprietary titles and Native Authorities still retain control over land administration. It should be observed, however, that while the Tongan system may work admirably so long as there is land to go round, it might be difficult to maintain in the face of any great increase of population. Moreover, the principle of taxing land

[1] See p. 133.

rather than the individual is open to criticism, and it would appear that in Tonga many young men have recently refrained from taking up holdings because of the tax that these entail.[1]

[1] See *The South Seas in the Modern World*, by Felix M. Keesing, 1942, p. 109.

CHAPTER XVIII

The British West Indies[1]

THERE is a general lack of reliable information relating to tenure in the British West Indies, but such as there is shows a remarkable variation both in the ownership and use of land.[2] In British Honduras most of the land is Crown land; in Barbados, the Crown owns no land at all. In Grenada land in possession of the Crown is small in area and consists principally of forest reserves and catchment areas in the mountains, which are unsuitable for cultivation. British Guiana and British Honduras are almost entirely composed of forest, and agricultural holdings are small;[3] Barbados has no forest, and three-fourths of its agricultural land is in the form of estates, the average size of which is between 200 and 300 acres.[4] In St. Kitts almost all the arable land is occupied by sugar-cane estates;[5] in Tortola all the land is owned by peasants. In St. Vincent agriculture is almost equally divided between estates and small holdings.[6] In Jamaica there are many

[1] For convenience the term 'West Indies' will be taken to include British Honduras, British Guiana and the Bahamas, which do not, strictly speaking, belong to 'The West Indies'.

[2] Attention is drawn to the absence of reliable data regarding land tenure in *Agriculture in the West Indies*—Colonial No. 182—(e.g. p. 15), Professor Engledow's *Report on Agriculture, etc.*, (e.g. pp. 1, 38, 215), and the *Report of the West India Royal Commission* (e.g. pp. 42, 43). The *1938 Report on Jamaica* states that 'there are no reliable statistics relating to the distribution of land in Jamaica'.

[3] 87% of the Colony of British Guiana is forest. Of the total cultivated area of 183,000 acres about 103,000 are small holdings and 80,000 are estates. But many small farmers reside on the sugar estates. British Honduras has an area of 6,000,000 acres. Of this some 560,000 acres are used for cultivation, but as a shifting system is practised only some 68,000 acres are actually under cultivation at one time. See Colonial No. 182, pp. 85, 91, 182 and 239.

[4] The figures for land ownership in Barbados are of particular interest. There are no Crown lands and ownership is almost entirely by freehold title. There are 280 estates, only 3 of which are operated under a lease. 9 of the estates are owned by companies and 271 by individuals or groups of individuals. Of the individual proprietors 16 are resident in England. On 130 estates the owner resides and manages the property, while 149 are managed by resident managers. One is managed by the lessee. 16,000 acres are owned by 18,805 peasants, so that the average size of a small holding is only ·85 of an acre. About 4,649 acres are leased by estates to their labourers at rentals of from £3 to £4 per acre. In 1938 the total number of labourers employed on estates was 37,550. Of these 15,000 were men, 15,300 were women, and 7250 were children. There are, therefore, more women labourers than men. The estates do not supply housing accommodation for labour. The general practice is for the labourer to build his own house with the aid of funds borrowed from the estate or a merchant, and to repay the cost by instalments. See *Agriculture in the West Indies*, Colonial No. 182, pp. 122-123.

[5] The labourers who work on the estates, some 7,400, are allowed to grow vegetables on 2,500 acres of inferior land.

[6] Prior to 1893 practically all the cultivable land in St. Vincent was owned by a small number of frequently absentee landlords. But since then many estates have

large estates, but considerable areas of these are rented to smallholders, and smallholding agriculture is, indeed, a predominant feature of the island. In most of the West Indian dependencies the small cultivators own their own properties, but many rent land for a cash rental or else work estate land on a crop-sharing system. In some islands, e.g. Trinidad, crop-sharing tenancy is not practised at all. In most of the islands, estates are held in freehold ownership, but in British Guiana some estates are leased from the Crown. There are also wide variations in the laws governing tenure, as well as in the basis and incidence of taxes and rates on agricultural property.

Much of this variety is due to the history of the various dependencies, which were acquired at various dates and have each pursued its own constitutional and economic career, without regard to its neighbour. Prior to the abolition of slavery there was greater uniformity, since agriculture everywhere was based on the estate system. The plantations were individually owned, and worked by slave labour. With the emancipation of the slaves there arose a movement towards peasant proprietorship and in many localities (e.g. Antigua, Nevis, Montserrat and the Virgin Islands) many of the estates were abandoned altogether. Where Negro labour remained on the estate it generally proved insufficient, with the result that additional labour had to be indentured from India. This in turn, when released from its contract, gave added impetus to the peasant movement, since most of the East Indians preferred to remain as permanent settlers rather than return to their own country. One of the major problems of British Guiana, Trinidad and to a lesser extent Jamaica (as of Fiji and Mauritius) has been, and will be, the social integration of these Indian immigrants. The West India Royal Commissioners have recently stressed the principle that Indian problems should not be regarded as distinct from those of the rest of the community.[1]

been acquired by Government and divided for land settlement purposes. Figures for land ownership may be misleading. A large proportion of estate land in St. Vincent is under forest or bush, being too steep to be profitably worked. In 1938 the following crops or agricultural commodities were, in order of value, produced by plantations and peasants respectively:

	Plantations	*Peasants*
Arrowroot	67%	33%
Cotton	40%	60%
Sugar	100%	—
Syrup	95%	5%
Sweet potatoes ..	20%	80%
Copra	98%	2%
Bananas	60%	40%

[1] *Report of the West India Royal Commission*, p. 454. This recommendation does not, of course, preclude the payment of special attention to the special problems of East Indians. In British Guiana East Indians constitute 42% of the total population, in Trinidad 34%.

Major Orde Browne, Labour Adviser to the Secretary of State, has drawn attention to one effect, in British Guiana, of the revolutionary change from a migrant labour system (as represented by indenture) to a resident body of estate labourers. Since the abolition of indentures free housing has been a gratuitous addition to the benefits of the labourers, who are now housed under conditions which give the ground landlord, i.e. the estate, the legal right to evict an occupant on the briefest notice. Estates are often embarrassed with superfluous workers and their dependants, and yet long enjoyment has naturally tended to create for these labourers a measure of prescriptive right. The removal of large numbers of these domiciled workers and their conversion into peasant proprietors would be an obvious solution, the nucleus left on the estates being obliged to accept a definite limitation of the security of their tenure. But the elaborate canal and drainage system of British Guiana is a serious impediment to the extension of peasant proprietorship in that dependency. Major Orde Browne has also drawn attention to another unregulated concession which takes the form of land given out to employees, for the purpose of growing rice or vegetables or pasturing stock. Here again the temporary permission is apt to be regarded as a prescriptive right, and much resentment is shown when it is withdrawn. Local custom, however, allows an evicted occupant the right to reap his crop.[1]

Throughout the West Indies tenure has also reflected the many changes in the conditions of cultivation, processing and sale of the various crops. Thus, developments in the system of manufacturing sugar have led to the conversion of many individually-owned plantations to joint ownership by registered companies, and the creation of these large organizations has in turn created problems of labour which are closely interwoven with those of tenure. Many individually owned sugar plantations still remain, acting as feeders for the central factory, and, in the case of crops other than sugar, the proportion of individually-owned plantations is higher, since less capital expenditure is required for processing. Many of the cocoa and coco-nut plantations are owned by individuals, the size varying from fairly large properties covering hundreds of acres to those which are no bigger than an average peasant holding. In the case of these crops the capital cost of planting and tending during the early stages can commonly be met by mortgage, where private funds are not available. In the case of cocoa, however, although processing entails no heavy expenditure it does entail the most careful regulation of fermentation. The control of this delicate process is one of the main problems which have to be faced

[1] *Labour Conditions in the West Indies*. Report by Major G. St. J. Orde Browne, O.B.E. Cmd. 6070, p. 168.

under all systems of tenure which are based on peasant cultivators.[1]

Although large-scale factory work is necessary for the efficient production of sugar, yet much of the cane required is grown by peasants on small holdings which they own or rent, selling their crops to neighbouring factories for which they may also work as wage-labourers.[2] In Trinidad, for example, 44% of the sugar grown in 1938 was produced by peasant farmers, most of whom are East Indians. Their holdings vary from one quarter of an acre to fifty acres, and on the larger holdings the farmer may employ wage-labour. The yields are low, being from half to two-thirds of yields from estate land on similar soil. The management is poor, cultivation is by hand, no fertilisers are used, and it is necessary, therefore, to rest the soil periodically. Many of the holdings and their occupants are stated to be in a wretched condition, and debt is universal. Professor Engledow has observed that 'the essential feature of the cane-farming situation in Trinidad is that it formerly paid estates to encourage cane farmers, but now, because of greatly increased efficiency of working, estates can produce cane at prices which peasants are reluctant to accept'.[3]

It is interesting to compare the conditions under which sugar cane is grown by peasants in Fiji and the West Indies. Under the Fiji system previously described practically all of the cane is grown by peasants under Company supervision, on holdings which are systematically leased and are provided with houses. The Company also undertakes the transport of the cane and the supply of fertilisers on favourable terms. It carries out its own cane breeding and research. The peasants in Fiji are able, therefore, to obtain high yields and to live in considerable comfort.

The possibility of transforming the West Indian system to that of Fiji has been carefully considered, but the provision of technical supervision and of transport would be impracticable in the case of holdings widely scattered. Moreover, there would appear to be, in some of the West Indian islands, imperative reasons for abandoning the growing of any single crop, cane or other, by peasant farmers, and for substituting the system of mixed farming. Professor Engledow has remarked that the greatest help that estates can give to cane farmers would be the encouragement of mixed farming and that for this purpose two elements of the Fiji system might well be adopted, namely, the provision of an adequate staff of skilled supervisor-

[1] See Dr. H. M. Leake in *Tropical Agriculture*, Vol. XV, No. 7.

[2] There are Government Ordinances for settling the price to be paid to factories. Cane-farmers who are tenants on rented land may be dispossessed in accordance with conditions laid down in the Sugar Cane Small Holdings Ordinance.

[3] *Report on Agriculture, etc.* (West India Royal Commission), by F. L. Engledow, p. 87.

instructors, and longer tenure for holdings. He adds, as regards Barbados, that, where land is precious, it is wasteful to do on a small scale what the lightness of the soil allows to be better done on a large scale. Peasant agriculture should, therefore, be directed away from cane towards the production of food crops. In this connection it may be noted that recent research carried out by the British West Indies Central Sugar-Cane Breeding Station in Barbados has resulted in such high-yielding new varieties of sugar-cane that a reduction in the acreage under sugar-cane should be possible without curtailing the output of sugar.[1] This would release land needed for the cultivation of food crops, but it is also likely to have the effect of adding to the unemployment which has been one of the major problems of the West Indies in recent times.

Crop Sharing

In the island of St. Lucia, cane is cultivated on a system of métayage. The Sugar Company provides the peasants with land, seed-cane and the funds for cultivation, and at harvest claims one-third of the crop and buys the balance.[2] Share-cropping, indeed, is common all over the West Indies in a variety of forms. In some cases the landlord, in return for a share of the crop, grants grazing or fuel rights free, in others he arranges for the transport of the tenant's crop to the factory and for this service he extracts a commission, or he may insist that the crop may only be sold through himself. Professor Engledow has stated that inquiry into many cases of métayage produced convincing evidence that the system was bad in every way. For the tenant it is harsh and dispiriting, and since neither the tenant nor the owner believe in the security of the tenure neither will do anything to maintain fertility. The result is continuous cropping for a few years until the land is exhausted, the tenant then proceeding to take over another piece of land on the same or a neighbouring estate.[3]

Professor Engledow suggested two remedies for 'this ruinous system'. The owner might be encouraged and financially assisted to restore his land to good order and manage it on an improved cash or share-rent basis; or the Government might acquire the property and settle it with the present share-croppers. In either case many

[1] See *The Times*, 16th January, 1943.

[2] There is a variant of métayage which is known as the 'contributor' system. In this the cultivator uses his own land and sells the whole of his cane to a factory at the current rates. Advances for cultivation are made by the factory usually free of interest, but the cultivator is under the same obligation to sell his canes to the factory as is the métayer.

[3] F. L. Engledow, op. cit., p. 38.

difficulties would have to be met. But in the meantime there was an urgent necessity for protective measures for tenants.

The crop-sharing system occurs in many forms all over the Colonial Empire. In Nigeria some ot the royal estates are cultivated by ex-slaves who may pay to the chief as much as one-third of the total annual produce.[1] In the Gold Coast, absentee proprietors often employ a head labourer and assistants under their own periodic supervision. But more commonly they adopt some system of share-cropping. A usual arrangement is for a relative to occupy the farm as a tenant or bailiff, hire the necessary labour, and pay the owner one-third of the crop or its proceeds. Under the more traditional system known as 'abusa', one-third goes to the land-owner, one-third to the farmer and one-third to the labourers. Many evils may arise under this system, and, quite apart from the misuse of the land, it is said that the commutation of debt by 'abusa', since it leaves the lessor in absolute possession, has been a principal cause of 'stool' land passing out of 'stool' control.[2] In other colonies the share-cropping system is criticized on the ground that it fosters among agricultural workers a disinclination for growing any form of crop that cannot be easily shared in kind on the field. It may delay the development of a money economy, or if this economy has already developed it may turn the share-tenant into a wage-earning labourer.

Métayage, however, is not under all conditions an unsatisfactory system of tenure. Dr. Martin Leake has observed that if the landlord remains resident and invests his capital in the land and its improvements; if he advances seed, manure, etc., to his tenants, and if he sells the crops and divides the proceeds fairly between himself and his tenants, he will contribute more towards attaining the goal of maximum excess produce than could any other person or organization.[3] It is in this way that métayage is successfully conducted in France. It depends for its success on the personal interest of the landlord in his estate, and on his close association with his tenantry. A further essential condition for the success of any system of métayage is complete security of tenure.

There is another aspect of métayage. When there has been a sudden depression in the price of produce the loss is, under this system, shared both by the landlord and the tenant. It does not fall wholly on the tenant as it would otherwise tend to do. Lord Hailey

[1] S. F. Nadel, *A Black Byzantium*, p. 199.

[2] *Europe and West Africa* (Meek, Macmillan, Hussey), p. 90.

[3] *Land Tenure and Agricultural Production in the Tropics*. H. Martin Leake, p. 101. But Dr. Leake has also observed (in speaking of India, p. 23) that although the métayer system, based as it is on a certain proportionate division of the actual produce, appears to be free from subjection to the rules of supply and demand, yet in practice this is not so. The proportion is altered, cess is added to cess, and so on.

has observed that on this account métayage has proved of the greatest value in India, during times of stress.[1] In the West Indies, crop-sharing appears to have arisen largely as a mode of accommodation to trade depression. Low prices had forced the estate-owner out of business, for the time being at least, and he was compelled to make what he could by letting out his land. The tenant, too, was often a former wage-labourer of the estate, endeavouring to tide himself over a period of unemployment.

It should not, therefore, be impossible to adapt the West Indian system of métayage, so that it will satisfy the needs both of landlord and tenant, and at the same time be agriculturally sound. Sir Frank Stockdale suggested (in 1938) that plantation owners who take up the system should be obliged to maintain areas in cultivation as home farms, to provide vocational educational services for their tenants, and to arrange for the marketing of all produce grown. In other words, it should be possible to develop the same relationship between a home-farm unit and tenants as is being built up in the United Kingdom under the Land Settlement Association.[2]

Small ownerships in the West Indies are described by Professor Engledow as those on which a family cannot sustain itself without extraneous income from wage-work. They range in size from five acres to one, but many are no more than one-quarter of an acre, or even less—hardly more than is sufficient for a house and vegetable garden. A peasant may own several pieces of land, an acre here, half an acre there, and a quarter of an acre somewhere else. In addition he may have a fourth plot in the hills, while his house may be in a fifth. The situation may be further complicated by the fact that part of the peasant's holdings may be let or sub-let. Or there may be multiple ownership. Cases occur in which several sons have become joint heirs to half an acre. All of them work on the plot in the intervals of wage-work or of fishing or some other occupation.[3]

Insecurity of Tenure

On rented land conditions are often ill-defined and insecure.[4] Written contracts are rare. The West India Royal Commissioners

[1] But Lord Hailey considers that, generally speaking, the métayage system in India only works well in certain parts where estates are small and there is a close relationship between the landlord and tenant. Where estates are large, or landlords are absentee, the system has great disadvantages, and the revenue law has rightly been directed to substitute cash rentals, under proper provisions for preventing rack-renting.

[2] The Fiji system described on p. 204 and the Gezira and Alternative Livelihood Schemes of the Sudan described in the Appendix are other examples of successful forms of share-tenancy.

[3] F. L. Engledow, op. cit., pp. 24 and 35.

[4] See *Agriculture in the West Indies*, pp. 16, 91, 212. Also *West India Royal Commission Report*, p. 43.

stated also that there was a lamentable lack of trust between owner and tenant.[1] Professor Engledow observed that, although in some of the colonies there were far-reaching Ordinances to provide security, the whole state of affairs was obscure and unsatisfactory, and that for the understanding of the situation at large there was often no other guide than individual opinion. Reform, he said, was undoubtedly needed, but 'nothing but harm could come from hasty legislation, and rental values and needs and possibilities of security must be added to the wide scope already recommended for a survey of peasant agriculture'.[2]

One of the chief causes of complaint in the West Indies is the absence of adequate provisions for compensation for unexhausted improvements in the case of rented lands. This undoubtedly has contributed to the demand for freehold rights. It is a subject to which attention has long been drawn, and is given special prominence in the latest report of Sir Frank Stockdale, who states that 'there can be no agricultural advance or a contented peasantry until the relations of landlord and tenant are placed on a satisfactory statutory basis, which provides for compensation for unexhausted improvements'.[3]

In some islands (e.g. Grenada) occupation of rental land may be on the basis of a yearly tenancy. But if the lands have been planted by the tenant in permanent crops the tenancy can only be terminated if compensation is paid for the crops which have been established.[4] Tenants on estates sometimes cultivate catch crops between the lines of permanent crops planted by the estate, and the tenancy expires when this form of cultivation is no longer possible. Many of the small rentings are worked on some form of shifting cultivation. The tenant, says Professor Engledow, argues that, as there is neither security of tenure nor compensation for improvement, any other system would be folly. He pays anything from ten shillings to twenty-five shillings an acre for land of moderate quality. The labour of clearing the bush is partly repaid by the timber. His main purpose is to exploit the land to the utmost and then proceed to do the same with another renting. From the owner's point of view a rent of twenty shillings a year for two years, followed by a resting period of five or six years, works out at an average rent of five shillings an acre for eight years. He contends, moreover, that an offer of a lease at even three shillings an acre for a term of eight years would be unsafe, since the tenant would, from ingrained habit, filch what he could from the land in the first two years, and then do

[1] p. 43.
[2] F. L. Engledow, op. cit., p. 38.
[3] Col. No. 184, op. cit., paras. 120 and 136.
[4] *Agriculture in the West Indies*, p. 142.

nothing further with it, and leave the balance of his rent unpaid.[1] The remedy for this state of affairs is the creation of a sense of partnership between landlord and tenant, built up on a knowledge of sound agriculture and respect for the land. The success of any system of tenure must ultimately depend on the way in which it is worked. Education, therefore, with the purpose of creating a sound tradition, must be considered one of the principal means of solving many of the problems of land tenure.[2]

Land Settlement

In the British West Indies there are large problems of settling unemployed, or under-employed, persons on the land, in order that they may provide their own food supplies. In Jamaica this policy has been pursued for some time and estates have been bought up for this purpose. In 1938, the Government embarked on a scheme estimated to cost £650,000, of which £400,000 was to be spent in the purchase of land. In Trinidad and Antigua, Crown land has been made available at from £4 to £10 an acre. In St. Vincent settlement schemes have been in vogue since 1899, while in St. Kitts and Grenada settlement has been assisted (in 1931 and 1934) by loans from the Colonial Development Fund.[3]

The West India Royal Commission, however, expressed the opinion that land settlement was only one of several ways by which the number of peasant holdings could be increased and their yield improved, and that for some time to come the betterment of existing peasant agriculture would be more practicable and fruitful than the undertaking of new schemes of settlement.[4] The outstanding agricultural need, indeed, appeared to be a more intensive use of land, with increased production of food in order to support the rapidly growing population.[5] Estate agriculture also seemed to be economically essential to the British West Indies, and essential too for the expansion of peasant agriculture. Professor Engledow observed that a regular weekly wage, even if small, was a most valuable financial pillar for the peasant farmer, while work on a

[1] F. L. Engledow, op. cit., p. 37.

[2] 'Community education should be provided if the results of investigation and science are to be translated into practice and the agricultural activities of small holders improved.' Sir F. A. Stockdale in *Agriculture in West Indies*, Col. No. 182, p. vi.

[3] In 1938 there were 19 land settlements in Grenada and Carriacu with a total area of 3,868 acres. No one who possesses land in excess of 10 acres is permitted to become an allottee, and priority is given to the deserving landless. The purchase is arranged on a 15-year amortization plan.

[4] *West India Royal Commission Report*, p. 323.

[5] 'An increased production of food supplies is most necessary and the development of mixed farming is essential if soil fertility is to be maintained or improved. Sir F. A. Stockdale, in *Agriculture in West Indies*, p. v.

good estate was instructive and set before him a pattern of industry, resource and efficiency. Thus estate and peasant agriculture should be regarded and developed as complementary elements.[1]

Freehold versus Leasehold

In the West Indies leasehold tenure has been viewed by the peasantry with suspicion and there has been an insistent demand for freehold.[2] The West India Royal Commission did not consider that governments should commit themselves to the grant of freehold tenures, but should experiment with both freehold and leasehold. Moreover, if freehold grants were made they should be accompanied by conditions which would prevent fragmentation and ensure the maintenance of soil fertility. When settlers were given freehold tenure on conditions of repaying the cost of the land by instalments, repayment should not begin for three years, thus allowing the settler reasonable time in which to make a profit, and should be spread over longer periods than those now customary. Where rapid repayment is required the settler may impoverish his holding in the early years in the attempt to meet this obligation, and the consequent process of restoring the soil may be prolonged and expensive.[3] In making this observation the Royal Commission was in fact drawing attention to one of the principal evils of unconditional freehold.

In his recent (1943) report, Sir Frank Stockdale, the Comptroller for Development and Welfare in the West Indies, states that the unrestricted freeholds which have been granted under land-settlement schemes have been subject either to excessive subdivision on the death of the owner, or to undue concentration of ownership as the result of indebtedness to traders and by sale to larger interests. "It is clear," he says, "that the freehold system of land-settlement is likely to lead to greater economic and social ills than is the case even to-day, and that the Governments of the future may be faced with the necessity of taking back into public ownership settlements which have failed through lack of control in the disposition and utilisation of the holdings."[4]

There has been considerable vacillation in policy regarding this

[1]The United States Government has recently embarked on an interesting experiment in land re-distribution in the West Indian island of Puerto Rico. Plantations have been bought and are being developed as proportional benefit farms 'designed to preserve the advantages of large-scale operation and skilled management with the sharing of profits between the workers on the farm'. (See C. W. W. Greenidge's Fabian pamphlet *Land Hunger in the Colonies*, p. 14.)

[2] See F. L. Engledow, op. cit , p. 35, para. 14. Also Sir Frank Stockdale's recent (1943) report on *Development and Welfare in the West Indies*, Colonial No. 184, para. 126.

[3] *West India Royal Commission Report*, pp. 316 and 447.

[4] Colonial No. 184, para. 135.

important matter. In British Honduras the system of Crown land leases for agricultural purposes was quite recently (in 1935) replaced by one of freehold grants, with payments in half-yearly instalments spread over ten years, and subject to a condition that at least half the land should be planted.[1] On the other hand in British Guiana the sale of Crown lands was suspended in 1938 (by Government Notice No. 233), pending a reconsideration of the land policy.[2] In St. Lucia also the Government has recently announced that Crown lands would in future be leased and not sold as before.[3] In this island out of a total area of 152,320 acres, 139,499 had, in 1937, been alienated to private freehold ownership. Of the land alienated by the Crown it was officially stated (in 1940) that practically the only criterion adopted with regard to its disposal had been the ability of applicants to pay the purchase price. Serious abuses had in consequence arisen and the whole question of the ownership of small holdings had become chaotic.[4]

The most recent pronouncement regarding the freehold system in the West Indies is contained in Sir Frank Stockdale's Development Report. He observes that the only alternative to freehold had been unsatisfactory forms of leasehold or unsatisfactory forms of share-cropping. The leaseholds accorded neither security of tenure nor compensation for unexhausted improvements. But when the evils of the freehold system had been explained to the people there had been a general readiness to consider other forms of tenure.[5] It would appear, therefore, that the problem of the replacement of freehold tenure in the West Indies is largely one of (*a*) education and (*b*) improvements in the leasehold system. But, if the replacement of freehold is to become a general policy, it may be necessary in those islands in which ownership of land is a qualification for a vote to introduce some modifications into the franchise.

Further observations on the general question of freehold versus leasehold in other colonies will be found in Chapter XX.

Food Production

In recent years much stress has been laid on the paramount necessity of widening the range of agriculture in the West Indies,

[1] See *Agriculture in the West Indies* (Colonial No. 182), p. 239.

[2] See Colonial No. 182, op. cit., p. 90. Practically the whole of the cultivated part of the coastal belt in British Guiana has been alienated under freehold title. Some of the coastal lands immediately behind the front lands have also been sold, but the majority are held on leases or licences from the Crown for varying terms, usually 21 or 99 years. These normally contain provisions that a specified fraction of the leased area must be placed under cultivation or beneficially occupied within a stated interval.

[3] See *St. Lucia Gazette* of 10th January, 1942.

[4] See Colonial No. 182, op. cit., pp. 175 and 176.

[5] Colonial No. 184, op. cit., para. 126.

particularly in the direction of growing more foodstuffs. The Agricultural Advisers to the Secretary of State, The West India Royal Commission, Professor Engledow, and more recently Sir Frank Stockdale (the Comptroller of Development and Welfare in the West Indies), have all insisted that increased food production must form an essential feature of any reform of the agricultural system. Most of the troubles of the West Indies have proceeded from excessive specialization on a single crop (sugar) which has lost its monopoly in the world market, and from the fact that on their present productive capacity most of the islands are over-populated. Relief must be sought through diversification, and the encouragement of subsistence husbandry.

The case for increased food production is well stated by the present Agricultural Adviser to the Secretary of State (Dr. H. A. Tempany, C.B.E.) in the following passage. 'The dominant principle has always been that a country should concentrate on the production of the staples for which it is by nature best fitted, and should depend on exports of these to supply the exchange necessary to enable it to import its requirements in other directions, including the bulk of its food. Obviously in these circumstances prospects depend on the relative market prices of exports and imports; when the ratio is favourable a satisfactory standard of living is assured, when it becomes unfavourable standards inevitably decline. During the past 100 years the ratio in the West Indies has on balance been unfavourable, and consequently conditions have been unsatisfactory.

'This position is in marked contrast to that which occurs, for example, in the Netherlands East Indies, where for many years the basic consideration has been the production, within the countries, of the bulk of the food of the population, and export production has been subordinated to the satisfaction of this requirement in the first place. The underlying economic consideration has been that, provided the primary requirements of the population in the matter of food supply are largely met by domestic production, slumps in the prices of export commodities can be faced without severe privation. Since the food of the people has been assured at all times, labour supply for export agriculture has been consequently benefited.'[1]

War conditions have already forced the change-over in the West Indies to increased food production. But it is necessary that mixed farming should become a permanent, and not merely a temporary, feature of the agricultural system. On the other hand, care will have to be exercised that production for export does not become so reduced that the material benefits of the outside world are placed beyond the reach of the islanders. The Secretary of State (Colonel

[1] *Agriculture in the West Indies*, p. 266.

Oliver Stanley) has recently observed that 'To depend for everything on what they could get from the soil would be to condemn the West Indies to an intolerable standard of life.'[1]

Conclusion

Summing up the main lessons of recent investigations into West Indian conditions, there would seem to be a need, firstly, for a redistribution of land, so that more of the labouring population may be settled on the land as small peasant proprietors; secondly, for a more intensive use of land, a greater diversification of agriculture, a greater production of subsistence crops, and a greatly increased use of livestock; thirdly, for a much more extensive knowledge of the conditions of tenure; fourthly, for greater security of peasant tenure; fifthly, for statutory provision for compensation for unexhausted improvements; and sixthly, for the abandonment of freehold grants in favour of long-term leases under which an hereditary class of contented and efficient tenants can be developed.[2] To this list may be added the need for more effective control of Crown land. To this the Agricultural Advisers and the West India Royal Commissioners have drawn attention.[3] Professor Engledow has also reported that authority to lease Crown land has been habitually exercised without collaboration between the various Departments concerned, that the Ordinances governing Crown lands have been imperfectly enforced, that there have been numerous cases in which the boundaries between Crown and private lands have been imperfectly defined, and that squatters have been allowed to use Crown land in an improvident and irresponsible manner.[4]

[1] *The Times* of 17th March, 1943.
[2] The possibility of large collectivized farms should also be considered.
[3] See e.g. *Agriculture in the West Indies*, pp. 176 and 189, and *West India Royal Commission Report*, p. 41.
[4] F. L. Engledow, op. cit., p. 31.

CHAPTER XIX

Land and Muhammadan Law[1]

MR. VESEY-FITZGERALD has pointed out that the conceptions by which English and European lawyers are dominated in their approach to many legal issues, including contracts, and especially those affecting immovables, are conceptions of sovereignty, allegiance, nationality and domicile, all of which are, in origin, alien to Muhammadan ideas. Although Islam has known many despots, it has always insisted that sovereignty belongs, and allegiance is due, only to Allah. Nationality is impossible in a world-wide brotherhood, and domicile is unimportant compared with religious belief. And so, in many Muhammadan countries, land is regarded as the property of *God*. In Northern Nigeria to-day, uncultivated land is spoken of as 'Allah's forest', and under a strict application of the Maliki system of Islamic law, which was followed by the Fulani conquerors of Northern Nigeria, all cultivated lands were, on conquest, treated as 'wakf'.[2] In practice, however, all over the world, Muhammadan law has had to accommodate itself to the demands of the local situation; native customary systems of land tenure and transactions in land have been retained, and Muslim law has also learned to keep pace with new commercial conditions, receiving, where necessary, the assistance of English mercantile law.[3] Even as regards the law of evidence, Muhammadan law has been modified by local law. Mr. Vesey-Fitzgerald states that Northern Nigeria is the only territory under British control where the Muhammadan law of evidence is still in force in its entirety;[4] yet even there, a number of unorthodox practices are permitted, particularly in the manner of swearing oaths.[5] In East Africa the Muhammadan law of evidence has recently been repealed

[1] In this chapter the writer has relied largely on, and quoted freely from, Mr. Vesey-Fitzgerald's standard work on *Muhammadan Law*. Further information will be found in Chapter VI dealing with Cyprus, and to some extent also in Chapters III and IV (Malaya).

[2] *An African Survey*, p. 771. The 'wakf' theory was equivalent to a claim of State ownership and served as a justification for imposing a system of land revenue, as well as for appropriating, if need be, the lands of non-Moslems. In 1902 the British High Commissioner in N. Nigeria was able to declare as public lands all lands which had formerly been the property of the conquered Fulani rulers. Compare the evolution of Mirie or State lands under the Ottoman Empire (see e.g. p. 63-4).

[3] See e.g. Sir R. K. Wilson, *Digest of Anglo-Muhammadan Law*, fifth edition, pp. 27-71.

[4] Op. cit., p. 27.

[5] Mr. Vesey-Fitzgerald himself draws attention to the Nigerian practice of tendering an oath as to any part of a statement which appears doubtful (p. 33), and also to the use of assessors (p. 30).

by the Evidence Enactments of the East African territories, and this repeal has had far-reaching effects on land problems in Zanzibar, since it invalidates evidence of the true meaning of the contract in cases of so-called 'fictitious sales', which have been one of the contributory causes of agricultural debt.[1] In Muhammadan law written evidence does not take precedence of oral, and 'acknowledgement' or 'iqrar' occupies so important a place that it has even made inroads on substantive law, since formal acknowledgements are used fictitiously to enlarge, or to defeat, the provisions of the substantive law. Such fictitious acknowledgements would probably not, in Muhammadan courts, be allowed to defeat the rights of creditors, any more than they would in British Courts, but they have been used to defeat the rights of heirs to land and other forms of property. Apart from the Supreme Court of Cyprus, British Courts do not seem to have taken any firm stand against the formalism of this Muhammadan doctrine.[2]

Mr. Vesey-Fitzgerald states[3] that, except in the Gambia and Zanzibar, there are in the British dependencies no definite enactments recognizing Muhammadan law, though its continuance in practice does not require any formal recognition. This statement is, perhaps, a little misleading, since in many dependencies (e.g. Sierra Leone, Uganda, Kenya, Gold Coast, etc.) there are Muhammadan marriage ordinances which frequently contain important provisions regarding inheritance. Thus, the Sierra Leone ordinance[4] provides that the estate real and personal of a Muhammadan who dies intestate shall be distributed in accordance with Muhammadan law, and the Gold Coast ordinance[5] lays down that, on the death of a Muhammadan, whose marriage had been registered under the ordinance, the succession to his property shall be regulated by Muhammadan law. It would be interesting to know how, if at all, these ordinances affect inheritance of land. In Tanganyika the Deceased Natives Estates Ordinance provides for the application of Muhammadan law to the estates of Somalis and Arabs, and in other cases Muhammadan law may be wholly or partially applied according to the expressed intentions of the deceased.[6] In the Gambia the 'Mohammedan Law Recognition Ordinance' of 1905 (Cap. 20 Sec. 6) grants to the Muhammadan Court jurisdiction only in cases between Muhammadan natives relating to civil status, marriage, succession, donations, testaments and guardianship. The recognition granted to Muhammadan law does not, therefore, apply to

[1] See the Zanzibar Evidence Decree (sec. 2).
[2] Vesey-Fitzgerald op. cit., pp. 28, 177 and 178.
[3] Ibid., p. 31.
[4] *Mohammedan Marriage Ordinance*, Cap. 128.
[5] *Marriage of Mohammedans Ordinance*, Cap. 98 (sec. 10).
[6] *Laws of Tanganyika*, Cap. 16 (sec. 4).

civil contracts other than marriage, or to any criminal or quasi-criminal matter. In Zanzibar, the position is very different, for there the law of Islam is declared statutorily to be the fundamental law of the Protectorate in *all* civil matters.[1] Nevertheless, Muhammadan Law in Zanzibar has been modified in many important respects by English law, notably by the Transfer of Property Decree of 1917.

The extent to which the administration of Muhammadan law has been left in the hands of Muhammadan tribunals in the different dependencies varies greatly, as does the degree of control exercised over them by the Supreme Courts. In Zanzibar, Tanganyika and Kenya the Muhammadan Courts exercise jurisdiction over indigenous Muhammadans or Arabs in all matters of personal and family law and succession, but jurisdiction over British and Muslim subjects from elsewhere (e.g. Indian immigrants) is normally exercised by the ordinary courts. 'In cases between Arab or African Moslems it has been held both by the Zanzibar and the Kenya Supreme Courts that the decision of the Indian Courts and the Privy Council on appeal from India, though of extreme interest for purposes of illustration and comparison, are not binding. In such cases the Supreme Courts take the advice, in Zanzibar, of the Qadis, and, in Kenya, of the Chief Qadi, who bears the title of Shaikh ul Islam; but they are not conclusively bound by that advice. In several cases the Supreme Courts have claimed a jurisdiction as Courts of Equity to over-ride the strict provisions of Muhammadan law, where such provisions appear inequitable. But there is no reported case of their exercising such a jurisdiction.'[2] In this connection it may be observed that it is a first principle of Muhammadan law to endeavour to bring the parties together in a spirit of friendly compromise,[3] and it would be a good thing if this principle were more widely recognized in British courts. Much of the litigation, which is one of the principal causes of debt, might thereby be avoided.

With regard to the difference between precept and practice in Muhammadan law, Mr. Vesey-Fitzgerald observes that 'The market law as conceived by the lawyer-moralists of the Shari'a, and the same law as actually practised in the market, have never been identical. Interest on money, which the moralists stigmatized as usury; the taking of risks in forward contracts and the fluctuations in the rate of exchange, both of which they regarded as gambling; all these things are the life-blood of legitimate commerce. In this branch of the law we have always to inquire not merely what the

[1] See the *Courts Decree 1923* (sec. 7).
[2] Vesey-Fitzgerald op. cit., pp. 32-33.
[3] Ibid., p. 32. See also the Koran 4, 35.

lawyers say but what respectable merchants practise. Nevertheless the Shari'a has always been the nominal basis of, and a powerful factor in, the market law'.[1] Certainly as regards the law of sale and contract generally, the Koranic prohibitions against usury[2] and gambling[3] have had an immense effect, 'making sale the archetype and usury the antetype of conveyances and contracts alike'. Contracts are deliberately assimilated to completed transactions, and if this is borne in mind many of the so-called 'fictitious sales' need not be regarded as forms of commercial roguery.

It is a principle of the Muhammadan law of sale that transfer of ownership takes place at once. Usually both delivery and payment occur simultaneously, but the price may be made payable by instalments, and the seller may retain a possessory lien until paid. There can, however, be no such thing as a contract to sell, because the element of uncertainty thereby introduced would reduce the transaction to gambling. Mr. Vesey-Fitzgerald[4] quotes an interesting case from East Africa in which the defendant, Rashid, agreed to sell to the plaintiff 'subject to the claims, if any, of Rashid's relatives, ten thousand acres to the North of Kilifi harbour'. This agreement was held to be a nullity, on account of (1) futurity (since a sale must be a present transfer); (2) condition (since the claims, if any, of Rashid's relatives go to the root of the conract and a sale must be an absolute and unqualified transfer); and (3) uncertainty (since the ten thousand acres had not been demarcated). The last argument, viz. uncertainty on the ground of non-demarcation, is of interest from the point of view of need for the better marking of boundaries, particularly in West Africa.

Muhammadan law recognizes two kinds of sale for future delivery, under strict safeguards against gambling in options. These are known as *salam* and *istisna*. We are only concerned here with the former. Of this Mr. Vesey-Fitzgerald says that the price must be paid in cash at the conclusion of the bargain, which must be for a definite delivery at a definite future date of a *res fungibilis*—that is to say, something which is not specific but is sold by quantity and quality, such as corn. 'Thus if a cultivator wishes to sell his, as yet, ungrown harvest, he cannot sell the crop to be reaped from a certain field, because that is a specific item and it depends on an uncertain future event, namely the success of the harvest: he would be selling a risk, and the transactions would be akin to gambling. But he may sell for delivery at a certain future date so many bushels of such and such a quality of corn: he anticipates that by that date he will have

[1] Vesey-Fitzgerald op. cit., p. 181.
[2] II, 275-6: III, 129: XXX, 39.
[3] II, 219: V, 90-1.
[4] Vesey-Fitzgerald op. cit., p. 183: Cobb *v.* Rashid, 3. E.A. 35.

reaped that quantity and quality of corn from his own field, but he keeps the risk and makes an unqualified promise to deliver. And from the side of the purchaser the method of gambling on settlement of differences, favoured by speculators all over the world, is prevented by the requirement of an immediate cash payment in full.'[1]

In sales of land (which are of course lawful under the law of Islam) the trees upon the land are included in the sale, whether specified or not: but neither the grain growing on the ground, nor the fruit growing on the trees, are included, unless specified. But in the case of the fruit or corn being purchased with the land it must be gathered or cleared away at one. Land may be resold previous to seizure or possession by the first purchaser, according to Abu Hanifah; but the Imam says it is unlawful.[2]

As regards the letting or leasing (*ijara*) of land, it is to be observed that this also is treated in Muhammadan law as analogous to a contract of sale. The *Mejelle* (art. 405) even defines it as the sale of a known benefit in return for its known equivalent[3]. In leases the period must be specified[4] and the lease is not lawful unless mention is made of the crop to be raised upon it. Moreover, at the expiration of the lease, the land must be restored in its original state (see *Hidayah*, Vol. III, p. 314). In Zanzibar, an alleged custom that a lease of land could be terminated by the lessor selling to a third party was held to be unreasonable, as also the custom that a landlord should continue to carry out repairs even if the lease was proved to be, for all practical purposes, in perpetuity.[5] Agricultural leases on a part profits basis are treated not as leases but as forms of partnerships, of which there are apparently three separate types.[6]

The cultivation of waste and unclaimed lands may be carried out with the permission of the ruler of the country, and the act of cultivation invests the cultivator with a right of property in them. But if the land be not cultivated for three years after it has been allotted, it may agian be claimed by the State. It would appear (*Hidayah*, Vol. IV, p. 128) that mere enclosure of waste land is insufficient: the squatter must break up the land and cultivate it.[7] Buildings upon, or trees planted in, land are separate from the land itself, and may be, and commonly are, held by a separate title—even where the title to the land is due to the planting of the trees. And

[1] Vesey-Fitzgerald, pp. 185-6.

[2] The authority for this is *Hidayah*, Vol. II, pp. 372, 481, 503—quoted in Hughes's *Dictionary of Islam*.

[3] Vesey-Fitzgerald, p. 186.

[4] Neverthless custom in Hanafi countries, both India and the ex-Ottoman dominions, has for centuries recognised leases in perpetuity.

[5] Vesey-Fitzgerald, p. 187.

[6] Ibid.

[7] Sultan of Zanzibar's Govt. *v.* Attorney General 4 E.A. 142.

since the buildings and crops are not regarded as part of the land, a 'trespasser' who owns buildings and crops on that land is as much entitled to the peaceful possession of his buildings and crops as is the owner of the land to the land itself. A gift of land which is uncultivated cannot be retracted after houses have been built upon it or trees planted. But if the donee sell half of the granted land the donor may, if he wishes, resume the other half. But a gift of land to a close relative may never be resumed (*Hidayah*, Vol. III, p. 302).

Coming now to the all-important subject of loans and security for debt, land may be lent and the borrower may build upon it. But when the lender receives back his land, he can compel the borrower to remove his house and trees. Land lent for tillage cannot be resumed by the lender until the crops sown have been reaped.

The lending of money at interest is strictly forbidden, and the prohibition is widely respected. In Northern Nigeria claims for interest are commonly dismissed, and usury is an offence, though in practice offenders may escape with a warning.[1] Mr. Vesey-Fitzgerald states that when the Government of India opened a general provident fund for its employees, offering handsome interest on compulsory deductions from their pay, many conscientious Muslims, even those in the poorest grades of Government service, refused to accept the interest. Nevertheless in the practical conduct of commerce the prohibition against usury has in most Muslim countries been found impossible to enforce, and attempts to enforce it, such as have been made in the East Africa Courts, have ended capriciously. On the other hand, it has been commonly observed in many countries that agricultural moneylenders are non-Muslims, since the Muslim law, while forbidding the taking of usury, does not forbid the paying of it.

Numerous devices to evade the prohibition have received the sanction of the schools. Commonest of all is the fictitious acknowledgement by the borrower of a larger sum than he actually receives. Reference has already been made to the conclusive character of acknowledgement (or *iqrar*) in Muhammadan law, which, even under English ideas, can hardly be displaced except by proof of undue influence.[2] The simplest form of security for debt is the *rahn* or pledge. Mr. Vesey-Fitzgerald states (p. 197) that the contract of pledge is naturally based upon sale, since it is by sale that the security can in the last resort be enforced. Accordingly the thing pledged must be capable of being sold. But if this is so, it can only be concluded that in many Muhammadan countries, where land can be pledged but may not be sold, the Muhammadan law has

[1] See M. Perham's *Native Administration in Nigeria*, p. 93.

[2] Vesey-Fitzgerald, p. 197.

had to be modified in this as in other respects, by local custom. Pledging in any case differs from sale and resembles gift, in that, until possession has actually taken place, the pledger may always withdraw and leave the pledgee with an unsecured claim for the money he has lent.[1] The continued possession of the pledgee is also essential to the maintenance of his rights, and it follows, therefore, that second mortgages are not permissible under Muhammadan law. But the Hanafi and Shafii rules regarding possession appear to be at variance with those of the Maliki school, and an East African decision permits a pledgor to continue using the property pledged, by arrangement with the pledgee.[2] This would seem to open the way for the non-agriculturist moneylender, but foreclosure of the property is not permitted, nor can the pledgor or pledgee sell, even after expiry of the period named for repayment, except by the consent of both parties or by a judicial decree.

The pledgee's right is said to be, normally, the right of retention only, though by agreement both enjoyment and periodical fruits may belong to the pledgee.[3] In practice, it is the usufruct that matters most, and as this is not taken into account against the principal debt it provides a profit for the lender without infringing the law against usury.

It only remains to add, as regards the pledging of agricultural land, that the custom appears in English law as a usufructuary mortgage. Thus, in the Zanzibar laws, there is formal recognition of the practice in the following definition (Cap. 83, Sec. 58 (4)): 'Where the mortgagor delivers possession of the mortgaged property to the mortgagee and authorises him to retain such possession until payment of the mortgage-money, and to receive the rents and profits accruing from the property and to appropriate them in lieu of interest, or in payment of the mortgage in money, or partly in lieu of interest and partly in payment of the mortgage-money, the transaction is called an usufructuary mortgage and the mortgagee is an usufructuary mortgagee.' In section 67 of this law, which confers on mortgagees the right to foreclose, there is an express statement that nothing in the section shall be deemed to authorise an usufructuary mortgagee, as such, to institute a suit for foreclosure or sale.

The forecloseable mortgage of Muhammadan law is the mortgage by conditional sale, that is to say, any agreement whereby in default of payment of the mortgage money or interest at a certain date the land would be transferred absolutely to the mortgagee.

[1] Vesey-Fitzgerald, p. 197; and Jaffer *v.* Mahomed, *East African Law Reports* (Kenya) 6. E.A. 170.

[2] Vesey-Fitzgerald, p. 198.

[3] Ibid.

Such mortgages are known in the Shafii School as *bai'khiyar* (sale option), to the Hanafi as *bai'bi'l wafa*, and to the Maliki as *thaniya*. Originally, the transaction in all its forms was considered illegal, as a breach of the law against usury. But it was gradually introduced under the plea of necessity, and is now regarded as a legitimate form of commercial enterprise. In a mortgage by conditional sale the mortgagee may be put into possession and obtain the use and enjoyment on conditions similar to those of pledging. Or he may lease the property to the mortgagor, thereby obtaining, under the name of rent, what is in reality interest on his loan. And he is saved the trouble of managing the property.[1]

But according to Muhammadan principles a sale must be absolute, and any sale with a promise to cancel, dependent on a future event, is null and void. To meet this difficulty, moneylending transactions of the conditional-sale type are usually embodied in two separate contracts—one for sale and the other a collateral promise to reconvey. This has led to a great deal of confusion, particularly in East Africa. In some cases the courts have permitted evidence to show that the real intention of both contracts was a mortgage, while in others (following Sec. 92 of the Indian Evidence Act) the written document of absolute sale was alone admitted, the oral evidence of reconveyance being disallowed.[2] This latter ruling was endorsed by the Court of Appeal of East Africa, and by section 2 of the Zanzibar Evidence Decree the Muhammadan law of evidence was in this respect virtually repealed. Nevertheless, mortgage by conditional sale continued to be recognized under the laws of Zanzibar. It is defined as follows: "Where the mortgagor ostensibly sells the mortgaged property—on condition that on default of payment of the mortgage-money on a certain date the sale shall become absolute; on condition that on such payment being made the sale shall become void; on condition that on such payment being made the buyer shall transfer the property to the seller; the transaction is called a mortgage by conditional sale and the mortgagee a mortgagee by conditional sale.' (Cap 82, Sec. 58 (3)). Section 67 of the law confers on other classes of mortgagees the right to foreclose, but does not extend this right to mortgagees by conditional sale.

The ruling given in the Appeal Court of East Africa held sway in Zanzibar for sixteen years, but in 1934 was superseded by the Land Alienation Decree, under Section 18 of which apparent vendors were enabled to obtain from the Court a declaration that the instruments of conveyance amount to a mortgage and not to an absolute sale. Under the new Land Alienation Decree of 1939 no permanent

[1] Vesey-Fitzgerald, p. 198.

[2] See Said *v.* Mahfuz, *Zanzibar Law Reports* I, 12 E.A. 189; Brit. Res. *v.* Hafiz, ibid. I, 12 E.A. 526; Rashid *v.* Salem, ibid. I, 12 E.A. 614.

alienation of land and no mortgage thereof shall, where the alienor is an Arab or African, have any effect without the approval of the Board for the area in which the land is situated. The Board may withhold its consent where it has cause to believe that the proposed transfer is intended to take effect as a mortgage. Under the Land Protection (Debts Settlement) Decree (No. 2 of 1938) specific permission is given to the Court to permit oral evidence in variation of any written acknowledgement by the debtor of an amount stated therein to be due (Sec. 7, 3 (c)). But, in the adjudication of debts under the Decree, oral evidence of any undertaking to pay interest is inadmissible (See Schedule III, 4 (11)).

It would be of interest to know what has been the course of legislation with regard to mortgages by conditional sale in other Muhammadan areas of the Colonial empire.[1] In Cyprus fictitious sales are, or were until recently, of common occurrence. A creditor instead of accepting a mortgage would insist on the transfer of the property as security for the loan, on the condition that he would resell to the debtor. Or a mortgage debtor might himself voluntarily transfer the mortgaged property to the creditor who would simultaneously, by an 'agreement of sale', resell to the debtor or to some member of his family.

It is perhaps worth adding that in the legislation of dependencies where conditional or fictitious sales are practised the words 'debt', 'debtor' and 'loan' may require special definition. Thus in the recent legislation for the settlement of agricultural debts in Cyprus (No. 12 of 1940) debt is defined as 'all liabilities of a debtor arising out of any transaction which is, in the opinion of the Board, in substance a loan'. It does not include 'any amount the liability for the payment of which is only contingent'.

Waqfs

Waqf—or habs—to use the common West African expression—is the name given to Muslim foundations or endowments. It occupied the place which in other legal systems is filled by non-trading corporations, trusts, religious offices and family settlements. Property which may be made waqf must be of such a kind that perpetual use can be made of it, whether movable or immovable, and so includes land and even houses and plantations on land leased from another.[2] A man may establish a waqf not merely as an insurance for himself and against his future debts, but also against spendthrift successors. He can guarantee the permanence of his family from generation to

[1] In the Punjab future mortgages by way of conditional sales were forbidden in 1900 (by Act XIII).

[2] Vesey-Fitzgerald p. 214.

generation in spite of all rules against successive estates,[1] and he can also, by a waqf, evade the strict letter of the law of inheritance and in particular the fractional subdivision of his property. A waqfif, or founder, in fact (as Mr. Vesey-Fitzgerald has observed)[2] possesses a power of legislation such as probably no other legal system concedes to a private individual. Except for the fact that it is doubtful if he can completely exclude his own children from benefit in his estate, he can provide for the succession in almost any way he likes.

Waqfs for the erection and upkeep of mosques, and also for graveyards, are common in all Muhammadan communities, and in Zanzibar a dedication of land to public use as a right of way has been treated as waqf.[3] In order to dedicate land there must, of course, be unrestricted ownership of the land to be dedicated. That is to say, the waqfif or founder must be under no legal disability to transfer. Mr. Vesey-Fitzgerald states[4] that in the Ottoman Empire tithe-paying land could not be dedicated, since the ultimate ownership was held to reside in the ruler, a claim which is frequently and often quite unjustifiably made in some parts of Africa. Nor could a mortgagor or mortgagee of any kind of land in the Ottoman Empire dedicate the mortgaged land, since such a grant would be contingent and the dedication could only be made by both parties agreeing to convey a complete title. In India there is no objection to the dedication of revenue-paying land, and a waqf may even be valid when made under an existing mortgage, provided there is no other legal disability to transfer.

A beneficiary under a waqf has no right to assign, encumber, or lease the property, and a trustee has no power to hypothecate, sell or exchange. A mosque, the land on which it stands, or a graveyard can never be lawfully sold, though some jurists hold that, if a locality intended to be served by a mosque becomes completely deserted by Moslems, the court may order the land on which the mosque stands to be sold and the proceeds used for the establishment of another mosque elsewhere.

In a number of British Colonies there are statutory provisions for the control of waqf property. Thus, in Kenya, by the Wakfs Commission Ordinance (Cap. 28) a body of four commissioners control all waqfs created for public purposes, or for private purposes which have expired. Where it appears to the Commissioners that the intentions of the founder of the waqf cannot reasonably be

[1] Vesey-Fitzgerald (op. cit., p. 218) remarks that similar inconsistencies are common in all legal systems. In England the power to bar an entail and the power to make a strict settlement were the invention of the same great equity lawyer. Even the property legislation of 1925 presents a similar conflict of ideas.

[2] Op. cit., p. 218.

[3] Barton *v.* O'Swald & Co., *Zanzibar Law Reports* I, p. 420.

[4] Op. cit., p. 208.

carried into effect the Court may order a sale. All property of deceased Muhammadan natives to which no claim can be established is vested in the Commissioners, as also waqf property for which there are no properly constituted trustees, or of which the trustees have misbehaved.

In Zanzibar, under the Wakf Property Decree (law 53 amended by 21/1927), a register is kept giving full details of all waqf property and of all persons owning buildings on, or occupying, waqf land; and the Commissioners are empowered to order the removal of any unauthorised building. All trustees of waqfs are under complete control of the Commissioners, who are authorised also to prevent any alienation by a trustee for a period exceeding one year. The provision in Zanzibar law requiring the registration of a waqf, if it is to be legally binding, is of considerable importance, and it would be interesting to know to what extent registration is the rule, either under British or native local law, in other Muhammadan areas of the Colonial Empire. In Zanzibar many waqfs have not been registered, particularly those relating to lands for freed slaves. It is worthy of remark that, in Zanzibar, the registration of waqfs was one of the early instances of the recognition of freehold by the Government.

In most Muhammadan countries the Muhammadan law of inheritance, with its insistence on the equal division of property among children, has been responsible for much uneconomic subdivision of land. It has been estimated recently that in Egypt two-thirds of the landowners own no more than two-fifths of an acre each, an area much too small to be profitable even under the most favourable marketing conditions. Many of the farmers are therefore in the hands of moneylenders and there is little possibility of improving the land.[1] In Zanzibar in 1933 much of the island's agricultural debt was attributed (by Messrs. Bartlett and Last) to the multiplicity of holdings, and consequent absenteeism, occasioned by the provisions of the Muslim Shari'a. In Northern Nigeria, at the 1939 Conference of Chiefs, the Chief Commissioner observed that, when the Islamic law of inheritance was established, estates consisted largely of camels and other livestock, and division was comparatively easy. But, now that they consisted of immovable property, division according to the letter of the law had become attended with infinite difficulties. He quoted cases of Kadis in Malaya being obliged to count even the leaves on a tree in order to divide an estate in strict accordance with the provisions of the Shari'a. Much harm had been done to agriculture through this excessive subdivision. In Malaya a solution to the problem had been found by

[1] Information obtained by Dr. Keen, F.R.S., from the Research Department, Foreign Office.

allowing local custom to take precedence of the provisions of Islamic law.

The position in Malaya has been well described by Mr. G. A. de C. de Moubray[1] who observes that, while puritanical Muhammadans would purge the legal system of all custom, particularly if it conflicts with texts of the Koran, nevertheless local custom regarding inheritance is in practice followed by Muhammadan peoples all over the East. The general Islamic system, moreover, allows for statute law overruling the Shari'a or canon law, and in Malaya this is what had happened in the case of 'The Customary Land Enactment' of Negri Sembilan and the 'Malacca Lands Transfer Ordinance'.[2] According to the Hidayah, custom holds the same rank as Ijma' (consensus of juristic opinion) in the absence of any express text. There is agreement also among the Sunnis that custom over-rides analogical law, and Hanafi writers on jurisprudence include custom as a source of law, under the principle of 'istihsan' or juristic preference.[3] In almost every Moslem country there have grown up at least two systems of law, the one administering canon law, the other based on local custom or the decrees of the local rulers.[4]

In Northern Nigeria, according to Dr. Nadel, new economic conditions have led increasingly to the adoption of the Muhammadan law of inheritance, as against the local custom by which land is inherited not by sons but by the brother, the sons and brothers' sons staying on the land and working under the heir as under their sociological father. 'Were individuals to attempt to enforce the traditional rule, dissatisfied family members could easily obtain a reversal of the decision by appealing to the Mohammedan court.'[5]

On the other hand, definite steps have recently been taken in the most orthodox areas of Northern Nigeria to modify the formal law in certain conditions. At the 1939 Conference of Chiefs, the Emir of Kano stated that the strict application of the Muhammadan law of inheritance had led to over-crowding and insanitary conditions. The Emir suggested that all such cases should be brought to his notice and he would cause an inquiry to be made as to whether the house in question could be subdivided without causing insanitary

[1] Op. cit., pp. 213-217.

[2] See pp. 42 and 35.

[3] Abdur Rahim, *Mahomedan Jurisprudence*, p. 136.

[4] See the article 'Islamic Law' in the *Encyclopædia Britannica* (14th edition.) There it is pointed out that 'In modern times demands have been made by liberal Muslim thinkers that the principle of agreement (*ijma*) should be so extended as to render possible changes in the Shari'ah, so as to bring it into harmony with modern conditions: but the orthodox legists have steadily resisted any such change. In 1926 the Turkish Republic solved the problem by adopting the Swiss Civil Code and the Italian Penal Code, thereby abolishing the sacred law of Islam altogether.'

[5] *A Black Byzantium*, p. 173.

conditions. If it could not, then the house would be sold and the proceeds divided among the legatees. To this the Conference agreed, and in their resolution included farms as well as houses. In 1940 the subject was again raised and Sheikh Bashiru of the Law School of Kano proposed that Muslim Courts be instructed not to divide what would be useless or insanitary, but either to persuade the heirs to an amicable agreement (e.g. some taking real property and others movable—adjustments being made by cash also) or, if this was impossible, to make a compulsory arrangement without sub-division (the real property being sold—perhaps to one of the heirs—and the proceeds divided). To this the Conference agreed. The Sheikh further proposed that a minimum figure of area for farms and houses should be laid down. The Khartum minimum was stated to be 200 square metres.[1] The Nigerian Conference, however, decided that the extent to which an estate might be divisible must be left to the Local Authority.[2]

It is clear from this restricted account that there is scope for a comprehensive, comparative study of the relationship of Muhammadan law to problems of land throughout the Colonial Empire, particularly with reference to the points raised above, namely, usury and mortgage, fictitious sales, waqfs and the excessive sub-division of estates. The subject of pre-emption, which is a characteristic feature of Muhammadan law, though by no means peculiar to it, has already been dealt with.[3]

[1] In the Sudan, under the Land Registration Rules of 1925, the registration minima for plots to be registered separately, or for divided shares in plots, shall be (*a*) town lands, 200 sq. metres, and (*b*) agricultural lands, .5 of a feddan (a feddan being slightly more than an acre). The registered minima for undivided shares shall be (*a*) town land 25 sq. metres, and (*b*) .1 of a feddan.

[2] In the Muhammadan State of Kelantan (Malaya) the minimum area into which a plot may be divided is one-fourth of an acre, though the Sultan may, in any particular case, authorize a smaller sub-division (see p. 48).

[3] See p. 69.

CHAPTER XX

Freehold versus Leasehold Tenure

IN many British Colonial dependencies there has been a persistent demand that agricultural land should be alienable in freehold grants to those who wish to obtain this form of title. Thus, in Kenya, a recent Government Committee on Land Tenure recommended, by a majority of six to two, that every lessee should have the right, on the fulfilment of certain conditions, to obtain a grant of his land in freehold: and the Committee was unanimous in the opinion that opportunity should be given for agricultural land to be held on title in perpetuity, with freedom from annual rental payments.[1] One of the members of the Committee observed that, in Nairobi, every lease for land, with everything the lessee had placed upon it in the way of improvements, automatically reverted to the Crown when the term of ninety-nine years was completed, and that it was only countries which were under the heel of bureaucratic government—the Federated Malay States, Tanganyika, Kenya and the West African dependencies—which were condemned to 'leasehold servitude'. In the West Indies there is widespread 'mistrust of any kind of holding by lease, even from the Government', and it would seem that the only form of title acceptable to the people is that of freehold.[2] In British Honduras, owing to the opposition to leasehold tenure, the former system of Crown land leases for agricultural purposes was, in 1935, replaced by one of freehold grants.

There are certain obvious advantages in freehold. It provides the best form of security for credit, and the sense of absolute ownership is a powerful incentive to development. When Arthur Young declared that 'the magic of property turns sand into gold', it was freehold property that he had in view.[3] Freehold provides opportunities for large profits when the value of land has substantially increased. It confers freedom from control by landlords, whether they are private individuals or Governments. In many dependencies it confers social status, and in some is even considered to be the hall-mark of political freedom. In the British West Indies the demand for freehold by Negro small-holders has not been unin-

[1] *Kenya Land Tenure Committee Report 1941*, paras. 5 and 24.

[2] *West India Royal Commission Report on Agriculture, etc.*, by F. L. Engledow, C.M.G., p. 35. See also Sir Frank Stockdale's *Report on Development and Welfare in the West Indies* (Colonial No. 184 of 1943), para. 126.

[3] Young also said: 'Give a man the secure possession of a bleak rock and he will turn it into a garden. Give him a nine years' lease of a garden and he will turn it into a desert.'

fluenced by the desire for political equality with Englishmen. In some of the islands the ownership of land is an electoral qualification.[1]

Yet in England and elsewhere many farmers prefer tenancy to ownership, since capital expended on development is more productive than when sunk in the purchase of the land.[2] More particularly in the case of small-holders, the purchase of freehold may entail the exhaustion of capital resources. In all the colonies where agricultural debt has become a State problem, the excessive buying (often for social reasons) of more land than could be developed has been one of the principal causes of indebtedness. The ability to borrow money on freehold property has everywhere been a curse to peasant proprietors who had not learned the proper use of credit. Freehold opens the door to speculation and under-development. A recent land Commission in Northern Rhodesia observed that it was monstrous that 80,000 acres of land, much of it more suited for cattle than for tobacco, should be lying idle at a time when land was so urgently needed; and they added that, since there were many other extensive areas held by companies and individuals for purposes of speculation, the Government should seriously consider the introduction of a tax on undeveloped land.[3] In Kenya, for the same reason, a similar measure is under consideration.[4]

There are other obvious dangers in freehold. In the absence of specific laws against partition there is the danger of excessive fractioning, so that what is left of a holding may no longer be able to support the farmer and his family. This danger is everywhere increasing, with the increase in population and the decrease in available land. Under a leasehold system the State is more able to ensure an economical use of land, to take steps to meet new conditions, and to insist on measures which will prevent the impoverishment of the soil through bad husbandry, overstocking and the

[1] In Bermuda (which is not part of the British West Indies) the right to vote is restricted to those who are in possession of freehold property of not less than £60 value. The qualification for membership of the House of Assembly is the possession of freehold property rated at £420.

[2] It is generally agreed that in England during the last century, before farmers possessed any statutory rights in their holdings, the tenancy system resulted in the highest development of the art of husbandry. Flanders provides another illustration of the same fact. (See Sir Henry Rew's article, 'Land Tenure' in the *Encyclopædia Britannica*, 14th ed.) In the United States of America the proportion of tenant farmers (25% in 1880) has almost doubled in the last 65 years.

[3] *Report of the 1942 Commission on the North Charterland Concession.* The 1943 Land Tenure Committee of Northern Rhodesia also stated (para. 14 of their Report) that as a result of the freehold system 'there are at present approximately three-quarters of a million acres of alienated land in the Territory lying completely idle and unoccupied, while there are places where land is being so misused that its destruction can only be a matter of time.'

[4] Under a recent Ordinance (No. XXII of 1944) the Land Board in the Highlands area may refuse to give its consent to any transaction in land if it considers that the applicant already has sufficient land.

destruction of forest.[1] Under a leasehold system adequate security of tenure can be given, and any substantial increase in land values, which are generally due to expenditure by the State, will accrue to the State and not to the individual.

In the political sphere there are weighty arguments against any extension of freehold. The peoples of the British dependencies are not culturally homogeneous, but fall into racial groups which are not all equally capable of holding their own. The local Colonial Government is the only authority which can protect the rights of the various component sections, and at the same time promote their integration. But it would prejudice its ability to do this if it were to grant, or continue to grant, extensive rights in freehold, more especially if the grants were made to one section of society and not to another.

In England present-day opinion regarding freehold may be gauged by the Uthwatt Report. In this the Committee puts forward, for the consideration of the Government, the proposal that 'all land in Great Britain be forthwith converted into leasehold interests, held by the present proprietors as lessees of the State at a peppercorn rent for such a uniform term of years as may reasonably, without payment of compensation, be regarded as equitable, and subject to such conditions enforceable by re-entry as may, from time to time, be applicable under planning schemes'. In commenting on this proposal the Committee remarked that 'intelligently administered, the proposal should not hamper the operation of private enterprise in regard to the development or use of land or otherwise fetter its enjoyment. Subject to compliance with planning legislation the leaseholder would be equally free to make the same use of his land as if he had remained a freeholder; and if in the future new developments are desired and the remaining period of the lease is insufficient to justify the expenditure, application for renewal could be made. . . . No compensation would be paid and the term of years to be fixed, therefore, would be such that the market value of the lease from the State was not appreciably less than the market value of the freehold interest. For this purpose the conventional term of ninety-nine years would certainly be long enough'.[2]

It is hardly necessary to observe that many of the arguments which can be brought against freehold are equally valid against very lengthy leases. It may be held, for example, that it is indefensible to commit the public interest for 1,000 years, particularly in new

[1] The Inspector-General of Agriculture in the West Indies (Mr. A. J. Wakefield, C.M.G.) has recently stated that the unrestricted grant of freehold had led to wholesale destruction of the soil even within a period of ten to fifteen years. Sir Frank Stockdale has also stated that, 'It is becoming increasingly clear that freehold tenure, except under very careful management, has been adverse to the interests of the owner and his descendants and also of the community.' (See Colonial No. 184 of 1943, para. 120.)

[2] *Uthwatt Report*, Chapter X, pp. 154-156.

countries like Kenya,[1] where immense changes may be expected to occur within a comparatively short time. Leases of ninety-nine years, with a reservation to the State of regulated opportunities of reviewing the return which they make to the public revenue, would offer sufficient security for any enterprise, provided that they included (as they seldom do at present) certain safeguards in favour of lessees. In England the Agricultural Holdings Act of 1923 recognizes both the tenant's claim to the value of unexhausted improvements and the landlord's claim to dilapidations at the termination of the lease. Similar provisions would seem to be required in the agricultural leases of a number of Colonies, as well as other changes, giving additional security, while retaining for the State the power to step in at the end of a lease, if the public interest so required. The Secretary of State for the Colonies has recently suggested that the State could declare its intention five years or so before the expiry of the lease, and if it had decided to take over the property could pay the outgoing leaseholder a properly assessed market value for his unexhausted improvements. Alternatively the State might announce its preparedness to grant a new lease for a further term. It could then enter upon negotiations with the tenant, stating its conditions (e.g. renovation of the property and a revised rent). If the tenant considered the conditions unattractive he would still be entitled to payment for his unexhausted improvements, and the State would have these to offer to the new lessee: or a lease of the improved property, subject to the State's new conditions, might be offered by tender or auction and the sum realized passed on to the outgoing tenant. On the other hand, the State would have to protect itself against an outgoing tenant who, as the lease neared its end, might endeavour to extract as much as possible from, and expend as little as possible upon, the leased land.

These arguments would apply with even greater force to building land. For with freehold or leases for 999 years there would almost certainly arise in the newer colonies, as in England and in India, a class of ground landlords, and while the real development would be carried out by tenants or sub-tenants their reversions would fall, not to the State, but to individual landlords with no interests but their own to consider.

In a number of dependencies the freehold system has already been abandoned. In Northern Nigeria, Tanganyika, Nyasaland and the Northern Territories of the Gold Coast, freehold is not granted under the land laws. In Northern Rhodesia the accepted policy has been that freehold should not be granted, though, as in Kenya,

[1] As already noted, leases in Kenya are normally for 999 years. There are, however, qualifying conditions regarding development and subdivision. And rents are subject to revision.

leases are granted for 999 years.[1] In Uganda sales of freeholds, though legally permissible, have been suspended since 1916, on the instructions of the Secretary of State. In St. Lucia (Windward Islands) a recent order has declared that Crown Lands will henceforth be leased and no longer sold,[2] and a similar order was promulgated in British Guiana in 1938.[3] In other Colonies there has been a general narrowing of the rights that normally go with freehold. In Ceylon, for example, we have seen that a new type of tenure was introduced in 1935 by which grants of land are given in perpetuity on conditions which include a small annual payment to the Crown, as well as measures to secure that the land shall be used in a specific manner, and that it shall not be alienated or subdivided. In Malaya grants of Crown or State land are given in perpetuity, but the grant is subject to the Land Code and any provisions in the grant itself. Rents are revisable and there are implied conditions regarding good husbandry. For the West Indies the Royal Commission of 1939 recommended that freehold should not be granted unless accompanied by conditions which would prevent fragmentation and safeguard good husbandry, including the prevention of erosion and the maintenance of soil fertility.[4] In some European and American countries freehold rights are only granted after certain measures of development have been carried out. But conditions precedent to a grant of freehold can only serve as a temporary safeguard and cannot ensure the continuous development upon which the State can insist under the leasehold system.[5]

From this summary it would appear that the whole weight of agricultural opinion is directly opposed to the freehold principle, that modern political and economic theory is consistently in favour of the increasing control of land by the State, and that British Colonial governments are becoming more and more committed to the leasehold system. Where freehold rights are still being granted they are being so narrowed that it is doubtful if they can be described as freehold at all. Moreover, much of the unpopularity of leasehold tenure can be removed, particularly if proper compensation is paid for unexhausted improvements. Sir Frank Stockdale has observed that in the West Indies when the objectives for

[1] See p. 126.

[2] See *St. Lucia Gazette* of 10th January, 1942. Prior to 1942 Crown lands were sold to peasants and others without any reservations except as to tracks, roads and mineral rights. The purchaser could do as he pleased with the land.

[3] See British Guiana Government Notice No. 233 of 1938.

[4] *West India Royal Commission Report*, p. 316.

[5] But it has been argued that the function of the State in protecting the land from misuse can best be fulfilled by *ad hoc* legislation, which would be applicable to all land whether freehold or leasehold (see e.g. the *Kenya Land Tenure Committee Report*, 1941, para. 8). In Kenya the Land and Water Preservation Ordinance (No. 11 of 1943) is an example of such legislation.

agricultural development have been explained and illustrations given of the disastrous results to the community of the freehold system, especially the fragmentation of holdings, the indebtedness of the land and the accumulation of land by mercantile interests at the expense of the agricultural community, the representatives of the people have shown themselves ready to consider alternative forms of tenure.[1]

[1] Colonial No. 184, op. cit., para. 126.

CHAPTER XXI

The System of Revisable Rents

THE revisable rent system is found in many of the British Colonial dependencies,[1] and there is very considerable variation in the methods of its application. In the Straits Settlements rents are revised at periods of thirty years (from 1915), but the rent payable in any term of thirty years must not exceed by more than 50% the rent which was payable in the immediately preceding term. In making the revision, no improvements are to be taken into account. In the Federated Malay States the provisions are similar,[2] but the Land Enactment does not prescribe any maximum percentage by which rents may be raised. In the Unfederated State of Kelantan revisions may take place at intervals of not less than fifteen years and no revisions shall have the effect of increasing the rent by more than 25%. In Perlis the rent, which is described as 'quit rent', may not be revised until after the lapse of thirty years and when revised it may not exceed by more than 50% the amount of rent imposed in the previous period.

In Uganda a covenant in Crown leases provides that rent shall be revised at specified intervals to a sum not exceeding 5% of the unimproved value. Considerable discretion is therefore left to the land administration authorities. The normal agricultural lease is for ninety-nine years, with revision of rent at thirty-three year intervals. Building leases, which may run for ninety-nine years or forty-nine years, are subject to rent revision at intervals of twenty-five years. Little attempt is made to adjust rent meticulously to area, nor to impose the maximum rate that each plot can carry. Rents in Uganda are undoubtedly low. No great body of rents has yet come up for revision, though some experience has been gained with a group of cotton ginnery leases. These were typically of five acres for forty-nine years at an initial rate of £1 10s. per acre, with a right of revision at the twenty-fifth year to a sum not exceeding £7 10s. an acre. Conditions would appear to have justified the raising of rents on the first revision to the maximum figure, but the Government decided to limit the revision to £4 an acre for the next ten years, when the rent would again be subject to review.[3]

In Kenya no provision existed for rent revision in the ninety-nine

[1] The system is also found in many parts of India, where cultivators hold occupancy rights in land direct from the State.

[2] The first revision may take place on the 1st of January, 1940, and subsequent revisions at intervals of *not less* than thirty years.

[3] Information of Mr. H. B. Thomas, O.B.E., formerly Director of Surveys and Land Officer, Uganda.

year leases issued under the Crowns Land Ordinance of 1902, and one of the reasons for the abandonment of the Land Bill of 1908 was the opposition raised to the rent revision proposals. The principle was, however, applied by the Government between 1911 and 1914 in certain Rules under which a number of leases were issued, and it was formally adopted in the Crown Lands Ordinance of 1915—the revision periods being fixed at thirty years, beginning in 1945. It was laid down that the annual rent should be, for the first period, at twenty cents per acre, for the second period at 1% on the unimproved value of the land in 1945, for the third period at 2% (in 1975), and for each subsequent period of thirty years at 3% (assessed every thirty years). If a lessee objected to the new valuation the question of the value of the land would be settled by arbitration.[1]

In Tanganyika, the Land Ordinance of 1923 (Chapter 68 of the Laws) provides for the auctioning of rents in the first instance and for fixing the rent then, and upon subsequent revision (at intervals of not more than thirty-three years), at the highest amount that can reasonably be obtained from the land, subject to certain provisos.[2] In practice, revision has been fixed for intervals of twenty years, with special provision (following the German system) for earlier revision in the event of the opening of a railway within a certain distance of the land. In revising the rental no account may be taken of any value due to capital expenditure, but the occupier may surrender his lease if he considers the revised rent excessive. In that case he is entitled to compensation for the unexhausted improvements.

In Northern Rhodesia the Tanganyika system of leaseholds for ninety-nine years, with rents revisable at intervals of thirty-three years, was applied to Crown lands in 1929. Since then new areas opened up for European Settlement have been subject to leases for 999 years with rents revisable after thirty years, the revision being based on the unimproved value of the land, following the Kenya model. Ranching land, when the acreage is from 6,000 to 20,000 acres or more, is granted under lease for a period of thirty years only, renewable at a revised rental, whether the ranches are inside or outside the settled areas.

In Nyasaland, under the Crown Lands Ordinance, 1912, the Governor was empowered to grant leases of land up to ninety-nine years for slowly maturing crops, such as tea and rubber, and other leases up to twenty-one years. In the case of the former the rental was made liable to re-assessment at the end of thirty-three and sixty-six years, while in the case of the twenty-one year leases the

[1] *Crown Lands Ordinance, 1915*, Secs. 35-38.
[2] See Amendment to the Ordinance (No. 17 of 1930).

rental was liable to re-assessment at the end of seven years. It was laid down that the re-assessed rental for all agricultural leases should be 5% of the value of adjacent undeveloped agricultural land of equal quality. The Crown Lands Ordinance of 1912 was repealed in 1931 by Ordinance No. 1 of that year (Cap. 56) and under the new Ordinance every lease may be for any definite term not exceeding ninety-nine years, rent being subject to revision at intervals of *not more* than thirty-three years. In determining the initial or upset rental of any lease, and on every subsequent revision, the Governor has to take into consideration the rent obtained or obtainable in respect of any other like land in the immediate neighbourhood and to fix the rent at the highest amount that can reasonably be obtained (without taking into consideration any value due to capital expenditure).

Coming now to West Africa, in the Colony and the two Southern Provinces of Nigeria there is provision for the revision of rents leased under Section 4 of the Crown Lands Ordinance (Cap. 84). The intervals between revisions are specified in the leases. In the Northern Provinces the revision provisions were formerly[1] the same as those described for Tanganyika (whose land legislation was largely modelled on that of Northern Nigeria). Building leases were revisable at intervals of not more than twenty years, while all other leases were revisable at intervals of not more than seven years. In 1929, however, rents were made revisable at such intervals as might be specified in the grant.[2] In 1941 legislation was passed (for the whole of Nigeria)[3] by which the revision of rent might be postponed at the Governor's discretion—a war-time measure which has been found necessary in other dependencies, since it appeared undesirable that rent revision should be mandatory under disturbed conditions.[4]

The general justification for a system of revisable rents is that the State, being the trustee of land for the people, has a right to participate in any increase in the value of land, particularly in new countries where the increased value of land is so often directly due to development carried out by the State.[5] Moreover, under a system

[1] Under the Land and Native Rights Ordinance of 1916.

[2] By Ordinance No. 23 of 1929.

[3] Ordinances Nos. 2 and 3 of 1941.

[4] In Sierra Leone the rent reserved under any lease of land in the Protectorate is subject to revision every seven years, by the District Commissioner, from whom there is a right of appeal to the Provincial Commissioner. (See Ordinance No. 16 of 1927, Sec. 5 (1)).

[5] Lord Lugard observes in *The Dual Mandate* (p. 302) that 'The owner of freehold land obtains without any effort on his part any increase in the value of land due to the expenditure of public funds or the industry of the community. It is reasonable and just that the community as a whole—viz. the State—should participate in these increased values by periodic revision of rentals, or preferably by a graduated income tax.'

of revisable rents the State is enabled to exercise necessary measures of control, such as the prevention of excessive accumulations of land in the hands of individuals.

But the revisable rent system has aroused a good deal of criticism at various times in a number of British dependencies. Thus, the Central Development Committee of Tanganyika observed in 1940 that, whether land in Tanganyika were alienated by auction or by tender, by variable stand premium and fixed rentals or by variable rentals, the condition that rent was revisable after a period not exceeding thirty-three years had the effect of reducing the value of the leasehold title as a security. The condition was imposed because of the possibility that development unassociated with the holding might affect the value of the holding, as when remote areas were opened up by the development of ports, railways, or all-weather roads; or a country holding came under the influence of urban development. The Committee considered that the factors which were intended to be taken into account should be clearly stated.[1] The Land Tenure Committee of Northern Rhodesia (1943) also observed that the rent revision system necessarily involved some insecurity of tenure and complicated mortgage transactions. In the long-term agricultural leases which the Committee recommended, there would be no justification for rent revision, since the lessee would have paid a premium equivalent to nine-tenths of the freehold value of the land. In the short-term lease, on the other hand, with the period of the lease limited to sixty years, there was no necessity for any rent revision.[2]

In commenting on the fact that, in Nyasaland, rentals on recent leases and conversions were liable to re-assessment in 1939 and at subsequent intervals of thirty-three years, Sir Robert Bell, who had been commissioned by the Secretary of State for the Colonies to report on the financial position and further development of Nyasaland, doubted the wisdom of a system by which the rentals of all estates were made liable to revision in one particular year. Quite apart from the fact that this might induce something like political pressure, it was obvious that if rentals fell due for revision from time to time for different estates, and not all simultaneously, then when the rental of any particular estate fell due, the revising officer and the Government would have before them for guidance the results of revising, at different dates, the rentals of practically every other estate in the territory. Moreover, with a rigidly fixed period

[1] *Report of the Central Development Committee, Tanganyika Territory*, 1st May, 1940. Para. 232.

[2] *Report of the Land Tenure Committee, Northern Rhodesia*, 1943, para. 25. The Committee observed, as regards township plots, that the appreciation of land values in a township is largely due to the improvement of the amenities provided by the local authority, at the expense of the inhabitants; and in any case the Government benefits indirectly as a town grows in size and prosperity.

after which the assessment *must* be revised, it was not clear what the legal position would be if the Government, for any reason, failed to effect the revision at the due date.[1] It would be clearly inconvenient and disadvantageous to the Government if the year of revision occurred during a slump and it would be difficult for them, and might be disadvantageous to the leaseholder, if the revision had to be effected on the crest of a boom.[2] Leaseholders are entitled to a degree of certainty, and it would be better policy if rentals were guaranteed for a *minimum* period of, say, thirty years, after which they would again be liable to revision with the same guarantee. As a further protection to the leaseholder the increase in rental should be limited to some pre-determined amount.[3]

Sir Robert Bell was clearly not criticizing the system of revisable rents as such, but rather the manner of its administration. But in Kenya a Land Tenure Committee has recently (1941) recommended the abolition of the system itself, in so far as agricultural rents are concerned. They considered that the existing revisable rent conditions were a hindrance to new settlement, a cause of uncertainty and dissatisfaction among existing settlers, and a deterrent to the investment of capital in farming enterprise. Their objections were based largely on the fear that when the revision took place rents would be increased, and that, although in theory the revision would be based on the unimproved value of the land, the settler would, in fact, have to pay an enhanced rental on the value of his own pioneering work, since his efforts to prove the potentialities of the land (often at a heavy cost) would increase the so-called 'unimproved' value. Furthermore, there was the impracticability of determining with any degree of accuracy the unimproved or prairie value of developed farms in widely differing classes of land. It had been suggested that reasonable values could be obtained by an examination of the farmer's balance sheets, but, bearing in mind the notoriously sketchy manner in which farmers' accounts were often kept, this method of valuation was more likely to accentuate than solve the difficulty. Whatever the method of assessment, there would always be wide scope for differences of opinion, resulting in a continuing series of appeals after each revision. As for the claim of the State to share, by means of a direct levy, in the unearned increment attaching to agricultural land, it should be remembered that the State derived benefit from increases of land values in many other ways. It was true that the farmer depended on an adequate road and railway system to get his produce to market, but he, like other members of the public, contributed, through taxes and railway rates,

[1] Since, presumably, rents are not necessarily enhanced on revision but may be reduced (C.K.M.)

[2] Or, as observed above, during a war (C.K.M.).

[3] Colonial No. 152, 1938, paras 83 *et seq.*

for the privileges enjoyed, and it was unfair that he should be additionally taxed by means of increased rentals on the enhanced value of his land, resulting from improved communications. The Committee concluded by saying that many farmers whose land was held on leases of ninety-nine years under the Crown Lands Ordinance of 1902 had refused to convert these into leases for 999 years under the Crown Lands Ordinance of 1915, precisely because the rentals of the former were fixed, whereas those under the latter had been made subject to revision. On the whole of the evidence the Committee was unanimous in recommending that the revisable rent provisions of the 1915 Ordinance should be repealed. They added the recommendation that agricultural lessees should be permitted to commute the whole or any part of their annual rent. The principle of rent redemption had been accepted by the Government in the case of township plots, and if it were extended to agricultural land one of the main objections to the investment of English trust moneys on the security of agricultural leases in Kenya would be removed.[1]

The Secretary of State (Colonel Oliver Stanley) considered that, since the greater part of available land in Kenya had been alienated, the abolition of revisable rents would be conferring an unwarranted benefit on existing landlords at the expense of the future revenue of the State. There was a tendency for money to depreciate in value. If the State abandoned its right to review rents, a gap would arise between the economic rent and the rent payable to the State, and this would open the door to intermediate trafficking in the value of this gap—as had happened in England and in India. It should be possible to devise a less rigid system of revision which, while maintaining the fundamental principle that substantial increases in land value should accrue to the State and not to the individual, would be less objectionable to the leaseholder. Thus, dates of revision might be 'staggered' in the manner suggested by Sir Robert Bell, and this system had in fact been followed in Uganda with regard to township plots.[2] As for the recommendation that permission should be given for the redemption of rents, the Secretary of State considered that many of the arguments for retaining the system of revisable rents were applicable in the case of rent redemption, which if permitted might prove a very bad financial

[1] *Land Tenure Committee Report, Kenya,* September, 1941, paras. 9-15.

[2] In Uganda, when a block of plots is thrown open to allotment, a date, say 99 years hence, is fixed for the termination of all leases in that block, with revision at 25 years. All leases subsequently granted in the block have correspondingly shorter terms, and so all expire on a common date. But the full 25 years between rent revision dates is accorded to these later leases. Thus, while spreading the rent revision dates, and so avoiding the difficult task of simultaneous re-assessment of the unimproved value, it is possible for the Government to consider the replanning of the whole block at a common date.

bargain for the Colony, in view of the steady depreciation in the value of money.

The Secretary of State did not deal with the objection that rent revisions were often arbitrary, and it would appear to be doubtful if in any of the tropical African dependencies there is any adequate machinery or technique for dealing with re-assessments. In the *Nyasaland Development Report* quoted above, Sir Robert Bell makes some interesting observations on the Indian method of fixing and revising the assessment, which is related to two factors: (*a*) the soil, and (*b*) the locality. The soils are classified field by field, deductions being made for poor quality, lack of depth, excess or deficiency of certain elements, e.g. stone, gravel and lime. The classification is done by experts and the rules have been worked out as a result of many years of constant modification. Furthermore, each area is divided into zones according to economic and climatic factors and to each zone is assigned a zone rate. In revising assessments zone rates are revised every thirty years for one, two or more zones at a time, the principal factor in making the revision being the level of prices of staple products in the zone for five or more years preceding the revision, as compared with the level of prices when the zone rate was last fixed. The soil classification is also revised. The re-assessment is based on the new zone rate, combined with the soil classification. Sir Robert Bell did not consider that this system could be applied wholesale to a country like Nyasaland, which had no experience of classifying estates or of demarcating and rating zones; but he thought that a beginning should be made and that on this account the policy of revising the rentals of *all* estates simultaneously should be discarded. If the revision fell due on different dates, each revision would help to build up a fund of experience from which formulae of scientific precision could be devised.[1]

Summing up the general argument regarding revision of rents, it may be said that present-day political and economic opinion favours the view that governments should be free to review the system of land utilization at reasonable periods and that any substantial increases in land values should accrue to the State and not to private individuals. Revisions should not, however, be open to arbitrary increase, but be made dependent on scientific principles worked out for each district. They should be restricted to a maximum percentage of the unimproved value of the land and be at fixed, but not simultaneous, intervals. In the case of agricultural leases the intervals should not be unduly frequent; but for town leases frequent revisions may be required, since urban values, particularly in the newer dependencies, are liable to increase with remarkable rapidity.

[1] Report op. cit. (Col. 152), paras. 86-92.

CHAPTER XXII

The Pledging and Mortgaging of Land

The Pledging of Land

The practice of pledging land is common in many regions of the British Colonial Empire. Where people have no other form of wealth but their land, and the sale of land is forbidden by native custom, the only means of raising money is by pledging the land or its usufruct. In its main features the pledging of land closely resembles a usufructuary mortgage, that is to say, a mortgage in which the mortgagor delivers possession of the mortgaged property to the mortgagee and authorises him to retain possession until the mortgage money has been paid, and to appropriate the profits accruing from the property in lieu of interest, or in payment of the mortgage-money, or partly in lieu of interest and partly in payment of the mortgage-money. Sometimes the pledgee's right is one of retention only, though by agreement both enjoyment and periodical fruits may belong to the pledgee. But in Africa, where the practice is widespread, it is the usufruct that matters most, and this is not taken into account against the principal debt. In Muhammadan areas the practice of pledging provides a profit for the money-lender, without infringing the Islamic law against usury.

Unlike the mortgagee of English common law, the pledgee of land in Africa obtains no permanent rights over the land; there is no right of foreclosure; the land remains redeemable for all time, although it is not restored to its owner until the debt has been paid in full. The African's 'right of redemption' is reflected in the Kikuyu proverb that 'A debt on land can never be finished',[1] in that of the Ibo of Nigeria that 'A thing which is pledged is never

[1] Kenya Cmd., 4556 para. 276. There was the same custom in India. Sir J. B. Lyall, writing in the middle of last century said, 'The commonest kind of mortgage in the Punjab is that by which the mortgagee takes all the rents and profits of the land in lieu of interest on the principal sum secured or towards the reduction of both interest and principal. Here no term is fixed within which payment is to be effected, and I understand that the custom of the country gives such a mortgagee no right to foreclose or ask for a sale. If ordinary mortgagees had such rights an immense amount of property would soon change hands.' Sir Richard Temple said he had known land mortgaged in one generation redeemed in the next, and Mr. E. Prinsep said he had known cases where redemption had been sanctioned by general consent one hundred years after the original transfer had been made, although no deed could be produced to support the fact of the mortgage. See *Punjab Customary Law*, by C. L. Tupper, Vol. II, pp. 226 *et seq.* It is interesting to note that it is not yet clear whether a Muhammadan mortgagor can make valid a gift of his equity of redemption in property of which the mortgagee is still in possession. See *Digest of Anglo-Muhammadan Law*, p. 326.

lost'.[1] and in that of the Gold Coast that 'Debt dries but never rots'. When proposals were made in 1927 for introducing into the Gold Coast a Statute of Limitations they had to be abandoned because of the opposition of the chiefs and people, who held that the proposals would upset the whole native system of holding land. Time, they said, is never of the essence of the native contract, and nothing but repayment can discharge a debt.[2]

Among the Kikuyu of Kenya,[3] land is frequently pledged in order to obtain cattle and sheep for the payment of a bride-price, rams for sacrificial purposes, or cash to pay fines or taxes. The person who is willing to dispose of his cultivation rights in return for such a loan is required to offer the first refusal to a member of his own clan. If no clansman is prepared to advance the loan, then, with the consent of the clan, he may hand over the land to some obliging neighbour. The rule of redemption is that, if the pledgee has exercised his rights of cultivation, then the exact number of animals lent must be returned. But if the pledgee has not exercised his rights of cultivation, then the original number of animals plus the natural increase must be returned. On this principle it might appear that a pledgor or his heritors would, in the course of even a few years, find it difficult to redeem the land. But it is said that, in practice, this seldom occurs, since, if a pledgee shows no intention of exercising his rights of cultivation, the pledgor will persuade one of his own clansmen to redeem the land and so save him from undue expense or the danger of losing the land altogether. Indeed, the clansmen would usually take this action on their own account. Moreover, land-pledging transactions are invariably carried out on a basis of friendship and not of private gain. Generations may pass before any attempt at redemption is made, and for this reason it is usual to include mere boys as witnesses to the agreement.[4]

It has often happened in the past that a clan has had to hand over a unit of land—in some cases practically the whole of its land—in order to pay blood-money, and in due course the pledgee may

[1] See *Law and Authority in a Nigerian Tribe*, by C. K. Meek, p. 103.

[2] Lord Hailey has observed that, 'The persistence of the right of redemption has in modern conditions frequently been pleaded as a defence against the recognition of sale when transactions, having all the appearance of complete transfers, have come before the European courts, and it has furnished the chief ground on which native opinion has argued the invalidity of the agreements made by chiefs for the surrender of land to non-natives.' (*An African Survey*, p. 836.)

[3] This information is derived from the *Report of the Committee on Native Land Tenure in Kikuyu Province*, 1929.

[4] But with the general rise in land values it may be expected that, where claims can be substantiated, pledged lands will be reclaimed. In the Kiambu district of Kenya, for example, it is said that as a result of the introduction of the plough and the consequent increase of the area cultivable by the family group, there has been considerable resumption of areas formerly pledged to outsiders. (See *An African Survey*, p. 849.)

himself be obliged to repledge the land to a third party. In cases of this kind there is no impediment to the redemption of the land by the clansmen: as soon as they are able they repay the original pledgee, who in turn must reclaim the land from the second pledgee. But pledgees must always be allowed to reap the harvest of any annual crop.

A pledgee may allow a third party a usufructuary share of the land he has obtained in pledge, and cases often occur among the Kikuyu of a single farmer being accorded cultivation rights in the holdings of several different individuals. If the land is redeemed the pledgee must remove his tenants, though the tenants would be given time to harvest their seasonal crops. If a tenant refuses to quit, the owner is, after redemption, entitled to graze cattle over the tenant's farm, and so drive him out.

As regards permanent crops, the variability of the rules in different districts, and even in the same district, is evidence of the difficulty of squaring native custom with modern progress. In some cases a pledgee, on relinquishing the land, is compelled to relinquish also the permanent crops which cannot be harvested or removed. In others he may be allowed to retain an interest in his permanent crops, or be given a sum of money as compensation; the amount being fixed by independent assessors. In others, again, he may be compelled to cut down his permanent crops. It was stated that, in Nyeri, an owner, on resumption, might allow land planted with permanent crops to lie fallow for a period, so as to avoid the charge of having resumed ownership in order to appropriate the occupier's crop.[1] On the other hand, cases appear to have occurred in which pledgees had sought to establish permanent rights, not only by planting permanent crops, but by building permanent houses.[2]

It is clear from these Kenya examples that the principle of redeemability, although it serves as a safeguard against speculation in land, has very serious drawbacks, in that it operates against security of tenure, and so against permanent improvement of the land. It is stated that in Kenya great difficulty may be experienced in obtaining land on satisfactory terms even for such public purposes as the building of a Church or School, since the native land official may revoke the right of occupancy at any time he likes.[3] The

[1] It is a common device in Africa for the owner of a piece of uncleared land to grant cultivation rights to another farmer, and then, at the end of a single season, reclaim the cleared land for his own use.

[2] In the Kano Emirate of Northern Nigeria 'the right to cultivate a farm may be assigned for any period or pledged as security for a loan, but the person to whom it is assigned may not erect permanent buildings on the land lest he prejudice the reversion to the original holder'. (Captain MacBride in *The Journal of the Royal African Society*, April 1938.) The question of compensation to pledgees who have built houses or made other permanent improvements has received little consideration in most African communities.

[3] Report, op. cit., p. 37.

'equity of redemption' may, indeed, work most inequitably, since a man with a well-kept garden or plantation may suddenly find himself under notice to quit, because of the repayment of a couple of goats borrowed from his grandfather fifty years ago. It is worthy of notice that among some related clans of the Kikuyu there is a private arrangement that if land is given in return for a 'loan' it can never be redeemed. In other words these related clans have agreed to permit the sale of land as between themselves.[1]

In Tanganyika the rules governing pledging are much the same as those in Kenya. Land may be mortgaged or pawned for a variety of reasons. The owner may wish to raise money for a bride-price, or to re-pay a debt, or to enable him to engage in trade. In the Bukoba district, according to Mr. Culwick, the avarice and improvidence of individuals have made it essential for the Native Authorities to draft rules limiting the sale, mortgaging and pawning of land held in individual ownership. Many persons, in their keenness to obtain money, had disposed of rights in land, the retention of which was essential for the maintenance of their dependants. A strong feeling had accordingly grown up in native society that such improvident persons should be restrained by law. Mr. Culwick considered that wherever the sale, mortgaging and pledging of land were already in full swing they should be allowed to continue, but that they should be rigorously controlled. No native should be allowed to engage in any of these transactions without the consent of the Native Authorities, who should withhold consent unless it could be shown that the land in question was not essential to the maintenance of the owner's dependants. All transfers should be registered by the Native Authorities. Mr. Culwick considered that these measures would tend to lessen the amount of land litigation. It would be interesting to know whether these suggestions were ever carried out, and also whether the rules drafted by the Bukoba Native Administration were ever put into force. It is easier to formulate rules of this kind than to put them into practice, as was found in Nigeria when it was proposed to place restrictions on the practice of mortgaging agricultural land.[2]

In Sierra Leone the practice of pledging land has become a problem of some importance. In the upland areas pledging is said

[1] Report, op. cit., p. 71.

[2] See pp. 166-7. It may be added that in their book just published (1945) on the *Customary Law of the Haya Tribe—Tanganyika Territory*, H. Cory and M. M. Hartnoll state that mortgages are now sometimes made 'with the condition that if the loan is not repaid within a certain date the plantation becomes the property of the mortgagee'. A form of procedure has been laid down for attachment and sale. There appears to be a tendency for some courts to regard land as irredeemable if it has remained unredeemed over a considerable period.

to be unusual, since land there is seldom cultivated more than one year in seven, and so is of relatively little value.[1] But with the advent of permanent swamp cultivation of rice, and the establishment of permanent tree crops in certain areas, agricultural holdings of considerable value have come into existence on which the money-lender will advance money, accepting land as security and generally demanding the entire[2] use of the land until the whole of the loan has been repaid. The use of the land serves as interest for the money-lender, and very profitable interest it usually is. The land is nominally redeemable by the owner or his successors at any time, subject to the interest of the occupier in the standing crop. But if the land remains long enough in the hands of the money-lender the claims of the original owner are likely to lapse. Wealthy men may hold a number of pledged farms; and so land is tending to fall into the hands of a wealthy few, with a corresponding rise of a landless class. Even traders are, through the practice of pledging, obtaining control over land, with a view to letting it out profitably on a yearly tenancy. Such is the report of Mr. A. F. MacKenzie, an Agricultural Officer who has made a special study of the Scarcies River area, where the cultivation of rice has made remarkable strides in recent years.

Mr. MacKenzie considered that it would be inequitable to pass a law prohibiting the practice of pledging, since the pledging of land was the only means a farmer had of meeting an emergency. But a grave defect in the native practice was, he considered, the indeterminate period of the pledge. Pledging should, and could easily, be regulated by law. There might be a scale so that after one year the pledged land would be handed back on repayment of the full amount of the loan, after two years on repayment of three-quarters of the loan, after three years on repayment of one-half of the loan, after four years on repayment of one-quarter, and after five years, without any form of repayment. As things were, the amount for which a rice farm could be pledged was usually rather less than the annual value of a single crop.

But any scale of terms would obviously be dependent on the amount lent, the condition of the land, and the character of the crop to be grown. As already observed, it is quite a common device in Africa for a farmer to pledge his land and resume it again as soon as it has been put into good cultivable condition. Moreover, in Sierra Leone, there is on the Statute Book a Money-lending and Standing Crops Ordinance (No. 12 of 1926), which allows for the

[1] Yet the upland areas are, by the same informant (the Director of Agriculture), said to be overfarmed.

[2] Sometimes the lender allows a borrower who is short of land to occupy a portion of the land which had been pledged.

re-opening by courts of harsh and unconscionable transactions of money-lending.[1]

On the Gold Coast the pledging of land has been practised from time immemorial, but it has taken on new forms in recent times owing to the introduction of permanent crops, and is, indeed, one of the principal means by which strangers from the Northern Territories and the French Sudan have acquired an interest in the cocoa plantations of the colony.[2] As in Sierra Leone, the amount lent may be no more than the average annual yield of the crop. The lender takes possession and reaps the crops until the debt is paid. Or he may take over the land for a specified number of years, though the crop itself is normally regarded as being no more than interest on the money borrowed.[3] Some borrowers may agree to repay the loan in cash, with interest at 25%, 50% or even 100% per annum. Or the sum to be repaid may be fixed without regard to time. In some cases, again, the borrower may remain in possession of his land and hand over to the lender two-thirds of his crop at each harvest—one-third being regarded as interest and one-third as repayment of capital.[4] According to Professor Shephard some members of Co-operative societies on the Gold Coast admitted that they had pledged all their cocoa farms and had joined the societies with the express purpose of borrowing money, having exhausted all the other possible sources of credit.[5] The West African Cocoa Commissioners also observed that 'The native small capitalist becomes possessed, either directly by purchase of land, or indirectly through the widespread custom of pledging farms for monetary loans, of numerous farms, often widely scattered'. The Commissioners cited an instance of one of these capitalists who owned no less than seventy-nine scattered plantations.[6] Data collected by

[1] It does not appear, however, that the Money-lending Ordinance is used in Sierra Leone, any more than in any other colonial territory.

[2] With regard to grants of stool lands to strangers seeking an interest in cocoa, Professor Macmillan has observed that the public interest has certainly suffered. (See *Europe and West Africa*, p. 86.) But a cultivator on stool land is not entitled to mortgage the land without the consent of the stool. (See Cmd. 6278, p. 59.)

[3] Formerly, if a mortgagor redeemed the land before harvest he had to pay interest in gold dust.

[4] Under the system known as 'abusa', if forest land is given for the cultivation of cocoa, one-third of the cocoa crop goes to the landlord. But food crops grown on the plantation belong wholly to the tenant. A tenant on the 'abusa' system may not alienate the property, but he may transfer his own share to a third person. It is an understood condition of the 'abusa' system that when permanent crops are cultivated the tenant's rights pass to his heirs. Under the normal system of mortgage the mortgagor on resuming the land is not required to pay for improvements made by the mortgagee, unless he has repaid the loan at an earlier date than would allow the creditor to reap his interest in full. In this case the mortgagor would be required to compensate the mortgagee. See J. B. Danquah, *Akan Laws and Customs*, p. 220.

[5] Sessional Paper No. 1, 1936, paras. 173 and 217.

[6] Cmd. 5845, p. 20.

Agricultural Officers in 1933 showed that 30 % of cocoa-farmers had pledged one or more of their farms and that, unless redemption were automatic, few of the debtors had any prospect of clearing themselves of their rapidly increasing indebtedness.[1] In some chiefdoms action had been taken by the Native Authorities to prohibit the pledging of land. It would be instructive to know the present position in this respect. In the past a good deal of land on the Gold Coast has been deliberately sold under the ægis of the custom of pledging. Vendors of land have purported to buy it back with an 'over-plus'—a legal fiction whereby it is assumed that the land has merely been pledged.[2] Similar fictions are used in Nigeria for the same purpose.

Coming now to Nigeria, the pledging or pawning of land, trees, crops and houses, and also of one's own person, has been practised from ancient times. It may be of interest to give some description of the pledging of the person, since, although the practice is forbidden by the Government, it is still carried out to some extent.[3] Thus, in some Ibo communities, a young unmarried man may pledge himself in return for a sum of money or even for a wife. He lives with and works for his master every day of the week, the master providing him with food. But he may find time to do some farming on his own account, the master providing him with the land. If the debtor is married, he and his wife work for the master three days in eight and they are provided with food on these three days only. When he is able to redeem himself by repayment of the loan, plus 50 % interest,[4] he is expected to present his master with a goat and some other gifts, while the master in his turn provides a feast to celebrate the occasion. Girls may also be given as pledges for a debt, and remain with their master or mistress under the same conditions as those described for an unmarried man. They may be redeemed before reaching the age of puberty, or may remain after puberty as the wives of members of the master's household, the difference between the bride-price and the amount of the loan being adjusted. It is said that, as a result of the prohibition of the pledging of the person,

[1] C. Y. Shephard, op. cit., para. 175.

[2] R. S. Rattray. (Unpublished material.) In the Punjab (Hazara district) 'Sales of land without reservation of any right to redeem were rare. In the occasional instances in which they occurred special terms were applied to them, which terms expressly indicated that the seller had foregone the customary right to redeem the land on repayment of the purchase money. . . . A practice of making conditional mortgages (*bai-bil-wafa*) under which the transfer becomes final, if not redeemed within a stated period, is now springing up.' See *Punjab Customary Law*, by C. L. Tupper, Vol. II, pp. 226-7.

[3] The West African Cocoa Commission quoted the case of a Gold Coast farmer who stated that he could always raise capital by pawning some of his nieces. (Report, op. cit., p. 24.)

[4] The normal rate of interest on loans among the Ibo is 100% per annum. See C. K. Meek, *Law and Authority, etc.*, p. 234.

there has been an increase in the pledging of land and of crops.[1] And the pledging of economic trees has now also become a common practice. The head of a family, for example, may pawn some of the family trees in order to defray the funeral expenses of his predecessor. It would be the concern of all the members of the family to endeavour to redeem the trees at some future date. Until this is done, the creditor claims the fruit of the trees, as interest on the loan. Creditors often obtain from the trees more in the way of interest than the whole of the principal sum, and in many cases the chances of repaying the loan are so small that the plantation becomes for all practical purposes the property of the creditor. Many complications may arise when the ownership of trees is not vested in the person who owns the land on which the trees grow. The owner of a plot of ground may allow a friend to plant economic trees on his plot. The owner of the trees may, in course of time, pledge his trees, and the owner of the ground may pledge his ground. The pledgee of the ground may, in turn, with the owner's permission,[2] plant economic trees on his own account, and later on he, too, may pledge his trees. It is easy to see how conditions so confused are likely to lead to continual disputes and litigation.

Among the Ibo of Nigeria, who are probably the largest tribe in Africa, the custom of pledging land has served to give flexibility to the system of tenure, and to relieve congestion in certain areas. But it has also led to the creation of large groups of landless people, and is liable, if uncontrolled, to encourage the commercialization of land.

In Ibo-land, there are, roughly, three classes of land, namely, land on which compounds are built, land held in common by an extended family or clan, and land held by individuals. As regards the first, if a household were to remove to another site it might give its land, or a part, in pledge; but as a rule a household prefers to retain full rights over former sites, for religious reasons. To give such lands in pledge would be regarded as offering a slight to the ancestors who lie buried there. There is also reluctance to pledge farming land held in common by the family or clan. But the head of the group may find himself compelled to pledge a piece of family land in order to pay off a debt left by the previous head, and he may insist on doing so against the wishes of the family, if the family has offered no assistance in paying off the debt. Cases have occurred in which family land has been pledged with the consent of the entire

[1] See e.g. H. L. Ward Price, *Land Tenure in the Yoruba Provinces*, p. 202-3. For a discussion of debt servitude in various countries the reader is referred to the article 'Peonage' by G. Mc C. McBride in the *Encyclopœdia of Social Sciences*. The International Labour Conference has recently thrown much light on the subject.

[2] An owner would not usually allow a pledgee to convert his food-producing land into a plantation of permanent crops like cocoa. But this has been done frequently without permission.

family, and redeemed many years later by a single member of the family, the others having refused to co-operate. The individual who redeemed the land has then claimed it as his own.[1] It will be seen that here a principle of some importance is involved, and it must become increasingly important now that an individual member of a family may attain a position of wealth, while the rest of the family may remain poor.

Land held by individuals may, among the Ibo, be pledged without reference to anyone, and it is common practice to pledge land in order to raise or repay a bride-price, or even to raise the means of paying the Government tax. Pledged land is often permanently alienated.[2] A landowner who wishes to hinder an ill-disposed relative from inheriting his land may fix the redemption price of land he has pledged at double the amount of the loan. Additional formal payments of hook currency or of a few yams are also sometimes made, in order to create the legal fiction that the transaction is a pledging of the land and not a sale—the selling of land being nominally a contravention of native custom.[3] Many farmers endeavour to obtain small additional plots in this way in order to round off their holdings.

Owing to the practice of pledging, many Ibo farmers own widely scattered pieces of land, and some may even own plots within the boundaries of villages other than their own. This complicates the problem of the local administration of land. Further complications arise when whole groups of people of one village farm on the lands of another village, leasing them for a season[4] or obtaining the use of them as pledge tenants. There is a great deal of temporary transference of rights in this way between the denser and less dense patches of population.[5]

[1] C. K. Meek, *Law and Authority in a Nigerian Tribe*, p. 102. In the Gold Coast, according to J. M. Sarbah, when any land lost by an ancestor has been recovered by a member of the family out of his own private resources, such land is considered to have been purchased on behalf of the family, unless it had been made clear to the members of the family that it was to be treated as self-acquired property. See *Fanti Customary Laws*, p. 89.

[2] Miss Margaret Green in her study of *Land Tenure in an Ibo Village* comments on the light-hearted way in which young men pledge pieces of land which they do not happen to require at the moment.

[3] See C. K. Meek, *Law and Authority in a Nigerian Tribe*, pp. 103-104. It is not contrary to native custom for a family to sell some of its land outright if all the members agree to do so. But in some Ibo communities if ancestral land is sold outright a goat is sacrificed on the land, presumably to pacify the ancestors. An individual may sell outright land which was self-acquired, i.e. if there are no family rights which over-ride his own. Self-acquired land is inherited by a man's sons and not by his family group.

[4] A landholder who wishes to raise, say, £5 may give leases of plots to a number of people for 5/- to 10/- a plot. The term of the leasehold varies with the character of the plot. The lessee may grow a crop of yams and resign the plot immediately after harvest. Or he may grow cassava and remain on the plot for three years. He may build a hut and endeavour to convert his leasehold into a proprietory title.

[5] Miss Green gives a number of instances. Op. cit., p. 4. As regards the Northern

From this review of the practice of pledging land in Africa it is clear that the subject is one of first-rate importance. On the one hand, pledging appears as a useful and indeed necessary institution in that it provides people with credit in times of difficulty and relieves congestion by making land available for those who require it. It serves as a safety-valve against the evils of outright sale. On the other hand, it is itself a step in the direction of the commercialization of land, for, while giving the appearance of protecting the land from alienation, it often in fact is tantamount to sale. It is an insecure form of tenure, and therefore militates against development. It is often an impediment to the adoption of plantation cultivation, and is also a fruitful source of litigation. Finally, it is a powerful incentive towards the contraction of debt. With the knowledge that his land can be redeemed at any time, the pledger keeps putting off the evil day of repayment, and so may lose his land altogether. The pledging of land, therefore, is a subject to which colonial governments, particularly in Africa, may well be invited to give attention. It would be useful if data could be provided showing the character and extent of pledging in each territory, and the measures taken to control the practice, where this has been considered necessary. Measures of control can well be left to the Native Authorities, but they should not be applied without full consideration of the alternative means of relieving congestion on the land, and of supplying the funds required by communities whose sole resources are their land and its products.

Mortgage

The mortgage of English law is the product of two distinct conceptions. By the common law the mortgagee was the owner of the estate conveyed in the mortgage; but in equity the mortgagor remained the real owner and the mortgagee was merely an encumbrancer. The Court of Chancery first interfered in the reign of James I, to decree a redemption after forfeiture; and the right of the mortgagor to redeem his estate after it had been forfeited became known as his 'equity of redemption'. The Law of Property Act of 1925 went further and secured to the mortgagor a legal estate and not a mere equity of redemption. Thus as the law now stands mortgagor and mortgagee have legal estates.[1]

In Ceylon, under the influence of Roman-Dutch law, which does not permit the transfer of the dominium, the mortgagee acquires no

Provinces of Nigeria the legal restrictions placed on alienation are indicated at p. 168.

[1] In many of the States of U.S.A., also, the common law mortgage no longer exists, a mortgage having the effect of giving the mortgagee a legal lien upon the property, the mortgagor still retaining his title.

interest in the land, but only a right to obtain a decree declaring the land bound and executable for the recovery of the amount due. Moreover, in Ceylon, the contract of mortgage is one which can be altered by a subsequent act of one of the contracting parties, which the other cannot prevent and to which he has never given his consent. By departures from the Roman-Dutch law and 'well-meant efforts by the Courts to smooth things for the debtor, often forgetting that mortgage is a contract like any other', the law of mortgage in Ceylon had become so complicated that it was described by the Judical Commission in 1936 as 'an ungodly jumble'. 'It is humiliating,' they said, 'to have to confess that our law is adapted to the protection of the dishonest debtor, and that it leaves the lender a precarious security or none.'[1] The Commissioners also observed that a common form of investment in Ceylon, prior to the great trade depression of the thirties, had been the concurrent mortgage under which several mortgagees invested funds upon security belonging generally to one mortgagor, one bond being executed in their favour. But in recent years the law had become so involved that concurrent mortgages were not considered safe by prudent investors. Another common form of mortgage in Ceylon was that described generally as 'an open bond to secure future advances, the aggregate of which may or may not be stated. The actual advances when made are sometimes made in exchange for promissory notes for the amount of the advances'. These transactions were declared by the Commissioners to be a fruitful source of litigation, owing to the uncertainty of the law. The public were showing an increasing reluctance to lend money on the security of land. This was particularly hard on the Ceylonese since, in the absence of a local stock exchange, land and mortgages on land were the usual forms of investment for savings. The Commission made a number of recommendations for the reform of the Ceylon law of mortgage but these do not appear to have been carried out. Evidence given at the time of the debt conciliation legislation (in 1938-39) indicated that the disinclination to lend money on mortgage had been very much less than the Commissioners supposed. It is noteworthy that under the Land Development Ordinance of 1935 (Cap. 320) land held on grant from the Crown may not be leased, mortgaged or seized in execution of the decree of any court.

In Nigeria, in 1922-23, an issue of considerable importance was raised by the Native Chief of the Egba and his Council who asked the sanction of the Government of Nigeria to modify the local land regulations so that property within the city of Abeokuta and other large trading centres might be mortgaged by their owners to anyone

[1] Ceylon Sessional Paper VI, 1936, *Report of the Judicial Commission*, paras. 123-145.

they pleased. Hitherto the sale, mortgage and lease of land had been confined to transactions among the Egba themselves, but the continuation of the limitation would, they felt, render the raising of money difficult and possibly extortionate. The people of Abeokuta desired to deal with the local European firms and banks without restriction. It was realized that foreclosure would follow mortgages in certain cases, and there might in consequence be a transfer of house property to Europeans. But nobody would lend money on mortgage unless foreclosure were possible. The Chief and Council did not recommend that similar rights should be extended to agricultural lands since 'we feel it a sacred duty to protect family property and communal land, and that, unless the precaution is strictly preserved, whole family properties would in a short time pass into the hands of European capitalists and our people become landless, and labourers on farms which were once their ancestral lands.'

This subject has already been discussed[1] and it need only be observed that in 1933 the Governor, Sir Donald Cameron, expressed the opinion that natives of the Yoruba Provinces of Nigeria should be allowed to deal freely with their land, farming or non-farming, *among themselves*, provided that under no circumstances should farming land become attachable for debt. They might mortgage their crops, but not their agricultural land. He would also allow natives to mortgage non-farming land to an alien, but only on the condition that if the mortgagee had to foreclose he would receive no more than a lease for a reasonable term. Natives should not be allowed to mortgage farming land to aliens. Some of these recommendations would, said Sir Donald, involve new legislation. But difficulty was found in framing the legislation and the whole question has been indefinitely postponed.[2]

It is perhaps worth pointing out that there may be difficulty in differentiating between agricultural and non-agricultural land, since agricultural land is liable to be diverted to non-agricultural purposes. In Kenya, in 1933, the Government found it necessary to appoint a committee on 'Change of User' of agricultural land, and it appeared that shops had been, or might be built on farms,

[1] See pp. 164-6.

[2] In the Punjab, under Act XIII of 1900, a member of an agricultural tribe is permitted to mortgage his land to one who is not a member of his tribe for a period of twenty years. At the end of the period fixed the mortgage debt is extinguished. But the mortgagor may redeem his land at any time. No interest accrues during the period for which the mortgagee is in possession. The same Act forbids any future mortgage by way of conditional sale, i.e. any agreement whereby in default of payment the land will be transferred absolutely to the mortgagee. No land belonging to a member of an agricultural tribe may be sold in execution of any decree or order of any court. It may be attached. But under the Debtors Protection Act of 1936 land required for the maintenance of a debtor may not be attached, nor may ancestral immovable property, standing crops (other than sugar or cotton), work-oxen or agricultural implements.

residential plots excised from farms, estates erected on the borders of townships, factories erected on farms for the manufacture of non-agricultural products, and so on. The Committee recommended legislation to meet this 'change of user'.[1] In Malacca it was found necessary to introduce a provision that if land held under native customary title had been used mainly for building purposes the Governor could declare that it was no longer held under customary tenure. In Ceylon it was found impossible to dissociate agricultural property from town property in mortgage transactions, since, in the absence of credit facilities for agricultural lands, agriculturists had often to mortgage town property in order to obtain necessary funds. Further, when agricultural property had been mortgaged, any depreciation in the value of that property might involve the mortgagor in a general insolvency, as his town property and his movables might have to be sold in execution of the mortgage decree. It was on this account that the Debt Conciliation legislation of Ceylon, which was intended solely for the relief of agricultural debt, had finally to be fashioned so as to effect the settlement of all classes of debts.

In Zanzibar, where agricultural debt had assumed serious proportions, a land commission recommended (in 1934) that agricultural property should be rendered inalienable to non-agriculturists, and should not be liable to attachment and sale for debt.[2] Three years later Sir Ernest Dowson expressed the opinion that the pledging of land for debt should be prohibited by law, observing that inability to obtain credit was the only possible preventative of any new growth of debt, and that one of the major causes of the accumulation of debt in Zanzibar had been the avoidance of foreclosure. In 1939, by the Land Alienation Decree, it was laid down that no land might be permanently alienated or mortgaged by an Arab or African without the permission of the Lands Alienation Board, and that in the case of a mortgage the purposes of the loan must be for the maintenance or improvement of the land or any other purpose approved by the Board; the mortgagor must be left in possession of land sufficient for his needs; the amount of the loan should not exceed two-fifths of the value of the land; interest on the loan should not exceed 9% per annum; and the mortgage deed should contain provisions for the amortization of the loan. No land of an Arab or African, or the produce of such land, might be made liable to attachment for debt.

In Kenya, under the Crown Lands Ordinance of 1915, the

[1] Report of Select Committee on 'Change of User' of Agricultural Land, Kenya 1933.

[2] *Report on the Indebtedness of the Agricultural Classes*, by C. A. Bartlett and S. S. Last, Appendix B., para. 5.

Governor may veto any sale, transfer, mortgage, assignment, lease or sub-lease, if the person to whom the land is to be transferred is of a different race from the person who proposes to make the transfer. Under the Crown Lands (Amendment) Ordinance of 1944 (No. XXIII) the Governor's consent is required before anyone may sell, lease, or encumber land in the Highlands. These restrictions do not, however, affect any transactions made by or in favour of the Crown nor any gift of land by way of testamentary disposition. Restrictions are also placed on dealings with shares and assets in companies owning lands in the Highlands. Furthermore under the Land Control Ordinance of 1944 (No. XXII) the Board established by the Ordinance is given wide powers regarding the alienation of land in the Highlands and may refuse to sanction a transaction which would confer on anyone more land than is considered necessary for his needs. In Uganda, under the Land Transfer Ordinance of 1916, no land occupied by any native, or any right, title, or interest may be transferred (either in perpetuity or for a term of years) to any non-native without the consent of the Governor. The Governor would not approve of a mortgage of *mailo* land (the Buganda native form of tenure) to a non-native unless the right of foreclosure and power of sale (except to other natives) were excluded. It is of interest to note also that one of the effects of the Land (Sale and Purchase) Law enacted by the Buganda native government in 1939 is the extinguishment of equitable as well as legal rights arising from unregistered documents. In some districts of Uganda Crown land is held under Certificates of Occupancy which do not permit the sale of land, though the holder may sell his crops or trees to another native.

In Cyprus, where no one may hold State land without a title deed, sales and mortgages must be carried out by means of a written document.[1] The accumulation of mortgage debt in Cyprus led, in 1940, to the enactment of an Agricultural Debtors Relief Law.[2] There is also a law (No. 29 of 1940) to restrict forced sales of immovable property in certain cases.

In the Federated Malay States, the owners of land held by entry in the Mukim register may charge or lease their lands, but all dealings have to be executed in a statutory form. Land held under native customary title may only be transferred or leased to a person of the same tribe, and then only with the consent of the headman of the tribe. There is special provision, however, permitting the charging

[1] The mortgage law of Cyprus is peculiar. Where a mortgage has been registered no subsequent mortgage can be registered unless the mortgage already subsisting is cancelled. The draft Land Code of 1934 made provision for the registration of second and subsequent mortgages, but a decision on this point had not been reached by 1939.

[2] See p. 69.

of customary land to the British Collector or to a recognized local co-operative society. In the Malay Reservations, also, there are restrictions on transfers, charge and leases to persons other than Malays. No lien by deposit of the issue document of title of any Malay holding as security for a debt is capable of being created in favour of any person: and no Malay holding in a Reservation may be attached in execution of a decree or order of any court. Reservations lands may, however, be charged to the Government or to approved co-operative societies. In Malacca, no transfer of customary title is valid unless it is made to a Malaccan. The rights of a customary landholder are registered and every registered holder may charge his interest by way of mortgage. But no mortgage or sale is valid unless it is carried out in the manner prescribed by law. In Fiji, under the new land law, native land may not be alienated by native owners (whether by sale, grant, transfer or exchange) except to the Crown, and may not be charged or encumbered by native owners; nor may any native Fijian to whom any land has been transferred by virtue of a native grant transfer such land or any estate or interest therein, or charge or encumber the land without the consent of the Board.[1] Moreover, Fijians farming in a Native Reserve under an Agricultural Licence are not allowed to mortgage their crops without permission.[2] On the other hand, farmers holding agricultural leases from the Crown—and these may apparently include Fijians—are accorded the right to mortgage.[3]

This chapter may be concluded with the observation that, in India, various enactments have from time to time been passed by different local governments to deal with the transfer, by sale or mortgage, of agricultural land to non-agriculturists.[4] In the opinion of the Royal Commission on Agriculture in India (1928) the desirability of extending the principle of statutory restriction on the alienation of land to districts or provinces other than those in which it is now operated must depend on local conditions, including the state of mortgage debt amongst cultivators, the extent to which land is actually passing from agricultural to non-agricultural classes, and the feasibility of defining with reasonable precision those agricultural tribes or classes whose interests it is sought to protect. The Commissioners considered that no usufructuary mortgage of agricultural land should be permitted by law unless provision were made for automatic redemption within a fixed period of years, of which twenty should be the maximum. This is a principle which may

[1] Ordinance 12/1940, Sec. 6.
[2] Native Land (Lease and Licences) Regulations 1940, Sec. 46.
[3] Ordinance 12/1940, Sec. 13.
[4] E.g. Punjab Alienation of Land Act, Bundelkhand Land Alienation Act, Bombay Land Revenue Act. See p. 277, footnote 2.

commend itself to some Colonial Governments and Native Administrations. There is an obvious risk of collusive evasion, and so the Indian Commissioners concluded that education and the development of character were the best specifics for the wiles of the lender and the recklessness of the borrower.[1]

[1] *Royal Commission on Agriculture in India*, 1928, p. 47.

CHAPTER XXIII

Land Titles and Registration

ONE of the largest and most complex problems of Colonial Administrations is the provision and maintenance of systems of land record which shall be adequate and appropriate to the needs of each territory. In any given territory these needs may be various since there may be many varieties of tenure, and a form of record which may be suitable to one category of land may not be suitable to another. Under some conditions there may not be any necessity for any written record. Where land is plentiful and is cultivated on a shifting system, there is usually no need for registration, nor indeed may registration be possible. Even where more settled conditions prevail, title may be adequately secured by the mere sanction of native custom. In Africa there are millions of holders of land rights which are continually changing hands, by inheritance or otherwise, without dispute, without the use of any written documents, and often without reference to any public authority. The ceremony and publicity which are attached to transactions in land in primitive communities themselves constitute a form of record. The parties meet on the land, accompanied by their witnesses, and perform certain ritual acts which are expressive of the intention to convey.[1] In this way ownership is registered in the memory of the general public, and in particular in the memory of certain elders who are traditionally trained to remember all the details of transactions in land.

There may be good reasons, economic, social and political, for postponing in any community the institution of a system of records. The poverty of the soil and of the people mat not justify the expense of survey and of registration. The local inhabitants may resent any inquiry about their lands, which in many parts of Africa are regarded as belonging to the ancestors. They may fear that the creation of title to land may be used as a basis for taxation.[2] In India land records were for long vitiated on this account.[3] A premature system of registration of title may tend to break down

[1] For an example of this ritual see J. B. Danquah's *Akan Laws and Customs*, p. 217. Cf. 'mancipatio' in early Roman law and 'livery of seisin' in early English law.

[2] It may be observed, incidentally, that the institution of land tax records tends to crystallize land-holding rights and so to become an incipient record of title.

[3] See *An African Survey*, p. 875. Lord Hailey there adds that in Palestine also, land records were vitiated for the same reason. This could hardly be true of the Ottoman Land Registers. Moreover, in Palestine, the operative tax until recently was the tithe—a tax on produce independent of the land registers and of land ownership.

the collective tenures which are common in Africa and to introduce an individualism inconsistent with the social grouping known as the extended-family, a unit of labour which is eminently suited for many forms of cultivation.[1] Individualization of title renders it readily transferable and this in turn leads to trafficking in land. In India the development of agricultural debt followed the recording of individual holdings in land revenue settlements.[2] In some areas of Africa registration of individual title has been sought as a means of escaping from the authority of chiefs and from the various tenure restraints imposed by native customary law. The formal creation of title may therefore create social disturbance, and if confined to one area of a territory may throw doubt on the validity of titles in neighbouring areas where lands are still held according to the traditional rules.[3]

But a need for registration may arise where the native customary law is no longer able to cope with new conditions, where land has become scarce, where well-defined boundaries have become imperative, where permanent crops have replaced seasonal, where credit is required on the security of the land, where in fact individual proprietary rights have arisen and land has acquired a negotiable value. The absence of effective settlement and registration of title may interfere with the provision of capital for development; it may, as at one time in the history of India, lead to incessant litigation and the clogging of the judicial machinery; it may, as in the Gold Coast, Uganda and other territories, lead to the flooding of the country with worthless scraps of paper purporting to be valid titles to land;[4] it may, as in Zanzibar and elsewhere, be held to be responsible for the excessive cost of credit and so for the growth of agricultural debt; or it may, as in Ceylon, render title so insecure that it would be unsafe to buy any land without heavy expense for legal advice.[5] Even if the system of tenure is such that it does not contemplate the transference of land by sale or exchange, the recording of titles may still serve an important function by promoting a sense of security, increasing the incentive to effect improvements, assisting the provision of credit by approved agencies, and reducing the scope of litigation.

In the more advanced communities of the world, where land is highly commercialised, and is held under European forms of tenure, there are two methods by which certainty of title can be sought:

[1] But if *suitable* and not *stereotyped* systems of land registration were applied they would preserve collective tenures in areas where this was necessary and would be recognized and supported by law.

[2] See *An African Survey*, p 872.

[3] *An African Survey*, p. 875.

[4] See pp. 135 and 171.

[5] The official *Handbook of Ceylon* admits (p. 249) that 'The purchase of land should never be undertaken except upon legal advice.'

(*a*) Private Investigation of Title, or (*b*) Public Registration of Title. Under the first the purchaser endeavours to assure himself by an exhaustive examination of all relevant documents that no loophole exists by which an adverse claim can be preferred, and in order to assist this investigation most governments provide a State system of *Registration of Deeds*, that is to say that the instruments affecting land are copied or abstracted in an official register, the entries being made in chronological order and indexed under the names of the transacting parties. In some countries registration is essential to the legal validity of the deed, in others it merely confers priority over an unregistered document.

The system of registration of deeds, which is voluntary in some countries and compulsory in others, is open to the objection that registration does not cure any defect in any instrument or confer upon it any validity which it would not otherwise have. Fraudulent documents may be, and often have been, registered in order to give a spurious appearance of genuineness. Indeed, the difficulties of private investigation of title have been found to be so great that in some countries (notably the United States) insurance companies exist for the express purpose of investigating title, charging a premium for the trouble and risk of error. Sir E. Dowson and Mr. V. L. O. Sheppard[1] have observed that the system of registration of deeds is an incomplete system since many rights and responsibilities affecting land do not in fact arise from deeds. Important effects may result from judgments, devolution by will, etc., not embodied in deeds and consequently not registered. Nevertheless, where records are well kept in co-ordination with a reliable cadastral survey, the system of registration of deeds can be effective. If obligatory, it ensures that the terms and date of every deed affecting land are officially recorded. There are sound systems of registration of deeds in Scotland and in Yorkshire, as well as in France, Italy, the Netherlands, Sweden, Denmark, Belgium, Spain and Portugal. In the Union of S. Africa, as in Southern Rhodesia, the system of registration of deeds is held to be as good as any system of registration of title, in so far as security of title is concerned. Systems of registration of deeds exist in most of the British dependencies except where they have been superseded by a formal registration of title. They are not, of course, applicable to native lands held under native customary forms of tenure.

Registration of title may differ in important features in different countries. But its effective characteristics everywhere are that the land is initially placed on the register as a unit of property, tran-

[1] The writer is much indebted to two valuable papers by Sir E. M. Dowson, K.B.E., and Mr. V. L. O. Sheppard, C.B.E.—(*a*) 'An Introductory Note on Registration of Title to Land,' (1929), and (*b*) 'The Establishment of Registration of Title to Land' (read at the sixth International Congress of Surveyors, 1938).

sactions are registered with reference to the land itself and not merely as instruments executed by the owner, and registration of transactions becomes essential to their validity and serves as a warranty of title and a bar to adverse claims.[1] The form best known in most parts of the British Empire is commonly called the Torrens system. During the fifties of last century Sir Robert Torrens had been first a Commissioner of Customs in Australia and later a Registrar of Deeds. In his former capacity he had observed the ease with which rights in ships were transferred, in the latter the difficulties attending the transfer of rights in landed property. In the case of ships all rights were recorded in a definite and easily determined place and no new legal right was acquired until it had been found to be in conformity with existing rights. In the case of land the record might be non-existent or embedded in an unknown number of documents kept by an uncertain number of persons in a variety of places. 'Title by deed,' he said, 'can never be demonstrated as an ascertained fact: it can only be presented as an inference more or less deducible from the documentary evidence accessible at the time being.' The basic factor in the Torrens reforms was that the parcellation of land became the basis of the record, instead of legal instruments or transacting parties. But great as Torrens's reform was, its fundamental features, as he justly recognized himself, were adopted from previously existing systems in Europe, and from English copyhold.[2]

Sir Ernest Dowson and Mr. V. L. O. Sheppard have summarised as follows the features of an efficient system of land registration. (1) An inspection of the register gives a true and exact survey of the legal situation of the land at any and every moment. Consequently any person dealing on the evidence of the register need have no fear of fraud or ejectment. The registered proprietor, and he alone, can dispose of his rights. (2) All dealings in land can be effected with security, speed and cheapness. (3) A registered proprietor can borrow money quickly, easily and cheaply on the security of the land. (4) Litigation about land is greatly reduced. (5) Absentee landlords and reversionary beneficiaries need have no fear that they will lose their rights. (6) The acquisition and holding of land by small proprietors is greatly facilitated. (7) Complete protection is given to persons who have restrictive rights over the land, e.g. a right of way, or water, or a restriction on building. (8) Absolute security is given to creditors who lend money on the security of the land. (9) Acquisitive prescription is abolished. (10) The administration of every public service and every branch of national activity

[1] These are the characteristics of registration of title as summarised by J. E. Hogg in *Registration of Title to Land throughout the Empire* (1920).

[2] Robert R. Torrens. *The South Australian System of Conveyancing by Registration of Title*, Adelaide, 1859.

connected with land is greatly assisted in the execution of its work by the existence of an up-to-date and unimpeachable map and record of landed property throughout the country.

All of these advantages can be secured under registration of title, and it is further claimed by the above that this system can be adapted to suit the land tenure, social customs, and economic conditions of any particular community. It can also be designed so as to be able to meet changes in those conditions. It gets rid of one of the greatest abuses of the Colonies, namely, the use among illiterate peoples of worthless documents purporting to be valid deeds of conveyance. The prevalence of these is a fruitful source of litigation, debt and insecurity of title—all of which affect the value of land.

There are certain obvious obstacles to the establishment of a general system of Registration of rights to land in many of the British Colonial dependencies. There is, first of all, the heavy initial expense, entailed primarily by the necessity of adequate survey. There is also the lengthiness of the process. Furthermore, it may be urged that over large areas of the Colonial Empire there is no need for any comprehensive settlement of absolute title. Where a settlement is necessary at all, the form of record need only be that of possessory or presumptive title, that is to say a title which holds good until questioned in the courts, when the burden of proof falls on those who contest it. This is the system which has been used effectively in India. In Egypt over 1,900,000 possessory titles were settled within a space of eight years (1898–1906), thereby enabling the state domain to be determined promptly throughout the entire country. In Palestine recently a Royal Commission recommended the substitution of a settlement of possessory, for one of absolute, title, owing to the excessive tardiness of the judicial proceedings necessary to the determination of absolute title: and Sir Ernest Dowson has stated, in connection with the difficulties of effecting a settlement in the Coastal belt of Kenya, that an expeditiously completed settlement of possessory title is of greater value to a country than a lethargic, incomplete and imperfectly maintained settlement of absolute title.[1] Lord Hailey has also observed that in India, where entry in the revenue record has carried only a presumptive value, the great majority of recorded titles have never been attacked. An uncontested title acquires a high evidential value and can, after a suitable period, be given the legal value of prescription. The process of inquiry before the record is made need not be elaborate, and the machinery for recording mutations can also be of a relatively simple character. But above all there is no need for the

[1] Sir Ernest Dowson, however, insists that a settlement of possessory title is not a final settlement but only a stage towards such a settlement, which requires to be brought to maturity by complementary measures, if its value is not to evaporate and the whole process be re-done.

meticulous, expensive and lengthy survey operations which are an indispensable condition of recording indefeasible titles. In India and Borneo a plane-table field survey carried out by a subordinate and relatively inexpert agency has provided sufficiently accurate data for the purpose of recording presumptive titles.[1]

But to this it may be objected that the reason why, in a settlement of possessory title, the initial inquiry need not be so thorough is because its conclusions are not final. The more imperfect the inquiry the more imperfect the results. If the initial imperfections are to disappear, and the register to mature into one that can be depended upon and accepted in law, then the settlement operations must be of the same quality as are required for a register of absolute title. Failing this the register must always remain one of prima facie claims which must be independently investigated before they can be safely accepted. Furthermore, meticulous and expensive surveys are not a necessary pre-requisite for the registration of all lawfully valid titles. The character and accuracy of the methods of cadastral survey must be economically, as well as technically, appropriate to the character of the terrain and to the parcellation. A plane-table is a perfectly appropriate instrument of cadastral survey, provided the conditions are suitable and provided it is trustworthily used.

Many legislators are opposed to acquisitive prescription as a general principle, holding that it leads inevitably to land-stealing by encroachment, particularly in undeveloped countries. Moreover, it is opposed to the principles of most native systems of jurisprudence under which long uninterrupted possession does not create an adverse title against the owner and no laws of limitation are recognized. On the other hand, native law is not rigid, and long occupation and use of land do in fact confer a title which is not easily assailed.[2] In India the objection to acquisition of title by prescription is largely met by the periodic checking-up of the record in the presence of right-holders and other members of the community. This provides a reminder to rightholders of the necessity of seeing that a title due to possession does not become absolute by prescription, and affords them an opportunity of raising the issue. The crucial point is the period fixed by law for the limitation of suits claiming an interest in land.[3]

A short review may now be given of the registration systems of a representative number of dependencies, with special reference to

[1] See *An African Survey*, p. 878.

[2] The Ottoman Land Law and Muslim religious law generally, as well as native practice in many areas, recognize acquisitive prescription where land is plentiful and neglected. This encourages useful production.

[3] The conversion of a possessory into an absolute title by efflux of time is not a simple automatic matter. The validity of any transfer or abrogation of right and the identity of the boundaries of the parcel of land alleged to be affected throughout the period of ripening maturity must be absolutely assured.

those in which special problems have arisen. It must be understood, however, that in many of the territories, particularly in Africa, the registration legislation is limited to lands held under European forms of tenure, and does not usually apply to those held under native customary tenures, though in some areas, e.g. Malaya and Buganda, native lands may also be included in the registration system.

Registration of deeds is common in some dependencies, registration of title in others, and in others again there may be a combination of both systems. In the British West Indies there is one statutory system of registration of title to land in Jamaica, the Leeward Islands and Trinidad-Tobago. These systems are of the Torrens type. In Grenada there is a deeds system and no will affecting land is admissible as evidence unless registered.[1] In the Bahamas registration takes the form of a Land Roll. Every year the occupant of any land is required to make to the land registrar of the district a return on a form which specifies the name of the occupant, whether he is an owner (sole or jointly), or tenant (and if so the amount of rent payable), the quantity of land and the boundaries (as far as possible.) British Honduras and Fiji both have systems of registration of title and were in fact among the first British Colonies to adopt the principles of Sir Robert Torrens. Tonga has a system of its own. The certificates issued to the holders of hereditary estates contain a description and diagram of the lands, together with a schedule of leases and allotments granted. A register of allotments is also kept and there is provision for the registration of leases, subleases, transfers and permits, as well as of all documents affecting leaseholds.[2]

There are systems of registration of deeds in Hong-Kong, the Straits Settlements, Ceylon, British North Borneo, Mauritius, the Seychelles, Gibraltar, St. Helena, the Gambia, Sierra Leone, the Gold Coast, Nyasaland and Northern Rhodesia. But in Nigeria, Tanganyika, Uganda, Kenya, the Federated Malay States, and Brunei, there is registration of title, based, with the exception of Nigeria and Tanganyika, on the Torrens legislation of Southern Australia; and in all of these territories the Land Book is public, publicity being regarded as one of the surest safeguards against fraud.[3]

In Ceylon a system of deed registration has long been in vogue, but it has not proved satisfactory, and uncertainty of title has been

[1] *The Deeds and Land Registry Ordinance*, Cap. 65 (Revised edition, 1934).

[2] A description of the Tonga land system will be found at p. 212.

[3] In England, Ireland, Palestine and Sarawak the Land Book is private. Palestine and Sarawak both have statutory systems of registration, the former having originally been introduced, like that of Cyprus and Transjordan, under the Ottoman Land Code and Land Registry Laws of 1858.

considered one of the principal obstacles to land development. In 1936 the Ceylon Judicial Commission expressed surprise that the island still lacked that 'necessary feature of a civilized administration'—a general cadastral survey and registration of title.[1] Since then fresh legislation has been prepared, but no steps have been taken (and none may be considered necessary) to effect a general settlement of rights in lands held under the various forms of customary tenure—and these constitute the major part of all the lands of Ceylon.

Coming to Africa, in the Gold Coast there is a system of registration of deeds, and an instrument cannot be registered unless it contains a description of the land. But there is no general system of registration, and in the Southern regions of the Gold Coast there has long been widespread confusion in the matter of titles to land.[2] This is partly due to the freedom with which chiefs have alienated tribal lands, partly to the wholesale commercialization of lands as a result of the development of the cocoa industry, and partly also to the widespread use of spurious documents purporting to be valid instruments of transfer.[3] It has been suggested that, although it would be premature to attempt any general registration in the Gold Coast Colony until the powers of chiefs over the disposal of land and the nature of the right which can be acquired by occupation have been legally defined, an experiment in registration might nevertheless be attempted in areas such as Accra, Takoradi, the former Crown lands of Kumasi, or wherever title has been validated under the Concessions Ordinance.[4]

In Nigeria the Registration of Titles Ordinance, which was enacted in 1935, has been applied only to a fraction of the territory where lands are held under European or statutory forms of tenure, namely, parts of Lagos Colony.[5] Here there has been a long-

[1] *Ceylon Sessional Paper*, VI, 1936, para. 122. The 'block survey' of Ceylon was a cadastral survey, but was concerned only with delimiting the Crown Lands.

[2] In the Northern Territories of the Gold Coast these difficulties have not arisen, since there the State assumed control of the lands and title is only granted in the form of a Right of Occupancy from the Crown.

[3] See p. 171.

[4] *An African Survey*, p. 858. As regards Kumasi a system of registration has in fact been carried on by the Government Lands Department and it is claimed that, under this, title is so secure that there is little land litigation and credit is easily obtainable—a matter of great importance to Africans who have to compete with Syrians. In 1943 the land on which Kumasi is built was placed under the control of the native ruler, the Asantehene, who has established a Lands office to take over the work formerly carried out by the Government Lands Department.

[5] Between 1863 and 1914 no less than 4,000 Crown grants were issued to owners of parcels of land in Lagos. Since the declaration of the first registration district in July 1936 until the end of 1938 (the latest date for which figures are available) 222 freeholds and 18 leaseholds had been registered. The Nigerian Ordinance appears to confer no more than a possessory title on first registration [see Sec. 48 (3)]. It makes provision *inter alia* for the registration of collective rights [see Secs. 10 (1), 10 (2) and 43 (2)].

standing need to clarify titles, the uncertainty of which, largely as a result of native attempts to use English forms of conveyance, has led to much expensive litigation. In the Northern regions of the Protectorate, where, in the words of Professor Hancock, there has been harmony between the trend of economic change, the tradition of the native Courts and the policy of the Government as over-proprietor, title to land is generally secure and there is no need for any system of registration.[1] But in the Southern regions, where the authority of the Crown over land is limited and where economic progress and the influence of English law have tended to outrun native customary law, there is no secure foundation on which to build a general system of registration of title, though here, as on the Gold Coast, experimental beginnings might well be made in certain selected areas.

In Tanganyika there are two systems of registration applicable to lands held under European forms of tenure. Under the Registration of Documents Ordinance registration is compulsory and essential to the passing of legal title to land or to any interest therein. Provision is also made for the registration, at the option of the holder, of any document of which registration is not compulsory. But registration, whether compulsory or optional, does not cure any defect in any document or confer upon it any effect or validity which it would not otherwise have had. Its purpose is mainly one of record. There is also a Lands Registry Ordinance, enacted in 1923 with a view to quieten title and so render dealings with registered land simpler and more economical. All grants of public land or leases of public land for a term of more than five years, and all mining leases made or granted after the enactment of the Ordinance, have to be registered under the Ordinance. Provision is also made for the recognition of former titles.[2] As regards native lands the position on the whole approximates to that of Northern Nigeria. No general system of registration is required.

In Northern Rhodesia a Lands and Deeds Registry Ordinance was enacted in 1914 (Cap. 68), but this has recently been amended with the object of simplifying the registration of documents and also of providing for the gradual introduction of certification of title.[3] Certificates of title are now required before registration, and may only be issued to a tenant of land held directly from the Crown in fee simple or as the original lessee or subsequent transferee of a

[1] In the crowded area round Kano there is a revenue survey system which constitutes a system of land registration. But this applies to little more than one-sixth of the area of Kano Emirate. The system is described at p. 155.

[2] This information is taken from the *1938 Annual Report of the Tanganyika Department of Lands and Mines*. By 31st December, 1938, the total number of certificates of title registered was 4,753, which included 335 freeholds.

[3] The Amending Ordinance, No. 5 of 1943, was based on the New Zealand Land Transfer Act of 1915.

Crown lease for life or for a term of years. Lands held under native customary tenures are not subject to registration.

In Zanzibar there has long been provision for the registration of documents affecting immovable property,[1] but there has been no record of titles to land. In 1937 the Government decided that the land situation called for a systematic settlement of rights, and a Bill was introduced for this purpose.[2] A Land Register was to be established, registered rights were alone to be valid, and no action was to lie in respect of unregistered disposition. This Bill has not, apparently, yet become law and it would seem that the Government of Zanzibar is doubtful whether the benefits to be derived from a system of survey and registration of title would be sufficient to justify the cost.

Zanzibar is, however, concerned in the larger proposal of Sir Ernest Dowson and Mr. V. L. O. Sheppard that there should be a co-ordinated programme of land survey, with the assistance of air photography, for all the East African dependencies. This proposal was being considered before the outbreak of war and it was suggested that, as a preliminary measure, a decisive test should be made of the value of air photographs for cadastral purposes on the Kenya Coast and in Uganda. To this reference has already been made in dealing with the problem of the settlement of rights in the Kenya Coastal belt,[3] and it need only be added here that if air photography should be found to provide a satisfactory and economical method of survey there should be no great difficulty in establishing a satisfactory system of registration.

The same problem was confronting the Government of Uganda in 1937 when they invited Mr. V. L. O. Sheppard to visit the Protectorate in order to ascertain in what ways the associated operations of land registration and cadastral survey in Buganda could be modified so as to conform better and more economically with the practical needs of the country, and also enable the conduct of these operations to be progressively entrusted to the Native Government. Mr. Sheppard found that the Registration of Titles Ordinance of Uganda (1923) had been copied from the legislation of the Australian State of Victoria, with little attempt to adapt it to the peculiar requirements of the 'mailo' tenure of Buganda.[4] The Registry was inaccessible to the mass of the people, the fees charged were exorbitant, and the country had in consequence become flooded with scraps of paper which operated illegally as private deeds of transfer. The Registry officials had made no attempt to check the illegal practice of the sale of land by private deed, but the parties to such

[1] Registration of Documents decree (Cap. III).
[2] A Bill for the Settlement and Registration of Rights to Land.
[3] See p. 95.
[4] For an account of 'mailo' tenure see pp. 131-6.

transactions had been advised to protect their interests by lodging caveats. The Register in fact had become, not a record of registered rights, but a record of claims to land protected by caveat. This was an improper use of the caveat. The law required that no dealing with any land should operate to pass any estate or interest whatever, until such dealing had been registered in the manner provided.

One of the greatest benefits of the ownership of land (said Mr. Sheppard) was the power of being able to borrow money on its security. This benefit became greater when the land was registered and carried a Government guarantee. Provision for such loans in Uganda had been made in the Registration of Titles Ordinance of 1935 (Sec. 113), but the practical application of this provision had been greatly restricted by Section 2 of the Land Transfer Ordinance of 1906 which prohibits the transfer of any land or any right of title or interest therein, held by a native of the Protectorate, to any person not a native, without the written consent of the Governor. The obvious intention of this restriction was to protect the native against himself, as was done, for example, in Tanganyika by Ordinance No. 16 of 1931 which provides that 'no debt for money lent, or goods supplied, by a non-native shall be recoverable from a native, unless the transaction creating the debt is in writing and approved in writing by an Administrative Officer'; and in the Native Areas of the Union of South Africa by Act No. 18 of 1936, the provisions of which enact that such Areas shall be held for the exclusive use and benefit of natives, that no dealings of any kind between natives and non-natives shall be valid, and that no such land shall be subject to any claim based upon prescription. In Buganda the effect of the restriction had been such that only one instance of a registered statutory mortgage could be found on the Register.

In practice the owner of 'mailo' land in Buganda, when in need of money, had been driven to borrow it either on an equitable mortgage by depositing his duplicate certificate of title, or else on note of hand. Both these forms of borrowing opened the door to grave abuse and usually ended in the sale of the debtor's land. It was true that the equitable mortgage had been expressly recognized in two of the Australian Acts,[1] and the right to create such a mortgage was implied in other Australian Acts. But in New Zealand it had been strictly prohibited; the equitable mortgagee, being unregistered, would there be told that he had no right to lose. Mr. Sheppard recommended that the New Zealand rule should be applied to Buganda, and that equitable mortgages should be abolished. He also considered that the attachment of 'mailo' land for debt should be prohibited. 'Mailo' owners could then be allowed to create mort-

[1] South Australia Real Property Act, 1886, Sec. 149, and Queensland Real Property Act, 1861, Sec. 30.

gages without the consent now required. They would thereby be able to borrow money on the most advantageous terms and the Government would be able to ascertain, at any moment, the total amount of agrarian debt. Measures could simultaneously be introduced to limit the improvident use of the freedom thus conferred.

As a result of Mr. Sheppard's report a new Survey Ordinance (No. 12 of 1939) was enacted, and the Native Government passed a new Land (Sale and Purchase) Law. The latter provides that 'no agreement relating to any dealing in "mailo" land shall have any validity or effect, to the prejudice of other persons who claim an interest in such land and have complied with this law, unless such agreement . . . has been lodged with the Registrar of Titles'. After the passing of the law it would be an offence for any person to purport or attempt to sell any 'mailo' land or to accept any money in respect of the purchase price thereof unless he were—(*a*) the registered proprietor of such land; or (*b*) the purchaser or donee of an unsurveyed part of 'mailo' land, and a memorial of his interest in such land had been entered in the Mailo Register. It would be an offence also for any person to accept any purchase money on account of the sale of any 'mailo' land unless all fees due to the Protectorate and Native Governments in respect of such land had been paid.

This new law of the Native Government is likely to have far-reaching effects, since it extinguishes equitable as well as legal rights arising from unregistered documents. As regards the question of statutory mortgages, the necessary statutory provision already exists, and the Governor stated that care would be taken that foreclosure and power of sale would not be exercised in such a way that land would pass into the hands of non-natives.[1] The manifest advantage of the statutory mortgage was that the amount of the debt and the rate of interest were set forth in the deed. A scheme for training African plane-tablers and registration clerks would also be prepared.

During the discussion of Uganda's survey and registration problems a suggestion was made (by Sir John Stewart-Wallace of His Majesty's Land Registry) that the registration system of Buganda might be rehabilitated on the basis of a law which did not envisage any guarantee of boundaries as a fundamental principle. In England the boundaries of parcels of land which are registered are not guaranteed, though any proprietor may, if he wishes to go to the necessary expense, have his boundaries guaranteed. Sir John emphasised that it was essential that there should be no room for doubt

[1] But the question still remains—what useful security can be offered by a native to a non-native lender if foreclosure and power of sale (except to other natives) are excluded, as indeed they must be, until the native is better able to look after his own interests?

about the actual extent, on the ground, of any plot to be registered and there must be boundary marks. Thus the plan attached to the document was merely a 'signpost', showing the way to the land itself. It was necessary, of course, that any parcel to be registered should be surveyed and that the proprietor should be able to point out the boundaries of his holding to a surveyor on the spot.[1]

It may be argued, however, that some forms of boundary (e.g. wooden fences) are apt to be moved, and that so slightly as not to compromise the general appearance of a plan, but quite sufficiently to rob the owner of a substantial part of what he had thought he had bought. An essential feature of an efficient system of land registration is that it defines in permanent terms the extent of the property to be registered. But in many of the Colonies the cost of survey of innumerable small holdings would be economically prohibitive.[2]

The further consideration of this and other problems of survey and registration in Uganda was interrupted by the war, but it would seem fair to conclude that most of the difficulties that have arisen over 'mailo' tenure in Buganda were directly due to the inexperience of the Administration in dealing with problems of land, particularly those relating to record. With a wider knowledge the Government would hardly have committed itself to a system which, because it set out to convey an absolute title, demanded an elaborate survey and minute inquiry into rights and was therefore too costly for native conditions. It broke down because transactions became too numerous for original record, and because no local agency existed for recording mutations due to inheritance or other causes. In 1940 the Governor of Uganda, in a despatch to the Secretary of State dealing with the general question of native land tenure, put this question: 'If the demand for individual ownership is likely to prove irresistible, must it, nevertheless, be associated with such incidents of tenure as freedom of disposition and control, the registration or other recognition of title, sale and purchase, survey, the creation of

[1] For a full presentation of Sir John Stewart-Wallace's views on land registration the reader should consult his *Principles of Land Registration*. It may be observed that in England the Lands Registration Act of 1925 consolidated previous acts. The machinery for the transfer of land is assimilated to that for dealing with stocks and shares. Absolute titles granted by the Land Registry are guaranteed by the State. The cost of buying, selling or mortgaging registered land in England is considerably less than when the land is unregistered.

[2] The Tanganyika Central Development Committee in their 1940 Report referred (para. 235) to the complaint that the cost of surveys of land in Tanganyika was a deterrent to development. The Committee considered that the remedy lay, not in the reduction of survey fees, but in reducing as far as practicable the need for precise survey. Already in Tanganyika surveys were not insisted on in every case where a complete adequate identifiable description of the boundaries was possible without survey, and the Committee considered that this principle should be extended.

encumbrances, the grant of easements, and the leasing and disposition by will? And if so, must these incidents be regulated in the complicated manner of European countries?' 'The conception,' he said, 'that, without survey, the resulting rights of natives *inter se* could never be satisfactorily settled, raises a fantastic prospect. A British Administrative Officer settles innumerable land disputes by demarcation on the spot: but without survey such decisions cannot be proved in a court of law: the British Courts in African territories usually lack both the knowledge for deciding, and the means of inquiring effectively into questions involving native land tenure.'[1]

The problems that have arisen in Kenya regarding land registration have already been discussed,[2] and it only remains to observe that in 1933 the Kenya Land Commission considered that in most of the districts of Kenya Colony the institution of registers of native rights in land would be premature.[3] But since, in their view, private right-holding should be developed as a general policy they suggested that, as an experiment, a register might be introduced in one of the subdivisions of Kiambu district, where private right-holding is already well established. Some years later the Kiambu Local Native Council passed a resolution favouring the introduction of a general system of registration, but there is no information to show whether this recommendation, or that of the Kenya Land Commission, was put into practice. It is hardly necessary to observe that no system of registering native rights should be introduced without close and expert investigation of the local systems of tenure. Where European forms of tenure are well established, or have been prescribed by statute, the task of registering rights is relatively easy. But in the case of native customary tenures the utmost caution is required, since the manner of recording rights necessarily affects the form that land-holding may take.[4]

[1] Advocates of registration of title might, however, retort that individual ownership *implies* freedom of disposition and control, recognition of title, and right of sale and purchase, and that a reliable and systematic record of these effects will alone prevent or minimize the complications which land dealings in so many countries show. Survey of any territory, they would insist, is the most elementary and essential of all preliminary stocktakings of the resources and potentialities of any country and, like other stocktaking, if carried out suitably and steadily, soon yields commensurate results. What, except as a temporary makeshift, is the use of a highly-paid officer deciding innumerable land disputes in an ephemeral way which cannot be sustained in the courts? If the British Courts in African territories lack both the knowledge for deciding and the means of inquiring effectively into questions involving native land tenure, then the remedy lies in a drastic revision of British judicial procedure.

[2] See pp. 92-6.

[3] Cmd. 4556, paras. 1662-5.

[4] When the Uganda Agreement was concluded in 1900 and Sir Harry Johnston had believed that he had given general security of tenure, the British Foreign Office expressed some misgivings, observing that 'the introduction of the law of England

In Malaya, systems of registration for lands held under native customary title have long been in use. These have already been described,[1] and it has been pointed out that in the Federated Malay States there were originally two types of titles, one suited to European and commercial interests and one to native occupiers. To meet the needs of the former a system of registration based on that of Sir Robert Torrens was introduced. This necessitated accurate survey and various other expensive items of procedure that accompany every up-to-date system of registration. In the case of native holdings no such elaborate procedure was considered necessary. A register of land held according to native custom was introduced and any person registered therein obtained a permanent right of occupancy, which, though transferable and transmissible, fell far short of ownership in the English sense and conferred no right to lease or charge the land. Accurate survey was not required and transfer was carried out merely by altering the name in the Collector's record. But the development of plantation crops in Malaya, coupled with the fact that the native system existed alongside one which depended on survey, tended to produce an assimilation of the native customary title to that of the European registered form, with the result that in 1930 the differences between the forms of title were considered by the Commissioner of Lands to be negligible. The occupant of land formerly held by native custom had now become the owner of land held by entry in the 'Mukim' or district register. He possessed a document of title, he could charge or lease his land, its area was surveyed, dealings had to be executed in a statutory form, and the instrument had to be registered before it became effective. The only notable difference in the system of registering grants and that of registering native rights was that in the case of the former the registration was centralized while in the case of the latter it was localized. It is claimed that the new system is superior to the old since it has got rid of the many difficulties created by unsurveyed land. But others maintain that the new system, by bestowing on the Malay peasants a valuable title which they had not been taught to protect, has delivered them, or many of them, into the hands of Chinese and Indian moneylenders.

Summing up the general situation regarding the machinery for recording titles to land, there is, on the one hand, the danger of merely providing for present needs, and of failing to make timely

in regard to land, which appears from the wording of the Agreement to be the intention of its framers, may create a very complicated system'. Events showed that Sir Harry Johnston's attempts to record rights had unfortunate results. This does not, however, affect the principle of registration. Registration is merely an orderly and authoritative record and can be readily adapted to record rights of any type, provided the trouble has been taken to understand those rights first.

[1] See pp. 36, 37, 40.

provision for changes, which may occur with great rapidity.[1] On the other hand, there is an equal danger of going beyond what is required, and setting up systems which may have disturbing or even disastrous effects on well-established institutions. It may not be necessary or desirable to institute registration at all, and if registration is required it may not be necessary to institute a fully developed cadastral survey, to guarantee boundaries, or to confer more than a presumptive or possessory title. In many areas the land is so plentiful and so poor in quality, and distances are so great, that the cost of registration could not possibly be justified. For primitive peoples the essential conditions are simplicity and cheapness. The registration should be carried out by local agencies and the cost should be such as can be borne by the poorest peasants. Particular attention should be given to the necessity of devising cheap and speedy methods of recording mutations which are occasioned by inheritance, partition between families, and surrender to the community, since it is this class of mutations, rather than those occasioned by sale and testament, which in the past, owing to inadequate provisions, have been the most prolific source of litigation.

The system of registration must of course be adapted to the systems of land-holding. It must, therefore, allow when necessary for family or collective rights as well as for individual rights. Nor should it necessarily have the effect of making the land subject to the English law of property.[2]

Finally, it would seem that a much greater degree of uniformity could be effected throughout the Colonial Empire, both as regards legislation and technical practice, by a general pooling of knowledge and by a concerted effort towards co-ordination.[3] The 'mukim' system of registration in Malaya, for example, might prove well suited to certain parts of Africa; or a number of dependencies might,

[1] One of the principal problems of Colonial Administration is the development of agriculture. This can only be done by settling the people on the land and giving them security of tenure—whether the tenure be of a community or individual character. In many dependencies shifting cultivation must give way to settled. Settled land immediately becomes a thing of commerce and so the law of tenure must contain provisions for the transfer of rights.

[2] Lord Hailey has drawn attention to a simple process introduced by the French as an alternative to the 'immatriculation' of native property. This consists of the issue to claimants of a 'livret foncier' which is applicable to the rights of groups as well as of individuals. Unlike 'immatriculation' it does not create an indefeasible proprietary title but is intended to secure the holder from dispossession by anything but judicial process, and has the advantage of leaving the land subject to native law. (See *An African Survey*, p. 860.) Registration of rights to land is not, *ipso facto*, a producer of individual ownership, but can be used potently to preserve collective rights, provided that public policy, the law and the Courts, work together to this end.

[3] Sir Ernest Dowson and Mr. Sheppard have contributed much towards co-ordination. In 1931 they arranged the first exhibits of cadastral maps for the Second Empire Survey Conference. See also their paper on 'The Collection and Study of Cadastral Maps and Records' at the 1935 Empire Survey Conference.

as Sir Ernest Dowson and Mr. V. L. O. Sheppard have suggested, join together to carry out co-ordinated programmes of aerial survey. Yet differences in environment, social habits, religion, systems of tenure, agricultural requirements and technical experience, all preclude any general application of stereotyped methods of recording rights to land.

CHAPTER XXIV

Changes in Native Land Law

IN the previous chapters many instances have been given of modifications of the native land law effected by statutory or other means. But as this subject is one of outstanding interest and raises many problems of administrative importance it will be well to draw the threads together, even if this entails restating much that has been said before.

Changes in tenure may be produced by many causes. Pressure of population may necessitate a switch from shifting cultivation on many scattered holdings to intensive cultivation on consolidated holdings: or it may lead to excessive subdivision, soil erosion and eventual abandonment. New methods of agriculture and of marketing may demand new methods of holding land. The introduction of a money crop may give a money value to land which it did not possess before. It may necessitate a new security of tenure which would be incompatible with any form of collective ownership; or it may, on the contrary, require an expenditure of capital beyond the means of any single proprietor. Thus, land may come to be held by companies or corporations in the form of large plantations. Again, changes in tenure may be produced by the direct action of local Colonial Governments, which, even if they have not assumed the ownership of the land and prescribed the manner by which it shall be held, may yet have assumed many other forms of control. Government Agricultural Departments may insist on methods of cultivation which require a departure from traditional methods of holding land, Veterinary Departments may introduce restrictions on the freedom of using pasture lands, Forestry regulations may entail a more economical use of arable land, and Land Departments may introduce systems of boundaries, survey and registration which are compatible only with the exercise of individual proprietary rights.

Local Native Authorities may also introduce far-reaching changes of their own. For, quite apart from the fact that Native Authorities may be required to administer the land regulations of the Central Government, they are usually also empowered to make new regulations of their own.[1] Native law, moreover, though it is sometimes described as native *customary* law, is not static, but is subject to change like any of the more developed systems of law. This is expressly recognized by Colonial governments in the

[1] The Nigerian Native Authority Ordinance, for example, empowers Native Authorities to make rules (subject to the approval of the Governor) providing for the fencing of land, declaring any land to be an open space, and so on. (See No. 7 of 1943, Sec. 25.)

permission given to Native Authorities to modify their native law. In Ashanti, for example, the *Native Law and Custom Ordinance* of 1940 empowers the Ashanti Confederacy to modify the customary law. In Nigeria the Native Courts Ordinance empowers a Native Tribunal to make rules embodying any law and custom 'with or without such additions or modifications as may be deemed expedient'. In Kenya the Native Areas Order in Council of 1939 directs that 'The Native Lands shall be subject at all times to such rights as are or may be enjoyed by native tribes, groups, families or individuals by virtue of existing native law or custom *or any subsequent modification thereon*'.[1]

Apart from the direct methods indicated above, there are many other ways in which native law is being continually modified. The day-to-day decisions of the Native Courts, based as they are on equity rather than on precedent, automatically reflect the changes that occur unconsciously in the social and economic structure. Native law is affected by the decisions of Administrative Officers who act as supervisors of Native Courts and themselves, in their executive capacity, settle innumerable disputes concerning land. The decisions of British Courts, the influence of English legal procedure and English conceptions of real property, coupled with the use, in many areas, of English forms of conveyancing, all tend to modify the character of the native law of land.

It is well to remember, however, that there is another aspect of the matter, and that Colonial Governments have often prevented change as well as fostered it. They have, for example, prevented the alienation of land to non-natives, they have placed statutory restrictions on chiefs from granting mineral or other concessions, they have placed restrictions on the granting of credit to natives, on the mortgaging of land or its attachment for debt, they have placed restrictions on sub-division and the local system of inheritance, and passed many other enactments and regulations which have interfered with what might be regarded as normal or spontaneous development.

The degree to which governments can influence the development of native tenures varies, of course, with their legal position as regards the land. In Fiji the control of all vacant lands has recently been

[1] There is, however, no generally accepted procedure for the determination of native law and custom regarding land among the various tribal groups. The Kenya Land Commissioners did not consider that Native Councils or courts should have the power to alter custom in respect of the tenure of land, though they thought that councils should be able to make a formal declaration that native custom had been modified in some particular respect. See Cmd. 4556, Sec. 1651. The West African Lands Committee considered that Chiefs and their councils should be encouraged to embody in a bye-law any local custom which it might be considered desirable to place beyond question. They did not consider that the rule of English law that a custom must be 'immemorial' should be applied to native African custom (as it had been in at least one Gold Coast Supreme Court judgment). See African (West) 1046 paras. 82 and 85.

vested in a Board, and the Government can therefore embark on a planned rural economy. In Malaya, apart from the Straits Settlements, land is vested in the Ruler of each State; but in the Federated Malay States the alienation of land is subject to the control of the British Resident, whereas in the Federated States alienation is not so closely controlled. In the Gold Coast Colony the land rights of the people are not qualified by any claim of superior proprietorship on the part of the Crown, and if land is required by the Government for public purposes it is obtained by voluntary agreement or through statutory procedure; land required by private parties for industrial or commercial purposes is obtained by direct purchase or lease, subject to the terms of a statute framed to safeguard the interests of the native vendors. Under such conditions native land law is relatively free to respond to changing economic conditions, though land rights may be subjected to legislation for the purpose of defining them (and so curtailing litigation), or in order to meet some new social or economic need, such as the regulation of the landlord-tenant relationship.[1] In Kenya, on the other hand, all land is Crown land (apart from alienation), but definite areas have been set aside as Native Lands and declared by statute (or Order in Council having the force of statute) to be held in trust for native use. Subject to this over-riding provision the land-holding rights of natives are those recognized by native law and custom. In Northern Nigeria, Tanganyika and the Northern Territories of the Gold Coast the legal position is that all lands are subject to the disposition of the Government, to be held and administered on behalf of the natives. The Crown is, therefore, a superior proprietor, and no title is valid without the consent of the Governor. But this provision was intended to prevent the alienation of native lands to non-natives, and not to invalidate rights recognized by native custom. This intention is evident from the Ordinances under which a formal Right of Occupancy is held to include the title of any native individual, family or group, holding land in accordance with native custom. Thus, although the Crown is the ultimate owner, this need not entail the curtailment of native rights. Indeed, where the rights of the Crown have not been actively exercised, private rights may become so stabilised that they may take a form equivalent to full proprietorship, even if they do not assume the technical form freehold tenure.

The Gold Coast provides the most outstanding example of change during the last fifty or sixty years. Here the demand for concessions by Europeans in the eighties of last century created among the native communities a new conception of land as a commercial

[1] In many territories where the landlord-tenant relationship has arisen, or is likely to arise, there is a need for legislation to provide tenants with the security which would enable them to obtain the funds necessary for development.

commodity. Many of the chiefs assumed a position of landlords rather than of trustees,[1] land was freely alienated and the theory was developed that every inch of ground was owned by some native unit—a theory which effectually prevented the British government from assuming control of the unoccupied lands. But the conditions of concessions as between grantor and grantee were made subject to some measure of government control by means of 'Concessions Ordinances' which required all concessions to be validated by the Supreme Court. The area of concessions for mining rights was restricted to five sq. miles and for agricultural land to twenty sq. miles, and protection was given to native rights of hunting, shifting agriculture and the collection of timber. Development provisions were also included, which would prevent the acquisition of land for speculative purposes. But the Concessions Ordinances have been criticized on the ground that the terms of concessions precluded the native communities from obtaining a fair share of the profits of development, and also failed to impose any adequate control over chiefs in disposing of community property.[2]

But it was the establishment of the cocoa industry at the beginning of this century that produced the most revolutionary changes in the native land law of the Gold Coast. Within a period of forty years cocoa-farming has developed from nothing at all until it now provides almost one-half of the world's requirements of cocoa and dominates the entire economy of the Colony. The introduction of a tree-borne crop which may occupy the same land for twenty to forty years or more has destroyed the balance of a system of tenure which was based on rotational occupation by short-term cultures. Where cocoa-growing has been taken up, shifting cultivation has been replaced by permanent cultivation, and collective ownership by individual ownership. The employment of wage-labour, almost unknown in former times, has become a regular feature of the land economy, and with that there have arisen also bailiffs, absentee landlords and multiple owners. Many of the wage-labourers are aliens who seek to become permanent settlers and obtain cocoa land on their own account. On the other hand, one of the effects of the new-found wealth is that it has sought an outlet for investment in the towns, largely in the form of house-building, with the result that there has been a keen demand for sites and a large increase in urbanization.[3]

[1] In Uganda, also, chiefs became landlords, and in Kenya the hereditary land administrators have sought to become landlords. On the other hand, persons who were formerly lent land as friends have tended to become tenants. See *Native Land Tenure in Kikuyu Province*, 1929, p. 13.

[2] See *An African Survey*, pp. 777 and 1527.

[3] Professor Hancock has drawn attention to this and pointed out that between 1921 and 1931 the number of towns of over 3000 inhabitants increased from 44 to 131.

But the full measure of the effect on land tenure of all these changes cannot be assessed, since the subject has received little study, and the most elementary facts are still unknown. In many of the chiefdoms formal recognition has been given to the principle of exclusive individual ownership. In 1912, the Chief Commissioner of Ashanti stated that, in Ashanti, a rule had been made that 'where a man had properly planted a cocoa plantation it should be regarded as his own, so as to give him the fruits of his labour. That was the beginning of individual ownership'.[1] By 1928 English methods of sale and conveyance had become firmly established in Akan law, and English forms of mortgage were also in use.[2] By 1936 steps had been taken in some chiefdoms to check the growth of landed debt by forbidding the pledging of land—a drastic innovation into native law.[3] Reference has already been made to the proposal in 1927 to introduce into the Gold Coast a Statute of Limitations. The absence of this principle from native law had been considered a bar to security of tenure and an encouragement of recurrent legislation and many forms of fraud, such as the postponement of claims to land until the land had been extensively improved. But the proposal was vetoed by the Councils of Chiefs on the ground that it was contrary to several principles of native law, and would force the people to adopt English methods of tenure and of transfer. The Government Anthropologist (Captain R. S. Rattray) also opposed the measure since, in his view, it would encourage persons holding rights of occupancy from the 'stool' to claim ownership under the time limit of the Statute. The Bill was accordingly dropped. About the same time proposals were made for introducing into the Gold Coast a general system of Registration of Title, but this measure was also abandoned, since it was considered that titles were insufficiently defined to make registration effective.

Many of the changes that have occurred in the Gold Coast have occurred also in Sierra Leone and in the Southern regions of Nigeria. In Sierra Leone, for example, English conceptions of real property have been introduced, so that, e.g. under the Protectorate Land Ordinance of 1927, there are provisions relating to 'tenants-at will' and 'tenants-on-sufferance'. Aliens may not acquire a greater interest in land than a lease for fifty years, and every alien settler who does not hold a lease of land must pay a settler's fee to the

[1] Cmd. 6278.

[2] See J. B. Danquah's *Akan Law and Customs*, p. 219. Among the Akan, land had long been sold by the 'fathom' and there was a customary method of giving 'livery of seisin'. See also H. W. Hayes Redwar, *Comments on Gold Coast Ordinances*, p. 75.

[3] *Gold Coast Sessional Paper No. 1*, 1936, para. 175. Some Native Administrations have also introduced maximum amounts for expenditure on funerals—one of the principal causes of indebtedness on the Gold Coast. In Kenya some Native Councils have proposed to do away with the principle of redeemability, where land has been mortgaged.

paramount chief in lieu of the customary presents or contributions of labour authorised by native law.[1] Rents payable by aliens are revisable every seven years, and there are provisions regarding fixtures which were formerly unknown to native law. In the case of tenants-at-will or tenants-on-sufferance, the reversion in all fixtures, buildings and economic trees is in the tribal authorities: but in the case of a tenancy created by lease the fixtures and buildings may (with certain provisos) be removed by the tenants, or sold to the tribal authorities, who in any case are required to pay to the tenant the fair value (to an incoming tenant) of any economic trees which had been planted by the tenant. These modifications of native law are the direct result of the introduction of commercial or plantation crops. Another result of the establishment of permanent tree crops, and also of the permanent swamp cultivation of rice, has been the wide extension of the practice of pledging land, since holdings have come into existence on which money-lenders are ready to advance money, accepting the land as security and its use as interest. In the swamp rice areas, moreover, there is a notable departure from native custom in that strangers from neighbouring chiefdoms have been allowed to clear plots for themselves, while still residing in their own homes. In this way a single individual may, and often does in fact, own farms in two chiefdoms and is therefore subject to two distinct Native Authorities. There is no information to show the extent of these developments or how they are being met.

Coming to Nigeria, in the Colony of Lagos and some areas of Southern Nigeria, much expensive litigation has arisen as a result of the fusion, or confusion, of English and native conceptions of land ownership. Lagos was ceded to Queen Victoria by King Docemo in 1861, but the precise nature of the rights and powers which passed to the British Crown were not clearly defined and are still in some respects a subject of dispute. Many lawyers and officials have assumed that the 'sovereignty' which King Docemo had exercised over land in Lagos was of the same character as that exercised by the Crown in England, and that when he had made a grant of land he continued to retain the 'ultimate title'. This view was supported by the further misconception that native rights in land were solely of a usufructuary character and that 'strict native law and custom did not allow of the alienation of land'.

In point of fact there is no reason for supposing that the land law of Lagos prior to the date of the Cession differed materially from that found in any other part of West Africa, wherever there is pressure of population on the land. The political chief was the grantor on behalf of the community of vacant or unclaimed land, but once land had been granted he lost all further right of control. Land

[1] See p. 196.

granted to a family or sib became the property of that family or sib. It could not be alienated except with the consent of the family or sib as a whole.[1] But land acquired by an individual through his own efforts or money became his allodial property which he could dispose of as he pleased, though in the absence of testamentary disposition it would revert to the category of family land, to be used and inherited according to the well-recognized rules of native law. At the time of the Cession, therefore, there were well-established *private* rights both of a collective and individual character, and these, by a fixed principle of English law, could not be affected by a change of sovereignty, though a new sovereign could of course alter the conditions by statutory or other juridical means.[2]

Between 1868 and 1912 the British authorities in Lagos issued some 4000 'Crown grants'. The issue of these grants was in many ways unfortunate, for although 'in their inception they were no more than confirmatory of the rights, titles and interests of persons in possession and occupation of the land to which they related at the time of cession'[3] they were used by many individuals as a fee simple title for land which in fact belonged to families or a series of families.[4] They also created the impression that the Government claimed absolute ownership of all the land ceded by the Treaty of Cession.

Another disintegrating factor was the introduction of English conceptions of mortgage. Under the native law land might be pawned but it always remained redeemable.[5] But largely as a result of the issue of Crown grants, and in order to meet the credit requirements of Europeans, foreclosure followed by public sale became common throughout the Colony. In 1912 Mr. (later Sir) W. Buchanan Smith, the Acting Commissioner of Lands, stated that 'the modern system of mortgages and sales by order of the Supreme Court, especially when they affect land outside Lagos proper, must

[1] Family lands have been freely alienated with the consent of the whole family during the last 80 years. Many of the business premises in Lagos have been acquired in this way, with title deeds made out in English form and duly registered. See Lord Maugham's judgement in Oshodi *v.* Brimah Balogun and Anor.

[2] The leading authority on this subject is the Privy Council judgment in the so-called Apapa Case of 1921 (Amodu Tijani *v.* The Secretary, Southern Nigeria, 1921, 2 A.C. 399).

[3] The Hon. K. Ajasa—a distinguished member of the Lagos Bar—in a statement to the West African Lands Commission 1912. In the Apapa case (1921) (*African* (*West*) No. 1048, p. 243), Lord Haldane observed that 'The introduction of the system of Crown grants . . . must be regarded as having been brought about mainly, if not exclusively, for conveyancing purposes, and not with a view to altering substantive titles already existing.'

[4] See *African* (*West*), No. 1048, p. 226. In Idowu Inasa *v.* Oshodi (11 Nig. Rep.) Lord Blanesburgh said that the issue of Crown grants to the headmen of compounds was 'a source of misunderstanding as each grant, on its face, purported to be a disposition in absolute terms in favour of the grantee'.

[5] See p. 256.

inevitably tend to cause hardship in a country where family proprietorship is more often the rule than the exception. It is of course always open to the members of the family to recover in Court land alienated through the fault of the individual debtor, but it is probable that in many cases this is not done, either through ignorance or in order not to embarrass the debtor. It is also true that in some instances creditors have been deprived of their just rights by means of such applications to the Court, the difficulties in either case being due to the fact that both mortgage and compulsory sale are quite foreign to the native conception of the principles of land tenure, even in their modified form'.[1]

Much confusion has also been caused by the presumption that lands which have been dealt with by written instruments can no longer be regarded as lands 'held under native tenure'. Yet the use of written documents is a natural development of native law. In 1909 Mr. H. W. Hayes Redwar, a former Puisne Judge of the Gold Coast, pointed out that written documents among natives, evidencing the transfer of land, had become common and although the documents were often clumsily prepared the Courts had endeavoured to give effect to their manifest intention. 'It is clear,' he said, 'that writing not being necessary by the Native Law to the validity of a dealing with land, this indulgence is rightly extended to conveyances otherwise imperfect.'[2] In 1912, in a Gold Coast judgment, Chief Justice Crampton Smyly and Mr. Justice Gough observed that: 'In the present case we are invited by the appellant to say that from the moment any transfer in land held by native tenure is effected, or purports to be effected by writing, the Native Tribunals have no jurisdiction, and from this contention it logically follows that an interest in land previously held by native tenure ceases to be held by native tenure. The far-reaching consequences of a judicial decision to that effect can readily be imagined.'[3]

[1] *African (West)*, No. 1048, p. 226. Compare the following extract from *Modern India and the West* (edited by L. S. S. O'Malley), 'Peasant proprietors also lost their lands as they were sold in pursuance of decrees issued by the Civil Courts for non-payment of debts. Expropriation on account of private debts was a Western and not an Indian practice. Formerly there was no such thing as the forced sale of lands for debts or eviction from an ancestral holding by legal process. Debts were limited in amount because of the poor security which could be offered, viz., cattle and personal property' (p. 715).

[2] *Comments on Gold Coast Ordinances*, p. 76. Sir W. H. Rattigan in his *Digest of Civil Law for the Punjab*, states that 'Since the introduction of British rule the practice of executing formal transfers in writing has become common and is sometimes asserted to be essential for the validity of the transfer. . . . The customary law ordinarily recognizes no distinction between the power of making verbal or written transfers of property *inter vivos*, nor where an unrestricted power of transfer is recognized to exist between a transfer *inter vivos* and one to take effect upon the death of the transferor. The form of alienation is treated as immaterial. (7th edition, 1909, p. 89).

[3] Azzu *v*. Akardiri (1912).

In 1914, Sir W. Brandford Griffith, a former Chief Justice of the Gold Coast, in a memorandum written on the meaning of the word 'tenure' in Section 19 of the Supreme Court Ordinance (No. 4 of 1876), stated that land held by a native under an ordinary English mortgage or an equitable mortgage would not in his opinion be land held under native tenure since these forms of tenure were unknown to native law. 'If, however, land is conveyed to a native by deed, or if he buys land in execution and obtains from the Court a certificate of purchase, such native holds land so conveyed by a form of tenure known substantially both to the English law and the native law. But, in view of the native law of inheritance and of the local legislation with respect to marriage and concessions, the tenure approaches more nearly to native tenure than to the law of England. In such a case it would be difficult to say that the land was not held by the native purchaser 'under native tenure', but it would be easy to say that it was not held under English tenure.'[1]

The conclusion then would seem to be clear that the use of a document does not of itself alter the incidents of tenure or cause land held under native tenure to cease to be such.[2]

Some thirty-five years ago the Acting Chief Justice of Nigeria, Sir Edwin Speed, referred to family ownership of land as a dying institution and observed that 'sooner or later the legislature of the Colony, or the Supreme Court in the exercise of its equitable jurisdiction, will have to give the *coup de grâce* to the whole system'.[3] This view has since been shared by other judges.[4] Yet there is plenty of evidence to show that even in the progressive Colony of Lagos family ownership continues to be an integral feature of the social life and that any sweeping change in the system of land tenure would cause widespread disturbance. So long as the social system of Africans continues to differ from that of Europeans the African system of land-holding cannot be assimilated to that contemplated by English law. The whole history of land legislation and litigation in the Colony of Nigeria during the last eighty-five years provides a signal example of the necessity of a sociological rather than a purely legal approach to problems of tenure in African communities.[5]

[1] *African (West)* No. 1048, p. 306.

[2] For further observations on this subject see pp. 179-80. In 1929 Sir Mervyn Tew did not consider that the equitable jurisdiction of the Supreme Court of Nigeria could be invoked to convert a mere right of occupancy into a fee simple because the occupier had purported to convey the freehold by means of an instrument drawn in the English form (*Nigeria Law Reports*, Vol. X, p. 43).

[3] Lewis *v.* Bankole (1 *Nigerian Report*, p. 83).

[4] See e.g. Brimah Balogun and Others *v.* Oshodi (10 *Nigerian Report*, p. 43).

[5] In 1936 the Privy Council stated that 'the wide differences of opinion of learned judges as to the titles to lands in Lagos . . . make it very desirable to deal with these questions by legislation'. But a necessary preliminary to any fresh legislation would be a thorough study of the systems of tenure in their social setting.

In the Southern Provinces generally the occupied lands are held by families, and over large areas where there is no great pressure on the land the sale of land would be repugnant to native sentiment.[1] But in some areas of higher density land is sold under various forms of legal fiction, such as the payment of some trifling sum by the vendor whereby he purports to redeem the property which he has 'pledged'.[2] In other areas, again, the sale of land is so well established in native law that sales have long been publicly advertised. In Abeokuta as many as a hundred auctions of agricultural land have been held in a single year, and in 1923 the Alake and his Council sought the permission of the Government of Nigeria to modify their local land regulations so that property within the city of Abeokuta and other large trading centres might be mortgaged by their owners to anyone they pleased. Hitherto the sale, mortgage and lease of land had been confined to transactions among the Egba themselves, but the continuation of this limitation would, they felt, render the raising of money difficult and possibly extortionate. It was not proposed, however, that these rights should be extended to agricultural lands, lest ancestral properties should pass into the hands of stranger capitalists. The Secretary of State agreed to these proposals, but insisted that, in the case of foreclosure, the land must not be sold to a non-native. In 1933 the Government of Nigeria proposed to give statutory freedom to natives of the Yoruba Provinces to deal freely with their land among themselves, provided that under no circumstances should land become attachable for debt. It was also proposed to allow natives to mortgage land to non-natives, provided that, if the mortgagee had to foreclose, he would receive no more than a lease for a reasonable term. But it was found difficult to give legal effect to these proposals, which were accordingly dropped.

In 1935, however, a remarkable piece of new legislation, applicable to certain areas of the Southern Provinces, was enacted. This was the 'Kola Tenancies Ordinance' (No. 25 of 1935) which provides for 'the extinction of certain holdings of land commonly called kola tenancies'. A 'kola tenancy' is defined as 'a right to the use and occupation of any land which is enjoyed by any native in virtue of

[1] The writer has recently been informed by Mr. G. I. Jones, an Administrative Officer with an extensive knowledge of S.E. Nigeria, that even in some densely populated areas of Iboland native opinion is becoming increasingly opposed to the outright sale of land. In the Bende Division as soon as land becomes insufficient for the needs of the village group the sale of land is forbidden.

[2] Or the vendor may agree that if he wants to recover the land later he will repay double the amount of the 'loan' he has received for the 'pledged' land. This would be tantamount to an admission that he had parted with the land for good and all. It is hardly necessary to add that legal fictions affect to conceal the fact that a rule of law is undergoing, or has undergone, alteration—the letter of the law remaining, but its operation being modified.

a kola or other token payment made by such native or any predecessor in title or in virtue of a grant for which no payment in money or in kind was exacted'. The Ordinance is to apply to any kola tenancy (*a*) where the tenant or any predecessor in title has granted interests in the land to any person for a consideration other than a token payment, and (*b*) where it is reasonable to suppose that the payments in money or in kind which are made to the tenant constitute a benefit more substantial than the grantor anticipated would be derived from the grant. Under such conditions the grantor is enabled to apply for the extinction of the tenancy. His rights may be transferred to the tenant for a price assessed by a tribunal (consisting of the British Resident and two assessors) or if the tenant fails to pay the assessed price the grantor may resume the land, provided he pays an assessed sum as compensation to the tenant. If the grantor or tenant fails to pay the assessed purchase price or assessed compensation by the date fixed, then the rights of the grantor shall be deemed to be transferred to the tenant at the end of five years from the date fixed. An appeal lies to the Supreme Court.

The purpose of this legislation is obvious—namely to enable grantors of land rights to receive a fair share of the benefits of any subsequent increase in land values. It is a principle that is becoming increasingly important now that Native Administrations are assuming greater control over vacant lands and it is of course the principle behind the system of revisable rents followed by most Colonial governments.[1]

But the Kola Tenancies Ordinance appears to be an ambiguous enactment, based on a one-sided interpretation of native law. Is the intention of the Ordinance to compensate families or communities who had parted absolutely with land which had no cash value at the time but had since become valuable? If so, it would be attempting an impossible task. Moreover, the use of the word 'tenancy' would be a misuse of language. But if the grantors have in fact remained landlords why, it may be asked, have they not exercised their rights as such? If the grants they made were merely tenancies which have been passed on by one occupier to another, why have the landlords failed to obtain from each successive occupier the same token of ownership? And, finally, why has a matter of such supreme importance been removed from the realm of native law and the

[1] See Cap. XXI. In India, tenancy acts (e.g. the Punjab Tenancy Act of 1887) make provision for the enhancement of rents. But the rent of a person who had made improvements can only be enhanced in the manner provided by the Act. In the Punjab, incidentally, it is laid down that a tenant is not considered to have a 'right of occupancy' in the land he occupies if the landlord proves that the tenant was settled on land previously cleared and brought under cultivation by, or at the expense of the founder. (See the Punjab Tenancy Act, 1887, Sec. 5. 1.)

decision of those most competent to deal with it, namely, the Native Authorities? It would be interesting to know how this Ordinance has been working in practice, if it has been working at all.

In Northern Nigeria, as a result of the British conquest at the beginning of this century and the assumption of the control of all lands by the British Government, land tenure has undergone a profound revolution. Under the former régime of the Muhammadan Fulani overlords, land had been, to a large extent, cultivated on a basis of slave labour. The demand for slaves had led to the perennial harrying of the pagan tribes who were often compelled to live on hills and subsist on meagre plots close to their homes. But with the abolition of slavery and the establishment of the *pax Britannica* Northern Nigeria became a land of independent peasant farmers, though on many of the estates the ex-slaves remained as tenants on a métayage basis, paying to the chief or other landlord a proportion of their crops.

It was commonly assumed, and reported, during the early days of British administration in Northern Nigeria that land rights were essentially usufructuary and that the sale of land was unknown, but it has since been ascertained that in the highly fertile areas around Lake Chad land had long been bought and sold, and that in many of the pagan tribes, also, land has had a transfer value. Moreover, since chiefs normally lose all right of control over lands that they have once conferred, occupancy in practice has conferred a right which has been practically proprietary.[1] Nevertheless, over the greater part of Northern Nigeria, the sale of farm land is still contrary to local law, and at a recent conference of Chiefs (1939-40) the Sultan of Sokoto held that sale should not be permitted without the consent of the local Native Authority and then only for exceptional reasons.[2] At this conference the question was considered whether some minimum limit should be put on the extent to which agricultural land might be sub-divided, since the strict application of the Muhammadan law of inheritance had led to overcrowding and insanitary conditions. The Conference decided that the extent to which an estate might be divisible must be left to the local Native Authorities and that, where necessary, these Authorities might order

[1] Compare I. Schapera's statement that under the traditional law of Bechuanaland 'once a man has cleared a field he retains the title to it, even if he neglects it for many years.' Schapera, however, adds that in some tribes this old rule has now (owing to the increasing demand for land) given way to the view that land should be continuously used or handed over to someone else. See *Native Land Tenure in the Bechuanaland Protectorate*, pp. 181 and 177.

[2] The Land and Native Rights Ordinance permits sale under conditions specified on p. 168. It is interesting to note that in the French Cameroons native owners may sell land (see *P.M.C.* (28), 1935, p. 115) and, by a decree of 1938, individuals may acquire an area of 20 hectares inalienable for 25 years.

farms to be sold and the proceeds divided among the legatees. This is a good example of the way in which local custom adapts itself to circumstances and may, in Muhammadan areas, over ride the provisions of Islamic law.[1]

In the crowded areas around Kano city the tenure of agricultural land has developed along lines which are unique in Nigeria. Here, prior to the British occupation of Kano in 1903, the Fulani Government had imposed a farm tax which was additional to the Muhammadan tithe on harvested grain and cattle. It consisted of a basic assessment on cultivated land, plus a surtax on crops other than cereals. The British Government took over this system and converted it into one of revenue survey, the details of which have already been given (p. 157). It is claimed that this system is more suitable for the area around Kano than the income-tax system prevalent elsewhere in Nigeria, since the farmer's tax liability is clearly defined and his efforts to improve his land are not penalised, as they might be under an income-tax system.

There is one further observation regarding recent tenure changes in Nigeria.[2] The *pax Britannica* has enabled pagan tribes, particularly in Northern Nigeria, to descend from the hills and distribute themselves widely over plains which were formerly unoccupied. A direct result of this has been the disruption of thousands of village communities. Large extended-families have also tended to break up into small family farming units. Administrative difficulties

[1] For further observations on the modification of Muhammadan land law by native custom and by statute see Chapter XIX, *Land and Muhammadan Law*. There it is pointed out, for example, that in Zanzibar although Muhammadan law is declared statutorily to be the fundamental law of the Protectorate in all civil matters, it has been modified in many ways by local custom and by British Law (e.g. by the Transfer of Property Decrees). Even the fact that the Muhammadan law of evidence has been repealed by the Evidence Enactments of the East African Territories has affected land problems, since it invalidates evidence of the true meaning of the contract in cases of 'fictitious sales' of land, which were one of the contributory causes of Zanzibar's agricultural debt. On the other hand, Dr. Nadel has recently stated that in Nupe-land (N. Nigeria) modern economic conditions have led increasingly to the adoption of Muhammadan rules of inheritance as against local custom. See *A Black Byzantium*, p. 173.

[2] An Ordinance of great importance (No. 73 of 1945) has recently been enacted in Nigeria. This empowers Native Authorities to make rules, subject to the Governor's approval, relating to the use and alienation of lands within the area of their jurisdiction: and in particular for controlling the use of communal and family land; for controlling mortgages and sales; for the recording and filing of documents relating to alienation; and for regulating the allocation of communal and family land and the area over which rights may be exercised. It will be interesting to see how far these powers will be used and whether they will tend to promote or hinder uniformity. There is considerable danger in allowing a large number of Native Authorities to evolve their own land law. Statutory Native Authorities do not always coincide with those recognized by native custom. Moreover, rights over family lands are normally regarded as private rights with which Native Authorities, statutory or other, are not entitled to interfere.

have followed on this development, and in Nigeria, as in Northern Rhodesia,[1] attempts have been made by some Native Authorities to preserve social cohesion by compelling farmers to return to their villages during some of the dry-season months. The wisdom of this policy must depend on local circumstances. Its general application would, in many cases, be a serious interference with economic development and the flow of population from congested to undeveloped areas. In Bechuanaland, where chiefs have insisted on the return of farmers to their parent village for certain months of the year, this rule has proved an obstacle to the adoption of winter ploughing and other improved methods of agriculture.[2] It has been argued, too, in favour of decentralization, that it leads to more sanitary conditions and a healthier dietary. On the other hand, there is much to be said for the view that living together in villages is the very foundation of the African's social life and provides the best basis for its future development, including the provision of educational and medical facilities.[3] Moreover, co-operation is likely to play an increasingly important part in the development of agriculture in Africa and may well assume the rôle that has been attended with so much success in Russia.[4]

In East Africa there is the same general tendency towards a diminution in the size of the land-holding unit and the emergence of individual proprietary rights. In the Kiambu district of Kenya for example many of the family lands have been converted into private individual holdings, with complete freedom of transfer.[5] Farms are being bought and sold: they are often sold to pay off debts, and cases have occurred of farmers selling their holdings in order to meet their Government tax. Fenced-in holdings are also appearing, and even pasture lands are being enclosed.[6] The introduction of the

[1] See p. 124 (footnote 2).

[2] See I. Schapera, *Land Tenure in Bechuanaland Protectorate*, pp. 267 *et seq.*

[3] In the Transkei territories of the Union of S. Africa a policy of concentration into villages is being followed in order to facilitate adequate reservation and rotational use of the land.

[4] Co-operation is already a feature of certain forms of African agriculture, and is being increasingly exploited for Government schemes connected with soil erosion, the redistribution of cattle, and agricultural development generally.

[5] But from some reports it would seem that, in Kiambu, land cannot be sold to a stranger without first being offered to members of the kinship group. It is important to note that the Kiambu practice of selling farms is no recent innovation, but was followed in pre-British times. See the *Report on Native Land Tenure in Kikuyu Province*, p. 11. In Sukuma (Tanganyika) land was also sold, in congested areas, prior to the German occupation.

[6] I. Schapera states that in Bechuanaland there is nothing in native law to prevent a person from fencing-in his land. But some chiefs seem to have prohibited the fencing-in of land, lest this should lead to a lessening of their control over land. See *Native Land Tenure in the Bechuanaland Protectorate*, p. 175.

plough has led in places to a new disparity in the division of land. Wealthy natives have been buying ploughs, breaking up large areas, and planting them with wheat, maize and wattle. These new capitalists, if unchecked, may acquire, as their own, land which is or was the public property of the tribe. In some cases the Native Authorities are said to be parties to this form of exploitation. In Tanganyika, also, Mr. Culwick has drawn attention to the danger of allowing monied natives (e.g. retired clerks) to acquire rights over large areas of land and to levy what amounts to an annual tax on the cultivator.[1] In Nyasaland, wealthy natives are obtaining more than their fair share of land and using it to cultivate cash crops by means of paid labour, much of which is immigrant. In consequence, many of the poorer farmers have insufficient land for their meagre requirements. Moreover, in the absence of supervision, the labourers on the lands of the wealthier natives make little attempt to follow sound methods of husbandry, thus adding to the amount of land that is being lost through erosion.

Developments of this kind are being viewed with concern by the local governments, since they may portend the rise of agrarian debt, the creation of a landless pauper class and the various other evils that accompany unrestricted freedom to traffic in land.[2] In Kenya (and Tanganyika) consideration has been given to the introduction of legislation to control the sale and mortgage of land, to prohibit its acquisition by absentees, to limit the maximum and minimum acreage of native holdings, to limit the amount of rent, and to provide greater general security to tenants.

In most areas of Kenya, and indeed of East Africa as a whole, the sale of agricultural land is still contrary to native custom, and it would be unnecessary to introduce rules forbidding it.[3] But rules

[1] Mr. Culwick also reports that, nowadays, in Bukoba, anyone can sell, mortgage and pawn his plantation (banana, coffee, etc.) provided it has not been acquired by inheritance. Plantation land can be taken in satisfaction of a Native Court judgement. Another novel feature of Bukoba tenure is that land can be obtained from the Native Authorities on payment of a fee.

[2] In 1938 the Governor of Kenya in Council decided that it should be the Government's aim to secure that the real title to land occupied by a native community should continue to be based not on individual ownership, such as English law has made familiar, but on a usufructuary occupation. It was further decided that a Committee should be appointed to examine and report on the following questions: (1) Whether tribal customs can be relied on to limit the right to disposal of land and if any form of legislation is desirable whether it would be practicable to enforce it; (2) How the problem of individual ownership has been dealt with in tribes in which it has occurred; (3) Whether there is any practicable method of presenting excessive acquisition of land by individuals; and (4) To make recommendations for methods of recording land transactions, if land transactions are to be recorded, indicating what precautions are desirable. (See the *Kenya Annual Report on Native Affairs 1938*, para. 12.)

[3] But among the Kikuyu some of the Native Councils have made rules regulating sales. It is of interest to observe that in Bechuanaland some of the tribal courts have been imposing fines for attempts to sell land. It appears also that persons who have

may become necessary as a preventive measure, though, where this is so, concomitant steps should also be taken to introduce a suitable system of credit, through co-operative societies, or possibly through the local Native Authority.[1]

There are difficulties in fixing maximum and minimum acreages of holdings on account of the varying quality of the soil, the varying requirements of crops, the practice of shifting cultivation, and the fact that family and individual rights over land may already be well established. In Kenya many of the tribal communities would resent a restriction of acreage as an unjust impediment to enterprise which would not be imposed on their European neighbours. The imposition of a minimum acreage, on the other hand, would, if it were effective, deprive many peasants of their only means of existence. It would not be effective unless some restriction were also put on the number of those who worked the land and drew their subsistence from it.

Nevertheless, in many African tribes the tribal authorities are entitled by native custom to withdraw land from anyone who is not using it beneficially.[2] In Bechuanaland this principle has recently been reaffirmed (at a meeting of the Advisory Native Council in 1940) in consequence of complaints that some individuals were in possession of more land than they could plough and would not surrender, or even lend, to others who required land. There is, however, no tendency as yet in Bechuanaland to restrict the amount of land that a single individual or family may hold, provided it is being fully used. In Basutoland, on the other hand, farmers are normally limited to three fields, and periodical inspections are made by the Native Authorities in order to see that no one is holding more. Should such a person be found he would be deprived of his excess land, which would be given to others with fewer fields or none at all.[3] The Basutoland rule might well be adopted by other African

cleared fields, and subsequently transferred them, are beginning to demand very substantial compensation for the work of clearing. On the whole, however, the people of Bechuanaland are still opposed to the use of land as negotiable property and on this account are also opposed to any system of individual tenure. See I. Schapera, op. cit., p. 178.

[1] In Northern Nigeria and Tanganyika some Native Authorities are already undertaking the financing of peasants who wish to take up mixed farming but lack the necessary capital. See p. 155; also the 1933 *Report on Tanganyika*, p. 21.

[2] See p. 24. In Kenya the 'muramati' of Kiambu have considerable powers of redistribution, but these are becoming more and more limited as shares are becoming more precisely defined. See *Kenya Land Commission Report*, Sec. 507. It is interesting to note, as regards land held by Europeans in the Highlands of Kenya, that under the new Land Control Ordinance (No. XXII of 1944) the Land Board may refuse to sanction a transfer of land if it considers that the applicant already has sufficient land.

[3] See I. Schapera, op. cit., pp. 181 and 182, and Sir A. W. Pim, *Financial and Economic Position of Basutoland* (Cmd. 4907), 1935, p. 46.

communities, where local circumstances make this possible. It may be recalled that in Tonga (Friendly Islands) the normal agricultural holding is limited to eight and one quarter acres, that in Malaya grants of village lands are limited to ten acres, and may be withdrawn if the land is not being beneficially used, and that in Fiji there is provision (in the 1940 Ordinance) for the redistribution of land, according as the land-owning group decreases or increases in numbers. In South Africa the Glen Grey Act of 1894 provided for allotments of a standard size of eight acres, but the Native Economic Commission of 1932 recommended that this restriction on the size of holdings should be relaxed.[1]

With regard to the question of the excessive subdivision of land and the fixing of a minimum acreage, this is a problem which is becoming acute in many parts of Africa. In Western countries the soil is not the only means of livelihood and co-heirs on an overcrowded farm may agree that one of their number should buy out the others, who would seek alternative employment elsewhere. But in tropical Africa this may not be possible owing to the absence of other industries and the nature of the social organization. On the other hand, native African law makes varied provisions to meet the problem. There is the system of periodic redistribution of land, and there is also that of primogeniture, by which the general control of family lands passes to the eldest son or senior heir. In this connection the Kenya Land Commission recommended that in areas outside Reserves, where leases have been issued to a family or family group, the title, as embodying the seignory, should pass to the senior heir, but that the right of use should be distributed. In other words the land would be impartible in respect of title, but partible in respect of use.[2] If however a right-holder were absent from the land for more than three years, and had made no use of it, then he should lose his right. The lessee, moreover, should be given the power to buy out superfluous right-holders. In the case of land held individually (outside the Native Reserves) it was important that this should be maintained as such, and the Commissioners accordingly recommended that when a lessee died intestate the title should pass by primogeniture. But they considered that a lessee should be able to dispose of his land by will—an inroad into native law—though in this case he should not be allowed to bequeath it as an inheritance in common. And although he might dispose of it by specific bequest

[1] See *An African Survey*, p. 844.

[2] The recommendation that titles should be issued to families accords with native social conditions. Lord Hailey has observed of The Glen Grey Act of 1894 (S. Africa), which initiated a system of individual allotments of 8 acres, that this experiment had been criticized because it missed out an essential stage in the evolution to individual title, namely the allotment of plots large enough to accommodate extended-family groups. See *An African Survey*, p. 845.

of particular shares, no share should be smaller than a certain minimum.[1] In Malaya, as in Northern Nigeria, the Muhammadan law of inheritance is in practice overruled by local custom, with a view to preventing excessive subdivision; and in the State of Kelantan there is statutory provision for restricting to one-quarter of an acre the minimum area into which a plot may be divided.[2] In Ceylon primogeniture is foreign to all of the many legal systems of the island, with the result that excessive subdivision has long been a serious problem. The difficulty is sometimes overcome by joint shareholders agreeing to cultivate the land in turn, but this usually leads to over-exploitation. Under the new Land Development Ordinance (of Ceylon) severe restrictions are imposed on the tenure of land alienated by the Crown. The owner may not dispose of a divided share of the holding less in extent than the unit of subdivision specified in the grant, and no person may be the owner of an undivided share in the holding less in extent than the specified unit of subdivision.[3] In South Africa, under the Glen Grey Act of 1894, which introduced to the Bantu-speaking peoples a system of individual holdings, special provisions were made to prevent the subdivision of holdings. Among these it was laid down that succession was to be by primogeniture, and this principle was confirmed by the Native Administration Act of 1927. Lord Hailey has observed, however, that, although undue subdivision is nominally prevented, the density of population has become such as to deprive the regulation of most of its effect, since the landless members of the community continue to squat on the allotments. In the Transkeian Territories to which the Glen Grey Act was extended the restrictions against subdivision have had to be relaxed (by Proclamation No. 300 of 1913 as regards the Transkei, and in the Ciskei by No. 66 of 1936). In this area, also, many of the allotments granted under the Act have been cancelled for want of beneficial occupation.[4]

Before leaving the subject of inheritance in its relation to tenure, it may be observed that many problems of tenure are being created by changes in the system of inheritance, and that many problems of inheritance are being created by changes in the system of tenure. It has been shown, for example, that in some matrilineal communities of the Gold Coast it is becoming customary for sons, and not sisters' sons, to inherit plantation land. In Malaya, among the

[1] Cmd. 4556, paras. 1890-1907.

[2] See p. 48. The Ottoman Land Laws overrule Muhammadan law as regards the inheritance of State or 'Mirie' lands. See e.g., p. 64.

[3] See p. 59 (footnote 1).

[4] See *An African Survey*, p. 844. Lord Hailey remarks that the success of the Glen Grey Act as an experiment in the individualization of tenure was prejudiced by local circumstances.

matriarchal peoples of Negri Sembilan, there is precisely the same tendency. All land was formerly owned by females, and was transmitted matrilineally, but nowadays rubber land is inherited by males, and by sons in preference to sisters' sons.[1] In Nigeria there are tribes where one section has adopted patrilineal principles while the other has remained matrilineal. Among the Verre of Northern Nigeria there are at least three tribal groups with three distinct systems of inheritance, one of which is ultimogeniture or inheritance by the youngest son.[2] In Bechuanaland, Schapera has reported that there is much confusion regarding the inheritance of land owing to the fact that ward segregation has broken down in the villages, and in many of the tribes daughters are permitted to inherit land and to retain it after marriage. On the other hand, cultivation is no longer a predominantly feminine occupation, and men are taking an interest in possessing arable as well as grazing land.[3]

Fragmentation,[4] as distinct from subdivision of holdings, may also be produced by customary rules of inheritance, even where primogeniture is the rule. A man may have children by several wives and it may be the rule that the eldest son of each wife is entitled not merely to a share of their father's land, but to a share of each category of land, such as land suitable for cocoa-growing, land suitable for maize, and so on. In Kenya it has been reported that in the coastal belt a plot of three acres of land may in this way be held by ten or fifteen people. The problem of fragmentation has received little attention in any of the dependencies, and few if any attempts have been made to consolidate holdings. It may be added that, in some dependencies, plantations of cocoa, coffee or coco-nuts are often rendered valueless owing to the fact that the ownership of trees is divided among innumerable heirs. None may have a claim sufficiently large to induce him to keep the plantation clean.

Another factor in modifying native methods of holding land has been the introduction of systems of survey and registration of title. In the chapters dealing with Malaya it has been shown that the whole of the native system of tenure has been transformed by the fact that it has existed alongside and intermingled with a European system which depended on survey. This, coupled with the development of plantation crops, tended to produce an assimilation of the customary title to that of the registered title, so that, at the present time, the differences in the two forms of title are almost negligible. The occupant of land held by native custom has now become the

[1] See *Matriarchy in the Malay Peninsula*, by G. A. de C. de Moubray, p. 138.

[2] Ultimogeniture is found in English law under the name of 'Borough English.' (See Glossary.)

[3] I. Schapera, op. cit., p. 152.

[4] Fragmentation may be defined as the holding of small units of land in various parts.

owner of land held by entry in the Mukim register, he possesses a document of title, he can charge or lease his land, its area is surveyed, dealings have to be executed in a statutory form duly attested, and the instrument has to be registered before it can become effective.

In Uganda, in the same way, a new system of native tenure has been evolved under the direct influence of European methods of holding land. With the establishment of 'mailo' tenure in Buganda[1] land assumed a new character: it became a private possession at the complete disposal of individual owners; and with the simultaneous introduction of a money economy it also came to be regarded as a source of profit through leasing and sale.[2] By the Land Law of 1908, enacted by the Native Government of Buganda, 'mailo' land was made freely transferable and disposable (to natives), not merely by customary succession, but also by will. Succession need not, therefore, be to an eldest son, nor even to any other member of the kinship group—a very significant innovation. Another departure from native custom was the provision that the owner of 'mailo' lands need not give to a chief any portion of the produce of his land. Furthermore, the English law of easements was made generally applicable to 'mailo' lands; land falling into escheat was to be dealt with by the Governor and Native Council as trustees for the Baganda people; and provision was made for the resumption of land for public purposes, and (by the Land Survey Law of 1909) for the survey and registration of 'mailo' lands.

In Buganda the commutation into money of the traditional service due by a peasant to his landlord developed gradually into a regular system of rent, and some 'mailo' landlords became entitled to rent from several thousand tenants.[3] And so in 1927 (at the instance of the British authorities) the Buganda Native government passed legislation designed to give security to native tenants and regulate the payment of tribute and of rents. This measure, known as the 'Busulu and Envujo law', was probably the first enactment in Africa dealing with native rental conditions.[4] Under this law

[1] See pp. 132-3.

[2] Lord Hailey has also pointed out that one effect of the grant of estates to chiefs in proprietary title was to divorce land-holding from the exercise of their political functions, upon which control over land had formerly depended. See *An African Survey*, p. 851.

[3] With this we may compare the history of 'socage' and 'gavelkind' in English tenure. This latter word is connected with the Old English word 'gafol' which means rent or a customary performance of agricultural services. See W. S. Holdsworth, *Historical Introduction to the Land Law*, p. 133.

[4] The status of tenants on native lands in Kenya received a good deal of attention in the Reports of the Committees on Land Tenure in Kikuyu Province and in the North Kavirondo Reserve. In dealing with the question of evictions the latter committee suggested that these should be controlled by a specific statute. But native law should be able to cope with this problem. More knowledge, however, is required

tenants, in return for a prescribed rent, obtained for themselves and their successors a right of occupancy in their small holdings, revocable only for good and sufficient reasons and after reference to the Native Courts. Their right to improvements was acknowledged and it was laid down that no sale, exchange or gift of 'mailo' land should affect either the status or duties of peasant tenants. But tenants were obliged to continue to render to the 'mailo' owner all customary respect and obedience, and to take good care of the land and the buildings. They were prohibited from sub-letting their holdings or any part of them, for profit. In 1932 a Land Tax law was enacted by the Native Government, and this, among other things, established the principle that landowners should not be entitled to the whole incremental value of their land. Finally, in 1939, by the Land (Agreements) Law, all dealings in unregistered 'mailo' lands were prohibited. This law marks a further departure from native custom, and extinguishes equitable as well as legal rights arising from unregistered documents.

In Tanganyika the changes that have occurred in recent times have already been indicated,[1] and reference need only be made here to the evolution of the type of tenure known as 'nyarubanja'. 'Nyarubanja' were originally estates or plantations conferred on the sons or daughters or favourites of the chief, or on those who had proved successful leaders in war. When a 'nyarubanja' was granted the previous owners of the various plots included in the 'nyarubanja' were compelled to give them up or else remain as tenants or serfs of the new 'mtwaze' or grantee, to whom they paid gifts of beer, produce or service. In 1922 the Commissioner of Bukoba directed that all dealings in 'nyarubanja' should cease and that all 'nyarubanja' should be registered. In 1926 the Government issued instructions for the commutation of tribute and of service, thereby altering the whole character of the tenure. The landlords now claimed full control of the land, but this claim could not be admitted under the Land Ordinance. Finally, in 1929, rules made under section 15 of the Native Authority Ordinance required landlords to pay to the Government a peppercorn rent in recognition of the Crown's title to land, and in return the landlords were given certain produce rights. It will be observed that in the case of 'nyarubanja' the development of tenure has followed very different lines from that of the royal estates in Buganda.[2]

in most African dependencies of the native custom regarding ejectment and of the remedies open to landlords in cases where tenants have abused their rights, e.g. where, having engaged to pay their rent in kind, they have failed to cultivate the land in the manner and to the extent that is customary. The problem of natives resident on European estates has been discussed at pp. 81-4, 116 and 127.

[1] See pp. 108-113.

[2] In speaking of the Bemba of Northern Rhodesia Dr. Audrey Richards stated (in 1939) that while the native political machinery founded on the system of land

In Kenya, consideration has been given to the question of instituting local agencies for recording transactions in land, whether by way of sale, mortgage or other method. The Kiambu Local Native Council has passed a resolution in favour of registration of title, the South Nyeri Council in favour of registering all transactions including outright purchases, the Fort Hall and Meru Councils in favour of registering transactions other than outright purchases, and the Embu Native Council in favour of regulations covering the relationship of landlords and tenants. It has already been observed, however, that, while full play must be allowed to local initiative, there is nevertheless a need for caution in leaving such questions as the institution of systems of records to inexperienced Native Authorities, since the form of record adopted is likely to have a determining effect on the form that landholding shall take.[1]

We may conclude this summary of change in native systems of land tenure by two examples from the Pacific—Tonga and the Fiji Islands. Tonga is an excellent example of the way in which a primitive system of tenure may be adapted to twentieth century requirements. The change was effected voluntarily by the people of Tonga with the advice and assistance of the British. The Tonga land system has already been described[2] and it need only be observed here that all land in Tonga has been declared to be the property of the Crown; that it is divided into three classes, namely (*a*) hereditary estates held by royalty and nobles, (*b*) tax allotments and (*c*) town allotments; that the interest of the holders in each class is a life-interest only and is hereditary according to prescribed rules; that every male Tongan over the age of sixteen is entitled to a minimum of eight and one quarter acres of farming land which he must keep in good order; that no landholder may sell or mortgage his land; that rents are at a standard rate fixed by the State; and that all transactions in land are subject to registration.

The declaration that all land is the property of the Crown was not a mere imitation of the English doctrine that 'every acre of land

tenure was breaking down with changing religious beliefs and the Chief's diminishing power to exact his legal dues, nevertheless from the agricultural point of view the position of the commoner had remained secure. No Bemba chief had yet profited from changing conditions to limit his subjects' right of cultivation or had tried to exact a profit from his theoretical ownership of land. *Land, Labour and Diet in Northern Rhodesia*, p. 266.

[1] The people of Kiambu were asking for registration of their 'ithaka' or units of land tenure as long ago as 1929. The Committee on Land Tenure in Kikuyu Province considered this reasonable, but pointed out that registration would entail rules governing sale and conveyancing. They also considered that a careful watch would have to be kept to prevent registration of 'ithaka' developing into landlordism (see *Report on Native Land Tenure in Kikuyu Province*, p. 41). In some parts of Tanganyika (e.g. Bukoba) systems of registering transfers have been initiated, but these seem to be confined to certain forms of title only.

[2] See pp. 212-6.

is held of the king', but was a logical development of the older Tongan principle that the chief holds the land in trusteeship for the people. The setting aside of hereditary estates for the use of the royal family and members of the aristocracy was in accord with the social traditions of Tonga and follows closely the development that occurred in Buganda, as a result of the Uganda Agreement of 1900. But whereas in Buganda the estates assigned to the chiefs or aristocracy became purely private property which their owners could use as they pleased, in Tonga a life-interest only was conferred. Moreover, in Tonga, unlike Buganda, care was taken at the outset to prevent the dispossession of the peasant. By the grant to every grown-up male of a holding of his own, the Tongan has been enabled to pursue the path of economic individualism. But since his holding is a 'usehold' only, as Dr. Keesing has expressed it,[1] both he and the land are protected from the abuses incidental to the fuller forms of ownership.

In Fiji the development of the native system of tenure has been governed by two principal factors, (*a*) the sugar industry, and (*b*) the presence of immigrant Indians who are now almost as numerous as the Fijians themselves. The Fiji Islands were ceded to Queen Victoria in 1874, but the Fijians retained the ownership of their lands. The land legislation, however, prohibited the alienation of native land by sale, grant or mortgage, except to the Crown, and it was laid down that when a 'mataqali' or land-owning group became extinct its land automatically became the property of the Crown as *ultimus haeres*. But natives were enabled to lease their land to anyone they pleased. Lands were freely leased to Indians for cane cultivation and were as freely resumed by their Fijian owners at the expiration of the lease. This led to much ill-feeling between Fijians and Indians and much improvident use of land.

In 1936 the Government of Fiji came to the conclusion that a greater measure of control over lands was necessary, if the interests of the Indians and Fijians were to be co-ordinated, if continuity of agricultural policy and security of tenure were to be attained, and if the existing wasteful system of agriculture were to be replaced by a planned economy. The Fijian leaders shared these views, and agreed to resign to the Government the control over all their unoccupied lands. In 1940 a new Ordinance was enacted, under which the administration of native land was vested in a Board. This Board will have the assistance of local committees which will advise it on questions of land tenure. The establishment of local committees to deal with land matters is an important innovation, long overdue in many of the dependencies. The Board may set aside any native land as a Reserve, and no land in any Reserve may be leased or otherwise

[1] See *The South Seas in the Modern World*, by Felix M. Keesing, 1942, p. 109.

disposed of, except to a Fijian. The Board may grant leases and licences of portions of native land not included in a Reserve. Thus, while all land not included in a Reserve will be available to applicants of any race, within a Reserve no one but a Fijian will be entitled to hold land. In cases in which the original area reserved appears to be too large for the present or future requirements of Fijians, the Board may exclude any portion of land from a Reserve. On the other hand, the Governor is empowered to set aside land for a 'mataqali' or land-owning group whose land is, or may be, insufficient for its maintenance. When a 'mataqali' dies out, the Crown retains its former right to become the 'ultimate heir'. Thus here, as in the Tonga legislation, important principles of native law have been retained. The Government's new policy provides adequate safeguards for native customary rights, but at the same time offers sufficient scope for individual enterprise.[1]

This review is a selection of some only of the changes that have occurred in native systems of land tenure. Nothing has been said about many important innovations such as the setting aside of land for special classes of natives, the special laws that have been made for native tenants on European estates, the effect on tenure of rules made to control erosion or of the innumerable ordinances enacted at the instance of the Agricultural and other Government Departments, of the effect of legislation restricting credit to natives, of debt legislation such as that recently enacted in Zanzibar, or of the establishment of co-operative systems of credit. But sufficient has been said to indicate something of the complexity of the many problems of change. It is clear, for example, that within a single territory the rate of change may vary widely and that the problems of each district may require separate treatment; that in most areas native law is well able to continue to deal with land administration, but that in some it will require assistance as tenure tends to pass from a basis of custom to one of contract; that in some territories (e.g. Nigeria and the Gold Coast) the legal position of the Government may enable it to control change more effectively in one area of the territory than in another; that problems of change in tenure cannot be considered apart from change in the other social institutions of the people and that drastic changes are therefore to be avoided; that, on the other hand, there is an equal danger in allowing many varieties of tenure to develop in a higgledy-piggledy

[1] In 1933 the Government of Fiji enacted legislation which enabled an individual Fijian cultivator to obtain security of tenure over a portion of tribal land and to enjoy the proceeds of his own efforts without interference from other members of his social group. In this connection it should be noted that in French North and West Africa there is a considerable body of legislation dealing with the transformation of collective usufructuary rights into those of purely private property (though restrictions may be retained on sale and mortgage). See e.g. *An African Survey*, pp. 858-63 and *l'Afrique française* for June 1937.

fashion.[1] It has been made clear also that under some circumstances the group may be a better farming unit than the individual, while, under other circumstances rights of co-ownership may be a definite bar to capital improvement. Finally, although many of the native systems of tenure appear to be passing through one or other of the stages traversed by all the developed systems of modern countries, it may be asked whether they must all necessarily arrive at the same conclusion as these modern systems. Must commercialization and urbanization lead inevitably to landlordism and tenant conditions? Must gifts in kind for the use of land become converted into money rents? Must the peasants of Africa accommodate their tenure to the capitalism of European countries, or may it be possible for them to follow the example of Russia, or else develop other systems of their own?[2] Must peasant farming give way to plantation or large-scale farming, and if so will the cultivator (as in Fiji and Russia) be given an individual interest in the land? As a part answer to some of these questions, and a conclusion to this study of the problems of land tenure in the British Colonial Empire, it may be appropriate to quote the following paragraphs from Dr. Felix Keesing's recent book on *The South Seas in the Modern World*. 'The average Westerner,' he says, 'tends to assume that his own particular property usages, with their attendant paraphernalia

[1] The Kenya Land Commissioners of 1933 declared that 'It is futile to imagine that an undirected mass evolution can solve the many new problems which have resulted from settled government and the impact of an industrial civilization on a primitive people and are entirely outside the range of tribal experience. . . . Government, by the very act of governing, has created the problems, and it is not unreasonable to expect that Government should solve them. . . . The function of Government cannot be discharged by marking and proclaiming the changes as they occur. Conscious regulation is necessary.' On the other hand, they observed that 'natives are entitled to be protected against the possibility of rash or ill-considered rules' and insisted that proposals for new Government rules should first be referred to the local Native Councils. Dr. Leakey, a well-known anthropologist with an intimate, knowledge of Kenya, stressed the danger of attempting to introduce modifications into native systems of tenure by means of Government rules. See Cmd. 4556, Secs. 1653-57. Dr. Audrey Richards has stated that among the Bemba and other peoples of Northern Rhodesia, although individual rights over land can become very clearly defined where ground for cultivation is scarce, the introduction of a rent-paying system and the right to sell or lease land is quite unnecessary to secure this end; the traditional system can be quite easily adapted without any need of Government interference. (*Land, Labour and Diet in Northern Rhodesia*, p. 276.) Sir Ernest Dowson has also observed that in Iraq the Ottoman Land Code had proved a failure because it had attempted prematurely to cast in a rigid mould the fluid practices of a still preponderantly primitive society. The establishment of security of tenure should be sought in conformity with existing custom, and in many areas it was essential that the tenure should be regulated locally if it was to be governed by law at all. Complete freedom of individual dealing with land should not be allowed until the mass of small-holders had attained greater economic stability and experience. (*An Enquiry into Land Tenure, etc., in Iraq*, 1932.)

[2] Dr. U. P. Mayer has remarked (in an unpublished manuscript) that 'In Russia the least collective type of collective agriculture, the *kolkhosi*, which preserves the individual holding of land but unites labour and management, may well be fitted to absorb certain tribal systems of cultivation which function on similar lines.'

of maps, theodolites, fences, and title deeds, have a kind of universal validity or even sacredness. Other systems of property holding, if they even come to his notice, are regarded as primitive, inadequate, and perhaps vaguely subversive. Yet, in reality, history shows that the present highly individualistic and legally complex system of the Western countries is a comparatively recent growth. It took form particularly from the sixteenth century, when the inclosure movement and its accompanying peasant revolts, together with the emergence of an increasingly large landless class signalized the main stage in transforming European feudalism and collectivism into private ownership in the modern sense. The customs of landholding before this were in many respects parallel to those found among Pacific peoples. It will be well to keep this in mind in exploring the problems of modernizing local systems of tenure, particularly as many of the difficulties and conflicts apparent in Colonial areas to-day resemble those occurring in Europe during the earlier centuries.' Again he says: 'It would seem that under these circumstances the official policies regarding land should be very elastic and adaptable, hence of a kind that would encourage native groups to try out for themselves which types of tenure might best suit their needs in the modern setting. On the one hand, the way ought to be open for persons who so desire to get individual holdings on government lands if native lands are not available. On the other, any experiments along collective lines could be encouraged, in order to test out their practicability.[1] Meantime, the traditional usages, so far as they are still vital, may well be respected and protected. In this, as in other matters of policy, dangers seem to lie equally in retarding indigenous development and in overstimulating it.

'In all such questions of land policy a primary need is for governing authorities to be expert in the traditional land usages within their jurisdictions and also to be in the closest touch with the trends of change under modern conditions. Either the local officials (judges, district officers, surveyors and others) should be thoroughly trained in these matters, or else specialists should be brought in to report on them. Ignorance on the part of administrators adds to the growing confusion and may dangerously undermine the prestige of a government, since landholding is so vital a matter.

'On the whole, the land question, except in a few regions, is still beset with difficult problems, especially in the sphere of native tenure. There can be no quick solutions, and, for the most part, resolving them depends on long-term education rather than immediate action. Indigenous land ideas and customs are an integral part of the whole cultural and psychological fabric now being tested

[1] An interesting example of experimentation (in the Indian State of Baroda) will be found in the Appendix (para. 7).

out for its survival value; nevertheless, upon the intelligent handling of land matters depends in large measure the future economic stability and social welfare of the peoples.'[1]

[1] *The South Seas in the Modern World*, by Felix M. Keesing, 1942, pp. 97 and 115. These passages are quoted by the kind permission of the author and of the publishers (George Allen & Unwin).

Appendix

Notes on some recent developments in tenure systems

1. *Collective Farming in Russia.* The following extracts are taken from a recent article by Sir E. J. Russell, F.R.S. They are reproduced here by kind permission of the author and of the proprietors of *The Geographical Magazine* in which the article appeared (December 1941).

'The whole of the farming land is vested in a selected group of peasants known as the "Collective"; if they had any agricultural property such as farm animals, implements, seed, etc., they had to bring it into the common stock. New members can be admitted, though some contribution is required, and some period of probation is usually necessary.

'The member of the Collective is assigned a house and fair-sized piece of ground; about ½ acre in the more fertile regions, up to about 2 acres in the less fertile districts; he keeps this as long as he remains a member of the Collective, but he cannot sell it, he has no proprietary rights. He is (or was before the war) allowed to possess one or two cows, a breeding sow and some chickens. On this little holding he may himself work, and his wife and family, but he may not employ anyone for wages.

'The management of the farm is in the hands of a Committee elected by the members themselves, presided over by a Chairman. . . . No wages are given to the workers but they are paid a share of the produce. . . . At the end of the season the total produce of the farm is estimated, the various State and other charges are paid, and the balance is shared among the members in proportion to their "labour days". During the year there are, of course, advances to enable the people to live. The direct Government demand for grain, potatoes and milk is about 4% or 5% of yields fixed by law and must be paid whether these yields are attained or not; the risk of the season thus has to be borne by the Collective, not by the Government. The Motor Tractor Station, the central body that hires out tractors to farms not possessing them, charges a percentage of the grain actually obtained. Other calls are for capital developments, insurance, seed, old and sick people, day nursery and crèche, etc. All these charges have to be met first, and then the balance is shared out.

'Some compromise has always to be made between the requirements of the Collective farms and of the land held personally, and there was a tendency for men to put in too little time on the Collective and too much time on their own land, which they found more profitable; this had to be stopped by a sharp law.

'Once the farms were collectivized the way lay open to the use of machinery and the introduction of modern scientific methods of farming; previously this had been possible only on the larger estates, not on the peasants' strips. Bitterly as the peasants resented collectivization—and well they might, for it was at first ruthlessly imposed upon them—they became reconciled when they saw the tractor coming forward and ploughing in a day what they knew it would have taken them weeks to do.'

2. *Communal Farming in Bechuanaland and the Union of South Africa.*[1] Apart from privately-owned farms there are in every tribe of Bechuanaland one or more

[1] This information is taken from *Land Tenure in Bechuanaland Protectorate* by I. Schapera (The Lovedale Press 1943), p. 157.

large farms specially cultivated every year for the Chief by his subjects. These farms are known as 'masotla'. They and their produce are tribal property of which the Chief is the custodian and administrator. Their cultivation is a communal enterprise undertaken to enable him to carry out the duty of providing for his people in time of need, of feeding the regiments that he summons to work for him and of entertaining visitors. In the Kgatla tribe there were formerly nineteen of these farms, situated in different parts of the country. Each was entrusted to a separate village or group of wards, so that practically the whole tribe took part in the cultivation. The British Administration, while restricting the Chiefs' use of forced labour in other directions, has explicitly recognized their right to demand this form of service from their people, on the ground that it enables them to maintain their position as heads of tribes and to discharge the duties of their office.

After the outbreak of the war, with a view to increasing agricultural production, a scheme was drawn up whereby special tribal lands should be cultivated communally along the lines of the 'masotla'. Ploughing and planting were to be done by a mass effort from all cultivators whose own holdings were situated close to where each particular 'war land' was situated. The weeding, thinning, cultivating, bird-scaring and so on were to be done by rotation of family groups, each being responsible for a few days' work. The harvesting and threshing would also be carried out by collective effort. Where necessary, seed would be obtained by purchase by means of an advance from the tribal treasury.

Although some of these 'war lands' did not receive the care given to land cultivated by individual owners, the scheme marked a new and important development in communal enterprise and land tenure among the people of Bechuanaland. In 1935 the Director of Native Agriculture in the Union of South Africa observed that 'a very large number of natives have not the facilities in the way of draught animals to work their individual holdings efficiently. Moreover, a greater number are employed in industry and elsewhere away from their homes at a time when the individual arable holdings require their undivided attention. It is considered that the stage has been reached when collective crop farming by organized groups or associations of heads of families under a capable leader should be undertaken. The leader of such an association must be held responsible to, and controlled by, a representative body like a local or district council or, where no council exists, an advisory council or board under the Chief. The objects of the system are to arrange for the group of producers to pool their labour, their draught animals, their implements, tools and seed, and to undertake all operations of fallowing, ploughing, planting, etc., at the proper time and efficiently in order that optimum crops may be obtained. Collective crop farming as against individual farming would also appear to offer an opportunity for a definite saving of human and animal labour. In this connection it has been estimated that the proposed system will release approximately 50%-75% of the male labour units and 40%-50% of the draught animals annually engaged on ploughing and planting of food crops of individual holdings.'[2]

3. *Jewish Agricultural Settlements in Palestine.* These in 1937 covered some 126,600 acres and were occupied by 10,000 families. The farms fall into two main types: (*a*) the 'kvotzoth' or collective settlement for 40-100 families who, together, manage one large estate, and (*b*) the 'moshavim' or settlement of smallholders, each of whom manages his own farm, backed by a co-operative system. The general trend under this system is towards diversification of cropping, which is made easier

[1] See Proclamation No. 74 of 1934, Section 22 (1) (c).
[2] *Report of the Department of Native Affairs for the Years* 1935-36 (U.G. 41, 1937), p. 38.

by an extensive use of irrigation. Cereals represent only 11% of the farm income as compared with 50% under the Arab system.[1]

4. *The Latifiyah Estates, Iraq.* In 1928 this Company bought 60,000 acres from the Government of Iraq for the purpose of general arable farming, and at the outset managed the estate on plantation lines, the workers being employed as daily wage earners. The Company's machinery and capital, however, proved inadequate and the workers, who were unaccustomed to a daily wage, showed little interest in the estate. A system of tenant farming was accordingly introduced, the unit being 20 acres for winter crops, plus a maximum of 5 acres for summer crops. The winter crops are cereals (barley for the most part) while the summer crops are millet, sesame and cotton. The whole estate, which was originally desert land, is watered from flow or pump irrigation and the cropping system allows half the land to lie fallow each year. The head of a family group may acquire a number of units of land and the families are registered as partners in the lease. The Company provides certain services, such as power cultivation and threshing. Rent is taken in kind—50% as a rule, though the exact figure depends on the type of land occupied and the extent of the services rendered.

5. *The Gezira Scheme* (*Sudan*).[2] The Gezira is the name given to the triangle of 5,000,000 acres lying between the Blue and White Nile. The cotton cultivation scheme covers an area of 1,000,000 acres which are irrigated from the Sennar dam. It is operated on a share system by a triple partnership between the Government, The Sudan Plantations Syndicate and tenant cultivators, whose shares are respectively 40%, 20% and 40%. The Government has the right to rent land from the original owners, but the owners have a prior claim on tenancies, which are held in single units of 40 feddans (a feddan being rather more than an English acre). There are provisions to prevent fragmentation and the sale of the land to merchants or others who would be unable or unwilling to reside on the land.[3] The Government meets the interest on and the repayment of the capital cost of the Sennar dam and major canals, the running expense of the Irrigation Service and the rental to the original landowners. The Syndicate meets the cost of development and of the minor canals and undertakes the general management of the scheme, the heavy cultivation (with power machinery), the supervision of the farming operations, and the collection and marketing of the cotton crop. The tenant pays a proportionate share of the expenses and is allowed to grow food and fodder crops on his own account. He has full security of tenure and since he can obtain cash advances from the Syndicate at reasonable rates he is able to keep himself free from moneylenders. He has every inducement also to improve his holding. The scheme provides the Sudan Government with one-quarter of its revenue and so is one of the principal means of providing funds for development. But it has been criticized on the ground that it depends on a single export cash crop, that it offers insufficient opportunity for the maintenance and development of the social life of the people,[4] that it tends to promote an individualistic and mercenary outlook and that its dependence on foreign capital necessarily entails a considerable degree of local exploitation.

6. *The Alternative Livelihood Scheme* (*Sudan*). With the construction of the Jebel

[1] For full details readers should consult *Planned Mixed Farming* by I. Elazari-Volcani (Palestine Publishing Co., 1938) and *Economic Survey of Palestine* by D. Horowitz and Rita Henden (Economic Research Institute, Tel Aviv, 1938).

[2] This Scheme expires in 1950 when the contract between the Sudan Government and the Syndictate is terminated.

[3] It should be noted that in the Sudan generally no native may sell, mortgage, charge or otherwise dispose of any land or interest therein without the consent of the Government. But such consent is not required to a devise by will or a lease for a period not exceeding 3 years.

[4] Many of the tenant farmers are immigrant Hausa from West Africa.

Aulia dam a large tract became inundated and some 70,000 families were unable to pursue their semi-nomadic mode of life. Many of these have been converted into settled cultivators under a system whereby the best features of their tribal organization have been preserved and the corporate life of their compact villages developed on modern lines. The agricultural system is modelled on that of the Gezira scheme, with this difference, that the Government, in addition to its own duties, assumes those also of the Syndicate. The scheme is therefore a partnership between the Government and the tenants, the Government taking 60% of the cotton profits and the tenants 40%. No large scale machinery is employed, but the tenants are encouraged to form co-operative societies for ploughing. There is a cess of one piastre per bag of cotton harvested and this is set aside to form a Tenants' Welfare Fund. Tribal discipline is fully maintained and there are courts for this purpose. An administrative Sheikh presides over the village council, and a feature of the scheme is the appointment of an agricultural Sheikh for each thirty holdings, who acts as an intermediary between the tenants and the Government Agricultural Officer. The various agricultural Sheikhs together form a court which is empowered to inflict fines for agricultural offences.[1]

7. *The Baroda Scheme.* The State of Baroda in India has recently embarked on a novel experiment in land tenure. It has bought out five villages which had fallen into the hands of moneylenders and proposes to rehabilitate the cultivators in five different ways, with a view to determining the most suitable system of tenure. In the first village each family will be given a consolidated holding of fifteen acres, which may not be subdivided, and must be cropped according to a programme fixed by the State. The cultivators will eventually buy out their holdings. The system in the second village will be similar but the cultivators will remain tenants of the State. In the third village all crops will be grown in blocks by the community, the produce being shared in proportion to the area of land worked by each cultivator. In the fourth village the system will be one of collective farming, each cultivator receiving a share of the whole produce proportionate to the amount of labour contributed by himself and his cattle. In the fifth village a system of State farming will be followed. The land will belong to the village as a whole and the cultivators will receive a daily wage, together with a share of the profits at the end of the year.

[1] The above information concerning Jewish Agricultural Settlements in Palestine, the Latifiyah Estates in Iraq, and the Gezira and Alternative Livelihood Schemes in the Sudan, is derived from *The Agricultural Development of the Middle East* by B. A. Keen, D.Sc., F.R.S. (O.U.P., 1946) It is interesting to compare the three last mentioned schemes with the Fiji system described in Chapter XVI.

Glossary[1]

1. Absolute Title. The registered proprietor of lands registered with an absolute title (under the Land Registration Act 1925) has a State guaranteed title that there is no other person who has a better right to the land. (Osborn.)
2. Adverse Possession. An occupation of land inconsistent with the right of the true owner. (Osborn.)
3. Alienation. The power of the owner or tenant to dispose of his interest in real or personal property. Alienation may be voluntary, e.g., by conveyance or will; or involuntary, e.g., seizure under a judgment order for debt. (Osborn.)
4. Allodium (adjective=allodial)=lands not held of any lord or superior, in which, therefore, the owner had an absolute property and not a mere estate. (Osborn.)
5. Assign. To transfer property to another.
6. Attach. To take or place property under the control of a court.
7. Beneficial owner. The person who enjoys or who is entitled to the benefit of property. (Osborn.)
8. Borough English. A customary mode of descent under which the youngest son inherited land to the exclusion of his elder brothers. It was abolished in England by the Law of Property Act, 1922. (Osborn.) The name is probably derived from the fact that at Nottingham it was the custom of the English as contrasted with the French borough. (See W. S. Holdsworth op. cit., p. 136.)
9. Burgage Tenure. A form of free land-holding, generally at a money rent, peculiar to boroughs, similar to the modern tenure in fee simple, but subject to local custom. It was abolished by the Law of Property Act, 1922. (Osborn.)
10. Caveat. An entry made in the books of the offices of a registry or court to prevent a certain step being taken without previous notice to the person entering the caveat. (Osborn.)
11. Contract. An agreement enforceable by law.
12. Conveyance. A mode of transfer of property; the deed or instrument other than a will whereby an instrument in property is assured by one person to another. It includes a mortgage, charge, lease, assent, vesting declaration, vesting instrument, disclaimer, release, and every other assurance of property except a will. (Osborn.)
13. Coparcener. One who shares equally with others in inheritance of the estate of a common ancestor. (*S.O.E.D.*)
14. Copyhold. Tenure of lands being parcel of a manor, 'at the will of the lord according to the custom of the manor' by copy of the manorial court-roll. (*S.O.E.D.*) Copyhold tenure was abolished by the Law of Property Act 1922 and existing copyholds were enfranchised.
15. Corporeal property. Property which has a physical existence such as land or goods. (Osborn.)

[1] This glossary of some terms used in connection with English land law is compiled from *A Concise Law Dictionary* by P. G. Osborn. A few of the definitions are from *The Shorter Oxford English Dictionary*. Some of the terms included are only of historical interest in so far as English law is concerned. But they provide parallels for many of the incidents of the developing tenures of the Colonial territories.

16. Custom. A rule of conduct obligatory on those within its scope, established by long usage. A valid custom has the force of law. A valid custom must be o immemorial antiquity, certain and reasonable, obligatory, not repugnant to Statute law, though it may derogate from the common law. (Osborn.)
17. Customary Freehold. A superior kind of copyhold. The tenants hold by copy of Court roll according to the custom of the manor, but not at the will of the lord. Abolished by the Law of Property Act 1922. (Osborn.)
18. Defeasible. An estate or interest in property which is liable to be defeated or terminated by the operation of a condition subsequent or conditional limitation. (Osborn.)
19. Demise. Originally any transfer or succession of a right; now the grant of a lease of lands or other hereditaments. (Osborn.)
20. Devise. A gift of land or other realty by will.
21. Easement. A right enjoyed by the owner of land over the lands of another. (Osborn.)
22. Emblement. The right of an out-going tenant to harvest the crop sown before the termination of his estate.
23. Emphyteusis. A grant of land for ever, or for a long period, on condition that an annual rent (canon) shall be paid to the grantor and his successors and that, if the rent be not paid, the grant shall be forfeited. (Osborn.)
24. Entail. To convert into 'fee tail'. To settle land on a number of persons in succession, so that it cannot be dealt with by any one possessor as absolute owner. (*S.O.E.D.*)
25. Equity of Redemption. The right of a mortgagor who has in law forfeited his estate to redeem it within a reasonable time by payment of the principal and interest. (*S.O.E.D.*)
26. Escheat. The lapsing of land to the Crown or to the lord of the manor, on the death of the owner—intestate without heirs. Escheat was abolished by the Administration of Estates Act 1925 and the right of the Crown to take as *bona vacantia* was substituted. (*S.O.E.D.* and Osborn.)
27. Escuage. A variety of tenure by knight's service. It imposed on the tenant the duty of accompanying the King to war for forty days, or of sending a substitute, or of paying a sum of money which was assessed by Parliament after the expedition. (Osborn.)
28. Estate. An interest in land. An *absolute estate* is one granted without condition or termination. An *estate in severalty* is one held by a person singly, and an *estate in common* is one held by several persons jointly in undivided shares. A *customary estate* is one that existed in manors and boroughs by virtue of local custom: now abolished by the Law of Property Act 1922. An *estate in fee simple* is one that is granted to 'a man and his heirs', and is the greatest estate a subject of the Crown can possess. An *estate of freehold* is one originally held by a freeman and subject to free services and of uncertain duration, e.g., for life, or for the life of another. An *estate tail* is one created by the grant of land to 'a man and the heirs of his body' or to a man and specified heirs of his body. Since 1925 the estate tail can be barred by will and will take effect as an equitable interest. A *legal estate* is one valid against all the world; it is the estate capable of subsisting or being created at common law. By the Law of Property Act 1925 the only legal estates capable of subsisting are (1) an estate in fee simple absolute in possession; (2) a term of years absolute; (3) legal interests or charges as follows: easements, rent charges in

possession; charges by way of legal mortgage; land tax; tithe rentcharge, etc.; rights of entry. All other estates, interests and charges are to take effect as equitable interests. An *equitable estate* is one created and recognized only by a court of equity, i.e. the Court of Chancery. (Osborn).

29. Estovers, Common of. The right of taking from the woods or waste lands of another a reasonable portion of his timber or underwood. (Osborn.) From the old French estovoir=to be necessary.

30. Expropriation. Compulsorily depriving a person of his property in return for compensation.

31. Fee. Originally a feudal benefice; land granted to a man and his heirs in return for services to be rendered to the grantor; now land or an interest in land, which is capable of descending to an heir. (Osborn.)

32. Fee-farm Rent. A perpetual rent issuing out of lands held in fee simple, reserved when the lands were granted, and payable by the freeholder. A fee-farm rent is included in the term 'rentcharge' (Law of Property Act 1925). (Osborn.)

33. Fee Simple. See Estate.

34. Feoffment. The overt or public delivery of the possession of land by the ceremony known as 'the livery of seisin'.

35. Feudal system. The system of political organization in the Middle Ages based on land tenure. The King was the ultimate lord of all land. He granted land to his lords in return for military and other services and they in turn made similar grants, the process being known as subinfeudation. The unit of land was the manor, each under its lord, who had a right to services in labour and in kind from the villeins, over whom he exercised full jurisdiction. The lord in return owed them a duty of protection. The King had an over-riding authority and claimed allegiance both from lords and their tenants. (Osborn.)

36. Fixtures. Anything annexed to the freehold. It usually becomes part of the realty and the property in it immediately vests in the owner of the soil. Tenant's fixtures are chattels annexed to land or houses and are removable by the tenant. They are not distrainable for rent, but may be seized in execution. Fixtures affixed to an agricultural holding by a tenant not under an obligation, and for which no compensation is received, may be removed, subject to conditions. See Agricultural Holdings Act 1923, Sec. 22. (Osborn.)

37. Foldage. The right of a lord of a manor of having his tenant's sheep to feed on his fields, so as to manure the land, in return for which the lord provided a fold for the sheep. (Osborn.)

38. Foldcourse. The right of the lord of the manor of feeding a certain number of sheep on the lands of the tenant during certain times of the year. (Osborn.)

39. Folkland (opp. to Bookland). The prevailing view of the antithesis has been that folkland was land belonging to the State, which the King or the witan might grant to a person for his life, but which did not descend to heirs, while *bookland* was held by charter or deed. Another view is that folkland was land heritable by *folkright* or common law, while the estate in *bookland* was confirmed by deed, and could be alienated freely. (*S.O.E.D.*) It may be suggested that a parallel may be found in the distinction, in many Colonial territories, between ancestral and self-acquired property, coupled with the introduction of documentary forms of conveyance. See e.g., pp. 307 (b), 185, and 54-5.

40. Foreclose. To bar the right of redeeming mortgaged property.

41. Frankalmoign or Frankalmoin (Free alms). The tenure by which Church lands were for the most part held. It originally involved no services except praying for the soul of the donor. Abolished by the Administration of Estates Act 1925. Is now socage tenure. (Osborn.)

42. Freehold Tenure. Under the feudal system land was held by military tenure, socage tenure or copyhold tenure. Both military and socage tenures were freehold tenures; they were held in return for services which a free man might not think it derogatory to perform. Military tenure was abolished in 1660 and the land became subject to socage tenure. (Osborn.) W. S. Holdsworth classifies the free tenures into four groups (frankalmoin, knight service, serjeant and socage) corresponding to four different types of social relationship. 'The unfree or villein tenant held of his lord a certain quantity of land in return for his services in cultivating the lord's demesne land.' His tenure developed into copyhold (q.v.).

43. Gavelkind. A type of tenure characteristic of Kent. Its principal incidents were (*a*) the land descended equally to all the sons; (*b*) a child could alienate his land by feoffment at fifteen; (*c*) there was no escheat of the land to the Crown on account of felony; and (*d*) the widow of the deceased tenant was entitled to half the land for dower or until remarriage. Irish gavelkind was a custom by which land, on the death of its occupant, reverted for redistribution among the members of his sept. Gavelkind was abolished by the Law of Property Act 1922.

44. Grant. The assurance or transfer of the ownership of property, as distinguished from the delivery or transfer of the property itself. A conveyance is a deed of grant. By the Law of Property Act 1925 all land lies in grant and is rendered incapable of being conveyed by livery of seisin. (Osborn.)

45. Hypothecation. A charge on property as security for the payment of a sum of money where the property remains in the possession of the debtor. (Osborn.)

46. Indefeasible. Not liable to be made void.

47. Lien. The right to hold the property of another as security for the performance of an obligation. (Osborn.)

48. Limitation, Statutes of. The Statutes which prescribe the periods within which proceedings to enforce a right must be taken.

49. Livery of Seisin. An 'overt ceremony' which was formerly necessary to convey an immediate estate of freehold. (Osborn.)

50. Métayage. A system of land tenure common in Western Europe and U.S.A. in which the farmer pays a proportion of the produce to the owner, who furnishes the stock and seed or a part thereof. (*S.O.E.D.*)

51. Mortgage. The conveyance of real or personal property by a debtor (called the mortgagor) to a creditor (called the mortgagee) as security for a money debt; with the proviso that the property shall be reconveyed upon payment to the mortgagee of the sum secured within a certain period. (*S.O.E.D.*) Formerly if the money was not paid on the day the mortgage became irredeemable at common law, but the mortgagor had an equity of redemption until foreclosure or sale. The right of foreclosure entitled the mortgagee to compel the mortgagor either to pay off the debt within a reasonable time or to lose his equity of redemption. But by the Law of Property Act 1925 a mortgage of an estate in fee simple shall only be made by a demise for a term of years absolute, subject to a provision for cesser on redemption, or by a charge by deed expressed to be by way of legal mortgage. A first or only mortgage shall take

a term of 3000 years. The object of the changes is to secure to the mortgagor a legal estate and not a mere equity of redemption as hitherto. (Osborn.)

52. Peppercorn rent. A nominal rent serving as an acknowledgment of the tenancy.

53. Pre-emption. The right to purchase property before on opportunity is offered to others.

54. Prescription. (*a*) Negative. Limitation of the time within which a claim can be raised. (*b*) Positive. Uninterrupted use or possession from time immemorial, or for a period fixed by law, as giving a title or right; hence title or right acquired by such use or possession. (*S.O.E.D.*)

55. Primogeniture. The principle by which property descends to the eldest son. Cf. ultimogeniture and Borough-English.

56. Profits à prendre. Rights of taking the produce or part of the soil from the land of another person, e.g. rights of common, pasture, vesture and herbage (Osborn.)

57. Quit-Rent. A rent, usually of small amount; paid by a freeholder or copyholder in lieu of services. (*S.O.E.D.*)

58. Rack-rent. A rent equal (or nearly equal) to the full annual value of the land. A very high excessive or extortionate rent. (*S.O.E.D.*)

59. Real Property. Lands, tenements and hereditaments. Immovable property (*res*=thing) as opposed to personal.

60. Reversion. Where land is granted by the owner for a less estate or interest than he has himself, his undisposed of interest is termed the reversion, because the land will revert to the owner on the determination of the particular estate. (Osborn.)

61. Seisin. Feudal possession: the relation in which a person stands to land or other hereditaments, when he has in them a state of freehold in possession. (Osborn.)

62. Severalty. Property is said to belong to persons in severalty when the share of each is ascertained (so that he can exclude the others from it) as opposed to joint ownership, ownership in common, and coparcenary, where the owners hold in undivided shares. (Osborn.)

63. Socage. A variety of tenure by certain fixed services other than knight service, frankalmoign, or serjeanty. Socage was originally either free socage or villein socage, according as the services were free or base. Generally a money rent was due, or occasionally agricultural service. The rent might be nominal or substantial, e.g. a rose or a pound of pepper. Sometimes no rent was exacted, only fealty. It was the least encumbered of all the tenures when land-holding involved public rights and duties as well as private rights of ownership. And so it developed into the ordinary freehold tenure of modern times. (See W. S. Holdsworth op. cit., p. 28-9.)

64. Squatter's Title. The title acquired by one who, having wrongfully entered upon land, has occupied it without paying rent or otherwise acknowledging any superior title for such time that he acquires an indefeasible title. (Osborn.)

65. Tenancy in Common. When two or more persons are entitled to land in such a manner that they have an undivided possession but several freeholds: i.e. no one of them is entitled to the exclusive possession of any part of the land, each being entitled to occupy the whole in common with the others. It is distinguished from joint tenancy by the fact that on the death of any one of them his share passes, not to the survivors, but to his heir or devisee, who then becomes tenant in common with the survivors. (Osborn.)

66. Tenant at Sufferance. A tenant who keeps possession of land after his title has expired.

67. Tenant at Will. A tenant who holds land at the will or pleasure of the lessor. Copyholds were originally tenancies at will.

68. Tenant for Life. One whose interest in land ceases at his death and does not pass to his legal personal representatives.

69. Tenant from Year to Year. A tenant of land whose tenancy can only be determined by a notice to quit expiring at that period of the year at which it commenced. An agricultural tenant (if a tenant from year to year) must, under the Agricultural Holdings Act of 1925, have twelve months' notice to quit. (Osborn.)

70. Tenure. The mode of holding or occupying land. By English law no person except the King can be the absolute owner of land. All lands in the hands of subjects are held of some superior, and mediately or immediately of the Crown. The possessor is merely a tenant. The manner of his possession is called a 'tenure', and the extent of his interest an 'estate'. Tenures were (*a*) temporal or lay, and (*b*) ecclesiastical or spiritual (tenure in frankalmoign and by divine service). The temporal or lay tenures were of two kinds according as their services were free or unfree. The frank or freehold tenures were (*a*) knight's service (including grand serjeanty, escuage, castle ward and cornage, all of which have been converted into common socage) and (*b*) free socage (including petty serjeanty, burgage, borough-English and gavelkind). The unfree tenures were (*a*) pure villeinage, which existed in the form of copyhold and customary freehold tenures; and (*b*) the obsolete privileged villeinage or villein socage, from which is derived 'tenure in ancient demesne'. The customary tenures were converted into socage tenure by the Law of Property Act 1922. (mainly Osborn.)

71. Ultimogeniture. Inheritance by the youngest of a family. See Borough English.

Index

H

I

J

K

T